"A brilliant description of the dark underbelly of modern democracy: dark money, influence games and the new tactics of the new far-right. Everyone should read it."

ANNE APPLEBAUM,
historian, author of *Gulag* and *Red Famine*

'Peter Geoghegan's investigations have been essential reading. Now this urgent, vital book is essential reading for anyone who wants to make sense of our politics.'

CAROLE CADWALLADR,
writer and winner of the Orwell Prize and
Stieg Larsson Prize, and finalist for the Pulitzer Prize

"There's a reason why 'follow the money' is such a good rule for journalism: donations to political causes tell us what private interests are at play. Peter Geoghegan's literally sterling work on the role of dark money in the Brexit upheaval is in the great tradition of investigative reporting. He follows the financial trails to reveal in compelling detail the nexus of international players for whom democracy is a game whose rules they could manipulate with impunity. *Democracy for Sale* is as urgent as it is illuminating."

FINTAN O'TOOLE,
author of *Ship of Fools* and *Heroic Failure*

"Democracy, we are told, dies in darkness. This forensic and highly readable book shows how so many of our democratic processes have moved into the murky, unregulated spaces of globalisation and digital innovation. It's time society took a good look at them and decided whether this is the sort of democracy we want."

PETER POMERANTSEV,
author of *Nothing Is True and Everything is Possible*
and *This is Not Propaganda*

"Geoghegan pulls off the ultimate goal of investigative writing. He not only exposes scandals – he enables us to witness the system that generates the wrongdoing and permits it. He does so by linking what once seemed isolated outrages into a compelling and very readable story of the ongoing corruption of our government and therefore ourselves."

ANTHONY BARNETT,
author of *Iron Britannia* and *The Lure of Greatness*

"Peter Geoghegan is one of our best investigative journalists; his work is careful, sober, non-sensational, and terrifying. *Democracy for Sale* forensically exposes the fault lines in our politics, and reveals how they have been exploited by the rich and the powerful to further their own interests. If you're concerned about the health of British democracy, read this book – it is thorough, gripping and vitally important."

OLIVER BULLOUGH,
author of *Moneyland*

DEMOCRACY
FOR SALE

PETER GEOGHEGAN is an Irish writer, broadcaster and investigations editor at the award-winning news website *openDemocracy*. He led *openDemocracy*'s investigations into dark money in British politics that were nominated for a 2019 British Journalism Award and the Paul Foot Award. His journalism has appeared in the *New York Times*, the *Guardian*, the *London Review of Books* and many other publications. His last book, *The People's Referendum: Why Scotland Will Never Be the Same Again*, was nominated for the Saltire First Book Award.

PETER GEOGHEGAN

DEMOCRACY FOR SALE

An Apollo Book

This is an Apollo book, first published in the UK in 2020
by Head of Zeus Ltd

9 7 6 8

A catalogue record for this book is available from
the British Library.

ISBN (FTP): 9781789546033
ISBN (E): 9781789546026

Typeset by Adrian McLaughlin

Printed and bound in Great Britain by
CPI Group (UK) Ltd, Croydon CR0 4YY

Head of Zeus Ltd
First Floor East
5–8 Hardwick Street
London EC1R 4RG

WWW.HEADOFZEUS.COM

Contents

For Mary

1

INTRODUCTION

A book about the dark money that is warping our politics could begin in many places. Our starting point might be a tour of Westminster, stopping to peer through the windows of the Georgian townhouses where well-heeled political consultants and think tanks plot out election-winning strategies. We could stroll around the backstreets of the City of London, searching for insights into the murky world of offshore finance amid the brash, overflowing bars and restaurants. Or head straight to the global capital of undisclosed political influence, the sleek glass and steel sepulchres of Washington DC's corporate lobbying firms.

The genesis of this book took place somewhere less obvious: Seaburn metro station on the outskirts of Sunderland, on 21 June 2016. Two days before the UK voted to leave the European Union, my editor had sent me to report on what voters thought in Sunderland. It was a warm summer's morning and there were only a handful of people on the open-air platform. I approached a middle-aged man with a soft face who was also waiting for the train to Newcastle.

"How will you vote?" I asked, falling into the only mode of conversation for a reporter in an unfamiliar place before a polling day. He wanted Brexit. He talked about pit closures and disinvestment, deindustrialisation and neglect. It was not hard to see why he felt politically abandoned. He had a particular worry about the

EU: that Turkey would soon join. He talked about how millions of Turkish workers could soon be coming to the UK in search of jobs. I asked where he had heard about this. "Facebook," he said.

A minute or two later the train arrived. I thanked my interlocutor for his time and sat down alone in an almost empty carriage. A well-thumbed copy of the free *Metro* lay on the adjacent seat. The front page was a wraparound advertisement calling on Britons to "take back control", the slogan of the official Vote Leave campaign. I turned the paper over. An imprint on the back said that the advert had been "paid for by the Democratic Unionist Party".

This was very curious. Since its foundation in 1971, the DUP had never run a single candidate outside Northern Ireland. Now it was splashing out on a massive ad campaign promoting Brexit in England. I knew that election spending in the UK is tightly capped. I also knew, having worked as a reporter in Belfast, that political donations to Northern Irish parties were kept secret under anachronistic local laws. Perhaps this was a way around campaign limits? I posted a photograph of the advert on Twitter, wondering aloud what was going on. Only a handful of people responded to my tweet.

Slowly, the suburban train cut through verdant countryside, past relics of former industrial glory. Sunderland was once, it is said, the largest shipbuilding town in the world. I forgot about the advert, opened my laptop and began drafting my report for the next day's paper.

Sunderland was one of the first places to declare on referendum night. Over 60 per cent voted to leave the European Union. It was a result that set the tone for a stunning political upset. Through the night, pollsters struggled to explain a vote that defied their predictive models. The next morning, markets nose-dived. The resignation of the prime minister, David Cameron, was only the third item on many news bulletins. The ensuing years of chaos laid bare the fault lines of modern Britain and have changed Europe forever.

In the months that followed the Brexit vote, my mind kept

returning to Seaburn station. How could the Democratic Unionists, a tiny party in the context of British politics, afford to buy hugely expensive ads in northern English newspapers? Why were voters in Sunderland seeing stories on Facebook about Turkey joining the EU? Who was paying for all this? My colleagues and I would spend much of the next three years asking such questions.

We found answers, but rarely those we had expected. The DUP's advertising blitz was bankrolled by the biggest donation in Northern Irish history, routed through a secretive Scottish group linked to a former head of Saudi Arabian intelligence. The Vote Leave campaign – led by its ruthless chief strategist Dominic Cummings – broke electoral laws on overspending when it bought highly targeted Facebook adverts with a Canadian digital company that almost nobody had heard of. Arron Banks, an insurance broker with interests in gold mines and a sprawling business empire registered in tax havens around the world, had become the biggest campaign donor in British electoral history. Banks was eventually investigated – and exonerated – by the National Crime Agency, amid concerns about the sources of his record Brexit contributions.

The trail continued, stretching far beyond Britain's shores – from Cambridge Analytica, Steve Bannon and leading figures in Donald Trump's America to Matteo Salvini, Viktor Orbán and Europe's insurgent far right. There were corporate-funded think tanks and lobbyists with access to the highest levels of government and networks of keyboard warriors in suburban bedrooms churning out hyper-partisan news stories that spread like digital wildfire. The more we uncovered, the more we became aware of serious concerns about central aspects of how democracy is supposed to function. Some of what we saw was illegal. Even more alarmingly, much of it was not.

Dark money is an American neologism for an increasingly global phenomenon: funds from unknown sources that influence our politics. This money gets into the political system in an increasing variety of ways, from loopholes in election law and online campaign fundraising through to anonymously funded, agenda-setting pressure groups. In her authoritative book on election finance, *Dark Money*, American journalist Jane Mayer outlines how US democracy was effectively bought by a cadre of the super-rich and their surrogates, often through faceless political action committees – so-called "super Pacs" – that can spend limitless amounts of money.

The sums involved in American political funding are enormous. The Koch brothers, David and Charles, co-owners of the second-largest private company in the United States with strong interests in coal and petroleum, spent more than $1.5 billion on Republican political causes until David's death in 2019. The pair bankrolled countless conservative think tanks and politicians. Trump's biggest backers included hedge fund billionaire Robert Mercer, whose data firm Cambridge Analytica also worked on Trump's presidential campaign. In America, elections involving hundreds of millions of voters have become contests decided, in key constituencies, by a handful of plutocrats.

In Britain, money has long played a determining role in politics. The 'rotten boroughs' of the 18th and 19th centuries were notoriously crooked, and their tiny electorates could be bought by influential patrons. The Reform Act of 1832 did not end corruption. Bribery was so endemic in an 1880 by-election in Sandwich that the constituency was subsequently abolished. David Lloyd George shamelessly sold peerages to wartime spivs and profiteers to fund his prime ministerial lifestyle.

You have to go back to the 1920s to find the last time a general election candidate was convicted of breaking spending limits, but only the most optimistic would believe that the financial restraints in British politics are not frequently exceeded. Money corrodes the political system in other ways, too. In the 1960s, architect and planner John Poulson and building firm Bovis bribed Labour politicians across the north-east to approve major construction projects. Three decades later, lobbyist Ian Greer gave Tory MPs cash in brown envelopes in return for asking parliamentary questions useful to his clients. More recently, former Labour ministers have compared themselves to cabs for hire, their wheels greased by generous daily retainers. When the MP expenses scandal broke in 2009, it revealed that parliamentarians had been claiming for everything from cleaning a moat on their country estate to mortgages on expensive second homes. Public trust in politics has never really recovered since.

British politics is comparatively low-spending, especially when set against the United States, but there is plenty of evidence that the American model of hidden finance and clandestine influence has traversed the pond. Britain, as the London-based American political analyst Anne Applebaum notes, "has become a place where untransparent money, from unknown sources, is widely accepted with a complacent shrug".[1] The relatively small sums involved can make it even easier to get access to the top table of British politics. US donors might be expected to spend hundreds of millions of dollars in a single election cycle. But for fifty grand pretty much anyone can get a seat with the British prime minister at a lavish Conservative Leader's Group dinner where discussions are kept strictly private, even if they touch on government policy.

The dark money playbook is straightforward. Take advantage of shady campaign financing; circumvent electoral rules where you can; and draw on a network of supportive think tanks, a receptive media run by a handful of magnates and hard-line caucuses within the long-established political parties. As we shall see, the same strategies and tactics are increasingly employed in the UK and across much of the world. From Vote Leave playing fast and loose with electoral law to the international influence campaign underpinning the rise of the populist right in Europe, politicians and their surrogates are increasingly willing to push the boundaries as far as they will go, and beyond. Donald Trump was elected US president in 2016 after a campaign marred by disinformation and electoral interference. Far from being an aberration, dirty politics is the new normal.

What's so bad about political campaigns not declaring the source of their funds? Does dark money actually matter?

It does, profoundly. Even relatively meagre sums can shift the political needle and generate highly effective lobbying operations. Small purposeful groups are adept at taking control of policy in ways that are very hard to see for those not regularly involved in politics. In Britain, a nexus of corporate-funded libertarian think tanks and transatlantic media moguls turned a 'no-deal' Brexit from what was in 2016 an outlandish proposal into a more or less explicit government policy option after Boris Johnson became prime minister in the summer of 2019.

These think tanks maintain that corporate donors do not dictate their views. Whether BP or big tobacco is giving them money, they insist, does not change their core commitment to economic freedom and small government. That is of course a reasonable position to take, but it ignores the pernicious way in which undeclared corporate donations buy privileged access to the political system. The amount of space and time in public debate is finite. Slots on crepuscular current affairs television programmes are limited (even if it doesn't always feel that way). Dark money gives these small, unrepresentative groups a marked advantage, pays for slick and articulate reports and polished media appearances, and accentuates the risk of the public sphere being captured by vested interests.

Dark money has gone hand-in-hand with the rise of digital disinformation. It is a truism that politics has been transformed in recent years. But it is not just the outcomes, the election of disruptive authoritarian populists, that have changed. Behind Brexit, Trump and a host of other unforeseen ruptures is a paradigm shift in the nature of political communication. The digital world offers voters the opportunity to live in echo chambers where their political prejudices are confirmed and reinforced daily. We can all choose a tribe now and decide not to hear any voices critical of our choice.

As politics is increasingly mediated through Silicon Valley tech giants, falsehoods and mistruths spread at light speed. So far, few political leaders have been willing to back down in a digital arms race in which every potential advantage is seized upon.

The communications revolution has changed our politics in ways we are still struggling to understand. Nigel Farage's Brexit Party may have ceded most of its power to Boris Johnson in the December 2019 general election, but the remarkable story of its short-lived success tells us a lot. In May of the same year, Britain's first 'digital party' topped the polls in European Parliament elections in the UK, less than four months after it was first registered. Inspired by Italy's Five Star Movement, the Brexit Party ran a sophisticated online campaign that tapped into widespread anger that Britain was still in the EU, nearly three years after the country had voted to leave.

This pop-up party was governed by a constitution that gave Farage almost complete control. Rather than members with internal voting rights, its supporters gave money but had no power. Ahead of the European elections, tens of thousands of people donated online through PayPal, with minimal checks. The electoral regulator warned that the Brexit Party's online fundraising could allow donors to evade the rules banning foreign contributions to British politics. But by then the votes had already been counted.

If the problem was just one of laws being broken, there would be a simple solution: tougher enforcement. Increase fines until the pips squeak. Introduce the threat of jail time. Former Trump fixer Michael Cohen was given a three-year prison sentence in 2018 for violating campaign finance laws during the presidential campaign. If British political operatives faced similar risks, then bad behaviours might swiftly change.

But the corruption of democracy is as much about perfectly legal abuse as it is law-breaking malfeasance. American religious funders have quietly pumped tens of millions of dollars into conservative campaigns across Europe, fuelling a reactionary backlash against women's and minority rights.

Already there are signs that faith in democracy has been badly shaken. Authoritarian attitudes are on the rise. From the election of Jair Bolsonaro in Brazil to Narendra Modi's Hindu nationalist government in India, voters around the world are increasingly turning to 'strongman' leaders. In developed nations, dissatisfaction with democracy is running at record levels. A study by Cambridge University's Centre for the Future of Democracy published in 2020 found that some 58 per cent of people were unhappy with democracy.[2] Discontent was particularly pronounced in two places: Britain and the United States.

The crisis in British democracy has become an increasingly partisan issue. Many prominent figures have been keen to silence any conversation about the flaws in our democratic system. Prime Minister Boris Johnson has kicked proposals for electoral reform into the long grass. All the while, democratic norms have been eroded. Judges were branded enemies of the people. The government shut down Parliament and attacked the apolitical civil service. As Johnson has shown, repeatedly lying is no barrier to the highest public office.

Against this backdrop of growing anti-democratic sentiment among both the public and politicians, political scientist Martin Moore warns that our democracy is no longer working as it should. "There is a genuine crisis of representation," he says. "How does democracy actually work in this new era? Right now it's not at all clear that we know."

Writing about politics in such a tumultuous period comes with obvious challenges. Prime ministers – and policies – have come and gone so readily. But behind the political theatrics, the underlying problems remain. Rules and regulations intended to manage a developed, properly functioning democracy have often been sorely lacking in a far more politically restive age. Ineffective checks and balances have been a boon for lobbyists and political opportunists.

The absence of a truly representative electoral system or a codi-fied constitution has only added to Britain's democratic malaise. Regardless of what the country's post-Brexit future looks like, its broken system needs radical surgery.

But before we open the patient up, we need to understand the disease's aetiology.

I have structured this book both chronologically and themati-cally. The opening chapters are directly concerned with the 2016 Brexit referendum and examine in some detail examples of electoral sharp practice that took place, from Vote Leave's law-breaking to Arron Banks's record spending to the DUP's dark money. These different stories are both crucial to understanding the context of modern British politics and illustrative of far deeper problems in our democracy. We will see how, time and time again, regulators have been found wanting, and almost nothing has been done to prevent future abuses.

The middle section of the book lays out how dark money has facilitated the growing American influence on British politics. We will explore the rise of the 'Anglosphere' – the idea that Britain's future lies with other English-speaking nations – and see how taxpayer and private money helped the European Research Group of pro-Brexit MPs become kingmakers at a crucial moment in British political history. We will also examine the influence of corporate-funded think tanks on Westminster, focusing in par-ticular on the role of the Institute of Economic Affairs. Born down an alleyway in the City of London in 1955, the IEA became the inspiration for many of the most influential obscurely funded think tanks operating in Washington DC today and has tried, with varying success, to be a major player in what its director unwit-tingly called "the Brexit influencing game".

The final third of the book examines how technology has trans-formed politics and created endless new opportunities for dark money to corrode it. From Cambridge Analytica to the British Con-servative Party 'shit-posting' on social media during the 2019 general election, we will see how online political advertising has been revolutionised and meet the digital campaigners that brought state-of-the-art political messaging from the US to Britain. Once again, we will find laws that are hopelessly out of date in the digital age.

We will delve into the world of online disinformation, meeting some of the people behind the online news sites that push populist messages across the Internet. We will chart the rise of Europe's populist right and trace the increasing international flows of unaccountable money, specifically from American Christian right-wing groups that have been funding campaigns from Eastern Europe to Latin America to back home in the US in the context of the 2020 presidential election.

Before our dark money tour gets started, I would like to take a moment to acknowledge the role of some of the many colleagues whose work I draw on in this book. This book would not have been possible without the team at *openDemocracy*, where I work. Without the dedication of a tenacious, far-sighted editor-in-chief in Mary Fitzgerald and a small band of talented colleagues, particularly Adam Ramsay, Jenna Corderoy, Jim Cusick and Claire Provost, many of the stories in this book would not have come to light.

Elsewhere, Carole Cadwalladr, writing for the *Observer* and the *Guardian*, has been a tireless campaigning journalist on everything from Arron Banks to Cambridge Analytica. BBC Northern Ireland's *Spotlight* team revealed crucial new material about the DUP's bank-breaking donations. The investigative unit at *Channel 4 News* broke major new ground. Reporters at the *Financial Times*, *Buzzfeed*, *Source Material* and *Byline* also pieced together important elements of the story.

All that said, I still find it remarkable that it was so often left to a handful of journalists, often in small, non-profits such as *openDemocracy*, to shine a light on the role of dark money in our politics. Many much larger outlets have shied away from investing their far greater resources in these stories, even though they raise fundamental questions about the foundations of our democracy.

Throughout what follows, I often draw on reports produced by parliamentary committees, regulators and NGOs, as well as secondary sources and original research. I would like to thank the dozens and dozens of people from across the political spectrum who spoke to me for this book, both on and off the record.

I should state at the outset, too, that I do not believe that Brexit was some grand conspiracy. The force of much of the British state apparatus and its political and business establishment was behind remaining in the European Union. Pro-Leave campaigns broke the law, but we cannot say with any certainty that the result would have been different if they had not. Instead, the referendum and its aftermath have revealed something far more fundamental and systemic. Namely, a broken political system that is ripe for exploitation again. And again. And again.

I grew up during one of the most optimistic moments in post-war European history: in a small town near the Irish border as the Troubles ended and the economy roared. My father was born in a cottage. I graduated from one of Britain's most prestigious universities. I lived most of my life with an almost Panglossian view of human potential. Bad things happen, but they can be stopped. New worlds, better worlds were possible.

It is only recently that I have started to appreciate how often this is not the case. That change is not always for the good. That advances once made can be lost again. That democracy is not something that can be left only to politicians, regulators and, a few days each decade, to voters.

I'm still an optimist. I believe our democracies can be defended, and even strengthened. Reform is possible. Tech companies can be reined in; regulations can be strengthened and properly enforced; new ways of democracy can be imagined and invoked. First, though, we need to understand how and why our democracy is on leave.

January 2020

2

DEMOCRACY ON LEAVE?

*However, there is another organisation that could spend your
money. Would you be willing to send the 100k to some social
media ninjas who could usefully spend it on behalf of this
organisation? I am very confident it would be well spent in the
final crucial 5 days. Obviously it would be entirely legal.*[1]

DOMINIC CUMMINGS, email to
Vote Leave donor, 11 June 2016

In late August 2019, Boris Johnson wrote a memo to the Westminster cabinet committee tasked with preparing for a no-deal
Brexit. The freshly minted prime minister had pledged to leave
the European Union "do or die". Now he told ministers to "act
immediately" to share all user data from their departmental websites. The government wanted to create a platform for gathering
"targeted and personalised information". Dominic Cummings, the
prime minister's chief advisor, emailed senior officials telling them
that the data collection was a "TOP PRIORITY".[2]

A few years earlier, a government plan to transfer masses of
data would likely have gone largely unnoticed. A privacy campaigner might have offered a comment; a lowly opposition politician would have raised a question without expecting much of
an answer. But the story of Johnson's diktat hit the headlines.

Labour deputy leader Tom Watson described the proposal as "very suspicious". Others complained that the government was secretly planning to hoover up detailed data about its citizens.

There were reasons for this heightened sensitivity. We are all (slightly) more wary of how our personal information is used, especially by political campaigners. Cambridge Analytica shut down in 2018, following a scandal about the massive misuse of Facebook data from tens of millions of users. But there was another reason the story of the prime minister's memo made waves. It had 'Dominic Cummings' and 'data' in the same headline.

Cummings has been the closest contemporary British politics has to a Machiavelli. Like the author of *The Prince*, he has a piercing stare and a prematurely receding hairline. The mastermind behind the unexpected vote for Brexit in 2016, Cummings presented himself as a British political strategist with an uncanny knack for tapping into voters' deepest desires. He read military historians, was inspired by Silicon Valley technocrats and wrote voluminous blog posts on everything from the Apollo space programme to Otto von Bismarck. Where others obsessed about appealing to the news media, Cummings – despite his well-heeled Oxbridge background – talked about opposing established elites. When then prime minister David Cameron described him as a "career psychopath", it only served to feed the Cummings mythology.

A former colleague said of Cummings: "He doesn't really believe in government at all."[3] If he had faith in anything, it was data. During the EU referendum, Cummings ran what he proudly called "the first campaign in the UK to put almost all our money into digital communication".[4] Vote Leave bought an estimated 1.5 billion Facebook advertisements directed at seven million people. Many of these targeted ads spread misinformation, particularly about immigration and the financial benefits of leaving the European Union. The campaign was also helped by massive illegal overspending, which paid for millions of digital ads. Cummings credited this almost invisible social media blitz, mostly delivered in the final days before the vote, with securing victory in a tight referendum.

Cummings's installation in Downing Street in July 2019 was followed by a sudden spike in digital activity by the new administration. Almost immediately, hundreds of targeted adverts promoting the new prime minister started appearing online. One Facebook ad paid for by the Conservatives trumpeted a BBC news story reporting a "£14 billion pound cash boost for schools". But it was not true. The BBC headline had been doctored. The actual figure quoted in the BBC story was just £7.1 billion. The ad was eventually taken down amid a chorus of criticism but it had run for two weeks before anyone flagged it.

This dissembling was a taste of things to come. A few months later, the Conservatives ran the most dishonest general campaign in British political history. Independent fact-checkers accused the Tories of misleading the public, after the party's official Twitter account was rebranded as a fact-checking website during a television debate. Dark money-funded pro-Johnson ads flooded social media. Conservative Party sources routinely lied to journalists. Many saw the spirit of Dominic Cummings behind the onslaught of disinformation.

Having vowed to "deliver Brexit" in government, Cummings was credited with instigating Boris Johnson's controversial decision to suspend Parliament in August 2019 in an unsuccessful attempt to force through an accelerated departure from the EU. (The Supreme Court later ruled the prorogation unlawful.) Twenty-one Tory MPs who voted to block a no-deal Brexit had the whip removed. "Dominic Cummings has been hired by Boris to lay waste," complained Winston Churchill's grandson, Nicholas Soames. "He is doing the job he was asked to do."[5]

Cummings was not the only Vote Leave alumnus that Johnson brought into the heart of his administration. Press officer Lee Cain became the prime minister's head of communications. The Leave campaign's youthful social media maven Chloe Westley took up a similar role at Number 10. So many former campaign staff were given jobs in the new administration that *Guardian* columnist Jonathan Freeland declared it "a Vote Leave government". It didn't seem to matter much that the campaign had in fact broken the law in 2016. Pumping hundreds of thousands of pounds more than the legal limit into millions of Facebook adverts targeted at undecided voters was treated as an historical footnote, if it was mentioned at all.

But precisely how Vote Leave broke the law and pushed the boundaries of digital campaigning matters a great deal. Not because it shows that the Brexit vote was fraudulent, but because it's one of the clearest examples of why our electoral system is broken. It demonstrates how even relatively small sums of money can influence our politics – and how our system is still wide open to abuse, especially through digital means.

Vote Leave's story is a parable about how modern campaigns, of all kinds, can bend and break laws drafted for a very different era, and how regulators have failed to get to grips with the rapidly changing realities of democratic consultation. To understand all this, we first need to understand how leaving the European Union went from a dream shared by a small band of largely libertarian Eurosceptics to a campaign that changed the face of Britain.

The 2016 vote to leave the European Union was a culmination that many Brexiters had spent their lives working towards. A political project long dismissed as the preserve of what then Conservative prime minister David Cameron called "fruitcakes" and "loonies" had won the day. More than anything else, the result was a vindication of the much derided official 'out' campaign, Vote Leave, and particularly its bosses Matthew Elliott and Dominic Cummings. Few had given them a chance.

Vote Leave was both the product of decades of Eurosceptic agitation and rhetoric and, not unusually in British politics, a conversation between a small group of confidants. On a warm summer's day in 2012, Matthew Elliott met Daniel Hannan in a summer house belonging to a septuagenarian Eurosceptic merchant banker named Rodney Leach.[6] For two decades, Hannan had been the nearest thing to an intellectual motor behind Conservative opposition to the EU. In that time he had progressed from the debating halls of Oxford to the chambers of the European Parliament, but his core beliefs about 'restoring' national sovereignty had remained unaltered. "Daniel wanted to destroy Brussels," one former colleague told me.

Now the push for a referendum on Europe was gathering pace. Cameron would soon commit to holding a vote. But the nascent campaign for withdrawal needed a front man. Hannan wanted Elliott to take on the role. "I knew it had to be Matt," he would later tell *Sunday Times* journalist Tim Shipman.[7]

In many ways, Elliott was an obvious choice to lead what became Vote Leave. He was young, had Westminster experience and was steeped in Euroscepticism. He was also a devoted free marketer. Growing up in a solidly middle-class family headed by a trade unionist father in 1980s northern England, Elliott picked up his politics outside the home.

"I remember at Leeds Grammar School there was an economics teacher called Terry Ellsworth, and he basically taught us A-Level economics using Milton Friedman's *Free to Choose* books and video series. I think a lot of my free market economics came from that," Elliott later recalled.[8] He went on to the London School of Economics, where he became president of the Hayek Society, named after the Nobel Prize-winning Austrian economist and polemicist against government intervention.

From the beginning of his career, Elliott worked to apply North American libertarian methods to British politics. Shortly after graduating from university, he paid his first visit to Americans for Tax Reform, a conservative Washington DC "taxpayer advocacy group" set up by Grover Norquist in the 1980s at the behest of president Ronald Reagan. Its corporate funders have included the Koch brothers' various foundations.

Elliott brought Norquist's model to Britain.[9] In 2004, aged just 25, he co-founded the TaxPayers' Alliance to campaign in favour of tax cuts and privatisation. The TPA called for the television licence fee – which pays for the BBC – to be abolished and the National Health Service to be replaced by private provision.

Like its American counterparts, Elliott's pressure group was adept at capturing media attention. There was almost nothing on which it would not offer a comment. In 2008 alone, the *Daily Mail* quoted the TaxPayers' Alliance in a staggering 517 articles. The *Sun* did so 307 times.[10] When the TPA published a denunciation of green taxes, a topless blonde model named Keeley on the *Sun*'s now-defunct Page 3 asked readers: "Why should Britain pay over the odds when our energy usage is lower than other countries?"[11] Even the revelation that one of the TPA's founders, Anthony Heath, did not actually pay any tax in the UK did little to dent the group's media reach.[12]

Elliott grew the TPA into a £1 million-a-year operation employing over a dozen staff. The impressive growth was undergirded by dark money. Although the TPA campaigned for greater transparency in government, Elliott always refused to say who funded it. "I think people have a right to donate to charities and campaigns anonymously," he said when pressed.[13]

Money did come from leading Conservative donors, including JCB tycoon Anthony Bamford, former Tory co-treasurer Peter Cruddas and the secretive Midlands Industrial Council, initially set up in 1946 to oppose Clement Attlee's nationalisation programme. The TPA was part of a lattice of libertarian and climate-sceptic outlets that often operated in tandem, pushing similar policies and causes. Many are based at the same address, 55 Tufton Street, a four-storey Georgian townhouse on an elegant Westminster side street. The house is owned by Conservative businessman Richard Smith.[14]

Washington lobbyists frequently pass through Tufton Street and its environs. In September 2010, Elliott hosted a huge "free market roadshow"[15] in central London featuring a raft of influential American libertarians: the Cato Institute, the Heritage Foundation, the Krieble Foundation and many more. Pride of place was reserved for the conservative movement sweeping across the United States, the aggressively anti-government Tea Party. A Tea Party-aligned consultant said that she had wanted to "identify groups in Europe" that "could start activist wings"[16]. At the time, Elliott said: "It will be fascinating to see whether it will transfer to the UK. Will there be the same sort of uprising?"[17]*

It was not just Elliott's familiarity with transatlantic libertarianism that would have appealed to the ardent Atlanticist Daniel Hannan as he set about building a campaign to leave the EU. Elliott's CV also contained a particularly rare qualification: he already had experience winning a British referendum.

In 2011, Britain held its first national referendum since the vote on joining the European project more than thirty-five years earlier. This time around, the proposal was more narrowly procedural. Should Westminster switch from the first-past-the-post electoral system to the slightly more proportional alternative vote?

The proposed alteration was a fudge. The Liberal Democrats, who wanted full proportional representation, had agreed to a referendum on a less democratic electoral measure as part of their coalition agreement with David Cameron's Conservatives.

Matthew Elliott led the campaign against the measure. In a foreshadowing of Vote Leave five years later, NO to AV quickly framed the terms of the debate with dubious figures and kept to a small number of simple messages. Elliott claimed that the alternative vote would cost £250 million to introduce. The claim was

---

* Elliott's American wife, Sarah, previously worked as a Republican lobbyist in Washington DC. After the vote to leave the EU, she often appeared on British political talk shows as chairwoman of Republican Overseas UK, talking up the prospects of a post-Brexit trade deal with Donald Trump.

refuted by the Electoral Commission and the non-aligned Political Studies Association. It didn't matter. Billboards ran photographs of a sick child in an incubator alongside the slogan "She needs a new cardiac facility, not an alternative voting system." 'Yes' lost by a crushing two to one on polling day.[18]

NO to AV also provided a trial run for the Brexit referendum in other ways. Elliott focused heavily on digital campaigning. He pushed messages on Facebook and built online applications that encouraged voters to attend real-world campaign events. It was cutting-edge for the time.

"Matthew was one of those people who saw early that we needed to put digital at the heart of the campaign. He had seen what was happening in the US," says Jag Singh, an American digital expert who worked on NO to AV and later set up a digital political consultancy with Elliott and Paul Staines from the right-wing website *Guido Fawkes*.

Elliott did not immediately establish Vote Leave after his meeting with Hannan. Instead, in 2013 he set up a prototype campaign called Business for Britain, again based at 55 Tufton Street. By then Cameron had pledged to renegotiate Britain's relationship with Brussels. The aim of Business for Britain was to subtly force Cameron's hand. "I realised that business was the way into it," Elliott later said. "We did not do it as a hard Brexit campaign but went along the lines of the renegotiation, albeit pushing further what the PM would be thinking."[19]

In May 2015, the EU referendum went from a remote possibility to imminent reality. After the Conservatives won a surprising majority, Cameron found himself having to call a referendum he had never expected or wanted. During the coalition years, Eurosceptics were often left on the backbenches as Liberal Democrats took up payroll posts in government. The attitude of Conservatives hostile to Brussels had hardened from a wariness about federalism into a full-throated demand to leave the EU itself. Business for Britain morphed into Vote Leave.

Then Elliott made his boldest move: he hired Dominic Cummings, once a pugilistic special advisor to education secretary Michael Gove, to run the Leave campaign. It was a decision that would come to define Vote Leave and even Brexit itself.

In person, Cummings and Elliott are very different. Elliott is often circumspect and serious. He prefers to operate behind the scenes. Cummings is truculent, controversial and wildly divisive. As Tim Shipman writes, Cummings is "viewed by his allies as one of the most talented public policy professionals of his generation". To his enemies, he is "a raging menace, a Tory bastard love-child of Damian McBride and Alastair Campbell".[20] One-time Vote Leave board member John Mills remembers Elliott as "a very nice person to work with"; Cummings, by contrast, was "difficult to manage" and "opinionated".

A young member of the Brexit campaign team, who spoke on condition of anonymity, had a rather different experience. "Matthew Elliott barely spoke to junior people, just the board and the funders. Dominic Cummings was hands-on. He was the one who was there for you."

Politically, however, the two men had much in common. Like Elliott, Cummings's background was solidly Eurosceptic. At Oxford, he studied under right-wing Scottish historian Norman Stone,[21] a leading member of the Thatcherite Bruges Group. After a failed attempt to set up an airline in post-Soviet Russia, Cummings had taken over Business for Sterling, an anti-euro lobbying campaign also set up by Rodney Leach. (The same small groups of people recur in a bewildering number of different combinations in recent British politics.)

Like Elliott, Cummings also had experience with British referendums. In November 2004, he had led the campaign against setting up a North-East Regional Assembly, intended as the first step towards English devolution. Cummings had other ideas. He came up with a catchy slogan to capture the key local objection: "Politicians talk, we pay."[22] There were negative billboards and television adverts, as well as photogenic stunts. To illustrate how much the assembly would cost taxpayers, campaign chairman John Elliott – no relation to Matthew – delivered a short talk on local government finance while standing next to a bonfire onto which blonde girls from Durham University wearing tight t-shirts threw bundles of fake £50 notes. Cummings brought an inflatable white elephant on a tour of the north-east. As he would in 2016, he said that the money saved on another layer of government could be used to hire additional doctors, teachers or police.[23]

In another echo of the Brexit referendum, the campaign was also dogged by arguments with the Electoral Commission and fellow campaigners against the assembly over designations and spending. In his insider account of the North-East referendum, Cummings's "ground war commander" William Norton writes that the regulator was "utterly useless". "It had no power to act as a referee, only as an auditor," he notes. Norton later became Vote Leave's legal director.

In the end, the disputes mattered little. Those hostile to a new North East Assembly won a resounding 78 per cent of the vote. English devolution was abandoned. The No campaign's chief spokesperson, Graham Robb, described the operation as "Britain's first populist campaign". Cummings would later say that it had been "a training exercise for the EU referendum".

Along with campaign director James Frayne, Cummings set up a free market think tank called the New Frontiers Foundation. The name was taken from a celebrated 1960 speech by John F. Kennedy. The intention was to create a UK equivalent of the Heritage Foundation, the behemoth of the American conservative think tank world that had set the policy agenda for numerous presidents.[24] In late 2004, the *Financial Times* reported that "the New Frontiers Foundation, one of the most active Eurosceptic groups in Britain, has been energetically cultivating transatlantic ties in the US".[25]

But Cummings's new venture quickly ran into the sand. By the following year, the New Frontiers Foundation was out of money. Frayne went to work for the TaxPayers' Alliance. Cummings joined Michael Gove as an advisor, where he stayed for seven years before quitting in 2014, only coming out of self-imposed political exile to run Vote Leave.

There is a temptation to retrospectively view a successful political campaign as flawless. With hindsight, every move becomes the right one. This was certainly not the case with Vote Leave. There were internal difficulties, including a failed attempt by the board to sack Cummings. Elliott's fledgling campaign spent months fighting an often vicious internecine conflict with Arron Banks's Leave.EU operation over which should be classified as the lead campaign. The designation mattered – the lead campaign would have privileged access to media and could spend up to £7 million. These spending limits would become crucial during the referendum, and after.

The Electoral Commission eventually chose Vote Leave as the official pro-Brexit campaign. Vote Leave also had another major boost: Boris Johnson. On Friday, 19 February, the former London mayor and Conservative MP wrote two columns in the *Daily Telegraph* about the forthcoming referendum. (Until he became prime minister, the *Telegraph* paid him £275,000 a year to write a weekly column.) He sent both pieces to his then wife Marina Wheeler. The first was a jeremiad against EU law that opened with a curious section about buses and ended with a rallying cry for a Leave vote. The second was a rather half-hearted endorsement of Cameron's insubstantial renegotiations with Brussels.

The draft column is most memorable for outlining Johnson's policy on cake ("pro-having it and pro-eating it") and Britain's relationship with Europe ("It is surely a boon for the world and for Europe that she should be so intimately engaged in the EU"[26]). In the end, Johnson filed the original column, backing Brexit.

Suddenly, the referendum seemed winnable. By then, Vote Leave had moved out of 55 Tufton Street to larger offices in the

Westminster Tower beside Lambeth Bridge, right across the river from the Houses of Parliament. It was the same site used by Matthew Elliott's campaign against electoral reform in 2011.

Donations, initially slow, started to flow in. Much of the money came from major Tory donors who had also contributed to the anti-AV campaign. Jeremy Hosking, co-founder of the Marathon hedge fund, gave almost £1.7 million to pro-Brexit campaigns. Former Conservative Party treasurers Peter Cruddas and Michael Farmer contributed, as did Anthony Bamford. After Cameron's government sent a pro-Remain leaflet to every house in the country, the Midlands Industrial Council pledged to give up to £5 million to the Leave campaign.[27] As referendum day approached, Vote Leave had more offers of money than they could legally spend.

In January 2016, a slightly built, bespectacled young Brighton University student logged on to Facebook and set up a new account. Darren Grimes wanted to start a campaign to encourage young people to vote to leave the EU. It was called BeLeave – a knowing wink to the 'Beliebers' who flock to Canadian pop star Justin Bieber's concerts.

Grimes was an unlikely BeLeaver. He had been a Liberal Democrat activist. When Charles Kennedy died in June 2015, Grimes paid tribute to the former party leader's belief that "having Britain in Europe was the only way forward".[28] But six months later he had left the Lib Dems to join the Conservatives. In a blog post for a Tory website associated with Daniel Hannan and Eurosceptic Conservative MP Steve Baker, Grimes said the Lib Dems had lost "that classical liberalism that first attracted me to politics".[29]

Although BeLeave struggled to get much support online – the market for young, liberal Leave voters was narrow – its front man was making a name for himself. Grimes had a knack for crafting simple, stylish videos and graphics. He was also often invited onto broadcast media hungry for youthful pro-Brexit voices. Originally from county Durham, Grimes spoke articulately about working-class attitudes to the EU and their wider concerns.

BeLeave was also getting noticed at Vote Leave's London HQ, and not just for Grimes's burgeoning media profile. BeLeave's online campaign was cheap. The group could spend up to £700,000 during the campaign but in four months had spent just £21. BeLeave didn't even have a bank account. With Vote Leave starting to approach its spending limit in the weeks leading up to polling day, the larger campaign had an idea. It would transfer excess funds to its far smaller cousin. "When it became obvious that we were in surplus funding, we chose to donate to other campaigns," Vote Leave finance director Antonia Flockton would later tell a parliamentary public administration committee.[30] "There is a question as to whether they were independent campaigns acting independently. They were. Therefore, there is no issue in relation to our expenditure. The rules, to our minds, are quite clear."

But there was a problem with Vote Leave's plan. In spite of Flockton's confidence, it was against the law.

British election law is fiendishly complex. Around 50 Acts and 170 statutory instruments govern electoral contests. "Almost no one knows how it all works," Gavin Millar, a QC and expert in electoral law, told me when we met in his London legal chambers. A keen art lover, Millar compared the labyrinthine legislation to a work by Heath Robinson, the English illustrator best known for his whimsical drawings of elaborate machines constructed to achieve simple objectives. "Election law is like that. There are bits hanging off it everywhere."

One core tenet of this legislative maze is reasonably straight-forward: spending should be capped to ensure a level playing field. This principle dates back to the 1880s, when Parliament first legislated along these lines to try and prevent tyrannical landlords from buying up seats. Nowadays, the central plank of British electoral law is something called the Political Parties, Elections and Referendums Act 2000 (PPERA is its inelegant acronym).

The Act was introduced in the early years of the Blair government, spurred by press stories through the 1980s and 1990s about tax exiles funding the Conservatives. For the first time, political parties had to declare their donors, and overseas donations were banned. PPERA also established a regulator, the Electoral Commission, with the courts as a last resort to deal with any disputes. The regulator oversees general elections and referendums; for the former, the UK is split up into 650 constituencies each with its own spending constraints; for referendums the whole country is treated as a single constituency with no limit on the amount of spending until the ten weeks before polling day. In the EU referendum's 'regulated period', each of the two designated campaigns, for and against, could spend up to £7 million. Other registered campaigners could spend up to £700,000. In an effort to prevent campaigners breaking spending limits by giving money to front groups, any coordinated campaigning must be declared as 'joint working' and their spending must be counted together.

The idea of using third-party groups to bypass spending rules was not new. Matthew Elliott had once suggested setting up a slew of different organisations that would be "paper tigers" for the main Leave campaign. "He viewed everything as a front campaign," UKIP campaigner Chris Bruni-Lowe told the journalist Tim Shipman.[31] Elliott even proposed some potential names for these confected groups: Bikers for Britain, Women for Britain, Muslims for Britain. (Three days before the referendum, Vote Leave did actually donate £10,000 to a group called Muslims for Britain.)

In February 2016, Vote Leave coordinator and future Brexit Minister Steve Baker suggested in an email that the campaign could "spend as much money as is necessary to win the referendum" by creating "separate legal entities".[32] A former Labour minister reported Baker's statement to the police. Vote Leave issued a press release saying: "We never have and never will encourage people to break the law."

In the lead-up to the referendum, Vote Leave ran a raft of pro-Brexit groups to appeal to less traditionally Eurosceptic voters. They all had catchy names. Out & Proud. Green Leaves. Mark Gettleson, a former Cambridge Analytica consultant, designed the concepts for Vote Leave's faux grassroots groups. Gettleson and Darren Grimes had worked together before, on Norman Lamb's unsuccessful bid for the Liberal Democrat leadership in 2015 (along with future Cambridge Analytica whistleblower Chris Wylie). Gettleson's ginger groups would all fade into history, except for one: BeLeave.

In the crucial final weeks before 23 June 2016, BeLeave became increasingly important to Vote Leave's strategy to circumvent spending limits. In less than two weeks, the largest pro-Brexit campaign made a series of huge donations to Grimes's small youth-focused initiative. In all, BeLeave received an astonishing £675,000 in the weeks before the Brexit vote, mostly from Vote Leave. By the standards of the US these are tiny sums, but in Britain, where the average cap on constituency spending in general elections is around £15,000, it was a very significant donation. And even more importantly, none of the money actually went to BeLeave – instead it was all paid directly to AggregateIQ, the same obscure Canadian data analytics firm that Vote Leave used. This was never declared to the Electoral Commission as 'joint working', which is where unrelated organisations campaign together.

"Vote Leave didn't really give us that money," former BeLeave treasurer Shahmir Sanni later told *Guardian* journalist Carole Cadwalladr. "They just pretended to. We had no control over it. We were 22-year-old students. You're not going to just give nearly a million pounds to a pair of students and let them do whatever."[33]

As well as spending £625,000 with AggregateIQ on BeLeave's behalf, Dominic Cummings also brokered other donations for the youth campaign. In early June 2016, Cummings emailed a potential donor, hedge fund millionaire Anthony Clake, saying that Vote Leave had all the money it could use but "there is another organisation that could spend your money". Cummings suggested that Clake "send the 100k to some social media ninjas" in Canada. "Obviously it would be entirely legal," he added.[34]

On 15 June 2016, Clake wrote to Cummings, saying that he would split a donation between Vote Leave and BeLeave. Cummings replied the same day, saying, "We are also giving money to them – you can just send us the full amount and we'll add yours onto what we are giving them and save you the admin."[35] Clake later said that he wanted to give the money to Vote Leave but was discouraged from doing so by the official Leave campaign, as "they were close to their spending limits".[36] Cummings said, in a tweet subsequently deleted, that the Electoral Commission had given Vote Leave the go-ahead to give excess funds to other campaigners. The regulator strenuously denied that assertion.

After the referendum, the suggestion that Vote Leave and BeLeave had been working together hung in the air. There were press stories and calls for the Electoral Commission to step in. Nevertheless, the authorities were slow to investigate. One of the main sparks for action was a series of emails published by *openDemocracy* that shone a light on the internal workings of the Commission.[37] Staff thought the BeLeave donations "unusual" but that there were no grounds to suspect coordination between the campaigns.

In response, the barrister Jolyon Maugham threatened to pursue a judicial review, writing that BeLeave was in fact a puppet entity being used to breach spending rules. In November 2017, the Electoral Commission opened a formal investigation. There were "reasonable grounds", the regulator said, "to suspect an offence may have been committed".[38]

The investigation was slow, partly owing to Vote Leave's intransigence. Matthew Elliott later told the BBC that the Electoral Commission had refused to engage with his campaign, but the official report paints a very different picture: of Vote Leave repeatedly failing to cooperate. The regulator suggested dates for interviews; Vote Leave never responded. The campaign did not disclose documents. When they finally offered to give up the paperwork, it was only on the condition that they meet the regulator to discuss closing the investigation. The Electoral Commission sent authorised officers to inspect and take copies of these documents. "In the event, these documents were incomplete and some were not the correct documents," the regulator reported. Vote Leave sent legal letters to the Electoral Commission, threatening to judicially review the decision to investigate them. Proceedings were never initiated.

In a submission to the investigation, Cummings said that he "had zero to do with BeLeave's marketing, including what they did with AIQ". When I emailed Cummings requesting an interview for this book, he sent back a one-line response: "I've no interest in Remain campaigns." He never replied to my follow-up questions.

There were other allegations against Vote Leave. In early 2018, their former treasurer Shahmir Sanni claimed that Vote Leave had "tried to delete" key evidence after the Electoral Commission investigation had begun.[39] The whistleblower also said that he had been introduced to BeLeave by Stephen Parkinson, one of Vote Leave's best-paid employees and another veteran of the NO to AV campaign. Parkinson told the *New York Times* that he had been offering personal advice in the context of a romantic relationship with Sanni. Sanni said Parkinson's statement had forced him to come out to his family and put relatives in Pakistan, where homosexuality is illegal and gay people are persecuted, in potential danger. Parkinson was kept on as an aide to prime minister Theresa May. (In 2019, May appointed him to the House of Lords.)

After Sanni spoke to the press, alleging that there had been coordination between BeLeave and Vote Leave, he was dismissed by the TaxPayers' Alliance, where he worked on social media. Matthew Elliott's pressure group later accepted that Sanni had been unlawfully dismissed and that there had been an active campaign to discredit his allegations of electoral wrongdoing.[40]

In July 2018, the Electoral Commission investigation reported that there was "significant evidence" of joint working between Vote Leave and BeLeave. The largest Leave campaign had broken the law. Gavin Millar QC described the offences as being of "a scale and seriousness" with no parallel in modern British politics. But the penalties were minuscule. Vote Leave was fined a total of £61,000, barely a tenth of the amount by which it had overspent during the referendum. David Alan Halsall, a Conservative donor who was legally responsible for Vote Leave, was reported to the Metropolitan Police. That was the extent of the punishment. No one else in Vote Leave was sanctioned.

Running a campaign that broke the law was not an impediment to career progression. Matthew Elliott went on to a succession of prominent roles: at the Legatum think tank, as campaign manager for Sajid Javid's ill-fated Conservative leadership bid, as advisor to a hedge fund. Cummings joined Johnson's government. Darren Grimes became a paid-up culture warrior, first at Elliott's partisan news site *Brexit Central* then with the libertarians at the Institute of Economic Affairs. Boris Johnson – who had dismissed claims of Vote Leave's law-breaking as "utterly ludicrous" – became prime minister, with Michael Gove by his side.

One former Labour MP says that senior British government figures were aware of Vote Leave's overspending long before the Electoral Commission reported. "Johnson, Gove and Cummings all knew what was going on," Ian Lucas told me when we met a few days before the 2019 election general, in a bar near Westminster fitted out in shiny Christmas decorations. Lucas had been an MP for Wrexham for almost twenty years and was a member of the Department of Culture, Media and Sport select committee's inquiry into 'fake news' which had examined the Brexit referendum.

"I voted against the election because I thought we needed regulation before the election. It's a charade," he said. With a short, unkempt beard and a natty brown jumper, Lucas looked like a man pleased to be leaving the glare of frontline politics. Four days later, Labour lost Wrexham for the first time since 1935, one of dozens of so-called 'red wall' seats to fall in the Conservative surge.

Sipping a mineral water among a smattering of early afternoon drinkers, Lucas complained about the failure to hold the prime minister to account for Vote Leave's law-breaking. "There are still huge questions to be asked about what Vote Leave did, but they're not being asked. No journalist seems to ask Boris Johnson what he knew."

This lack of interest is revealing. Unlike in the US, breaking British election law is often treated as a bagatelle. The maximum fine is just £20,000. Louise Edwards, the Electoral Commission's head of regulation, told me that the fines she can levy are "scandalously low". For British political parties and campaigners, paying a few thousand pounds for breaking the rules has become the cost of doing business. "We are seeing people who don't want to work within the spirit of the law anymore," says Gavin Millar QC. "Once that consensus, that you won't break the rules, goes, you're stuffed."

Vote Leave was not the only campaign fined by the elections watchdog following the Brexit referendum. Arron Banks's Leave.EU was sanctioned, as were the Liberal Democrats and the official Remain campaign, for failing to provide receipts and invoices. A small anti-Brexit campaign was fined £1,800 for not declaring more than £50,000 of joint working. Campaigners complained that election reporting processes are overly complex and difficult to follow. "It is very easy to get it wrong and there is very little help," says John Mills, whose Labour Leave was fined £9,000 for failing to declare £20,000 worth of in-kind donations. Mills said that his sanction was "totally unreasonable given what Vote Leave was fined for".

A number of the Electoral Commission's decisions ended up in the courts. A judge overturned the decision to fine Darren Grimes

£20,000 for allegedly making a false declaration. Grimes, whose case was supported by Vote Leave, said that he was "relieved" at the verdict and that the sanction "was based on an incorrectly ticked box on an application form".[41] Vote Leave repeatedly denied that it had broken the law, but in early 2019 the campaign quietly dropped its appeal and paid the fine, as well as the Commission's £200,000 legal costs.[42]

The Metropolitan Police investigation into Vote Leave's breaches of electoral law was still going on as this book was being written. In November 2019, the police passed a file on Vote Leave and BeLeave to the Crown Prosecution Service "for early investigative advice".[43] "The time the police have taken has been absolutely ludicrous," Ian Lucas told me. "All these years on, we still don't know what happened." In an unguarded moment, a Scotland Yard spokesman admitted to an *openDemocracy* reporter that "political sensitivities" contributed to the glacial pace of the force's inquiries.[44]

Electoral legal expert Gavin Millar said "police are notoriously reluctant to get involved in this sort of thing. Understandably so." One option, he says, is to give Britain's electoral regulator the power to pursue criminal investigations. "Unless you put people in the dock and threaten them with prison, why will people play by the rules?"

In early 2019, *Brexit: The Uncivil War*, a feature film about the EU referendum, aired on British television. Cummings, played by Benedict Cumberbatch with a prosthetically enhanced receding hairline, is very clearly the protagonist. The drama closes with Cummings giving evidence at a future government inquiry into Brexit. The scene is fictional but most of the action that follows is largely factual (with some poetic licence).

In one of the most memorable moments, Cummings is told that there are three million people that do not traditionally vote who could be persuaded to support Brexit, if Vote Leave can reach them.

Instead of mail drops and billboard adverts, he decides to target the "missing three million" with ads on social media. "We are going to be making decisions based on science and data," Cumberbatch-as-Cummings tells the camera. "No advertisers, no snake oil salesmen, or fucking Saatchis. We're gonna follow algorithmic, statistical analysis."

In one of his many lengthy post-referendum blog posts, Cummings wrote that Vote Leave "spent 98% of its marketing budget" on Facebook in the final days of the EU referendum. This claim is almost impossible to verify due to the paucity of regulations governing digital politics in Britain, but Cummings certainly put a lot of money and effort into online campaigning. Vote Leave deluged around seven million swing voters with an unprecedented 1.5 billion pro-Brexit videos and messages on Facebook, mainly in the last three or four days of the campaign. "Adverts are more effective the closer to the decision moment they hit the brain," Cummings later wrote.[45] Internally, Vote Leave staff nicknamed the strategy 'Waterloo'.

Vote Leave and its sister campaigns spent more than £3.6 million on Facebook adverts. Cummings's decision to focus on Facebook was adroit. Around six in ten British voters use the social network. The platform is particularly good for reaching those that don't care much about politics. What was surprising, however, is how Vote Leave spent money on Facebook. All of the campaign's spending went through AggregateIQ, a company that, in early 2016, had no web presence and was based above an optician's in a shopping centre in the small city of Victoria, British Columbia. Cummings said he found AIQ "on the internet" before the Brexit referendum. "It was strange. Nobody in the UK had heard of AIQ. They seemed to come out of nowhere," says Sam Jeffers, an expert on digital campaigning in British politics.

Vote Leave was relatively late to the digital party. Both Arron Banks's Leave.EU and the Remain campaign already had access to large databases of supporters by the time AIQ began running social media ads remotely from Canada. AIQ staff soon moved into the campaign's London offices. They were even given their own room. "They were really the ones in charge of the online advertising," a Vote Leave insider told me.

AggregateIQ set about building an audience for Vote Leave's message. Co-founder Zack Massingham started by identifying people who expressed an interest in Eurosceptic causes online. This demographic was mainly middle-aged and older, less well-off and non-university-educated.[46] Once he had identified a core of potential voters, Massingham could use Facebook's tools to build much bigger 'look-alike' audiences to target adverts. Potential supporters were sent an increasing volume of online adverts. Messages were rigorously tested, and adverts that failed to get a response rate of at least 30 per cent were junked.

The size of this organic audience – well into the hundreds of thousands – allowed Cummings's campaign to drill down into highly specific sub-samples of voters. Then, in turn, the campaign could advertise directly to those groups of 'persuadables'. These key cohorts would be sent different messages. "We could say, for example, we will target women between 35 and 45 who live in these particular geographical entities, who don't have a degree," Cummings later explained.

He boasted of using physicists and experts in "quantum information" to crunch voter data. Vote Leave recorded spending over £70,000 with a firm called Advanced Skills Initiative.[47] The company is better known as ASI Data Science, a tech start-up that marketed itself as a world leader in artificial intelligence, and which employed a number of data scientists that worked for Cambridge Analytica.

Cummings also came up with clever ruses to find data on the "missing three million". He ran an online competition during the 2016 European Football Championship. Win £50 million, the advertisement proclaimed, by successfully predicting the winner of all 51 games. Entry was free; all you had to do was give your personal details. Nobody won – the odds were calculated at an eye-watering 5,000 trillion to one – but more than 120,000 participated.[48]

Cummings said the point of the competition was to gather "data from people who usually ignore politics".[49] Harvesting such personal information was not against the law, but Vote Leave was later fined by the data regulator for sending hundreds of thousands of unsolicited text messages to contestants. The texts contained a link to a website operated by Vote Leave.[50]

Leave's digital operation was not completely *sui generis*. Remain spent heavily on social media ads, too. It also had access to huge amounts of voter data from political parties. A former staff member of the Stronger In campaign told me that Vote Leave's big advantage was that it had much freer rein to craft messages without the involvement of political parties. There were no Conservative, Labour and Lib Dem MPs squabbling over what the campaign should and shouldn't say. Cummings used this space to run the biggest targeted digital misinformation campaign ever seen in Britain.

Vote Leave was often seen as the 'nice' face of an often vicious Brexit referendum campaign. Daniel Hannan preferred to talk about sovereignty and Brussels bureaucracy, rather than immigration. UKIP's only MP, Douglas Carswell, joined Vote Leave ostensibly because it offered a respectable alternative to Nigel Farage and Arron Banks.

But many voters looking at their Facebook news feeds in the final days before the vote saw a very, very different face of the campaign. In the final 72 hours before polls opened, Vote Leave placed millions of ads that spread wildly fantastic narratives about immigration, particularly from Muslim states. One Facebook advert claimed: "Turkey's 76 million people are being granted visa-free travel by the EU." The accompanying graphic showed a map of Turkey with *Dad's Army*-style arrows heading towards Britain. Other variations on the same advert featured maps of Syria and Iraq.

Vote Leave's ads were textbook examples of misinformation.

They took a kernel of truth – Turkey had applied to join the EU – and distorted it by removing any actual political and historical context. By 2016, Turkey's bid for EU membership, first made as long ago as 1987, had completely stalled. Prime Minister Recep Tayyip Erdogan was increasingly seen as an autocrat. He had suppressed protests in Istanbul's Gezi Park with tear gas and water cannons, killing 22 people. In Brussels, Turkey's accession was firmly off the agenda.

But in Vote Leave's offices, "every week was Turkey week", according to a former employee. Head of media Rob Oxley bought yellow rubber turkey masks for his staff. Politicians and campaign surrogates were encouraged to focus on Turkey as much as possible. A few weeks before the vote, Conservative minister Penny Mordaunt told the BBC that Britain could not veto Turkey's membership of the EU. This was not true.

Cummings knew the political value of dividing voters by playing on their fears around migrants coming to Britain. "Fear is such a powerful driving emotion, especially online," says Claire Wardle, an expert in digital disinformation. Unlike in traditional campaigns, Vote Leave's emotive images were not seen on posters or buses. They appeared privately, on people's social media feeds, as I discovered in Sunderland. They were part of an invisible conversation conducted away from the media's prying eyes. "You put all the negativity on the Internet and you put it at arm's length from where journalists can see," explained Sam Jeffers.

The only reason Vote Leave's digital adverts did not disappear completely into the digital ether was Facebook's decision to release them – with the campaign's approval – to a Westminster parliamentary inquiry in 2018, two years after the referendum.[51] Some of the 1,433 ads published had no imprint, a breach of electoral law if they had appeared in a leaflet or a newspaper. But the requirement that voters be told who paid for political adverts does not extend to the digital sphere, even though this is where campaigns now spend huge chunks of their budgets.[52]

As well as immigration, Vote Leave made great play with the now notorious claim that Britain sent £350 million to Brussels every week, and that if this money was repatriated it could be spent on the National Health Service. The misleading figure was debunked almost as soon as it had been unveiled on the side of a red Vote Leave-branded bus. The UK paid around £250 million each week into the EU budget, as a consequence of the rebate negotiated by Margaret Thatcher in the 1980s. The chair of the independent UK Statistics Authority described Vote Leave's claim as "a clear misuse of official statistics" in a letter to Boris Johnson. Nevertheless, Cummings continued to push this message through targeted Facebook ads.

Cummings believed this was a crucial factor in winning a tight referendum. "If Boris, Gove and [Labour MP] Gisela [Stuart] had not supported us and picked up the baseball bat marked 'Turkey/NHS/£350 million' with five weeks to go, then 650,000 votes might have been lost," he wrote.[53]

That is not to say that a Facebook ad or a shonky figure on the side of a campaign bus is *the* reason the UK voted to leave the EU. Remain had countless advantages. Indeed, if anything the pro-EU campaign was exactly what it was accused of being: an establishment stitch-up. Cameron spent more than £9 million of taxpayer money sending leaflets to every household in the country, urging a vote to stay in the EU. Stronger In peddled its own line in dubious claims. Brexit would cost families £4,300 a year. Britain would go into recession overnight. Remain had access to the machinery of government and a trove of party data.

Unlike in the case of pro-Brexit campaigners, however, these attempts to load the dice in Remain's favour were clumsy and inefficient, analogue weapons in a digital war. The government-funded pamphlets motivated Vote Leave donors more than ordinary voters. 'Project Fear', as it was dubbed by Eurosceptic hardliners, repelled more than it attracted.

Leave's illegitimate overspending and misinformation, on the other hand, was targeted and effective. Here, in this new world of political campaigning, even small sums of money can go a long, long way, while multimillion-pound government public relations exercises can prove practically worthless.

Cummings led Vote Leave unilaterally. He ignored members of his own board who wanted to push sunny visions of a buccaneering post-Brexit Britain, dismissing what he called "'go global' trade babble". Instead, he kept buying huge numbers of Facebook adverts that played on voters' fears with simple, compelling messages. In the whirr of the referendum, this digital offensive hardly registered. By the time recalcitrant regulators started to ask what was happening, Brexit had won. The victorious campaigners had already packed up and gone home.

AggregateIQ largely disappeared too – until, in the spring of 2018, the company became embroiled in one of the most controversial political scandals of recent times: the operations of Cambridge Analytica.

As Carole Cadwalladr revealed, Cambridge Analytica had illegally harvested millions of US Facebook users' data for political advertising ahead of the 2016 US presidential campaign. The London-based company had also been involved in election 'black ops' around the world. Reports noted how closely connected AIQ was to Strategic Communications Laboratories, Cambridge Analytica's parent company. AIQ had the same phone number as an SCL subsidiary and had worked with Cambridge Analytica on Republican Ted Cruz's unsuccessful run for the US presidency in 2016.[54]

Amid a barrage of negative publicity, Facebook decided to suspend AIQ as it may "have improperly received FB user data". Vote Leave's biggest digital supplier had been banned by the platform on which it had pushed over a billion ads at British voters.

With Cambridge Analytica accused of everything from hiring prostitutes to bribing opposition politicians to coordinating voter suppression campaigns, the question of who the people behind AIQ were – and how Dominic Cummings found a firm so small that its Twitter followers in early 2016 would have fitted into the back of a London black taxi – suddenly became a matter of major interest. The British information commissioner, Elizabeth Denham, announced she was launching an investigation into AIQ.

Certainly, the exact relationship between AIQ and Cambridge Analytica was opaque. Chris Wylie, the sharp-suited, Brexit-supporting data scientist turned pink-haired Cambridge Analytica whistleblower, claimed that AIQ was essentially SCL's Canadian office.[55] Documents later provided by Wylie's friend and some-time business partner Mark Gettleson to a parliamentary inquiry suggested that it was Gettleson, a former Cambridge Analytica employee, who sourced AIQ for Vote Leave.[56] AIQ co-founder Zack Massingham maintained that his company "has never been and is not a part of Cambridge Analytica or SCL"[57].

In November 2019, an investigation by Canada's privacy commissioner found that AIQ had broken laws in its work for Vote Leave. AIQ, the Canadian watchdog ruled, did not have proper legal consent from British voters to disclose their personal information to Facebook for the Brexit advertising blitz ordered by Cummings. The company was also criticised for security failures. AIQ had failed to properly protect the data it had misused during the EU referendum.[58]

Immediately after the Brexit vote, AIQ put a quote from Dominic Cummings on its homepage: "Without a doubt, the Vote Leave campaign owes a great deal of its success to the work of AggregateIQ. We couldn't have done it without them." This testimonial was later removed.

On a warm afternoon in early September 2019, I arrived in Westminster to meet Conservative MP Damian Collins. It was noticeably quiet; Boris Johnson's prorogation of Parliament had not yet been declared unlawful. A handful of protestors waving starry EU banners stood in the autumn sunlight. Police in high-vis jackets leaned on bright red bollards blocking a road where they had, a few days earlier, clashed with far-right demonstrators chanting "We love you, Boris". When I asked Collins if he was busy, he smiled politely. "Always."

Collins had emerged as an unlikely poster child for anti-Brexit campaigners. A Tory MP for Folkestone, a heavily Leave-supporting southern English port town, he had voted for Theresa May's doomed withdrawal agreement with the European Union in the spring of 2019 and then backed Johnson's leadership bid. But as chairman of the Department of Culture, Media and Sport select committee's inquiry into fake news, the burly, cricket-playing former Saatchi advertising executive had overseen Westminster's only sustained examination of electoral malfeasance during the 2016 referendum and beyond. Everyone from experts in online mis-information to senior staff at Facebook and Cambridge Analytica had been brought before Collins's committee.

The inquiry initially began as a bipartisan examination of the spread of disinformation, inspired by the efforts in Washington of Democratic senator Mark Warner and his Republican counter-part Richard Burr to understand the role of Russia in the 2016 presidential election. Quickly, Collins's remit widened. "We realised that fake news was not just a content problem," he said, "but that the systems of social media could be used to create audiences and direct people to content."

As the biggest digital campaign in British political history to that point, Vote Leave swam quickly onto the committee's radar. Vote Leave's law-breaking was, Collins believed, "just a tiny example of something that is easily achievable at scale". Inspired by US political campaigns and Cummings and Elliott's own prior referendum experience, Vote Leave had imported "the cutting edge of American techniques of using data and micro-targeting to drive messages", he said.

But Collins's inquiry had very limited powers to delve deeper into Vote Leave. Witnesses were not compelled to give evidence. When Dominic Cummings refused to attend the inquiry, he was found in contempt of Parliament. That sounds very serious, but it was no impediment to becoming the prime minister's special advisor four months later. "We are still interested in talking to Cummings," Collins told me, almost wistfully. "There are still questions we want to ask him."

Despite the serious findings against Vote Leave, there was little political will in Britain for a major investigation into how election law was broken in 2016. Unlike a general election, which can be scrutinised by High Court judges if evidence of serious cheating emerges, only Parliament can investigate a referendum. Many commentators dismissed the criticism of Vote Leave's law-breaking as a displacement activity for those who did not like the result. That might be fair as a description of political emotions, but it is hardly the point. The law had been broken.

Imagine, as Chris Wylie does, if we were talking about sport rather than politics. "If an athlete in the Olympics is caught doping and using illicit drugs, we don't ask the question, 'How much has that drug influenced the result? Maybe they would have come in first, maybe they would have come in second?' If you cheat, you don't get your medal. And in something as important as our democracy, we shouldn't stand for cheating."

In December 2019, Boris Johnson won a general election landslide. The campaign was a ramped-up reprise of Vote Leave. There were dubious claims and disinformation, anonymous adverts on social media and incessant lying. Journalists who asked awkward questions were sidelined. On the morning after the vote, Dominic Cummings stood smiling outside Number 10 Downing Street. Asked if he should take any credit for the emphatic win, Johnson's special advisor said "no, not at all". But it was not hard to see his fingerprints on a campaign that more than any other had pushed the limits, willingly eroding voters' capacity to separate truth from falsehood. Vote Leave had taken over British politics.

3

THE BAD BOYS OF BREXIT

*Our skill was creating bush fires and then putting a big fan
on and making the fan blow. We were prepared to and if you
could criticise us for anything – and I am sure you would – we
picked subjects and topics that we knew would fly.*

ARRON BANKS, June 2018

Arron Banks likes to make a splash. On referendum night, 23
June 2016, the brash insurance mogul threw a typically outsized party on the 29th floor of Millbank Tower. The 400-foot-
high skyscraper overlooking the Thames in central London had
once housed Labour and Tory election operations. Now, the lofty
citadel was being stormed. The self-styled 'Bad Boys of Brexit'
had arrived.

The Millbank party was to be a celebration for Leave.EU, the
insurgent populist campaign that Banks had bankrolled with what
was often described as the biggest donation in British political
history. The world's media was there. Free drinks flowed. But at
11 p.m., the atmosphere became despondent. Shortly before the
polls had closed, Nigel Farage, by far Leave.EU's most recognisable
face, had told a television journalist that his side had lost.

The mood changed as the results started to trickle in. The vote
in Sunderland was expected to be close. Leave won by 22 per cent.

The pattern was repeated across England, outside London. Almost every declaration pushed Brexit closer. At two in the morning, the stocky Banks, his rangy press spokesman Andy Wigmore and Farage, wearing a pink tie and grey suit, took the elevator to the ground floor bar to continue watching on a bank of television screens. "The adrenalin and the alcohol were doing their work. Excitement was at fever pitch," Banks recalled in his campaign diary.[1] At 3.44 a.m., Farage announced on Twitter that he could "now dare to dream that the dawn is coming up on an independent United Kingdom".

Hundreds of miles away, on the outskirts of Bristol, the sun was about to rise over a beautiful Victorian mansion. As Arron Banks was drinking champagne in Millbank, dozens of staff from both Leave.EU and his insurance business were partying in his property at Old Down Manor. The referendum results were shown live on television screens. A DJ played pop music. The majestic Severn Bridge connecting England and Wales twinkled in the distance. Towards the end of the night, when it became apparent that the UK had voted for Brexit, Liz Bilney stood up to make a speech. "You've done a great job," the Leave.EU chief executive told her team. Many were in their early 20s, and had worked for little more than the minimum wage. As Bilney spoke, one of her staff drunkenly sat down on the polished wood floor.

Banks would later claim that his insurance empire was completely separate from Leave.EU. But that was not the case. Eldon Insurance had bootstrapped Banks's Brexit campaign with staff and data. This was not the only discrepancy in the account of his extravagant referendum spending. Over the course of the three years that followed the Brexit vote, Banks was seldom out of the headlines.

He was slapped with major fines for misusing voters' personal information and was investigated for breaking electoral law. He made Trumpian attacks on Twitter against the "fake news media" and ran attack campaigns targeting Tory MPs who he deemed insufficiently pro-Brexit. Speculation about the source of Banks's political donations was rife. He owned African diamond mines and had clandestine meetings with prominent Russian diplomats and businessmen.

Banks was eventually vindicated when a police investigation found that the Brexit donations had in fact come from within his labyrinthine business empire and not from any third party. He has long maintained that "no money came from the men with snow on their boots". But Banks's remarkable rise to prominence underscores the weakness and confusion of the laws and rules governing our politics. This isn't just a story about alleged interference from Moscow. It's about money and misinformation much closer to home.

A biographer would have a difficult time writing the definitive story of Arron Banks's life. Even in the *vérité*-fluid world of modern politics, few have mixed fact and fiction so readily. As Banks told a parliamentary committee in June 2018, he likes to lead journalists and politicians "up the country path".[2] If admitting to an inquiry into fake news that he created "bush fires" to get attention on social media fazed Banks, it didn't show. He walked out of the session, with his right-hand man Andy Wigmore, to go for lunch by the Thames with two senior figures from the Northern Irish Democratic Unionist Party. Afterwards, committee chair Damian Collins complained that it was hard to know what to make of Banks's and Wigmore's evidence as "they frequently lie, exaggerate, misspeak and misunderstand".

Even Banks's earliest days are obscured by a fog of myth-making and inconsistencies. Banks has said that he "grew up" in South Africa, and on other occasions that he only visited the country on summer holidays, flown in from the family home in Basingstoke like an "army brat" to visit the sugar estates that his father managed.[3] Regardless of which version is closest to the truth, Banks certainly did spend some of his formative years in Britain's former colonies. Many leading Brexiters had similar experiences: Douglas Carswell was raised in Uganda; Vote Leave's head of media Robert Oxley has strong family ties to Zimbabwe; UKIP's eccentric and short-lived post-Brexit leader Henry Bolton was born in Kenya.[4] As with these other ardent Eurosceptics, Banks's time in Africa seems to have left him with a distinct sense that Britain needed to regain its former imperial glory.

In his early teens, Banks was sent to Crookham Court, a draughty 19th-century private boarding school in Berkshire previously used for the children of armed forces personnel serving at nearby RAF Greenham Common. Banks was expelled from both Crookham Court and a subsequent school. In an interview, Banks dismissed rumours that he had been caught selling lead stolen from school buildings as "fake news". "I've never nicked anything," he said. But in his own book, *The Bad Boys of Brexit*, Banks writes that he was expelled for "pinching lead off the roof and flogging it on the side".

What is certain is that Crookham Court was shut down after an investigation revealed that its millionaire owner, Philip Cadman, was a paedophile. In 1990, Banks acted as a character witness for Cadman at Cadman's trial. Banks told the *New Yorker* that the curious decision "shows my independent streak. He was a decorated war hero. I was asked to say what did I think. I can only say what I thought, which was: I saw nothing."[5] Cadman was found guilty and sentenced to ten years in prison, reduced to six on appeal.

Banks has often spoken approvingly of authoritarian political figures and decried what he views as the 'snowflake' generation. In 2013, on a public Facebook group for former Crookham Court students, Banks hit out at those who had assisted in the child abuse prosecutions.[6] "Crying over spilt milk doesn't get you very far," Banks wrote in response to an appeal from a former teacher, Ian Mucklejohn, for victims of abuse to come forward to pursue compensation.[7] Mucklejohn later wrote a book about the scandal in which he says that even students who were not abused had been "brutalised by a regime in which physical abuse and absence of human feeling became the norm".[8]

Banks's education ended with secondary school. Afterwards, he went straight into business. He began by selling things. Paintings, houses, vacuum cleaners. "I was quite good at persuading people to buy things they didn't want to buy," he told the *New Statesman* a few months after the Brexit vote.[9] Attracted by Thatcher's economic policies, Banks joined the Young Conservatives, standing for election to Basingstoke council in the Labour-held ward of Norden in 1987, at the age of 21.

Banks pitched himself as a law-and-order candidate unafraid of political niceties. He distributed leaflets that played up comments made by Labour MP Bernie Grant about a riot on a predominantly black estate in Tottenham that led to the death of a policeman in 1985. Grant, who was born in British Guiana, said that the police deserved "a good hiding". (Grant said he had been misquoted.)[10]

Labour activists were incensed that the young Tory was dredging up a divisive issue that had no obvious link to the local area. Banks's combative campaign was run by Mark Fullbrook,[11] who would later go into business with Australian spin doctor Sir Lynton Crosby and become a senior advisor to Boris Johnson. Banks lost. The following year he stood again for the Conservatives in Basingstoke, this time in a neighbouring ward. He finished a distant second behind an independent candidate.

Abandoning electoral politics, Banks moved into insurance. A neighbour found him a junior position at Lloyd's of London. He was young, recently married and needed a steady income. At Lloyd's, Banks learned the insurance trade, watching how insurers spread risks and traded assets to cover their positions. After seven years he left the firm and relocated to Bristol, after separating from his first wife, Caroline, with whom he had two daughters.

What Banks did next is not altogether clear. Banks has claimed he led his own sales team at Norwich Union – now part of Aviva.

However, Aviva said they have no record of Banks ever having worked for Norwich Union.[12] He has also said he worked for Warren Buffet's prestigious investment outfit Berkshire Hathaway. Buffett, nicknamed the Oracle of Iowa for his market prescience, said that Banks "certainly never worked for me".[13] What we do know is that by the mid-2000s, he had remarried – to a Russian, Ekaterina Paderina, better known as Katya – and was running a successful insurance business called Brightside. He occasionally made small donations to the Conservatives.

Life was not all plain sailing. In 2011, Banks floated Brightside. The following year he was unceremoniously ousted from his role as chief executive by new investors who, Banks claimed, wanted to cash in on the business. Banks tells a story of how, after his sacking, he punched his friend and former partner, John Gannon, in the face: "I hit him as hard as I could and he went over like a bag of cement."[14] Banks kept his shares in Brightside. When the company was sold to a private equity firm in 2014, he received around £12 million. This appears to have been his biggest payday.

Estimates of Banks's overall wealth vary wildly. The admiring Brexit chronicler Tim Shipman introduces him as "a successful businessman who had made around £100 million from insurance firms"[15]. In 2017, the influential *Sunday Times* Rich List put his fortune at £250 million, but this was based primarily on a valuation of Banks's insurance business that he himself had supplied to newspapers. He was later quietly dropped from the Rich List.[16] Bloomberg estimated Banks's fortune at around £25 million, mostly holdings in insurance, financial services and diamond mines.[17] These are not assets that can be quickly and easily transferred into cash.

An analysis by *openDemocracy* quoted in the *New Yorker* found that Banks had spent around "half his lifetime earnings" on the campaign to leave the EU – "an amazingly generous amount".[18] After the *Financial Times* published an investigation into Banks's business empire, the paper's editor, Lionel Barber, asked: "How rich is he really?"[19] In reply, Banks accused the *FT* of spreading fake news,[20] which by then had become the standard populist response to any inconvenient revelation.

One of the difficulties in ascertaining the size of Banks's wealth is that his business empire is so complex and opaque. His interests have included a British firm that produces iodine,[21] a uranium mining operation in Niger[22] and an Isle of Man bank[23]. He has set up dozens and dozens of companies, primarily centred on insurance. Most are registered at Lysander House, a soulless glass box on the edge of a Bristol industrial estate, and are ultimately owned offshore by entities in Gibraltar, the Isle of Man, Bermuda and the British Virgin Islands.[24]

Like many British businessmen – and many British political donors – he avails himself of the financial secrecy that offshore holdings give him. Banks, who was named in the Panama Papers leak of sensitive financial information from the law firm Mossack Fonseca in 2016, has said of his offshore interests: "I don't give a monkey's. I live in England. I pay tax in England."[25]

Some of Banks's most active holdings have run into financial and regulatory difficulties. After being pushed out of Brightside, Banks concentrated on his best-known business, Eldon Insurance. But by 2013, the jewel in his business empire was in trouble. Authorities in Gibraltar had, for two years, been scrutinising Banks's insurance underwriter, Southern Rock. They questioned whether it had anywhere near enough capital to meet strict new rules introduced by the European Union, designed to avoid a repeat of the meltdown that followed the financial crisis. Southern Rock's own accounts warned that the company was "technically insolvent" under the new rules.[26] If Eldon suffered a run of claims, Southern Rock could in theory go under leaving hundreds of thousands of British drivers without insurance and Banks's business in peril.

Gibraltar is not renowned for its officious financial oversight, but the regulator decided to act. Authorities in London became interested, too. Banks voluntarily recused himself from the Financial Conduct Authority register[27] and, in 2014, he stepped down as a director of Southern Rock.[28]

On paper, Banks had barred himself from working in a role where he was in charge of insurance operations, but he remained in effective control of the overall business. Southern Rock, which posted a series of losses, still needed capital to stay afloat. The company addressed the shortfall, in part, through an accountancy sleight of hand. Assets owned by the firm, including shares of future income from insurance renewals, were sold to other firms in the Banks group – a strategy that led City journalists to question both the health of Banks's businesses and the purpose of some of these transactions.

Even by the standards of the insurance industry, Southern Rock's bailout was an obscured, convoluted arrangement.[29] Banks later said that the Southern Rock deal was simply a case of "money that went from one company I own to another company I own".[30] The insurance business continued to struggle. In 2015, Eldon put 150 of its 500 UK staff on redundancy notice after poor financial results.

When faced with questions about his business, Banks often displayed the combative style that he would later bring to the Leave campaign. When a report by Gibraltar's Financial Services Commission confirmed Southern Rock's vulnerability to shocks, Banks claimed that its authors, PricewaterhouseCoopers, had leaned on the regulator. A few months later, in September 2014, Banks took out a full-page advert in the *Telegraph* featuring a photo of a pie and a cryptic comment about PricewaterhouseCoopers receiving a multimillion-dollar fine from US regulators. The advert was signed "Friends of PWC Gibraltar". An insurance trade publication described the ad as "how shall we put it, enigmatic".[31] Soon many British political commentators would use similar phrases to describe the man who bankrolled one of the most confrontational and divisive political campaigns in British history.

*

Banks only came to political prominence in October 2014, a month after his bizarre *Telegraph* advert, when he announced that he was donating £100,000 to UKIP. The Bristol-based businessman said that he was tired of the Conservatives' milquetoast position on Europe. After meeting Nigel Farage for lunch, he had decided to switch his allegiance to UKIP. "My businesses in this country and overseas, where I own a number of diamond mines, were doing very well. I wanted to give something back, and help the fight to get Britain out of the EU," Banks writes in *The Bad Boys of Brexit*.[32]

The donation was carefully choreographed for maximum effect. Wigmore, a garrulous former aide to Conservative cabinet minister Michael Portillo,[33] summoned Britain's political journalists to a press conference at Old Down Manor, where Banks was hosting a gala for the Belize high commissioner that evening. Banks had taken out a loan of more than £3 million to buy the grand house, previously owned by musician Mike Oldfield. The morning of the UKIP press conference, Conservative Leader of the House of Commons William Hague told a radio interview that Banks was "somebody we haven't heard of".

Banks was livid. In retaliation, he increased his donation to £1 million. "Hague called me a nobody," Banks said. "Now he knows who I am."[34] A former Leave.EU staff member whom I met during months of investigations into Banks's commercial interests described the move as "classic Arron". "He was pissed off by the Tories. To make a point he went off and upped the ante massively. That's how he operates."

Banks continued to raise the stakes. After David Cameron's general election victory in May 2015, Banks set his sights on leaving the EU in the near future. The £1 million contribution to UKIP soon started to look like loose change. Over the course of the referendum, he registered donations of at least £8.4 million to various anti-EU causes.[35] Exactly how much Banks spent during the referendum is unclear. Much of his support was made up of 'in kind' donations – staff, office and other resources – and loans to his Leave.EU campaign that do not seem to have been drawn down. "We probably spent around £3 million in cash in the whole campaign," Wigmore told me over the phone from Belize.

For British politics, even £3 million is a very significant amount. By comparison, Vote Leave's largest donor, the hedge fund manager Jeremy Hosking, apparently much richer than Banks, spent just under £1.7 million campaigning for Brexit.[36] Banks's money bought him the political recognition that he had failed to win at the Basingstoke ballot box decades earlier. He was invited on to television debates and radio panels. Newspapers wrote quizzical profiles of the man with pockets deep enough to buy an entire political campaign.

Interest in Banks and his money grew after the Brexit vote, spurred by the fact that he refused to go into detail about how he financed his political spending. "I am an entrepreneur," he told the *New Yorker*. "With all due respect to journalists or anybody else, how the hell do they know what investments I've got? You know, I might be a good stock market investor. I might own bonds."[37]

The questions kept coming. In Parliament, British politicians asked how Banks could have afforded to spend so much on the Brexit campaign. Journalists turned up new information about his complex business arrangements, which did not always reconcile with Banks's own accounts of his wealth. In November 2018, the National Crime Agency announced that it was investigating Banks and Leave.EU for potential failings under electoral and company law. The Electoral Commission had asked the force to intervene after concluding that there were "reasonable grounds" to suspect that Banks was not the true source of all the political donations made in his name during the EU referendum.[38]

Banks said he was pleased that the NCA was investigating him. "There is no evidence of any wrongdoing from the companies I own. I am a UK taxpayer and I have never received any foreign donations," he said.[39] But the story of the biggest donor in British political history was about to take a few more twists.

Shortly after the National Crime Agency investigation into Banks was announced, I received an email to my secure account. A contact said they had something I might be interested in. A series of emails had been sent between Arron Banks, Cambridge Analytica and former Trump advisor Steve Bannon. The correspondence, from late 2015 and early 2016, confirmed what many had long suspected: the links between some of the key figures in the Brexit saga and Trump's victory were long-standing, and more extensive than previously realised.

Some of these secrets were hidden in plain sight. In an October 2015 diary entry in *The Bad Boys of Brexit*, Banks writes that Leave.EU had "hired Cambridge Analytica, an American company that uses 'big data and advanced psychographics' to influence people".[40] Cambridge Analytica, which went on to work for the Trump campaign, had a burgeoning reputation as the cutting edge in election black-ops. It was bankrolled by radical libertarian hedge fund billionaire and Trump backer Robert Mercer. His daughter Rebekah sat on the board, alongside Nigel Farage's friend Steve Bannon.

At the time, Cambridge Analytica was working on Republican presidential hopeful Ted Cruz's campaign, boasting of using psychological data gleaned from tens of millions of Facebook users.[41] This would later be at the centre of the scandal that brought down the company.

Arron Banks looked at Cambridge Analytica and liked what he saw. Banks thought the company could work on Leave.EU's data operation and help solicit donations from the United States. Accepting political donations from foreign nationals or companies and channelling them through a qualified donor – a company or individual based in the UK – is prohibited under British electoral law.

In late October 2015, Banks wrote an email to a handful of his closest associates including Wigmore, Liz Bilney and businessman Richard Tice saying that he "would like CA to come up with a strategy for fund raising in the states".[42] Steve Bannon was among the email's recipients.

Banks had hoped to raise money outside Britain before – in Belize. He writes that the idea for Leave.EU was hatched in July 2015 when he did "a runner from reality"[43] with Farage and Wigmore to the tiny Central American state. The 'Bad Boys' already had ties to Belize, famous for its light-touch regulatory regime. Wigmore was a representative for the Belize High Commission in London, and Banks had been in the country a year earlier attempting, unsuccessfully, to set up a bank. Three weeks before they travelled to Britain's last colony on the American mainland, Banks was made Belize's honorary consul to Wales.[44]

In Belize, the three amigos Banks, Farage and Wigmore stayed at a hotel owned by Francis Ford Coppola and went fishing on a beautiful desert island, before travelling to the fishing town of San Pedro to meet Tory donor Lord Michael Ashcroft. Banks said he asked the Belize-based Eurosceptic peer if he was "going to join the fight, perhaps even put a bit of money into the pot". Ashcroft demurred.[45] (Ashcroft did not fund Leave.EU, but his imprint published *The Bad Boys of Brexit*, which was ghost-written by his close collaborator Isabel Oakeshott.)

Cambridge Analytica appeared keener to help with US fund-raising. On 25 October 2015, the day after Banks had emailed his advisors and Steve Bannon about attracting American donors for his campaign, a Cambridge Analytica employee replied, saying that the firm could develop a proposal that would include "US-based fundraising strategies".[46] (Banks said that this proposal was never followed up.) Leave.EU's leadership had already met with senior Cambridge Analytica staff to discuss what Banks called a "two stage process" to "get CA on the team".

Cambridge Analytica also asked Leave.EU to "connect us" to

Matthew Goodwin, a political scientist who had conducted extensive research on UKIP voters. "He should have the raw data from that, which will be very helpful for us."[47] Former UKIP party secretary Matthew Richardson responded: "I have already spoken to Matt Goodwin and the data is incoming." (Goodwin said that to his knowledge the data he collected was never shared.)

Bannon was copied into many of the emails. Andy Wigmore later told journalist Carole Cadwalladr that the Mercers were "happy to help" Leave.EU.[48]

When Leave.EU went public, Cambridge Analytica was there. At the London press conference to announce the campaign's launch in November 2015, Cambridge Analytica's director of business development, Brittany Kaiser, sat on a panel that included Banks, Liz Bilney, Tice and American lobbyist and referendum specialist Gerry Gunster, who was working with Leave.EU. (Gunster later said that he brought Banks "the methodology and the science behind how best to win, based on my experience of running many ballot measure campaigns here in the US".[49])

Banks later told British regulators that after "initial discussions" Leave.EU decided not to work with Cambridge Analytica.[50] But the email correspondence I received from my source raised questions about the depth of this account. Banks had told the Information Commissioner that the final meeting with Cambridge Analytica was in early January 2016. But weeks later Matthew Richardson had emailed Cambridge Analytica's chief operating officer Julian Wheatland saying that Leave.EU "would like to talk about using the service and staging the contract".[51] Another email talked of "micro-targeting" British voters. In early February 2016, Banks tweeted that Cambridge Analytica's "experts" were working on Leave.EU's social media. Banks later said he didn't hire Cambridge Analytica because Leave.EU did not win the lead campaign designation. He also told the *New Yorker* that he had been concerned about Cambridge Analytica's techniques. The company, he said, promised to raise "six or seven million pounds for the campaign", using an algorithm derived from the Facebook data to micro-target donors. Banks said he turned the offer down "because it was illegal".[52]

Banks's account of his dealings with Cambridge Analytica has been contested by former Cambridge Analytica employees. In April 2018, Brittany Kaiser told parliament's fake news inquiry that Cambridge Analytica had been given UKIP party data to conduct modelling and analysis that would inform Leave.EU's communications strategy.[53] "The fact remains that chargeable work was done by Cambridge Analytica, at the direction of Leave.EU and UKIP executives, despite a contract never being signed," Kaiser wrote in a letter to chair Damian Collins.[54] (Arron Banks denied this.) Kaiser also claimed Cambridge Analytica had sent UKIP an invoice for £41,500, which Banks had given the party money to pay.[55] The bill was never settled, Kaiser said, because UKIP decided that "their party was not the beneficiary of the work, but Leave.EU was". UKIP said it never paid Cambridge Analytica because "we didn't think it was worth it".[56]

Damian Collins told me that "the oddest thing about the inquiry was the relationship between Cambridge Analytica and Leave.EU". The chair of parliament's fake news inquiry said it was "very odd, the way people have run away from this relationship".

Cambridge Analytica was not the only controversy that Banks faced. The National Crime Agency investigation into Banks was the force's most high-profile inquiry into a British political donor. The move followed months of mounting speculation, especially about his Russian connections.

Banks's Russophilia was hardly a secret. He had a Russian wife and an admiration for President Vladimir Putin's muscular foreign policy. Banks had acknowledged meeting Russia's ambassador to Britain, Alexander Yakovenko, months before the Brexit referendum. Over six hours in November 2015 that ended with shots of vodka from a bottle supposedly produced for Stalin, Banks and Wigmore discussed everything from the war in Syria to Brexit.

"We chose our words carefully, but we didn't mind telling him we think everyone's in for a shock," Banks writes. He said that the introduction to the ambassador was made through "a shady character called Oleg we'd met in Doncaster at UKIP's conference".[57] 'Oleg' was not just any old conference delegate. He was really Alexander Udod, a member of Russia's foreign intelligence service. Udod was later expelled from Britain after the poisoning of Russian-British double agent Sergei Skripal in 2018.[58]

Banks maintained that this "one boozy lunch" was his only contact with "the Russians" during the Brexit campaign. But this was not the case. Reports in the *Observer* and elsewhere revealed that Banks had numerous previously undisclosed meetings with Russian officials and businesspeople around the time of the Brexit referendum.[59]

He eventually admitted to having three meetings with the Russian ambassador in London. He soon revised that figure to four in a newspaper interview. Other reports suggested as many as eleven meetings between the Leave.EU campaign and Russian embassy officials. Why was Banks so coy about these contacts? Was he just equivocating, leading the media up the country path again? Or was there another reason?

Politics was not the only topic of discussion at the initial alcohol-fuelled meeting at Ambassador Yakovenko's Kensington Palace Garden residence. The possibility of a potentially lucrative gold deal was also floated. Over tea a few days later, the ambassador introduced Banks to Siman Povarenkin, a Moscow businessman with residency in the UK. Banks was shown a presentation sketching out a plan to merge a mining company owned by Povarenkin with half a dozen rivals to create a giant conglomerate. The proposal featured pictures of shiny gold bars and a Russian flag. The multibillion-dollar deal was ostensibly backed by Sberbank, the powerful Russian state bank by then under sanctions. Povarenkin subsequently offered Banks an opportunity to invest in the partly Russian state-owned Alrosa.[60] Two months before the referendum,

Banks was presented with a third Russian-backed investment opportunity. This time a London-based Russian businessman with a Belizean passport was selling a gold mine in Guinea.[61] Banks acknowledged that these business deals were proposed to him, but he said that he never acted on them. He denied any wrongdoing, noting that his opposition to the European Union long predated his meeting with the Russian ambassador.[62]

Experts on Russia said that the Kremlin, which had been accused of being pro-Brexit, would have been well aware of the business offers being made to Banks. Sir David Omand, former director of Britain's surveillance agency GCHQ, said the approach to Banks had the typical characteristics of a Russian influence operation.[63] Anne Applebaum, who has written about Putin's Russia, said the deals presented to Banks were "forms of political bribery", adding: "Why should someone whose sources of funding are completely unknown be allowed to influence British electoral politics?"[64]

Banks said that he had never invested in Russia and that his various meetings with the Russians were standard business practice. "As a businessman, you entertain and look at everything," he said. "You shouldn't be judged on what you *don't* do."[65]

Banks certainly developed a firm rapport with Ambassador Yakovenko. The pair often exchanged pally texts and emails,[66] and Banks invited the bespectacled Russian diplomat to the Leave.EU referendum party in Millbank Tower. (Commitments in Moscow prevented Yakovenko from attending.[67]) The two men also met shortly after Banks returned from meeting Donald Trump following his surprise election victory in November 2016.[68] Yakovenko asked Banks for phone numbers for the president's transition team. The ambassador was later reported to be on the radar of Special Counsel Robert Mueller's probe into Russian interference in the 2016 US presidential election.[69]

Banks and Wigmore seemed to enjoy the press attention on their Russian links. When parliamentarians on the fake news inquiry asked if Leave.EU was bankrolled by Moscow, Wigmore answered

"nyet".[70] So why did they visit the ambassador? It would be "nice",
Wigmore said, for Banks's wife Katya to meet Yakovenko, because
"she has never ever engaged much with the Russian diaspora".
Katya did not accompany her husband to the embassy.

The couple had a turbulent relationship. Banks has told inter-
viewers that he met Katya at a Britney Spears concert in London
in 2000.[71] For both it was a second marriage. Shortly after arriving
in Britain in 1998, Katya struck up a conversation with a retired
merchant seaman named Eric Butler while she was sunbathing
topless on the waterfront at Portsmouth.[72] She asked him to rub
sunscreen on her back; it was butter. "I can't afford the sun cream
in your country. I am Russian and I have no money," she reportedly
said.[73] The pair were soon wed. Katya was 25; her new husband
was 54 and living on benefits of £72 a week in a semi-detached
house near Portsmouth's huge naval base. The marriage did not
last long. Butler complained that his new wife soon began staying
out most of the night, without explanation. He claimed that Katya
was of interest to Special Branch, which deal with British national
security and intelligence.[74] She was threatened with deportation
by authorities who believed her marriage was a sham, but she
was allowed to stay after her local MP, Liberal Democrat Mike
Hancock, stepped up to defend her. Katya's name later emerged
in the British press during a parliamentary row about suspected
spying involving Hancock and a Russian aide with whom he was
having an affair.[75]

Banks liked to play up speculation that his wife was a spy.
Famously, she drove a Range Rover with the number plate X MI5
SPY and had an email address with the letters 007.[76]

Banks's comic-book villain persona extended to an interest in
African diamonds. He had bragged of owning "several old De
Beers mines" in southern Africa and a jewellery store in Bristol.[77]
The success of his diamond business had, he wrote, encouraged
him to donate to political campaigns. In 2018, he said that his mines
were worth a combined $100 million.[78]

But those who went looking for Banks's riches in southern Africa reported finding little more than slag heaps and padlocked gates. The Lesotho mine produced only a handful of stones, with an estimated value of just £28,000. Banks's colleague James Pryor, who had previously worked for Margaret Thatcher and F. W. de Klerk, said the mines were producing diamonds but "whether it's massively economical or whether he's making hundreds of thousands is another story".[79]

In South Africa, Banks became embroiled in a bitter legal dispute with a former business partner that led to yet more questions about his Russian links. In an affidavit, Chris Kimber claimed that Banks "had travelled to Russia" to discuss investment opportunities in the South African mines with, among others, the big Russian diamond company Alrosa.[80] Banks described the claims as "ludicrous" and a "concoction of nonsense" and said that Kimber had defrauded him out of his share of the diamonds found in their mines.[81] In September 2019, Banks put one of the South African mines up for sale for just over half a million pounds. (When I called the South African sales agent a few months later, he said he "didn't know" if the mine was sold, then hung up on me. He didn't take my follow-up calls.)

Wigmore told me that he understood why Banks had sparked such extensive interest. "You couldn't blame people for having a go at it. It was such a delicious story. It had it all. Russia, Trump, Brexit, diamonds, the Panama Papers." The pair had been "naive" and "possibly a bit arrogant" but "hadn't done anything wrong", Wigmore said. "We were victims of our own hyperbole."

In September 2019, the National Crime Agency reported on their investigation into Banks. The agency found "no evidence" of any criminal offences committed by Banks or his associates, or that a third party had funded his Brexit campaign loans. Banks had not acted on behalf of anyone else, the NCA said, adding that: "There have also been media reports alleging that Mr Banks has been involved in other criminality related to business dealings overseas. The NCA neither confirms nor denies that it is investigating these reports."[82]

Banks welcomed the decision and said that he intended to sue the Electoral Commission. He claimed that the investigation had cost his business more than £10 million in lost revenue.[83] "We knew we hadn't taken any foreign money, it was ludicrous, but I'm glad it's over," Wigmore said of the investigation.

The workings behind the NCA ruling are quite complicated but they are worth taking a moment to unspool because they show – once again – the fragility of British election law. The agency – which specialises in complex financial transactions – found that Banks's main Brexit campaign vehicle, Better for the Country Ltd, had been funded through another Banks company, called Rock Holdings, based in the Isle of Man. Banks had essentially taken out a loan from his own offshore business to cover the referendum spending. British election law prohibits firms outside the UK or Ireland donating to political campaigns. But because Banks was a British voter, and so a permitted donor, and the beneficial owner of the Isle of Man company, no laws had been broken. The rest was just a complex accountancy wheeze. (Banks had previously denied that his Brexit funding came via the Isle of Man. Asked in 2018 by the BBC's Andrew Marr whether his donations to Leave.EU were "connected in any way" to Rock Holdings, Banks had said "no, absolutely not".[84])

Banks and his supporters hailed the NCA ruling as a vindication of their Brexit campaign. Others saw it as a tacit acceptance that companies in offshore jurisdictions could underwrite political donations. Foreign interests could set up shell companies in the UK purely to fund politics. The Electoral Commission said that this "apparent weakness in the law" would allow "overseas funds in British politics". Transparency International's research manager Steve Goodrich said that the case showed that the rules preventing foreign funding of British politics were "non-existent".

There was some precedent for donors using foreign companies to contribute to British politics. In 2010, a long-running Electoral Commission investigation found that Michael Ashcroft had donated more than £5 million to the Conservatives through a series of complex transactions involving companies that the businessman controlled.[85] Again the chain ended offshore, this time in Belize. (Ashcroft had not broken any electoral laws in making these donations.)

In 2016, the far-right Britain First party created a UK shell company to hide £200,000 worth of donations. Albion Promotions had no website, never filed any accounts and its only director was Britain First's deputy leader. Bizarrely, the Electoral Commission told *Vice* that Albion Promotions was a permissible donor, as it was carrying out business in the UK. When asked how the watchdog assessed whether it was doing so, the regulator did not reply. Albion Promotions was dissolved without ever having to reveal the source of the donations it funnelled into the British far right.[86]

Preventing foreign donations is one of the primary goals of British electoral law, but political parties have shown no compunction about raising millions from donors abroad. A clause exists in British legislation prohibiting anyone not resident in the UK for tax purposes or not domiciled in the UK (so-called 'non doms') from giving more than £7,500 to a political party – but this legislation has never been implemented. Successive Conservative administrations claimed that the measure was unworkable as a person's tax status is confidential. Such concerns, however, have not prevented proposed recipients of knighthoods, peerages and other honours having their tax behaviour assessed. Certainly, closing these loopholes would cost some British parties; the Tories raised at least £5.5 million from Britons living in tax havens in the decade from 2009.[87]

The vast offshore empire that runs through Britain is tailor-made for secretive donations. Many of the most generous donors in British politics have significant offshore interests. If these companies became conduits for political donations, it would be nigh-on impossible to tell where the money originated. In the US, anonymous super Pacs are already used to funnel vast sums of dark money into the political system.

Many believe that the British electoral system is inadequately equipped to deal with the threat of foreign money. Damian Collins would like to see "a higher level of transparency" applied to large political donors to prevent the kind of questions that dogged Leave.EU and its related referendum campaigns. "You should have to demonstrate that you have the liquid funds and where those funds were generated if you are going to give a major six-, seven-figure donation to a political campaign," he said.

Arron Banks moved money around his on- and offshore business empire to fund his massive political campaign contributions. This was all technically legal, it turns out. But it was also opaque and almost impossible to decipher, even for the electoral regulator. Yet if Banks's political financing was difficult to follow, the campaign it bankrolled was anything but.

On Thursday afternoons, Jo Cox, the Labour MP for Batley and Spen, held a regular constituency surgery in a library on Market Street in the West Yorkshire village of Birstall. Cox was on her way there when, just before 1 p.m. on 16 June 2016, Thomas Mair shot her twice in the head and once in the chest with a sawn-off hunting rifle. He stabbed the MP 15 times, shouting "Britain first" and "keep Britain independent".[88] Cox died shortly afterwards, in the back of an ambulance.

The murder of Jo Cox stunned British politics. She was a vocal supporter of the Remain campaign who had spent the previous day with her husband and two young children on rubber dinghies on the Thames, disrupting Nigel Farage's flotilla of pro-Brexit fishermen. Now, exactly a week before the EU referendum, Cox was dead, killed by a loner who had links to neo-Nazi groups in the US and UK. Mair was later sentenced to life in prison. In court, when asked to confirm his name, he said, "My name is death to traitors, freedom for Britain."

In the wake of Cox's murder, both Vote Leave and Stronger In agreed on a three-day pause in campaigning, as a mark of respect. Publicly, Leave.EU followed suit. The campaign was under pressure. Farage had just unveiled a new poster that consciously stoked fears about immigration. The image featured a long line of refugees beside the slogan "breaking point". In a diary entry, Banks wrote that the MP's killing "has shaken us all to the core... Wiggy, [Leave.EU's Richard] Tice and I talked about how to respond, and all agreed we should suspend campaigning activities immediately".

Privately, however, the campaign's reaction was very different. The morning after the killing, Banks emailed Liz Bilney, Leave. EU's chief executive, and other staff, telling them to "keep pumping" pro-Brexit adverts on Facebook, according to *Channel 4 News*.[89] Banks told Bilney to "press it harder" and "boost it more". A Leave.EU staffer drafted a press release attacking the media for politicising the MP's murder. The statement was in the name of Labour Leave, a putatively separate campaign run by Labour Party Eurosceptics that shared office space with Leave.EU in Millbank Tower. Labour Leave subsequently disowned the comments. Leave.EU complained to Ofcom saying that *Channel 4* had taken the emails out of context. (The broadcast regulator did not uphold the complaint.)

Leave.EU was created very much in Banks's image: it was vulgar, confrontational and constantly trolling. Online, the campaign pumped out an almost endless stream of belligerent videos, graphics and text messages, mostly about immigration. In the wake of a deadly terrorist attack at a nightclub in Florida by an American-Afghani in June 2016, Leave.EU posted adverts warning: "Islamist extremism is a real threat to our way of life. Act now before we see an Orlando-style atrocity before too long."[90] An accompanying tweet claimed that "the free movement of Kalashnikovs in Europe helps terrorists".[91]

The campaign even created fake videos purporting to show how easy it was for migrants to sneak into Britain from France. This claim was fundamentally false – the whole thing was staged off the coast of Dover[92] – but was reported as genuine news by the *Mail* and the *Express*. Leave.EU's unstinting, often distorted, focus on migrants was the crucial factor in the Brexit vote, says Steve Bannon. "It was that billboard that Nigel put up and the immigration issue that brought Brexit to a culmination. Like Trump," the alt-right *éminence grise* told me in an interview.

After the EU referendum, I started investigating Leave.EU's operation. I spent months travelling back and forth to Bristol to meet former campaign staff. Many described an aggressive workplace culture that often verged on bullying. "There was pretty much nothing that we weren't encouraged to say," a junior employee told me. Like everyone else, this person asked to remain anonymous.

Many of Leave.EU's most combative and controversial messages came straight from Banks. On one occasion, a few weeks before the referendum, Banks invited a small group of insurance staff to view an anti-immigration video before it was posted to Leave.EU's Facebook channel. A young broker said that the short clip lacked concrete information. Banks snapped back: "It isn't meant to be informative. It's propaganda." The campaign later refused to provide details of the adverts it posted on Facebook to Parliament's fake news inquiry.

Leave.EU can be seen in part as Banks's reaction to being snubbed by the Conservative political establishment. There was a vicious battle with Vote Leave for the official designation – and to win the right to spend up to £7 million. Farage dismissed his rivals as "toxic Tory toffs from Tufton Street". Banks described Douglas Carswell as "borderline autistic with mental illness thrown in" when UKIP's only MP sided with Vote Leave. When a Vote Leave source told *The Times* that Leave.EU was racist and homophobic and hinted at potential data theft, Banks threatened to sue. After Vote Leave won the designation, Banks threatened to sue the Electoral Commission. In jest, a journalist called Leave.EU "the Provisional wing of the Leave campaign". Banks liked the description so much that he started using it in press releases.

Throughout this bitter internecine conflict, Leave.EU ran an astonishingly toxic campaign that appealed to voters' basest instincts. Almost nothing was beyond the pale. Banks might have been a recent arrival on the political scene, but he played the media to maximum effect. He also knew how to use his business empire to support his political interests. And vice versa.

On paper, Banks was involved in a dizzying number of Brexit campaigns: Leave.EU, Grassroots Out, Go, Better for the Country. In reality, there was little separation between these groups, or between the anti-EU campaign and Banks's insurance business.

In Parliament, Banks said that his insurance staff did not work on Brexit.[93] Around a dozen former employees told me a very different story. "I was supposed to be working on the insurance side, but I was always being asked to work on the political stuff, too. I had to if I wanted to keep my job," one former Eldon employee said. Another recalled being forced to push hardline anti-immigration messages on social media: "Some of these images were really horrible. The immigrants and refugee stuff. But there were always these urgent requests coming in. You were told to stop everything you were doing and do something for Leave.EU."

Just how much money Banks spent on Brexit is unclear. As we saw earlier, much of his headline-grabbing multimillion-pound contribution was made up of 'in kind' donations and loans that might never have been spent. But Banks's campaign was spending significant amounts of hard cash, too. A cache of internal communications provided by a source gave me a rare glimpse into the scale of its operations. According to one email, by December 2015 – two months before the date of the poll had been announced – Better for the Country had already spent £1.5 million on the Brexit campaign.[94] As none of this spending took place during the ten-week regulated period, it did not have to be declared.

This highlights a wider problem. As politics becomes increasingly voracious of time and occupies more and more space on digital media, the scope for hidden influence through spending outside of the narrow regulated window in the period before a vote is all too obvious. "This is a huge issue," says political scientist Martin Moore. "Campaigns can effectively spend as much as they want so long as it's not in this short regulated period."

Another blind spot is the use of data during the campaign. Banks may not have hired Cambridge Analytica, but he was definitely very interested in the potential of data in politics, and for his business. Two days after the referendum, Banks wrote to a *Daily Telegraph* journalist saying that his targeted data campaign had delivered the victory: "Using – new to the UK – social-media polling technology developed in the US and dismissed by the established polling companies, the Leave.EU team had at their fingertips the confident ability to understand exactly what was on people's minds, where they lived and how they would vote."[95] Banks boasted that he was considering starting a new political party leveraging the "huge database" he had built up.

By the end of the referendum, Leave.EU was one of the largest British political sites on social media, with more than 800,000 Facebook followers. A former UKIP data controller later claimed that the Leave.EU campaign had "hijacked" the personal data of UKIP's entire membership to build its huge online following.[96] (Banks said the allegations were "false" and "politically motivated".)

Banks had access to a frightening amount of information about British voters. Before the referendum, staff in his Lysander House headquarters were under pressure from management to gather the electoral rolls for the whole of Britain.[97] These electronic registers, held mainly by local councils, contain valuable information including voters' names, addresses and postcodes. Staff were never told the purpose of collecting the electoral rolls, but a handful of Leave.EU employees were retained after the referendum to format the electoral data. "There was a level of urgency with it," recalled someone who worked on the task.[98] After formatting, the rolls were sent to a senior Eldon employee.

What happened to all this data is unclear. Electoral rolls are only allowed to be used during campaigns. In September 2016, three months after the referendum, a Leave.EU staff member emailed chief executive Liz Bilney, saying that "the electoral data hasn't yet been deleted". A subsequent email reported that the spreadsheets had been destroyed. This message came from a Southern Rock email address. Banks declined to explain why his Gibraltar-based underwriter had authority to speak about control over sensitive data about millions of British voters.

Banks always maintained that there was no data sharing between his insurance business and the Brexit campaign. But in February 2019, Leave.EU and Eldon were collectively fined £120,000 for data protection violations during the EU referendum.[99] Leave.EU had sent more than a million emails to subscribers that offered deals on insurance, before and after the referendum. Eldon Insurance customers' details were unlawfully used to send almost 300,000 political marketing messages. The campaign negligently disobeyed electronic marketing regulations.

The Information Commissioner, Elizabeth Denham, said, "It was deeply concerning that personal data gathered for political purposes was later used for insurance purposes, and vice versa. It should never have happened." Leave.EU and Eldon appealed against the ICO fine. The case was thrown out of court.[100]

The Information Commissioner was not the only regulator with whom Banks tangled. In 2017, the Electoral Commission began looking into his campaign spending. The watchdog fined Leave.EU £70,000 for a range of offences including exceeding its £700,000 spending limit by failing to include a fee paid to Banks's campaign organisation, Better for the Country.* (Unusually, Banks recouped some of his political spending by charging his own campaigns administration fees.)

The Electoral Commission also referred Banks, Liz Bilney, Better for the Country and Leave.EU to the Metropolitan Police. After more than a year and a half, the force announced that no further action would be taken.[101]

Leave.EU's legal battles were over. But the campaign was not completely finished.

Like his bitter rival, Vote Leave's Matthew Elliott, Banks often looked to the United States for inspiration. He found it in slightly different places and people. In August 2016, Banks and Farage travelled to Jackson, Mississippi, for a Donald Trump fundraiser at the invite of state governor Phil Bryant. The UKIP leader – introduced by Trump as "Mr Brexit" – put in a barn-storming performance. "He got a thunderous standing ovation," recalled Trump advisor Steve Bannon. "He got more of a standing ovation than any politician besides Donald Trump."

A few months later, the 'Bad Boys of Brexit' were back in the US, this time as the first foreign politicians to meet Trump after his unlikely election victory. In a widely shared photograph, a grinning, bleary-eyed president-elect stands outside a gold elevator in Trump Tower flanked by Farage, Banks, Wigmore, Gerry Gunster and former UKIP advisor Raheem Kassam. Within days Trump was tweeting that Farage would do a "great job" as Britain's ambassador to the US.[102] Downing Street responded by saying that the UK already had an ambassador. The president

---

* The Electoral Commission fine was later reduced by £4,000 on appeal.

repeated the suggestion again in 2019 when career diplomat Kim Darroch resigned following a leak of sensitive diplomatic cables highly critical of Trump. That story was broken by Banks's ghost-writer, Isabel Oakeshott.

Leave.EU was at the vanguard of a populist awakening in British politics that exhibits many of the same traits seen in the rise of Trump in the United States. Banks continued to campaign after the referendum, using the social media muscle he'd built with Leave.EU to push the Conservatives to adopt a hardline interpretation of the Brexit vote. Leave.EU's hugely influential Facebook page instructed its now almost million-strong following to join the Tory Party as part of an entryist "blue wave".

As Theresa May's doomed Brexit deal struggled through Parliament in late 2018, Banks attacked anti-Brexit Tories as "traitors" and "enemies of the people". Voters in Damian Collins's Folkestone constituency received a letter from Banks calling the chair of the fake news inquiry a "snake in the grass" who had "never respected the Brexit result". (Collins voted for May's deal and never backed a second referendum.)

Leave.EU bought adverts on Facebook against liberal Conser-vative MPs: of the 29 Tory MPs targeted by Banks, 20 did not stand for the party in the 2019 general election.[103] Many reported being subjected to horrific abuse and threats. One man was jailed for sending one-time Tory MP Anna Soubry a letter saying "Cox was first you are next".[104]

Arron Banks embodied the increasingly aggressive mood of post-Brexit British politics. Having once courted the media, Banks became increasingly truculent with journalists. Like the incumbent in the White House, he singled out reporters on Twitter for vitriolic personal attack. He posted a spoof video of *Guardian* journalist Carole Cadwalladr being beaten up and threatened with a gun, as the Russian national anthem played on the soundtrack.[105] Banks later brought a libel case against Cadwalladr, who had revealed his meetings with the Russians and much else.

When it was revealed that he had spent £450,000 bankrolling Nigel Farage's lavish lifestyle after the Brexit referendum, Banks dismissed the story as "a smear".[106] He accused the established media of bias and even set up his own news site, *Westmonster*, modelled on Steve Bannon's *Breitbart*.

Alongside breathless reports on burqas, immigration and crime in London, *Westmonster* was – like Arron Banks – an early enthusiastic supporter of the Brexit Party. In May 2019, the site's editor, Michael Heaver, was elected as a Member of the European Parliament for Nigel Farage's embryonic party. Banks later distanced himself from the Brexit Party ahead of the British general election in December 2019, and hailed Boris Johnson's triumph as a victory for his own entryist tactics. "We set out to make the Conservative Party conservative again: job done!" he said while appearing as a guest on the BBC's election night coverage.

Questions still abound about Arron Banks. Is he a strategic mastermind or merely a supreme troll? Or both? Almost from nowhere, Banks became one of the most recognisable faces in British politics. His belligerent, populist tone became a constant on social media and beyond. But Banks's story tells us something bigger. Time and again statements he presented as fact were proven false. When truth and falsehood become so hard to disaggregate, many voters will decide to believe nothing. Politics becomes reduced to a partisan battle in which anything goes. Most worryingly, the outcome of the National Crime Agency investigation into Banks's cavalier use of funds underscores just how susceptible British politics now is to the threat of foreign money. While Banks has made clear his funding came from his companies, not elsewhere, the agency's ruling massively broadens the scope for untraceable dark money. Future political donors will be able to make campaign contributions through secretive companies in the Isle of Man, Gibraltar and other offshore vestiges of empire.

While speculation has swirled about clandestine Russian interference in European elections, evidence of the influence of the

American model of dark money has been hiding in plain sight. In July 2019, just as Boris Johnson became prime minister, a string of influential Trump-supporting Republicans met in the New York Athletic Club to hear Nigel Farage launch a new pro-Brexit lobbying outfit. World4Brexit promised to expose the funders of anti-Brexit campaigns, investigate media bias and "use paid research to get our message out".

The campaign was organized "at the American end" by former Leave.EU Strategist Gerry Gunster, Farage said.[107] Supporters included one-time Trump campaign manager Corey Lewandowski and Mississippi governor Phil Bryant. World4Brexit's chairwoman, Californian Peggy Grande, appeared in the British Press, quoting her former boss Ronald Reagan. Offices were listed in Washington DC and London.

Where the money was coming from was a mystery. Under US legislation, World4Brexit's funders were mostly anonymous. Its literature said: "We have donors from all across the United States and across the globe" and pledged to "follow the letter of the law in the eyes of the IRS".

Until recently, anyone could have funnelled dark money into British politics without all that bother. They could have gone to Northern Ireland instead.

4

THE DUP'S DARK MONEY

At a time when politics and politicians are widely discredited
it is vital that those seeking to rebuild the reputation of politics
demonstrate good judgement in order to prove to the electorate
that they are capable of representing them honestly.

RICHARD COOK, 30 November 2009[1]

If you arrive by train from Glasgow on a warm spring afternoon, Clarkston looks like a Home Counties suburb transplanted to the southern lip of Scotland's largest city. There are four-wheel drives and rows of immaculately potted plants coming into bloom in bright yellows and reds. An air of sleepy prosperity pervades.

Slipping off the well-kept main drag, you walk down one of Clarkston's more modest streets. It's a winding strip of post-war semi-detached houses, most painted in pastel colours and coated in pebbledash. It's the kind of street where young boys still play football on the road. Halfway down, in a garden with a manicured lawn, lives a man named Richard Cook.

Cook has long been a Clarkston fixture. A businessman of more than two decades standing, he ticks all the boxes that mark him as a pillar of the local community. Ruddy-faced tennis club president. Conservative activist. Rangers supporter. Parent and neighbour. He is also the man behind one of the most controversial anonymous donations in modern British political history.

Before 2017, Richard Cook was best known in this part of Scotland as a perennial local Conservative candidate. For decades, Clarkston was true-blue Tory. So much so that when Tory Scottish Secretary Ian Lang controversially restructured local government in the 1990s, he created a standalone local authority for middle-class East Renfrewshire. Clarkston, with its seemingly impregnable Conservative majority, would sit outside the clutches of Labour-dominated Glasgow.

The impact of this gerrymandering can still be felt. Many of the four-wheel drivers who make their way into Glasgow every day work in well-paid jobs in the city, but their local taxes go on better roads and public services in East Renfrewshire. Politically, however, Lang's move failed. When Tony Blair swept to power in 1997, the Conservatives lost all eleven of their Scottish seats. It would be another twenty years before the Tories held more than a single seat north of the border.

Cook's political career coincided with New Labour's dominance. He didn't let lack of prospects hold him back. Tall and broad-shouldered with a loud, easy confidence, Cook rose to become vice-chairman of the Scottish Tories. Former Scottish Conservative press officer Andy Maciver remembers Cook as "one of the few people you could rely on at election time. He understood politics. He was able to appear in front of the media without completely messing it up. There was no question he had political ambition."

Throughout the early 2000s, Cook combined a job in the accounts department of a large waste management company with frequent tilts at public office. On the campaign trail, he often cited former local Conservative MP Teddy Taylor as a personal mentor. Taylor had been one of the "bastards" singled out by John Major after their rebellion over the Maastricht Treaty in 1993 almost brought down his government. Scottish journalist and later Labour MP Brian Wilson once remarked that calling Taylor by a cuddly name like 'Teddy' was "like calling the hound of the Baskervilles 'Rover'".[2] In the mid-1980s, Taylor said that Nelson Mandela should be shot. (He later said he was joking.) A few years earlier, Glasgow had become the first city in the world to give the African National Congress leader the Freedom of the City.

Cook followed Taylor's rightward political path. He became Scottish spokesman for the Campaign Against Political Correctness, railing against "overpaid salary-justifying busybodies who should go and get a proper job in the real world". Like Taylor, Cook gravitated towards the libertarian pressure group the Freedom Association. Dubbed "the conservative wing of the Conservative Party", the Freedom Association was established in the febrile mid-1970s to oppose what it saw, with a strangely distorted optic, as abuses of individual freedom. The group campaigned against trade unions and in favour of making it compulsory for all Irish people in Britain to register with the police.[3] English cricketers should be free to tour apartheid South Africa.

As the Cold War thawed, the Freedom Association became pre-occupied with Europe. In 2006, its campaign to leave the EU was launched in Westminster by Tory MP Philip Davies. Daniel Hannan, Douglas Carswell and Nigel Farage all endorsed the initiative.[4] Its supporters went on "fact finding" missions to Northern Ireland with MPs from the Democratic Unionist Party.

The mix of strident unionism and Euroscepticism chimed with Cook's political outlook. In May 2009, he addressed a Freedom Association fringe event at the Scottish Conservative Party conference to celebrate the 30th anniversary of Margaret Thatcher's first general election victory. The room in the Royal George Hotel in Perth was full. Former Tory MP Bill Walker, another of Major's bastards, arrived in his kilt. Cook gave a short speech, glancing occasionally at his handwritten notes. The Freedom Association's chief executive praised Cook as "one of the hardest working PPCs [Parliamentary Prospective Candidates] anywhere in the country".[5]

But all the hard work never quite paid off. In the May 2005 general election, Cook finished a distant second behind Labour's Jim Murphy in East Renfrewshire. A few months later, he contested Glasgow Cathcart in a by-election for a Scottish Parliament seat. A photograph from the campaign trail shows Cook giving then Tory leader Michael Howard a tour of a housing scheme. Cook looks older than a man in his early thirties. Behind him, on a lamppost, is a blue placard with just one word: 'Cook'. Above it, in brighter colours, is a sign for the Scottish Socialist Party. Cook finished third.

By the time the 2010 general election came around, Cook's prospects in East Renfrewshire looked much healthier. After three terms in office, Labour was struggling. Cook was fast-tracked through selection and given soon-to-be-prime-minister David Cameron's imprimatur. Expectation of a Tory gain in Glasgow's 'stockbroker belt' was so high that BBC Scotland sent a film crew to follow Cook as he went from door to door. Writing from the campaign trail, Cook said voters had little time for concerns about political financing and international affairs. "It seems to me that the public simply couldn't care less about the G20 or MP expenses," the candidate said in a diary piece for the *Conservative Home* website.

But Cook's time had not come. While Labour lost badly in England, in Scotland the party's vote held up. Jim Murphy won East Renfrewshire again, with a greatly increased majority. Immediately after his defeat, Cook declared the need for a political party that would "represent the hundreds of thousands of Scots who believe in the same things we do".

Cook did not stand for election again. Following his second general election defeat, he drifted away from politics. Then, in the spring of 2017, Richard Cook was catapulted into the political spotlight. This time it was not of his own volition.

*

Only two parties with seats in Westminster endorsed a Leave vote in the 2016 referendum. One was UKIP, which had a single MP, Douglas Carswell. The other was the Democratic Unionist Party. The small Northern Irish party would go on to play a major role in Brexit and its aftermath.

The DUP had long been a political outlier. Founded in 1971 by the Free Presbyterian preacher Ian Paisley, from the beginning its politics mixed fundamentalist Protestantism and strident Ulster loyalism. The party abhors gay marriage and abortion and has called for a debate on the return of the death penalty to Britain. Where British politics is overwhelmingly secular, the DUP is staunchly socially conservative. Annual conferences start with a prayer, not a raucous pop song.

Paisley built the DUP in his own combative image. He believed that Northern Ireland's nascent civil rights movement – and European integration – was a front for Irish Republicans, the Roman Catholic Church and the Pope ("the Antichrist"). Compromise with Irish nationalism or the Dublin government was dismissed with a booming "never, never, never". Tacitly, Paisley gave succour and support to violent pro-British extremists. In 1998, the DUP was the only major party to reject the Good Friday Agreement that effectively ended the Troubles and 30 years of violence.

Paisley mellowed in his old age. Power proved alluring. In 2007, after the St Andrews agreement, the DUP did a deal with the devil, Sinn Féin, and joined the power-sharing government in Northern Ireland's devolved assembly at Stormont. But the "satanic" European Union remained beyond the pale. Brussels, Paisley said, was a stalking horse for Rome, "a beast ridden by the harlot Catholic Church, conspiring to create a Europe controlled by the Vatican". (This didn't stop Paisley drawing an EU pension after sitting in the European Parliament for a quarter of a century.)

By 2016, Europe was a side issue for the DUP. Paisley had died in 2014. The party had survived a series of financial scandals and accusations of cronyism and incompetence to become the dominant unionist force in Northern Irish politics. On the centenary of the 1916 Easter Rising, which paved the way for Irish independence, Northern Ireland's place in the union had rarely seemed more secure. There was almost no talk of 'border polls' on Irish reunification – or of Brexit.

The DUP only announced its intention to advocate a Leave vote in February 2016. By that stage, the party was under pressure to pick a side. The DUP still draws a third of its members from Paisley's tiny Free Presbyterian Church. While the party's Belfast-based leadership came to recognise the value of the EU while in power in Stormont, its religious grassroots were solidly Eurosceptic. Some of the party's own MPs were publicly endorsing Brexit, too. DUP veteran Sammy Wilson had joined Nigel Farage at a Leave.EU event in November 2015. The following January, the East Antrim MP signed the Kettering Declaration pledging to leave the EU, in front of a crowd of two and a half thousand. "It was such a success that Sammy has suggested we do something similar in Belfast," Arron Banks wrote in his campaign diary.

Few in the DUP's upper echelons believed the UK would vote for Brexit. "We probably didn't see it coming," one party insider told me. Some even quietly voted remain. Occupied by domestic issues in Stormont, the DUP hierarchy largely left the referendum campaign to the party's eight MPs, a group who had previously exerted little influence in London.

Many of these men – they were all men – saw Brexit as a chance for the DUP to play a role on the British political stage. Westminster leader Nigel Dodds joined the board of Vote Leave, as did London chief of staff Christopher Montgomery. Ian Paisley Junior would later urge Britain to adopt a "no surrender" attitude to Brussels, echoing his father's rhetorical intransigence and the history of unionist resistance to Catholic nationalism.

During the referendum, Northern Ireland barely featured in the British debate. Former prime ministers John Major and Tony

Blair jointly warned that leaving the EU could jeopardise the peace process, but this was widely dismissed as the latest instalment of 'project fear'. The fact that the DUP, Northern Ireland's largest party, supported Brexit was frequently cited by Leave supporters such as then Northern Ireland secretary Theresa Villiers as proof that concerns about the impact on Ireland and the border were overplayed. The DUP did not, however, throw the full weight of its electoral machine behind a Leave vote, at least not initially.

The Democratic Unionists only registered as a participant in the Brexit referendum a month beforehand. Becoming an official participant was significant – the DUP could now spend up to £700,000 on the campaign. But there was little sign of such largesse on the streets of Northern Ireland. A few weeks before the vote, I walked around a DUP-voting Protestant neighbourhood on the outskirts of Belfast. Only a handful of Vote Leave placards looked down from below lampposts topped with Union flags. Most of the people I spoke to were intending to vote for Brexit, but their enthusiasm was muted. "It's really an English thing, isn't it?" said one.

The DUP did not record spending any money during the referendum until just two weeks before the vote. Then it spent far more money than it had on any political campaign, ever, almost all of it outside Northern Ireland.

On referendum night, Ian Paisley Junior, Sammy Wilson and others on the right of the DUP celebrated as the votes came in at the Titanic Exhibition Centre, a draughty warehouse space in the shadow of the famous yellow Harland and Wolff cranes in Belfast's docklands. Northern Ireland voted to remain in the EU by 56–44 per cent, but the UK as a whole voted to leave. The DUP contingent "were cock-a-hoop", recalls a political journalist present. Party leader Arlene Foster was conspicuous by her absence.

The next morning, Foster appeared before the Northern Irish media. She was sullen and downbeat. The DUP leader had not expected Brexit. The result would place Northern Ireland at the front and centre of negotiations with the European Union, and eventually put the DUP at the heart of British politics and the British government for the first time. It would also raise serious questions about the party's unprecedented Brexit campaign spending.

A few months after the EU referendum, I got a phone call from a tenacious Scottish journalist named Adam Ramsay. He wanted to talk about the DUP's spending during the EU referendum. He'd seen Vote Leave placards with the Democratic Unionists' imprint in Edinburgh in the days before the vote. Why, he wondered, was a Northern Irish political party paying for campaign materials in Scotland? I told him about the wraparound advert in the *Metro* in Sunderland 48 hours before the polls opened. Adam and I began digging together.

In February 2017, *openDemocracy* published a long article about the funding of the DUP's Brexit campaign.[6] The piece laid out everything we knew about the party's spending. There was the newspaper advert. There were the Vote Leave placards with the DUP's imprint that Adam had spotted in Edinburgh. We found social media posts. Most importantly, we were able to put a figure on how much the DUP had spent during the Brexit campaign: at least £250,000.[7]

The story caused a commotion. A quarter of a million pounds was an unprecedented sum of money for a political party in tiny Northern Ireland to spend on any campaign. It was more than five times the amount the DUP had spent winning elections to the devolved assembly at Stormont the previous month.

The sheer scale of the party's spending also begged the question of where the money had come from. The DUP's entire income in 2015 was just over half a million pounds, according to the party's accounts. How could it afford to lay out such a massive amount of money on Brexit? In his campaign diary, Arron Banks claimed that the DUP asked for £30,000 a month over four months in order to back Leave.EU. Banks said that he told the unionists "that's not the way we operate". (The DUP denied this.)

The revelation of the huge cost of the DUP's Brexit campaign played into ongoing scepticism about the party's financial probity. In early 2017, Northern Ireland was in the midst of a full-blown political crisis. Power-sharing at Stormont had collapsed. Sinn Féin pulled the plug on its often acrimonious coalition with the DUP when it emerged that a botched green energy project could cost the cash-strapped local exchequer as much as £400 million. The renewable heating incentive – which would become known as 'cash for ash' – saw farmers and companies paid handsomely for burning wood pellets. For every £1 a business spent, they got £1.60 back. There was no cap on payments. The scheme was established during DUP first minister Arlene Foster's tenure as Energy Minister, and many of the beneficiaries were party supporters.

A snap election was called for early March. The Brexit funding story broke just two weeks before the vote. Irish media outlets sniffed blood. Was this another version of the 'cash for ash' scandal? During a live televised debate with other Northern Irish leaders, Foster was asked directly about her party's referendum spending. She stumbled, eventually saying only that the money came "from an organisation in England that wants to see the union kept and make sure we can have a United Kingdom". The following night, the DUP leader sat for a television interview. She was asked again how much the Brexit campaign had cost. "I have no idea how much was spent. This was last June," she said, appearing testy and uncomfortable.

There was a simple reason for all this secrecy. Political donations in Northern Ireland were allowed to be anonymous. The names and addresses of donors to Northern Irish parties and campaigns were not made public because of "special circumstances" – a euphemism for the political violence of the Troubles. Donors to parties on either wing of the sectarian divide would have laid themselves open to being murdered.

Legislation had been introduced in 2014 to close the loophole, but successive Conservative Northern Irish secretaries had chosen not to enact it. Instead, donations were reported to the Electoral Commission but kept sealed and not released to the public. Anyone leaking information about a Northern Irish political donation could face up to six months in prison.

This obscure lacuna in Northern Irish electoral law is largely irrelevant during general elections – which are fought in 650 seats across Britain – but for the 2016 referendum, the whole of the UK was treated as a single constituency. Donations made to a registered Northern Irish party could be used to fund campaigning anywhere in the country. Dark money could be funnelled into the Brexit campaign without anyone knowing where it came from.

Under mounting media pressure, the DUP unexpectedly went public on the Brexit donation. There was no great mystery, the party said. A group called the Constitutional Research Council had given them £435,000. It was by some distance the largest donation the party had ever received. "The DUP had to give up a name. If they hadn't, people would have started saying it was the Russians or something even worse," said a source close to Ulster unionism.

But who or what was the Constitutional Research Council? The DUP said it was "a pro-union, unionist organisation based in Great Britain" that had approached the party "to support our campaign during the referendum because it supports unionist causes in the United Kingdom".[8]

Anyone trying to find out more about the CRC had a hard time. The group was what electoral law calls an 'unincorporated association'. It didn't have to publish an address, list its members or file accounts. It had almost no Internet footprint. Many in the DUP hierarchy had never heard of it. "The first I knew of them was when I saw the name in the paper," said a well-placed party source.

The Constitutional Research Council did have one name attached to it: a chairman. He was Richard Cook, the diligent

Clarkston Tory. The DUP said that Cook was a "very credible, respectable person".

Richard Cook was largely silent when news of the DUP donation broke. Media requests to his Clarkston home went unanswered. When he did speak, he refused to reveal the source of the cash and said that, although he had administered the massive DUP donation, he had never received any money from his involvement in the CRC. "I just run a small consultancy company, doing some waste energy stuff internationally," he said.

Cook had not always been so modest about his business interests. In 2008, he became a founding director of a company called DDR Recycling. Recycling was a growth market, and after almost a decade working in waste management, Cook was well placed to move into it. On the general election campaign trail in 2010, he talked up his environmental credentials. Companies, he said, needed "to play their part in a cleaner, more sustainable planet". Cook had the backing of his party leader, who was urging British voters to "vote blue, go green". David Cameron was photographed hugging a husky on the Norwegian tundra.

Around the same time as Cook was promising to "clean up politics", his recycling business started to take off. From a small office in an unremarkable industrial estate on the outskirts of Glasgow, DDR signed multimillion-pound contracts around the world.[9] There were deals in Russia, Mexico, South Korea.

In April 2009, DDR shipped 250 tonnes of valuable hard rubber crumb to the Indian port city of Cochin. But there was a problem – the containers were filled with scrap tyres, which it was illegal to export to India. Cook's company had sent Indian authorities tests which supposedly showed that the cargo was high-quality rubber, not illegal scrap. These tests appeared to have been carried out by a company called Grapevine Networking. But Grapevine was actually a recruitment business based in Glasgow city centre run by Cook's fellow DDR director, Donald McCorquodale.[10] "Grapevine Networking never did any tests on any rubber at all," McCorquodale told me later. "It does seem strange, but I have absolutely no idea at all." Cook has said that he was "not involved in any illegal shipment to Cochin, India, against UK and Indian regulations". He also said that he had "no knowledge" of the certificate for the rubber sent to the Indian authorities and was not involved in the recruitment company.

Back in Britain, the Environmental Agency sent DDR dozens of increasingly testy emails through 2010 and 2011 demanding that the Scottish company repatriate the illegal shipment on the docks in Cochin. Cook told the regulator that the cargo was the responsibility of a Romanian company that was handling it. When British regulators pointed out that Cook was listed as a director of the Romanian intermediary on his own LinkedIn profile, he claimed that his social media had been hacked. Cook told the agency that he had "contacted LinkedIn to establish how a fraudulent entry could be made to my profile". LinkedIn said it had no record of receiving a complaint from Cook.

The scrap tyres were eventually shipped to Malaysia.[11] The cumulative transportation costs were over $1 million. DDR Recycling never paid the bill. Cook said that he had no knowledge of the company owing any debts for a shipment of rubber waste. The British environmental regulator appeared to lose interest in the case and ceased contacting DDR.

In all, from its small office in Glasgow, DDR Recycling signed contracts worth over $1 billion around the world. In 2013, DDR agreed a $80 million deal in Ukraine to ship 20,000 tonnes of railway tracks every month for a year.[12] The contract was with a German national who had previously been sentenced to eight years in prison for running an elaborate grain fraud that almost collapsed the EU's organic food market in the early 2000s. There is no sign that the railway sleepers existed. A retired FBI Special Agent who specialised in financial crimes and money laundering told BBC Northern Ireland that such high-value dollar contracts would likely be of interest to authorities in the US.[13] Cook has said that he had no knowledge of the Ukrainian contract and that he was not actively involved in DDR at the time of the deal.

Richard Cook resigned from DDR in February 2014. Later that year he was listed as a defendant in a court case in California taken by international logistics giant UPS after his recycling firm failed to pay over $450,000 for the transportation of steel wire to Busan, South Korea. A few months before the South Korean shipment, Cook had wired over $3,000 to UPS. The multinational claimed that this and other payments for much smaller shipments were "for the purpose of inducing UPS to provide additional shipping services to DDR". However, the Scottish company failed to pay the subsequent, much larger, bills. Court documents paint a picture of consistent avoidance by DDR. After a series of exchanges, in May 2013 a UPS lawyer wrote to Donald McCorquodale saying, "Your emails to date have provided UPS with no pertinent information and only seek additional non-relevant information in a transparent attempt to avoid your debt." A default judgment of more than $1.5 million was eventually awarded against Cook and a number of the company's associates.[14] Cook has denied any wrongdoing in relation to DDR Recycling. He said that at "no time" had he ever used UPS and that he was unaware of being listed as a defendant in the legal case in California. DDR went into liquidation in 2017, owing revenue and customs around £150,000.

At times Cook's business dealings read like excerpts from an airport thriller. His private consulting company was part of a $1 billion deal to develop drinking water facilities in Pakistan that never got off the ground. In 2013, Cook became the founding director of a wealth management company called Five Star Investment Management Ltd. Three-quarters of the business was owned by the former head of the Saudi Arabian intelligence agency, Prince Nawwaf bin Abdul Aziz.[15] The prince's son was the Saudi ambassador to the UK at the time. A third director was a Dane named Peter Haestrup who had previously been involved in a notorious Indian gun-running case known as the Purulia Arms Drop.[16] In December 1995, a consignment of 548 Bulgarian AK-47 rifles, 11.3 tonnes of ammunition, rocket launchers and anti-tank weapons were parachuted from a low-flying Russian-made plane over Purulia in West Bengal state. The arsenal was intended for a violent Hindu cult opposed to the provincial communist government. The Indian Central Bureau of Investigation named Haestrup in a probe into the arms drop. Haestrup was never charged. When I called his Danish home, Haestrup told me that he had done nothing wrong. "Have you been a soldier? A lot of things happen in the world," he said. "I was involved there but I [have] never been accused of anything. I have a 100% clean record."

Haestrup met Richard Cook through mutual banking connections in London. But the wealth management business didn't get far. "We had a lot of good talks, a lot of good dinners but we never got started on the business. We did not want to do business the way the Saudis did," Haestrup said. The company was dissolved in December 2014. Prince Nawwaf bin Abdul Aziz died the following year, aged 83.[17] Cook later dismissed questions about his links to Saudi Arabia as "just fake news".[18]

In 2017, Cook said that the Constitutional Research Council was willing to bankroll other Unionist political causes. He refused to name anyone else involved, or to say who had donated money to his organisation. He said that the CRC operated within the bounds of electoral law and only gave out money from eligible donors domiciled in the UK.

In the days leading up to the Brexit referendum, around five million voters – most of them in England – received targeted Facebook ads from the DUP.[19] Bright blue and red messages with the party's lion head logo promised that Brexit would be "better for jobs", "better for security" and "better for family budgets". One advert pledged that a Leave vote would be "better for our borders" – oblivious to the difficulties that the Irish border would later pose in Brexit negotiations. This massive social media campaign was run by AggregateIQ, the same analytics firm used by Vote Leave and its surrogates.

Hiring a data company thousands of miles away in Canada was highly unusual for the DUP. The party had always adopted a decidedly local approach to political spending and politics in general. In previous elections, the DUP had very seldom worked with companies based outside Northern Ireland. Every single penny that the party spent in the run-up to the May 2016 Stormont elections went to local firms.

The EU referendum was different. The party spent the vast majority of its massive budget outside Northern Ireland. The spending spree began on 9 June, exactly two weeks before the vote, when the DUP bought £100,000 worth of placards, bags, window stickers, t-shirts and badges from a small branding agency called Soopa Doopa in the Cambridgeshire cathedral town of Ely.[20] The campaign merchandise – paid for by the CRC – appeared throughout mainland Britain. Popular BBC Radio Ulster presenter Stephen Nolan would later invite his listeners to phone in if they had seen any DUP-branded material in Northern Ireland during the Brexit campaign. The lines were unusually quiet.

Soopa Doopa's location was not the only factor that made it a surprising choice for the DUP. The company was small and young, with little obvious experience in the world of political advertising. But during the Brexit referendum, various Leave-supporting groups spent more than £800,000 with the firm. Otherwise fierce rivals Vote Leave and Leave.EU both employed Soopa Doopa to produce election material.

As we saw earlier in this book, British election law has strict rules on campaign groups working together, to prevent one side gaining an unfair advantage by moving money around to circumvent spending limits. Using the same supplier is not in itself evidence of coordination, but quite how so many different campaigns all stumbled across the same small branding operation is not clear. Asked how Soopa Doopa was able to attract so much referendum business, owner Jake Scott-Paul said that his firm had been "lucky". The company was not hired by anyone during the 2017 UK general election, but it later worked for Nigel Farage's Brexit Party.

This allegation of joint working was at the nub of Vote Leave's violations of electoral law. The campaign failed to add its donations to the BeLeave youth campaign to its declared spending, which pushed it far beyond the £7 million spending limit. Did Vote Leave work with the DUP, too? Certainly, the official campaign in London was aware of the DUP's potential to spend significant amounts. Two months before the referendum, Matthew Elliott, Vote Leave's chief executive, wrote in an email to senior staff: "The DUP also have a £700k spending limit, which can be spent nationwide!"[21] At that stage the DUP had yet to register as a referendum participant. It only did so in late May.

When the CRC started giving money to the DUP, Vote Leave had almost completely exhausted its spending allowance. On 21 June, just two days before polls opened, the CRC donated a further £334,993 to the DUP. That very same day the DUP-branded wraparound *Metro* advert appeared carrying Vote Leave's key slogan: "Take back control". It was Richard Cook, not the DUP, who booked the front page advertisement.[22]

The similarities between the DUP and Vote Leave's campaigning did not end there. On 20 June, a day before the DUP had even received Cook's additional contribution, the party spent more than £32,000 on digital advertising with AggregateIQ. During the referendum, AIQ had bought millions of pounds worth of Facebook ads on behalf of a suite of pro-Brexit campaigns clustered around Vote Leave. These ads carried similar messages about the benefits of leaving the European Union, but were separately branded for the different campaigns.

How the DUP found AIQ is not clear. A DUP source would

later say that they could not remember where they had heard about the data analytics firm. Nevertheless, just 72 hours before the Brexit vote, the DUP spent almost as much money on Facebook ads with an unheralded company in British Columbia as it had invested in the entire Stormont campaign the previous month.

According to Cambridge Analytica whistleblower Chris Wylie, the DUP were simply a front organisation to allow Vote Leave to go beyond spending limits imposed by election laws. Wylie claimed that AIQ's Jeff Silvester told him that this was all part of a common plan that was "totally illegal". (Silvester denied this.) A computer expert who analysed source codes for AIQ's referendum work that had been uploaded onto the Internet said that he could find no mention of the DUP, but lots of references to Vote Leave. "I would conclude beyond a shadow of a doubt that there was some sort of collaboration going on," Chris Vickery told Parliament's fake news inquiry.[23] (The DUP and Vote Leave both denied this.)

There was more evidence that Vote Leave and the DUP could have been working to a common plan. They were supposedly separate organisations, but AIQ's Jeff Silvester told a BBC Northern Ireland documentary on the DUP's donation that the firm's contact person in the unionist party was local councillor Lee Reynolds, who had been seconded to head up Vote Leave Northern Ireland. Gavin Millar QC described this arrangement as "a sham" that suggested that Vote Leave was directing the DUP's spending – in contravention of the law. "It pulls Vote Leave and the organisation of the Vote Leave campaign Northern Ireland firmly into the activities of the DUP which are being funded by Cook's money," Millar said. (The DUP said that its work with AIQ was directed by the party. Reynolds said that he did not direct DUP activities with AIQ while he worked for Vote Leave.)

Had the DUP checked if the CRC donation was legal? Under British electoral law, the onus falls on political parties to make sure money they receive is permissible. When probed about the CRC donation, however, the DUP's treasurer, Gregory Campbell, said that he was under no obligation to verify political contributions. Campbell asked a journalist from the investigative news site *Source Material*: "How would I be or anybody in our party be expected to know who the individuals are that are involved in the organisation?"

The BBC Northern Ireland documentary was watched with interest by staff at the Electoral Commission in London. The morning after transmission, the watchdog's head of regulation wrote to colleagues saying that Campbell's comments were "sufficient for us to have concerns" about whether the DUP had carried out checks on the source of the CRC donation. The head of the Northern Irish Electoral Commission told senior staff that "the most compelling point they made was on potential joint working. There is new information there."[24]

So how did the elections regulator respond to this new information? With a robust investigation?

Not quite. The Commission contacted the DUP, warning that party treasurers were responsible for ensuring that all donations are permissible. Campbell replied, expressing his "disappointment" that the watchdog had written to him after a "biased BBC output". Campbell said his interview had been used "out of context" and "in an attempt to convey an incorrect impression".

The regulator seemed keen to limit its inquiries to letter-writing. Internally, the Electoral Commission said that even if Vote Leave had collaborated with the Democratic Unionists, "it would not be in the public interest to investigate" as the official campaign had already been fined for breaking electoral law.[25] Commission staff said that there were "a number of possible explanations" for why Richard Cook had booked the *Metro* ad. Rather than call the newspaper to ask, the watchdog decided that it would not be "appropriate" to inquire further about a crucial aspect of the biggest political donation in Northern Irish history.[26]

The regulator also noted Cook's business background, including DDR Recycling's alleged involvement in the shipment of illegal waste. The Commission concluded that British electoral law "is silent on whether or not money obtained from crime would make a political contribution unlawful". It seems that not even the body charged with overseeing British democracy knows if giving money derived from crime to political causes is illegal.

Less than three weeks after the BBC film aired, the Electoral Commission put out a short statement "to draw a line" under the issue. There was no further investigation of the DUP's unlikely Brexit campaign bonanza. At the end of the referendum, the party had £9,000 left over from the CRC donation. This was transferred to a DUP bank account "for pro-union campaigning".[27]

The Democratic Unionists' political fortunes were transformed on 8 June 2017. At 10 p.m. that evening, as ballot boxes closed across the UK, the BBC published a shock exit poll. Tory prime minister Theresa May had called a general election intending to cement her position. Some pundits predicted a 100-seat victory. Instead, she lost her majority. Parliament was hung. The Conservatives could only remain in power if they secured the support of the Democratic Unionists' ten MPs. That night the DUP was the most searched political party on Google in the UK.

May moved quickly to form a pact with the Northern Irish unionists. After two weeks of negotiation, the first parliamentary 'confidence and supply' arrangement in decades was agreed. The unionists had no interest in a formal coalition, which would have given the party the enhanced responsibility of ministerial portfolios. Instead, the DUP contingent in Westminster would support May's government on votes of confidence and budgetary matters. In return, the DUP would get £1 billion of concessions, mainly for infrastructure and health spending in one of the poorest regions in Western Europe. A hard-right party formed by a loyalist street preacher now had unprecedented clout inside the British government.

The DUP's newfound prominence also brought the story

of the unexplained Brexit money to a new audience. UK news outlets were now beating a path to Richard Cook's door. There were renewed calls to end donor secrecy. Secretary of State James Brokenshire announced proposals to finally bring Northern Ireland into line with the rest of the UK.

But there was a snag. Political contributions would only be published from July 2017. All previous giving would be excluded – including donations made during the EU referendum. This was particularly curious, as an Act of Parliament already existed allowing all Northern Irish political donations to be made public from January 2014 onwards. With a flick of a pen, the secretary of state could have enacted that legislation. But he chose not to do so.

So, in mid-December 2017, on the eve of Parliament's Christmas recess, 17 MPs met in a Westminster committee room to consider the order that would bring donor transparency to Northern Ireland. The debate was truncated and bad-tempered. Ben Bradshaw told the committee that the failure to backdate Northern Irish donations "stinks". The Labour MP said that:

> The only conclusion that any reasonable person can draw is that the DUP was used, with its knowledge, by the CRC to funnel money to the Leave campaign in a way that to this day keeps the source of that money secret. By refusing to make this provision retrospective, the Government are effectively complicit in covering that up.[28]

Labour MPs on the committee frequently clashed with the two DUP MPs present. Technically, Sammy Wilson and Ian Paisley Junior were observers, but they continually heckled and interjected. Both said that their party had been fully transparent about the £435,000 donation. After less than two hours of debate, the committee voted along party lines. Nine Tories in favour of not backdating, eight Labour against. Like Saint Augustine, Northern Ireland would have donor transparency, but not yet.

The move was greeted with fury across civil society in Northern Ireland. "The whole thing was a DUP stitch-up. It was a concession from the Tories to the DUP," Alliance Party leader Naomi Long told me. As an MP for East Belfast, Long had pushed hard for the inclusion of political donations in the original 2014 legislation. "The Conservatives said it wouldn't be fair on the donors, but we were all told by the Electoral Commission to warn them from January 2014 on that their names could be published."

The Northern Irish Electoral Commission was unusually vocal in calling for the power to retrospectively publish donations. Its former head, Seamus Magee, remarked that: "The deal on party donations and loans must be part of the DUP/Conservative deal. No other explanation."[29]

The £435,000 was not the only donation that the CRC made to the Democratic Unionists. Cook's outfit also made two further contributions after the Brexit referendum, totalling more than £13,000.[30] The last came just five days after the party lost eight seats in the snap 2017 Stormont election. The DUP said, in by now familiar language, that it had used the CRC money to "further the cause of unionism at home and abroad". Around the same time, the party spent just over £12,000 on social media advertising with AIQ.[31]

These donations were the last activity registered by the Constitutional Research Council. What became of the group is not clear. It may not even exist anymore. Or it could just have given itself a new name and continued its shadowy operation.

Privately, some within the DUP regretted accepting the CRC windfall. The £9,000 left over in party coffers at the end of the Brexit referendum was hardly consolation for the endless, at times hyperbolic, questions about dark money and dubious donors. The story broke at the very worst time for the DUP, just as their own political and financial mismanagement precipitated the collapse of Northern Ireland's devolved government. (Stormont was only restored in early 2020, after three years in abeyance.)

But the CRC cash did have a lasting impact on the DUP, and on the future of British politics. The money allowed the Democratic Unionists to play a prominent role in a UK political campaign for the first time in the party's history. That the DUP had worn 'Leave the EU' across their branded t-shirts added to a sense that the party was tightly bound to the referendum result. Politically, the DUP's influence over a minority Tory government – and their strident opposition to the Irish backstop, the provision that in order to prevent a hard border and maintain the peace agreement, Northern Ireland would remain aligned with the EU customs and trade rules – was a key factor in the failure of Theresa May to force her withdrawal agreement with the EU through Westminster.

The confidence and supply arrangement with the Tories boosted party coffers, too. A parade of senior government figures crossed the water for DUP fundraisers, including Michael Gove, Andrea Leadsom, Jacob Rees-Mogg and Priti Patel. Arlene Foster cancelled a scheduled appearance at the influential British Irish Association in September 2018 to host a gala dinner in Fermanagh for then Defence Secretary Gavin Williamson. Two months later, Boris Johnson was the star attraction at the DUP's annual conference in Belfast. The then former foreign secretary declared that May's withdrawal agreement was "a historic mistake". The speech ended with a line from Van Morrison and a standing ovation from the DUP faithful. Afterwards, Johnson flew back to London with Foster in a private plane belonging to Christopher Moran, a Conservative donor and chairman of Co-operation Ireland.[32]

Other senior DUP figures gravitated towards Nigel Farage and Arron Banks. In May 2018, the month before Banks and Andy Wigmore walked out of the fake news inquiry to have lunch by the Thames with Sammy Wilson and Ian Paisley Junior, the quartet were joined by Nigel Farage at a private DUP fundraiser in Ballymena. Paisley Junior played the role of compère in Antrim that night. At one point he told the packed room that "Ulster is not for sale" but he had "a little piece of Ulster" for Farage, Banks and Wigmore. He handed the Bad Boys of Brexit a stick made of blackthorn, saying, "I want you to take home a wee bit of Ulster. When you're out walking the dog, you need to slap the kids about, whatever, you have a wee bit of Ulster in your hand." The crowd broke into applause.

Later in 2018, Paisley Junior was suspended from Westminster for 30 days for failing to declare two family holidays paid for by the Sri Lankan government. The North Antrim MP narrowly avoided having to fight Westminster's first recall election. A recall petition fell 444 votes short of the 10 per cent of the electorate needed to trigger a contest. Paisley said he was "stunned" and "greatly humbled" to retain the seat.[33]

The DUP's influence in Westminster effectively ended in October 2019 when Boris Johnson returned from Brussels with a reheated version of May's agreement. This time Britain would leave the EU's single market and customs union, but Northern Ireland alone would stay in alignment with European rules. The British prime minister had betrayed the DUP.

It was not the first time that unionists had accused the Conservatives of abandoning them. In 1921, after partition and the creation of Northern Ireland, unionist leader Edward Carson lamented, "What a fool I was. I was only a puppet, and so was Ulster, and so was Ireland, in the political game that was to get the Conservative Party into power."

Johnson's withdrawal agreement cleared the first stage in Parliament, but when a timetable to force it through in just three days failed, he announced his intention to call a general election. The ten DUP MPs voted against the government. "I don't care if this deal is brought to us on Christmas Day, we will be there to vote against it!" declared Sammy Wilson.[34] In the subsequent general election in December 2019, the DUP's vote slumped. The party lost two MPs, including arch Brexiter Nigel Dodds.

From being kingmakers in Westminster, the DUP were back to being also-rans. Far from securing Northern Ireland's place in the union, Brexit had put the issue of Irish unification firmly on the political agenda.

The £435,000 that Cook's inscrutable Constitutional Research Council gave to the DUP is probably the most blatant example of dark money in recent electoral politics. "With the passage of time this scandal only grows in importance," former Scottish Labour leader Jim Murphy told me. "The most important vote in the UK's history was the subject of a concerted effort to disguise huge payments made to the DUP to get the UK out of the EU." Murphy said that Richard Cook, his long-time political adversary in East Renfrewshire, was "a bizarrely unlikely middle-man for this sort of money". Just how much control the DUP had over its record donation and how it was spent remains unclear. And who was behind the money is still a mystery.

There is an optimistic reading of this particular story. When pressure for transparency came from journalists and campaigners, closing Northern Ireland's donor secrecy loophole quickly moved to the top of the secretary of state's in-tray. The security situation had changed little from 2014 to 2017. What had altered was public awareness. People now knew that almost half a million pounds in anonymous cash had been funnelled through Northern Ireland to support a campaign that a majority in the region opposed. Politicians had to act.

But the story of the DUP's dark money also reveals a series of deeper systemic problems with British electoral law and with our politics more generally. Ending donor anonymity in Northern Ireland was a step forward, but it has provided little transparency. Under the laws adopted in 2017, all donations of £7,500 or more to Northern Irish political parties must be published. (The threshold for individual politicians is £1,500.) Those limits might be justified in England, where it costs £50,000 to have dinner with a Conservative prime minister.[35] But in cosy Northern Ireland, political access comes much cheaper. "For five grand you could meet every Stormont minister," says one Northern Irish civil servant involved in elections.

Even more significantly, the electoral loophole that allowed the Constitutional Research Council to come into being in the first place still exists. As we saw, the CRC was an unincorporated association. These are some of the oldest common-law structures in England and Scotland. Like the very name of the Constitutional Research Council, unincorporated association is a rather grand title for what is essentially a paper exercise. Unincorporated associations do not have any of the normal disclosure requirements that an incorporated company has to meet, such as publicly filing accounts. These are black boxes that can be set up for the sole purpose of funnelling money to political campaigns, with little or no transparency.

The unincorporated association is a popular way of organising fundraising within the Conservative Party. The Association of Conservative Clubs, which connects affiliated private clubs around the country, explicitly advises members to set up as unincorporated associations, not limited companies. These clubs have given well over £1 million to the Tories.[36]

Some basic rules govern unincorporated associations. They are supposed to notify the Electoral Commission if they make political contributions worth more than £25,000 in a calendar year. They must also tell the regulator of any gifts they receive. But the published register of donations to all unincorporated associations is less than half a page long. From 2013 to 2019, just six gifts were recorded. All were made to the same Conservative association, the Trevelyan Campaign Fund. The last gift was recorded in November 2014. At the time, Tory central office had encouraged candidates in marginal seats to set up unincorporated associations without the words 'Conservative' or 'Tory' in their title, to avoid scrutiny.[37] The donations ceased shortly after the practice was exposed in the press.

There is evidence that unincorporated associations have donated to British political campaigns without registering at all. In 2018, two separate Electoral Commission investigations were launched after it was revealed that Scottish Conservative fundraising groups that had collectively donated over £400,000 to the party since 2001 were not included in the regulator's register of unincorporated associations.[38] A fifth of all donations declared to the Scottish Conservatives before the 2017 snap UK general election came from an unincorporated association that had not even registered with the Electoral Commission.[39] The regulator subsequently fined the Scottish Unionist Association Trust for failing to report donations properly.

Richard Cook's Constitutional Research Council also fell foul of electoral law. The CRC was fined £6,000 for failing to register its donations to the DUP. The penalty was barely one-hundredth the size of the CRC's donation. We only know about the fine at all because of a legal challenge against the Electoral Commission.[40] Otherwise, even this shard of information would have been buried under Northern Irish donor secrecy laws.

The CRC story starkly reveals the limits of the rules governing our democracy in other ways, too. Official attempts to scrutinise the DUP donation floundered. When the fake news inquiry wrote to Richard Cook, he initially claimed that his response had been "lost" by the inquiry.[41] This was contradicted by clerks in Westminster. Cook then wrote a letter accusing chair Damian Collins of being "the source of the 'fake news' you claim to wish to investigate".[42] Cook refused to answer any questions about the donation. In its final report, the committee concluded that:

There is an absence of transparency surrounding the relationship between the Constitutional Research Council, the DUP and Vote Leave. We believe that, in order to avoid having to disclose the source of this £435,000 donation, the CRC, deliberately and knowingly, exploited a loophole in the electoral law to funnel money to the Democratic Unionist Party in Northern Ireland. That money was used to fund pro-Brexit newspaper advertising outside Northern Ireland and to pay the Canadian-based data analytics company, AggregateIQ.[43]

In February 2019, Martin Docherty-Hughes secured a Westminster Hall debate on unincorporated associations. The Scottish National Party MP issued a stark warning: "Dark money is a cancer in our political system, and unincorporated associations are the most prominent way in which that cancer enters the bloodstream. It is a malignancy that works by removing transparency and confidence in the system of political funding – something that undermines trust in the political system as a whole."[44]

5

THE PARTY WITHIN A PARTY

Only go over the top if you have some chance of success. If it's
just a futile gesture, everyone will say how tough you are, but
you'll have weakened yourself for the next time – and that's
when it might really have mattered.

MICHAEL SPICER, European Research
Group founder, *c.* 1993

On a sweltering summer's day in late June 2018, John Bolton arrived at a private meeting in London. There were no British officials to greet Donald Trump's bellicose national security advisor, just a small welcoming party from the increasingly vocal pro-Brexit cadre of Conservative MPs, the European Research Group. Leading the delegation was the one-time Tory leader and former cabinet minister Iain Duncan Smith, who had first met his "good friend" Bolton more than a quarter of a century earlier.

The Eurosceptic backbenchers were agitated. Theresa May was due to unveil her Brexit plans at Chequers a few days later. The ERG was worried that Britain might not leave the customs union and single market – which could severely limit any future free trade deals, not least with the US. Bolton asked, "Is there any way we can help?"[1]

Over the course of an hour, Bolton reassured his British friends that Trump was an enthusiastic Brexit supporter. The president would soon prove his commitment publicly. Two weeks after the ERG's meeting with Bolton, the US president caused a diplomatic incident during a visit to Britain when he told the *Sun* that May's Chequers plans for a customs arrangement with the EU would "probably kill" a deal with the US.[2] It was unusual for a president who so often showed little interest in the detail of major pieces of domestic legislation to take such a defined position on the prime minister's proposal. Many Brexit supporters held up Trump's comments as evidence of the need for a 'clean break' with Europe. Bolton would later say that Britain would be "first in line" for a trade deal with America if it left the European Union without a deal.

The ERG's private discussion with John Bolton was not a one-off. As we have already seen – and will see in more detail in the coming chapters – a small group on the libertarian and Eurosceptic right of British politics has long looked to the United States for inspiration. These transatlantic connections grew and strengthened rapidly, away from the public view, in the years before and after the EU referendum. A network of pro-Brexit politicians, journalists and lobbyists pushed for Britain to move away from European regulation, and towards America. They deployed the same tools that had proved so successful inside the Beltway for decades: relentlessly on-message think tanks and academics funded by corporate donors; well-organised 'astroturf' groups designed to look like grassroots supporters; and, crucially, small, highly organised groups of influential politicians.

A few days after his meeting with Bolton, Iain Duncan Smith dismissed the conversation as a "friendly chat". "Just because you're in government doesn't stop you talking with people you know and are friends with," he told a BBC reporter, adding, "I'm not in government, I'm not able to direct the government."[3] But over the following months, Duncan Smith and his colleagues in the ERG would show themselves to be increasingly capable of directing the British government. The ERG would eventually force May's Brexit deal off the table and the prime minister out of office, and pave the way for Boris Johnson. They would, for a time, become one of the most influential forces in British politics.

This is the story of how a fringe Conservative Party pressure group was transformed into a highly disciplined, secretive party within a party that changed the course of British politics – and how taxpayer money, anonymous private donations and a hidebound parliamentary system helped them do it.

The European Research Group began in the imagination of an idealistic Oxford undergraduate. It was the spring of 1993 and Daniel Hannan, who had been raised in Peru by British parents, was finishing a history degree at Oriel College. He was 22 and had a fondness for Aleister Crowley. Unlike the flamboyant occultist, who once described democracy as an "imbecile and nauseating cult of weakness", Hannan believed that the biggest problem with British politics was that Britons did not have enough say over their own affairs.[4]

A few years earlier, he had set up a Eurosceptic student society called the Oxford Campaign for an Independent Britain. Hannan was particularly vexed by the Maastricht Bill that led to the creation of the European Union. In Oxford's student union he quoted Aristotle, Shakespeare and William Pitt the Younger in tirades against deeper European integration. With his university days nearing an end, Hannan wrote to the 22 Conservative MPs who had rebelled against Maastricht, offering his services as a researcher. Around a dozen replied. The ERG was born, with Hannan as its first secretary.[5]

The ERG was not the only Eurosceptic organisation to emerge on the margins of the Conservative Party at that time. Traditionally, the Tories had been seen as the more pro-European of Britain's two major parties. Ted Heath's Conservative government brought Britain into the then European Economic Community. Margaret

Thatcher was an early, vigorous supporter of the common market at a time when many senior Labour figures such as Tony Benn were wary of a "capitalist club" led from Brussels.

This changed through the 1980s as Labour began to embrace the vision of a 'social Europe'. In September 1988, European Commission president Jacques Delors was given a standing ovation when he told delegates at the British Trades Union Congress in Bournemouth that Europe would guarantee workers' rights.[6]

Twelve days later, prime minister Margaret Thatcher offered a withering riposte. In a now famous address at the College of Europe in Bruges, Thatcher complained bitterly that she had "not successfully rolled back the frontiers of the state in Britain, only to see them re-imposed at a European level with a European super-state exercising a new dominance from Brussels". It was a watershed moment in British relations with the European project. A once vocally Europhile prime minister was turning her face against Brussels.

Shortly afterwards another precocious Eurosceptic Oxford undergraduate, Patrick Robertson, set up the Bruges Group.[7] By the middle of the 1990s, the Bruges Group's membership would include more than 130 Tory MPs. Thatcher, by then out of office, was the first honorary president.

Opposition to Europe – and particularly the threat of federalism – was growing across the political right. Robertson convinced expatriate financier James Goldsmith to set up the Referendum Party, in 1994. Goldsmith had been a notorious corporate raider and *bon vivant*. During the 1970s, he often played poker with Lord Lucan, who would later vanish after killing his children's nanny and trying to murder his wife, and spoke approvingly of a military coup to topple what he believed was a socialist conspiracy led by Harold Wilson's Labour Party.[8] Now the pugnacious tycoon put £20 million of his own fortune into Eurosceptic politics.

In 1997, Goldsmith's self-explanatory party ran almost 550 general election candidates on a single issue. (Future Conservative home secretary Priti Patel was the Referendum Party's press officer.) The party did badly but took Conservative votes in key seats. Most famously, Goldsmith himself ran against disgraced former Tory minister David Mellor in Putney. Mellor's concession speech after losing his seat to Labour is worth watching on YouTube. He bellows at Goldsmith to "get back to Mexico knowing your attempt to buy the British political system has failed" while a wild-eyed Goldsmith grins maniacally and claps his hands, leading the crowd in a chant of "Out, Out, Out".

Although Labour had swept into power with a thumping majority, Euroscepticism was stirring. Tory MP Zac Goldsmith, who inherited a £284 million fortune from his father, later described the Referendum Party as a "rebel army" of valiant Brexiters who saved Britain.[9] Historians have pointed to the Referendum Party as a catalyst for UKIP's later success.

The European Research Group, by contrast, was a far less showy affair. Through the 1990s, a dozen or so Tory MPs met regularly to discuss European politics at breakfast meetings in the Attlee Room in the House of Commons. Guests included members of the Bruges Group, the libertarian pressure group the Freedom Association, and a young journalist named Michael Gove.[10]

The first chairman was Tory MP Michael Spicer. Educated in Vienna and at Cambridge, Spicer had been removed as a minister in 1990 over his opposition to the Exchange Rate Mechanism. He believed that the EU was fundamentally undemocratic, later comparing it with China and Russia.[11] The real driving force, however, was Hannan. At the time, he was sharing a flat in Soho with future Conservative and UKIP MP Mark Reckless. The pair hung a huge Union Jack over the fire escape and threw parties. Destiny was calling. "Don't ever make the mistake of thinking Dan was a young fogey," Douglas Carswell, who credited Hannan with converting him to Euroscepticism, told the *Guardian*. "This was a radicalised streak of thinking."[12]

Instead of radical Conservative change, British voters shifted to the pro-European New Labour. The challenge for the ERG and others became keeping the Eurosceptic debate alive. Hannan rallied around opposition to the proposed European single currency, which Tony Blair had praised. The ERG published a paper making the business case against the euro. Hannan helped set up the pressure group Business for Sterling to fight a widely expected referendum on joining the European currency – in the end, it never materialised.

Business for Sterling was in some ways a prototype for Vote Leave. Dominic Cummings was the campaign director, and below him were many of the same staff and supporters. The anti-euro campaign, however, also took pains to say it did not want to leave the EU. "I got involved initially in Business for Sterling," one-time ERG member Guto Bebb told me. "I thought that Europe needed reform. I wanted a two-speed Europe, not Brexit." In 2018, Bebb resigned as a Conservative minister to campaign for a second EU referendum.

In stark contrast to its very public presence in the years after the Brexit vote, the ERG flew almost entirely under the radar during Hannan's tenure. Occasionally, its links with like-minded European movements did raise quizzical eyebrows. Jörg Haider, former leader of the far-right Austrian Freedom Party, claimed that he had been in frequent contact with the group during the mid-1990s.[13] In 1998, Labour MP Andrew MacKinlay told the House of Commons that he had received a mysterious package at his Westminster office addressed to the treasurer of the European Research Group. Inside were one hundred cheques and a Midland Bank paying-in book for an account in the name of the Danish Referendum Campaign Account.

"Someone is running a fund-raising exercise from the House for that group, which could bring the House into disrepute," said MacKinlay.[14] At the time, Hannan was still in charge of the ERG from Westminster. Two years later, the Danes rejected adopting the euro in a referendum, by 53 per cent to 47.

By then, Hannan had stepped down from the European Research Group to become a Conservative member of the European Parliament. Hannan railed against the "illiberal" and "Bonapartist" European project. He had always maintained that the goal of the ERG was reform. "From day one it was conciliatory, the idea was to build a consensus around a looser relationship with the EU," he later said.

A former colleague describes Hannan's agenda as far more radical. "He wanted to take the institutions down from the inside," says Edward McMillan-Scott, a former Conservative MEP who served alongside Hannan in Brussels and Strasbourg before defecting to the Liberal Democrats in 2010. "He used to say, 'I don't want to do anything but get out of the European Union, and if possible break the European Union up.'"

In the European Parliament, Hannan aligned himself with right-wing politicians opposed to immigration and regulation. (A parliamentary group he led was ordered to return more than half a million euros after an investigation into its spending, which included a quarter of a million euros on a conference in Miami.[15]) Hannan was particularly obsessed with restoring the sovereignty he believed had been lost to Brussels. His incessant attacks on the European Court of Justice and the role of EU institutions in British life were later picked up by Nigel Farage and others who added a nationalist edge to Hannan's rhetoric about sovereignty. When the *Guardian* published a long feature about Hannan in September 2016, the paper titled it "The man who brought you Brexit".[16]

Through the early 2000s, there was little sign that the ERG would become anything more than a recondite backbench outfit. With Hannan away in Brussels, and with domestic politics dominated by a stridently pro-EU Labour party, Eurosceptics struggled to get attention. The ERG was run by a succession of less distinctive characters, the most noteworthy of them being Matthew Glanville, future brother-in-law of the future chair Jacob Rees-Mogg. (Glanville's wife, Annunziata, became a Brexit Party

MEP in May 2019 before leaving Nigel Farage's party a few months later to advocate a Conservative vote in the general election.)

Guto Bebb was introduced to the ERG by his friend, then ERG chair Chris Heaton-Harris, shortly after becoming an MP in 2010. At the time, the group met around twice a term, often on the terrace at Westminster. "The European Research Group was exactly what it was. There was a lot of research," recalls Bebb. "It was really good at going into detail of things like what was happening at the European Council. It was pretty nerdy. Which appealed to me."

The group's headcount hovered around 20 Conservative MPs and a handful of Eurosceptic peers. Members included a number of Tories who would later be branded as sell-outs for their opposition to a hard Brexit: John Bercow, Oliver Letwin, David Gauke.[17] Their ethos was less 'Brexit do or die' and more 'what do the latest reforms to the Common Agricultural Policy mean for British farming?'

Conservative Eurosceptics did have one notable success in these wilderness years: they convinced David Cameron to make his ill-fated pledge to give British voters a say on EU membership. Wary of the pressure from the increasingly organised right of his party, the prime minister's 2015 general election manifesto committed to a referendum on Europe. When the Conservatives won an unpredicted majority, the ERG was ready. Bebb received a phone call from Heaton-Harris. His old friend asked if he would support a Leave vote. Bebb declined, and left the group. The ERG did not take a public position on Brexit, but it campaigned vigorously behind the scenes. Prominent members such as Michael Gove, Chris Grayling, Iain Duncan Smith and Liam Fox joined Vote Leave.

After the shock result, the ERG quickly changed shape, emerging as a vocal and highly organised opponent of a soft exit from the EU, pushing the Tory party ever further to the right and, eventually, toppling Theresa May. Its members started to appear frequently on television, listed as ERG spokespeople. Supporters such as Dominic Raab, Priti Patel and Jacob Rees-Mogg were given key cabinet roles. None had been involved with the group before the referendum, said Bebb. "The ERG was taken over as an already existing vehicle. It morphed into a no-deal Brexit sect."

In American politics, small, influential bands of Republican legislators have often acted as outriders. The Freedom Caucus, and others, have adroitly used the conventions of Capitol Hill to steer the GOP in their preferred direction. It turns out that something similar had been happening in Britain, too – led by a baby-faced, sky-diving Tory backbencher named Steve Baker.

If Daniel Hannan created the ERG, it was Steve Baker who moulded it into what the *Economist* has described as "the closest thing Britain has produced to *sans-culottes*".[18] Baker is easily underestimated. Slightly built, with a piercing stare and a keen eye for detail, the Conservative MP for Wycombe since 2010 can come across more like a zealot than a sharp political operator. He once said that the EU "needs to be wholly torn down".[19] But the former Royal Air Force engineer has a flair for organisation that would be the envy of any Leninist sect.

In September 2015, Baker led a successful rebellion over David Cameron's proposals to loosen the strict ban on government institutions being involved in campaigning – known as 'purdah'.[20] What looked like a rather technical victory severely curtailed the prime minister's ability to use the machine of government to push pro-EU messages in the crucial final month before the referendum.

Baker is often said to possess an innate understanding of the concerns that motivate grassroots conservatives. "Steve Baker is very good at talking to the Conservative mind," remarked veteran Eurosceptic Roland Smith. "If you feel you are one cog in a historical enterprise that is the United Kingdom, he completely taps into that." Daniel Hannan's old friend Mark Reckless privately described the ERG as "a backwater with little real influence on policy till the arrival of Steve Baker".[21]

Baker took over as ERG chairman in late 2016. On his watch, it mushroomed from a talking shop with a dozen active members into a well-drilled political machine that could persuade as many as a hundred MPs to toe the line. "They have their own leader, their own whip, MPs are furnished with what to think and what to ask. Nothing is ever made public. They don't even say who is a member and who isn't," said one source close to the inner workings of the group.

Baker reorganised the ERG into an inner core comprising a handful of MPs, Eurosceptic Tory MEP Syed Kamall, peers such as David Owen and Nigel Lawson, and trade lobbyist Shanker Singham.[22] The steering committee, chaired by veteran Eurosceptic Tory MP Bernard Jenkin and aided by former cabinet ministers such as Owen Paterson and Theresa Villiers, met weekly in Iain Duncan Smith's parliamentary office to plan strategy. Notes were never taken. A much wider group of ERG 'supporters' was organised through a very active WhatsApp group, incongruously titled 'ERG DExEU/DIT Suppt Group'.[23]

The ERG had one main aim: to ensure a hard, clean Brexit with a minimal role for the EU in British affairs and maximum flexibility to deregulate and sign free trade deals around the world.

The fervour with which Baker approached the task of leading the ERG mirrored other aspects of his life. He is a born-again Christian; baptised by full-body immersion off the coast of Cornwall, he has spoken of being guided by a higher power.[24] He is also a committed disciple of the laissez-faire Austrian economics advocated by Thatcher and Reagan. Baker has called for the deregulation of carcinogenic white asbestos and has consistently argued for an end to the state's involvement in the banking system.[25]

"The bail-out of the banks incensed him as being a flagrant abuse of power by one class of people over another. This was a key motivation, in my opinion, for him to go into politics," says Toby Baxendale, who first met Baker a few years before he became an MP and has remained close to him ever since. In the EU, Baker also saw "an elite political class enriching itself as the expense of the poorest", Baxendale told me.

Baker keeps a silver coin in his breast pocket[26] to remind him of what he believes to be an impending financial collapse, and has advocated a return to the gold standard. (After the EU referendum he invested £70,000 in a company that urged people to buy gold as "insurance" against a no-deal Brexit. The firm later went into administration.[27]) This faith in monetarism brought him into the orbit of dark money-funded US conservative groups. In 2015, American Principles in Action paid for Baker to attend a conference on global finance in Jackson Hole, Wyoming. The conservative think tank has received funding from Robert Mercer and the Koch brothers. Another libertarian outfit, the American Liberty Fund, picked up the tab for Baker's attendance at similar events in Britain, Italy and the US.[28]

Baker has also spoken at the Antigua Forum in Guatemala. Billed as "the accelerator for freedom", this invitation-only gathering has featured an unlikely smattering of libertarians from around the world. Guests have included a former advisor to Vladimir Putin credited with implementing Russia's flat income tax, an Ivorian politician close to the country's former president Laurent Gbagbo, who was once acquitted of crimes against humanity at the International Criminal Court in the Hague, and staff from British free market think tanks such as the Adam Smith Institute and the Institute of Economic Affairs.

Baker was also a member of the Freedom Association. When writer and comedian David Baddiel described the Freedom Association, set up in the 1970s by right-wing Tories vehemently opposed to trade unions and Irish Republicanism, as a "slightly posher version of the BNP" in a radio interview in 2011, Baker wrote a letter of complaint to the BBC.[29] The broadcaster apologised.[30]

After the vote to leave the EU, Baker saw the ERG as a chance to shift Conservative Party policy from within. British politics has had pressure groups in its major parties for a long time. The Trotsky-ist Militant Tendency was a constant thorn in the side of Labour leaders before being purged in the 1980s. Alex Salmond was briefly expelled from the Scottish National Party for his membership of the 79 Group. The League of Empire Loyalists and the Monday Club kept a strain of imperial white supremacist nostalgia alive in the Conservative Party from the 1950s through the 1970s.

But rarely has a pressure group exerted as much influence on a governing party as the ERG. Conservative ministers and whips felt compelled to work with them. ERG members had advance notice of key decisions. The group was even given a private briefing before Theresa May delivered her key Lancaster House speech in January 2017, which committed to leaving the European Union's single market and customs union. It was Eurosceptic red meat. As the prime minister would soon discover, the ERG would accept nothing less substantial.

When May lost her majority in June 2017 and needed to soften her stance to have any hope of getting a Brexit deal through a divided Parliament, she sought to pacify the ERG by bringing them into government. Steve Baker was made a junior minister in the Department for Exiting the European Union (DExEU). In January 2018, Suella Braverman, Baker's nominal successor as ERG chair, joined him in the increasingly powerless Brexit depart-ment. The archly reactionary investment banker Jacob Rees-Mogg became the public face of the ERG. May and her whips hoped that ministerial baubles would placate the Eurosceptics.

The plan backfired completely. Baker showed scant regard for ministerial rules and conventions and continued to effectively lead the ERG from inside government, organising briefings for the group and attending meetings in the Commons that were not recorded in his ministerial diary.[31] When this was exposed, Baker faced no sanction. Instead he resigned in July 2018, saying that he had been "blindsided" by May's Chequers proposals that would have seen Britain remain in a customs arrangement with the EU, limiting the scope for free trade deals.

Baker was replaced in DExEU by another ERGer, Chris Heaton-Harris. A few months earlier, Heaton-Harris had written to every British university demanding lists of academics who were teaching about Brexit.[32] Steve Baker was soon followed out the ministerial door by Braverman and fellow ERG supporter Dominic Raab. Both resigned in November 2018 in protest at the withdrawal agreement that May negotiated with Brussels, based on her Chequers proposals. Far from neutralising the ERG's threat, May had increased the ERG's standing.

"[Conservative chief whip] Julian Smith and the other whips took the view that they could get the ERG to fall into line by bringing them into government," says Bebb. "It simply didn't work. It was a disaster."

The ERG's red line was trade. Trade had scarcely featured during the EU referendum, but in its aftermath it was often cited as the most compelling reason for Brexit. Britain had to be free to strike trade deals around the world. (The irony of leaving the world's largest free trade block of near neighbours in the name of free trade with countries thousands of miles away was occasionally commented on.) As May's withdrawal agreement, and the benighted Irish backstop, would have limited Britain's ability to sign trade deals – particularly with the United States – the ERG opposed it implacably.

Baker, Jacob Rees-Mogg and other senior ERG figures secured a vote on the prime minister's leadership under Conservative Party rules in December 2018. Although May survived, the ERG would soon effectively end her premiership. When Tory MP Anna Soubry resigned from the party in February 2019, she decried the ERG as "a party within a party" with "its own damaging agenda based on blind ideology". One-time member Guto Bebb agrees. "There was never any intention to support May's deal."

The ERG's fervent opposition – and tight whipping operation – ensured that May's withdrawal agreement suffered two crushing defeats. The prime minister's Brexit bill fell for a third time in March 2019, this time by 58 votes. Some senior ERG figures, including chair Jacob Rees-Mogg, did switch to support the government. But 28 ERG members – the so-called 'Spartans' led by Baker – voted against, as did the group's close colleagues in the Democratic Unionist Party. Had these pro-Brexit factions supported the prime minister, her deal would have gone through. May later announced her intention to resign and was replaced by Boris Johnson, a late convert to Brexit.

The ERG, a party within a party born in Daniel Hannan's student digs, had brought down a Conservative prime minister and changed the course of Britain's most significant peacetime policy. And it had achieved this thanks to a little-used Westminster convention that effectively allowed MPs to set up powerful caucuses funded by taxpayer money.

Despite being formed in the early 1990s, the first time many people heard of the European Research Group was in early September 2017, when its then chair Suella Braverman appeared on *Channel 4 News* live from the lobby in the House of Commons. The ERG had started flexing its muscles publicly. The pressure group had circulated a letter warning Theresa May against signing a transitional deal with the EU that would keep the UK in the single market. Braverman, a junior government aide, trotted out familiar lines. "No deal is for sure better than a bad deal." The prime minister must "do justice to Brexit". But then news anchor Krishnan Guru-Murthy changed the subject – to the ERG itself.

"Could you just explain to us what is the European Research Group," Guru-Murthy asked, "because a lot of people are saying it is effectively a party within a party, it is a group of hardline Brexiteers, some of whom are government ministers operating within the

Conservative Party and taking public money, because a lot of you use public money as MPs to fund this group, the ERG."[33]

The inquisition seemed to catch Braverman off guard. Pressed about why the ERG's membership was secret, the ERG chair struggled to answer. She would, she said, "definitely provide" a list. None was ever published. Already people were starting to ask who the ERG were, and why a partisan pressure group within Parliament was being underwritten by taxpayers.

Officially, the ERG is one of five parliamentary research services; the others are connected to the four largest political parties in the Commons: the Conservatives, Labour, the Scottish National Party and the Liberal Democrats. The ERG is funded by MPs paying an annual subscription of £2,000 each, which they claim as an expense. Writing on *openDemocracy* right before Braverman's appearance on *Channel 4 News*, veteran lobby journalist Jim Cusick detailed how more than 50 Conservative MPs had claimed subscription money from their expenses for ERG membership.[34] At £2,000 each a year, this works out at around £340,000 in taxpayer money between 2010 and 2018.[35]

"The public purse has been underwriting the ERG's so-called research for years," says Cusick. "And for years nobody knew anything about it. It was hiding in plain sight."

In theory, every time an MP claimed £2,000 from their expenses for an ERG subscription the information was publicly available. But it was veiled in secrecy. Many Tory MPs listed their ERG payments simply as "other pooled research" on their public record, rather than as donations to the European Research Group. "When I phoned Jacob Rees-Mogg's office staff, they told me that he wasn't a member of the ERG and he hadn't contributed. Even though he was," recalls Cusick.

The true extent of the ERG's funding is likely to be far higher than a few hundred thousand pounds. Data for payments to the ERG only goes back to 2010, when MPs were forced to publish details of their spending for the first time in the wake of the expenses scandal. Prior to that, almost no information had been published about the ERG at all. The group also has a separate bank account for private donations.[36]

Taxpayer funding was crucial to the ERG's success. It paid for the staff that oversaw the group's transition from talking shop to well-drilled political force. In June 2015, committed Brexit supporter Christopher Howarth, son of long-term ERG member and former Tory defence minister Gerald Howarth, joined as a researcher. His arrival coincided with a pronounced change in ERG message discipline. Research briefings started to look more like public relations than analysis. Members were fed with statistics that supported leaving the European Union.

Whereas previously the ERG met at the occasional breakfast briefing, now they were in continual contact. The group's constantly updated WhatsApp conversation provided briefings for its MPs before they did interviews, offered rapid rebuttals and agreed responses to breaking events. Senior members coordinated complaints to media that they felt had been negative about Brexit. After reviewing a tranche of ERG WhatsApp messages, Steven Barnett, a communications professor at the University of Westminster, told *Buzzfeed* that he had never seen a political movement "coordinated with such apparent dedication outside of an election campaign".[37]

Detail of the ERG's private funding is scant, but occasionally some scraps of information have fallen into the public domain. In 2014, the group's then researcher Robert Broadhurst disclosed to Parliament that his salary was partly funded by private donations. One donor was Norman Lamont, the Eurosceptic former chancellor of the exchequer. Lamont, a member of the House of Lords, said that he remembered contributing "about £1,000" to Broadhurst's pay. "I probably felt that it was wrong that I was not contributing, and MPs were," he said.[38]

Lord Lamont also noted how the ERG had changed after the 2016 referendum. Whereas before it had, he said, largely consisted of "having breakfast once a month and hearing from Robert

Broadhurst, and making up our own minds" and did not have a "collective policy", after the Brexit vote it became "more of a sort of campaigning thing".[39]

The strident Euroscepticism of the ERG's post-referendum incarnation proved far more attractive to private donors. Paul Dyer, a pro-Brexit businessman, gave £10,000.[40] The ERG also received cash from the Constitutional Research Council, the shadowy group behind the Democratic Unionist Party's huge Brexit donation. In December 2016, the CRC gave £6,500 to then chair Steve Baker for an ERG Christmas party. It was the only other donation on record from the CRC.

By then, Baker's Eurosceptic cadres had become increasingly close to key figures in the DUP. Nigel Dodds, the party's Westminster leader, was a regular at ERG meetings. Former DUP Westminster chief of staff Christopher Montgomery joined the ERG staff, alongside Howarth. Like Dodds, Montgomery was a former Vote Leave board member. He had a long-standing personal relationship with the CRC's chair Richard Cook, who was also a member of the ERG's WhatsApp group. In December 2018, as Theresa May struggled against Eurosceptic opposition to her withdrawal agreement, Cook applauded Baker's "outstanding leadership of Brexit" in the WhatsApp group.[41] Baker was "a superstar in a parliament with too many political pygmies!" the Scottish businessman wrote.

Private money allowed the ERG to broaden its horizons. The group commissioned expensive private polling and drafted alternative proposals for the Irish border. Front groups such as StandUp4Brexit – coordinated by staff who worked for former Vote Leave chief technology officer Thomas Borwick – gave the appearance of a groundswell of popular support on social media for key ERG policies. Other similar 'astroturf' campaigns sprang up opposing Chequers and May's withdrawal agreement. The ERG was even reported to be working with CTF Partners, the public relations firm run by Australian spin doctor Sir Lynton

Crosby which ran the 2015 and 2017 Conservative general election campaigns, and which later donated money and staff to Boris Johnson's successful Tory leadership bid.[42]

Just how much money the ERG raised from private donors is impossible to gauge. The European Research Group is an unincorporated association. Like Richard Cook's similar Constitutional Research Council, it doesn't have to publish accounts or list its members. This means it was able to exert an outsized influence on British politics with very little oversight or transparency about where its money came from.

The ERG had two bank accounts – one for private donations, the other for public funds. Asked about this arrangement in 2018, then chair Jacob Rees-Mogg said: "The research is publicly funded, but everything else isn't and we've always been very careful to differentiate and make sure anything that isn't justifiably a public and parliamentary expense is dealt with separately."

Westminster has a regulator that oversees how taxpayer-funded parliamentary groups like the ERG operate. But the watchdog seems to take a very curious view of what the public should be told about how its money is spent.

In January 2018, Jenna Corderoy, my colleague at *openDemocracy*, wrote an email to the Independent Parliamentary Standards Authority (IPSA). Citing the Freedom of Information Act, Corderoy asked the parliamentary watchdog for copies of research submitted to it by the ERG. IPSA had been set up in a hurry in 2009, as the MPs expenses scandal rocked Westminster. Amid a seemingly endless drip feed of stories about taxpayer-funded second homes and bath plugs charged to the public purse, the Labour government announced that it was establishing a watchdog to monitor MPs' spending. For the first time, expenses would be scrutinised and published. Part of the remit of the Independent Parliamentary Standards Authority was to oversee research services funded by MPs' expenses – like the European Research Group.

For years, IPSA had taken a very light-touch approach to the ERG. It asked few, if any, questions. In 2017, however, as press attention intensified on the ERG's increasingly public Brexit lobbying, the regulator wrote to the group saying that it wanted reassurance that public money was not being misspent on party political campaigning. In response, the ERG sent the regulator samples of its publicly funded research output.

Although Freedom of Information is often used by journalists, the law allows anyone to request information from a public body. A decent rule of thumb for FOI is that if the information has been paid for by taxpayers, then you should have a right to access it. The parliamentary watchdog took a different view. Releasing the documents it had received from the ERG could damage its relationship with the group, IPSA said in response to the request.

Corderoy, one of Britain's most experienced FOI journalists, was undeterred. She appealed to the Information Commissioner's Office, whose job it is to adjudicate on access to information. The timid regulator upheld the original judgment that research funded by taxpayer money should stay private. She appealed once again.

In early May 2019, Corderoy walked into a drab central London court where an information rights tribunal was being heard to decide her case. She was 29 and representing herself. Wearing black jeans, a white shirt and a pair of shiny Doc Martens, Corderoy was the only one not in a suit. Over many months, she had fought the case in her spare time, reading previous judgments, constructing skeleton arguments. She told the court that the public must have access to the ERG's research "in order to understand what kind of research these MPs have relied upon to mould their views on Brexit. And for history's sake, we must be able to access these materials to understand how we have got to the point where a no-deal Brexit is a very real possibility." The judges agreed.

Dozens of ERG briefings were released. Most were quite short and read more like talking points than research. There were lines for MPs to take on key Brexit issues. ERG notes frequently accused the Conservative government – of which the ERG's MPs were members – of failing to "address the positives" and "distorting statistics".[43] Reports by business groups were dismissed as false forecasts. Post-Brexit job losses should be described as jobs that would no longer be needed for EU migrants. IPSA had found that one briefing – which attacked the Labour Party for voting against a Brexit bill – had crossed the line into party politics, but on the whole the ERG's output was, the regulator said, "factual and informative".

Independent trade experts came to a very different conclusion. The ERG's research was "superficial and selective", said former UK trade official David Henig. The British taxpayer had spent a small fortune underwriting a highly political party within a party, and the regulator had fought tooth and nail to prevent any of its work from being released to the public.

It had taken Corderoy a year and a half, and countless hours of work, to force Parliament's putative watchdog to hand over basic information. Her experience is far from unique. British government departments refuse to comply in full with more than half the Freedom of Information requests that they receive.[44]

I have lost count of the number of times I have asked for documents from ministerial meetings, only to be told that none exist. No minutes were taken. No notes were kept. Increasingly, there is no paper trail for crucial decisions.

Laws supposed to make government more open have had the opposite effect. Supposedly publicly accessible information, such as the register of MPs' interests, is so poorly presented as to be almost unusable. Freedom of Information, the legislation that led to the MPs' expenses scandal, "doesn't work properly", transparency campaigner Tamasin Cave told me. Government departments routinely obfuscate. Regulators err on the side of institutions, not the public that they are supposed to protect. "The system is broken, and nobody intends to fix it," said Cave. "In all the windows of government, the curtains have been closed."

The success of the ERG demonstrated how a small, disciplined pressure group could pull British politics in directions that would have been unimaginable a few years earlier. The parliamentary convention for funding pooled research services provided an ideal vehicle for a committed band of ideologues, with the public picking up the tab. Anonymous private funding and a constant stream of WhatsApp messages helped the ERG to push their agenda even more effectively. Without all this, Britain would almost certainly have left the European Union as planned at the end of March 2019 with the agreement negotiated by Theresa May.

Politically, the ERG often found itself outmanoeuvred. The attempt to unseat May in late 2018 was a tactical disaster, at least initially. The group's epitaph was written countless times. Yet when Boris Johnson unveiled his first cabinet in July 2019, the European Research Group was at the top table. Dominic Raab was back, this time as foreign secretary. Priti Patel was given the key home office role. Jacob Rees-Mogg became leader of the House of Commons. Steve Baker took up the chair of the ERG again, a role he had never really left. Johnson's strident determination to leave the European Union "do or die" could have come from a taxpayer-funded ERG briefing note. In October 2019, the ERG conspicuously backed the prime minister's proposed withdrawal agreement.

Johnson's hastily rewritten text was almost a carbon copy of May's original, except in one crucial respect: by acquiescing to bespoke arrangements for Northern Ireland, it would leave Britain free to sign trade deals around the world. The ERG threw their former comrades the Democratic Unionists under the bus. "I would ask the DUP to accept this compromise," Steve Baker pleaded on *BBC Radio 4*. The DUP said "never". In January 2020, Johnson's withdrawal agreement passed the Commons with the enthusiastic backing of the ERG. The DUP voted against, but it didn't matter.

So why was the ERG so opposed to Theresa May's deal but so supportive of Boris Johnson's? The group's motivations were often discussed on late-night talk shows and in the pages of political magazines. Sovereignty. Identity. A dash of xenophobic Little Englandism. But when I asked former member Guto Bebb what drove the ERG he gave me a one-word answer: "deregulation". May's agreement would have bound Britain to continental standards that many in the ERG wanted to see loosened. Johnson's kept alive the ERG's vision of a deregulated "Global Britain".

Daniel Hannan frequently talked of post-Brexit Britain imitating Singapore's low-tax, low-regulation economy. "The ERG is Singapore on steroids," says Guto Bebb, adding that many in the group were "climate change deniers" who "were quite happy to see Trump win". Another Tory MP, Tom Tugendhat, said that the ERG represented a corruption of British Conservativism: "It is rampant libertarianism. It's the very opposite of what it means to be a Conservative."

Tugendhat's point is a crucial one. The ERG did not just provide a home for fervent Brexiters; it was also the first really cohesive pressure group inside the Commons since Thatcher that strongly identified with American libertarianism. During the long years of arguing over Brexit, the ERG was the most vocal proponent of prioritising a trade deal with the United States. ERG top brass frequently travelled across America spreading their message to receptive audiences. Boris Johnson's sweeping victory in December 2019 meant that the ERG no longer held the balance of power, but by then it didn't matter. The hardliners' job had already been done.

As Tea Party-aligned caucuses had done on Capitol Hill, the ERG had successfully used the machinery of British party politics and funding to push their radical Brexit agenda. And they were not the only ones dreaming of a new transatlantic alliance.

6

THE ATLANTIC BRIDGE
TO GLOBAL BRITAIN

*While we have been hectored and insulted by Eurocrats, our
old friends in the Anglosphere have been waiting with touching
patience. We let them down in 1973. Let's not let them down again.*

DANIEL HANNAN, the *Telegraph*,
4 November 2018

There are many different ways to buy political influence. I first
encountered the most obvious method when I was young. It
was sometime in the mid-1990s. I had just started secondary
school, and Irish local news was dominated by a scandal involving
a senior politician accused of receiving backhanders from a
property developer. The politician, a government minister, denied
the charges and refused to resign.

I asked my mother if she believed him. I expected her to say
she did – she was usually quite trusting of authority. Instead, she
solemnly shook her head. "Sure, your uncle paid him to rezone
those fields he has as industrial," she replied matter-of-factly.

My uncle was a farmer. Land classified as agriculture was
worth only a fraction of industrial holdings. A few years later,
construction began on a new motorway. The proposed road ran

straight through my uncle's farm. His land, freshly rezoned, was subject to a compulsory purchase order. My uncle made a fortune.

If you want to influence politics beyond a planning decision or a dodgy public contract, doling out cash to politicians is a very blunt tool. Politicians might not do what they say. They might get voted out of office or be demoted.

And besides, what if instead of getting a strip of land rezoned, you want to change the entire political culture? You could try bribing a gaggle of venal politicians to vote for, say, a single tax-lowering measure, but what if you wanted to change the whole political conversation so that low taxes across the board became the norm?

The way to do that isn't to buy the politicians. It's to own the ideas that dominate the political conversation. Richard Fink realised this four decades ago, and it made him one of the most influential people in modern American politics. He was the man who showed the billionaire brothers David and Charles Koch how dark money could buy political control.

Fink was an unlikely Koch *consigliere*. He was a teenage tearaway who injured his back loading freight cars in his native New Jersey. Needing something else to occupy his time, Fink enrolled in an economics course at university. He would later say that he didn't even know what economics was.[1]

Fink soon learned. He developed a particular passion for the Austrian school that underpinned most libertarian political philosophies. The state should play a minimal role, and the fewer regulations the better.

After college, Fink started a postgraduate course in New York University and was struck by the paucity of schools teaching courses in Friedrich Hayek and Ludwig von Mises. He decided to ask Charles Koch for money to start a programme in Rutgers, where he was teaching part-time. In the late 1970s, he flew out to Wichita, Kansas, the centre of the oil empire that the brothers had inherited from their father in 1967.[2]

Fink was 27 years old, with long hair, a beard and a black polyester suit with white piping that wouldn't have looked out of place on *Saturday Night Fever*. Charles Koch stumped up $150,000, and Fink repaid the mogul's faith in him.[3] He developed a theory of how political change could be manufactured, just like any one of the many products that Koch Industries produced every single day.

In the mid-1990s, Fink, by then president of the Charles Koch Foundation, summed up his strategy in a paper called 'The Structure of Social Change'.[4] Behind the dry title was an ingenious three-tiered model for how to bring about a libertarian revolution.

The first stage was investing in academics who would produce "the intellectual raw materials".[5] Money poured into universities from libertarian donors. Graduate programmes in Austrian economics started opening across the United States.

Step two in Fink's process was refining the "often unintelligible" intellectual output of these academic programmes into a "useable form".[6] Think tanks were key. Independent research institutes had existed in the United States and elsewhere since the turn of the century. Organisations such as the Brookings Institute professed to follow facts and reason to understand social problems, even if the solutions they offered almost always involved government playing a greater role in public life.[7]

Fink's think tanks, by contrast, were intentionally partisan. Like the grand dame of the libertarian think tank world, the Institute of Economic Affairs in London, these institutes preached the undiluted doctrines of Hayek and Friedman. The American Enterprise Institute, the Cato Institute, the Heritage Foundation and dozens of others in Washington DC are more like lobbying organisations than research centres. They push often heterodox positions – such as minimising the human role in climate change – that at times conflict with one another but chime with their sponsors' overall libertarian aims.

The third part of Fink's strategy was subsidising citizens' groups that would pressure politicians to adopt particular policies, and funding fringe political movements to lobby inside the established parties. These political outriders pulled the Republican party base and their political representatives further and further to the libertarian right.

Guided by Fink's insights, a tiny group of American plutocrats invested billions in think tanks, universities and election campaigns over the last four decades. Before this methodical and precisely targeted spending spree, libertarians had been largely thought of as cranks.[8] Afterwards, the limited space within which policies are created and publicly discussed was filled with proposals that they wanted. The deregulation of Ronald Reagan and George H. and George W. Bush often came straight from blueprints drawn up by libertarian institutes. Donald Trump campaigned to "drain the swamp"; in office he rolled back roughly 85 environmental rules and regulations in his first two years.[9] The US pulled out of the Paris climate accord and loosened domestic laws on toxic air pollution. These moves were applauded by the foundations and very rich activists, like the Mercer family, who backed Trump's 2016 campaign.

Could Richard Fink's dark money playbook travel across the Atlantic? In many ways, it already has. After Washington, London is home to the largest concentration of libertarian think tanks. The nest of institutes – mostly housed in those Tufton Street townhouses – are committed to open markets and perfect information in all areas except one: their own funding. Legally, they are not required to identify their donors, and very few do.

Centrist and left-wing think tanks, which did well under the Blair and Brown Labour governments, are often equally desperate for money but generally more transparent about where it comes from, largely because they rely more heavily on public funding and donations from trusts.

"There is definitely an asymmetry in funding of think tanks on the right and the left," says Nick Pearce, Professor of Politics at the

University of Bath and a former head of the left-leaning Institute for Public Policy Research. "On the left, private donations are not anywhere near as important."

It's been like this from the very beginning. Madsen Pirie, the Adam Smith Institute's dapper founder, recalled visiting "all of the main companies" soliciting donations for his new think tank in 1977. Some twenty responded with cheques. The most enthusiastic supporter was future Referendum Party leader James Goldsmith. Pirie recalled that Goldsmith "listened carefully as we outlined the project, his eyes twinkling at the audacity and scale of it. Then he had his secretary hand us a cheque for £12,000 as we left."[10]

Such candour about think tank funding is rare. In Pirie's own account of the history of the Adam Smith Institute, any references to donors cease from the early 1980s. The money just miraculously appears and keeps on coming.[11]

The willingness to accept anonymous funding makes think tanks the ideal vehicle for companies and business interests to quietly influence government policy. "These think tanks wouldn't function without corporate donors," says Pearce. Words like 'institute' and 'centre' give an appearance of academic rigour to what is essentially paid-for lobbying.

This kind of criticism has even come from within the think tanks themselves. John Blundell, former head of the influential Institute of Economic Affairs, complained that corporations were buying up these 'research' groups "left, right and centre".[12] David Frum, formerly a fellow at the Koch-funded American Enterprise Institute, has said that think tanks "increasingly function as public-relations agencies".[13]

In the UK, anonymous corporate money has often helped set the political agenda in ways that are subtle yet highly effective. A good example of this is the rise of the very notion of the 'Anglosphere'. In two decades, the idea that Britain should leave the European Union, deregulate and form a new trading relationship with predominantly white English-speaking nations went from a fringe concern to a widely held political aspiration. As we shall see later, the Anglosphere's success was the product of dedicated transatlantic networks of think tanks, politicians and media.

"Brexit is a big example of centre-right think tank success," a former staffer at a British libertarian think tank told me. "When people like Dan Hannan were the only ones seriously talking about leaving the EU, and the Anglosphere, the think tanks were behind it, too."

Of course, ideas have always come and gone in politics, aided by a combination of money, good timing and clever communications strategies. From Thatcher to Blair, British politicians have picked up – and often discarded – proposals generated by small cadres of highly motivated corporate, political and other players. Blair's flirtation with Anthony Giddens's 'Third Way' is a case in point.

But what's changing is the growing role of private money in producing the ideas that are gaining traction. If anything, British politics is even more vulnerable to corporate capture than America's.

"A little bit of money goes a long way," says former Conservative MP Guto Bebb. "We are not America. You don't have to spend half a billion on a general election campaign. If you are willing to put a quarter of a million into a think tank, you can get a lot of bang for your buck." Or, as many do, you can donate directly to political parties or, increasingly, give money to individual politicians.

But before we delve into spreadsheets of political funding data and the murky history of the Anglosphere, let's take a look at a story that encapsulates how British politics has become increasingly Americanised: the rise and fall, and rise again, of Liam Fox and his dream of the Atlantic Bridge.

On a clammy evening in July 2018, Liam Fox stood up to deliver the tenth annual Margaret Thatcher Freedom lecture at the Heritage

Foundation in downtown Washington DC. Britain's international trade secretary was formally dressed – blue suit, white shirt, a chequered tie the only nod to the possibility of mischief – but he looked relaxed. Fox was among friends. "Liam has been a frequent visitor to the Heritage Foundation for the last two decades," the compère said as he handed over the lectern. Over the course of the next hour Fox, flanked by an American flag, made the case for a "trailblazing" post-Brexit free trade deal between the US and the UK.[14] The applause at the end of his speech was long and warm.

At Heritage, Fox was speaking directly to some of the best-connected people in Washington. Heritage provided many of the top personnel for Trump's transition team. The president's commitments to slash trillions off the federal budget and bin environmental protections were lifted straight from the think tank's policy proposals,[15] which are inspired by the radical egoism of Ayn Rand, one of the most important propagandists of unfettered capitalism and a major influence on the modern American right.

Heritage is one of the biggest beasts in DC, with an annual budget approaching $100 million. Visitors talk of a cavernous office that feels more like a megachurch than a lobbying operation. The list of its funders reads like a who's who of American libertarianism: the Coors brewing dynasty, the Kochs, hedge fund billionaire Robert Mercer and his daughter Rebekah, who bankrolled Cambridge Analytica, *Breitbart News* and Donald Trump. The Mercers were also fond of British Conservatives: in 2005, Robert funded the creation of the Margaret Thatcher Center for Freedom inside the Heritage Foundation. A UK equivalent struggled to get off the ground amid questions about how the funds were spent.[16]

Heritage was also interested in Brexit. A few months after Fox's visit, Heritage was one of more than half a dozen transatlantic think tanks that published a detailed joint blueprint for an "ideal" free trade agreement between the US and post-Brexit Britain.

The paper was co-authored by Daniel Hannan and published by his own recently created think tank,[17] the Initiative for Free Trade.* It was cited approvingly by members of the European Research Group. One newspaper report coyly noted that the researchers behind Hannan's free trade paper had "exceptional access" to government ministers, including Liam Fox.[18]

Fox's interest in American libertarianism was not a recent development. In 1997, as a young Conservative MP, Fox set up an educational charity to lobby against those who "would like to pull Britain away from its relationship with the United States". He called it the Atlantic Bridge. Margaret Thatcher was its honorary patron.

Atlantic Bridge would later become a byword for lobbying scandal, leaving a trail of dark money and influence-peddling stretching from Washington to London and around the world.[19] But before that, Fox's think tank played a key role in building links between British and American libertarians, neo-conservatives, Tea Party enthusiasts and their mutual corporate interests. Many of Atlantic Bridge's most prominent British supporters would later play leading roles in Vote Leave and the ascendant Brexit-supporting wing of the Conservative Party, including Boris Johnson and Michael Gove.

That Atlantic Bridge got off the ground at all is a testament to Fox's determination. The first decade of this century was not a propitious one for British Conservatives. Out of power in Westminster, Tories also struggled to get a hearing in George W. Bush's administration. Except for Liam Fox. Fox was briefed in the White House by the president's senior advisor, Karl Rove.[20] Henry Kissinger received Atlantic Bridge's Margaret Thatcher Medal of

* Daniel Hannan's think tank, which was launched by Boris Johnson on Foreign Office premises in 2017, was initially called the Institute of Free Trade but was forced to change its name as it did not have permission to call itself an institute. The word 'institute' is protected in British law and can only be used by organisations "that typically undertake research at the highest level, or are professional bodies of the highest standing".

Freedom. Rudy Giuliani gave the inaugural Margaret Thatcher lecture in London.

Fox's strategy of connecting US and British conservatives echoed Richard Fink's approach. As Fox explained to a local journalist in Pittsburgh, he wanted to create a network of individuals "in politics, and in the media, and in the military, and in academia" to push the Atlanticist message and fight off the threat of being "dragged" into European integration. The reporter's description of Fox as "almost the Donald Rumsfeld of Great Britain"[21] was more accurate than he might have realised, at least in terms of Fox's aspirations: at the time, the shadow defence secretary's Westminster office was decorated with a detailed map of Afghanistan and a photograph of himself with President Bush.

Fox's transatlantic relationships were not merely personal. In 2007, Atlantic Bridge established a "special partnership" with the American Legislative Exchange Council, one of the most influential forces in US conservative politics. ALEC, whose funders have included the Kochs, the Philip Morris tobacco conglomerate, ExxonMobil and the National Rifle Association, is famous for aggressively lobbying state legislators to adopt corporate-backed policies. The tactic is very successful: ALEC claims that around a thousand bills based on its drafting are introduced each year, with a fifth being enacted,[22] including laws to restrict the minimum wage[23] and to promote 'stand-your-ground' gun legislation (which has been cited in numerous vigilante killings).

As part of its tie-up with Atlantic Bridge, ALEC set up a US charity, also called Atlantic Bridge. Although legally separate, the two Atlantic Bridges effectively operated in tandem. The American arm even paid for Fox and other senior Tories to fly to America.[24]

Atlantic Bridge's anonymous funding increased dramatically after its relationship with ALEC was established. The charity's US arm hired a raft of well-connected lawyers and lobbyists with links to America's military-industrial complex.[25] Catherine Bray was brought in to run international affairs. Bray, who later worked for Daniel Hannan, had previously been employed by Tory MEPs Richard Ashworth and Roger Helmer, who later defected to UKIP. Atlantic Bridge researcher Gabby Bertin – whose post was funded by pharmaceutical giant Pfizer[26] – became David Cameron's press secretary.

In the US, Atlantic Bridge was close to central figures in the Koch-supported Tea Party insurrection that swelled after Obama became president. Its advisory board included South Carolina's Jim DeMint, described by Jane Mayer as defining "the outermost anti-establishment fringe of the Republican Party".[27] Another US advisory board member, Oklahoma senator James Inhofe, had spent years arguing that climate change was a hoax. Inhofe's stance was supported by big oil companies, and his 2014 re-election campaign was funded by BP.[28]

Fox's American connections began to prompt questions back home. David Cameron, who was attempting to detoxify the Tories, was accused of supporting privatised healthcare after another Atlantic Bridge-advising Republican senator wrote that he had concluded that Obamacare was "nuts" after Daniel Hannan told him "about the socialised medicine in Britain". The pair had met in the green room of a Fox News studio.[29] Cameron publicly admonished his MEP.[30]

After the Conservatives' narrow election victory in 2010, the Atlanticists finally had a place in the British government. Liam Fox became defence secretary in the coalition administration. Atlantic Bridge had gone from a small Tory charity handing out Margaret Thatcher medals to a sophisticated network connecting the British cabinet, global corporate interests and US libertarian donors.[31] Fox travelled the world spreading the neo-conservative message, almost always accompanied by his close friend and Atlantic Bridge's £90,000-a-year chief executive, Adam Werritty.[32] But Fox's moment of triumph would be brief.

The first sign of trouble was a complaint to the Charity Commission that Atlantic Bridge was breaking the rules by adopting a pro-Conservative political stance. The regulator suspended the charity.[33] Rather than change how it operated, the trustees just shut Atlantic Bridge down.

But this did not stop the questions. The press smelled a story, and homed in on Werritty. It emerged that Werritty, who did not have security clearance, had been using Fox's office in Portcullis House as the charity's official headquarters. Even though he worked for a private think tank, he had been handing out business cards embossed with Parliament's logo, describing him as an "advisor to the Rt Hon Dr Fox MP". And he had indeed been advising: Werritty accompanied Fox on over a dozen foreign visits. He even brokered a meeting in Dubai with a potential defence contractor and met the Sri Lankan president.[34]

Days after the charity watchdog suspended Atlantic Bridge, a new company called Pargav Ltd was created specifically to fund Werritty's first-class travel around the world. The firm's sole director was an employee of British-Australian hedge fund manager and major Tory donor Michael Hintze.[35] The money came from four high-profile businessmen who were also donors to the Conservatives,* and from an international investigation outfit staffed by ex-MI6 agents.[36] Fox arranged for one of the funders, a secretive organisation called the Iraq Research Group, to meet with junior Minister of Defence Gerald Howarth.[37]

Fox was forced to resign amid mounting inconsistencies in his statements about Atlantic Bridge and his relationship with Werritty. An official report found that Werritty was not a lobbyist himself, but that he was used by defence lobbyists to gain access to the minister.[38]

---

* Venture capitalist Jon Moulton, who gave Pargay £35,000 believing it was for "back office" costs, said he felt "mugged". "If you look at the dictionary, the definition of 'foxed' is 'discoloured with yellowish brown staining', and I fear it might be reasonably appropriate," he said. Moulton later donated to Vote Leave.

Atlantic Bridge showed how a US-style think tank, funded by anonymous private donors, could gain influence in the centre of British politics. Despite ending in disgrace, Fox's outfit played a crucial role in building relationships between British Conservatives and American political and corporate elites that continued long after the Atlantic Bridge had crumbled into the sea.

Just weeks after the Brexit vote, Liam Fox was brought back into the cabinet by Theresa May, as international trade secretary. One of his first visits was to Heritage in Washington, where he met the foundation's president, former Atlantic Bridge board member Jim DeMint. Afterwards, Fox wrote to DeMint, saying how much he was looking forward to working with Heritage. During his three years in post, Fox, a vocal supporter of leaving the European customs union and the single market, frequently shuttled to Washington to meet lobbyists inside and outside the Trump administration.

Steve Bannon recalled that when Theresa May visited Donald Trump for the first time, in February 2017, Liam Fox was in attendance, too. "I got [Fox] in a room with Reince Priebus, the chief of staff, and said 'we will make a deal with you in 90 days. Trump has given us the order. Let's get on with it,'" Bannon told me. The former Trump advisor complained that his British interlocutors "just kinda mumbled and said they had to check the rules".

Bannon was not impressed by the calibre of the British contingent. "Trump was giving Theresa May negotiating tips. You could tell they weren't focused. They weren't engaged. They didn't have a plan. I thought the team was extremely mediocre," said Bannon.

One of Boris Johnson's first acts as prime minister in July 2019 was to sack Fox. But Fox's libertarian friends on Capitol Hill remained firm supporters of Brexit. In August 2019, less than two weeks after Johnson had succeeded Theresa May, 45 Republican senators signed a letter to the new prime minister pledging unconditional support for a free trade deal with Britain after a no-deal Brexit. The letter quoted Winston Churchill's over-familiar lines about finest hours and Britons possessing the hearts of lions. Among the signatories were senators James Inhofe and Lindsey Graham.[39] Both had been US advisors to Atlantic Bridge.

Through the early 2000s, Atlantic Bridge had worked behind the scenes to shift Britain's horizons away from Europe and towards a new special relationship with the United States based on deregulation and free trade. They were not the only ones. Quietly, with little fanfare, a small network of corporate-funded think tanks, politicians and media commentators on both sides of the Atlantic had a similar goal. Their project even had its own catchy name: the Anglosphere.

In December 1999, Margaret Thatcher arrived at the English-Speaking Union in Midtown Manhattan amid a cloud of controversy. A few months earlier the former prime minister had thrown the Conservative conference in Blackpool into chaos by declaring that the US and Britain were responsible for the world's greatest achievements. "In my lifetime, all the problems", Thatcher told the faithful at a Tory fringe event, "have come from mainland Europe, and all the solutions have come from the English-speaking nations across the world."[40] Now, on the eve of the new millennium, Thatcher was expanding her transatlantic thesis. She outlined for her American audience a vision for "a new international alliance", a union of English-speaking people as a bulwark against "the ambitions of bureaucrats in Brussels".[41] The Anglosphere, an idea that first emerged in the dog days of the British empire, was back.

Thatcher was not on a solo run. A few months earlier, the historian Robert Conquest, chronicler of Stalin's purges and famines, told the English-Speaking Union that the European project was an "anti-American" scheme born of "extreme regulationism". The only solution, he said, was to replace the "grotesque rigours of the European Union" with a new Anglophone alignment:

> It hardly needs saying that what comes to mind is some form
> of unity between countries of the same legal and political – and
> linguistic and cultural – traditions: which is to say an Association
> of the United States, the United Kingdom, Canada, Australia
> and New Zealand – as well as, it is to be hoped, Ireland and the
> peoples of the Caribbean and the Pacific Ocean.

Conquest's arguments were not new. In his iconic *A History of the English-Speaking Peoples*, Winston Churchill presented the idea of the Anglosphere to a mass audience. Britain, the wartime leader wrote, should retain a special bond with its former territories, even as it moved closer to Europe. A distinct undercurrent of imperial nostalgia has long run through the modern Conservative Party.

But at the start of the 21st century, there was little popular support for such flights of fancy. Tony Blair was a vocal proponent of the 'special relationship' but had no intention of leaving the EU. Even among British Eurosceptics, Conquest's racially tinged Anglosphere was very much a fringe idea. There was little interest in America, even among the incoming Bush administration. But a small, well-connected network of journalists, politicians and intellectuals were starting to talk about a realignment of Anglophone nations. As had happened in US politics since the 1970s, libertarian-minded universities and think tanks were helping to nurture an outsider idea that would later come to prominence during the Brexit referendum and, especially, in its aftermath.

As might be expected, the Anglosphere had support from the dispensers of American libertarian dark money. Conquest was a fellow at the Hoover Institution at Stanford at the time of his New York speech. The Hoover Institution's main funders include major conservative donors such as the Mellon Scaife oil dynasty. Conquest's speech mentioned support for his ideas from the American Enterprise Institute. One of the oldest and richest conservative think tanks in Washington, the AEI provided senior staff to Bush's government, including Dick Cheney, John Bolton and Paul Wolfowitz. The AEI's funding is opaque, but it has received money from a range of corporate and wealthy libertarian donors including Philip Morris, ExxonMobil, the Kochs and the Scaifes.

In 1999 and 2000, the Hudson Institute, a think tank whose funders also included Richard Mellon Scaife and the Koch brothers, organised two conferences in Washington and Berkshire to bring together leading figures in British and American conservatism.[42] As authors Michael Kenny and Nick Pearce note in their history of the Anglosphere, the Hudson conferences proved crucial to the idea's revival. Among the delegates were Thatcher, future Brexit minister David Davis, the influential *Daily Telegraph* owner Conrad Black, and prominent commentators such as James C. Bennett, John O'Sullivan and Francis Fukuyama, the neo-conservative historian who had prematurely prophesied the "the end of history" after the fall of communism.

Many of the main contributors subsequently wrote books and articles proselytising for the Anglosphere, which often appeared in outlets owned by Black and Rupert Murdoch.[43] In Washington, John Hulsman, a policy analyst at Heritage, called on "Britain to join an alternate future path, one that recognises that its natural economic and political partner remains the US, and not the European Union".[44]

Somewhat ironically, it was the global financial meltdown from 2008 that propelled the Anglosphere into the centre of the conservative imagination. The crash was largely a product of deregulatory Anglo-American capitalism, but it triggered a run of sovereign debt crises across the eurozone. As the very future of the European Union came into sharp focus, British Euroscepticism enjoyed a resurgence. The imperial yearnings of those committed to the Anglosphere became a major plank in the case for Brexit among small but influential sections of British conservatism. Prominent supporters included Gove, Fox, John Redwood, Norman Lamont, Michael Howard and conservative leaders in Canada, New Zealand and Australia.

As in the United States, corporate-funded think tanks played a key role in pushing the idea of the unique identity of the English-speaking peoples. The Institute of Economic Affairs, the Adam Smith Institute, the Henry Jackson Society and Policy Exchange and their transatlantic cousins in the Cato Institute, the Heritage Foundation and the American Enterprise Institute reimagined the UK as 'Global Britain' striking deals around the Anglophone world. At the root of this shared vision was a heavily deregulated economic model with low taxes and minimal state intervention.

In 2017, Matthew Elliott wrote a blog post reflecting on the lessons of Brexit for the Atlas Network, an umbrella group for more than 450 libertarian think tanks and campaigns around the world which has its headquarters in Arlington, Virginia.[45]

"Major policy changes are never impossible," declared the founder of the TaxPayers' Alliance and Vote Leave. "Who would have thought that a coalition of people working over two decades could convince a country to leave a major international organisation? But with a lot of perseverance, we managed to make history."[46]

The Young Britons' Foundation exemplified the growing American influence on the Eurosceptic fringes of the David Cameron-era of 'compassionate Conservatism'. Lawyer Donal Blaney set up the Young Britons in 2003 after visiting the annual Conservative Political Action Conference in Washington DC. The Young Britons was badged as an educational think tank, but the real aim was to "import American political techniques into the UK".[47] Like Richard Fink, Blaney realised the importance of spreading libertarian ideas through grassroots activists. The YBF sought to place "young radical free-market Anglosphere Conservatives in public life", Blaney said. "Some might become Members of Parliament, some might become councillors, some might become journalists and some might go and earn a packet of money in the City."[48]

At times the YBF looked more like a Tea Party offshoot than a Tory think tank during Cameron's attempted detoxification of the Conservative brand. Global warming was a "scam"; waterboarding prisoners wasn't all that bad; environmental protesters who trespass should be "shot down" by the police. "We have been described as a Conservative madrasa," Blaney once said. "We bring the next generation out to the States and bring them back radicalised."[49]

These Young Britons' strident politics started to get an audience. Ahead of the 2010 general election, around a dozen Tory parliamentary candidates attended YBF training courses. In the last days of the campaign, its activists delivered over half a million leaflets in Liberal Democrat/Conservative marginals warning of the dangers of a hung parliament.[50]

As in America, regular conferences were a central part of the YBF strategy for building a grassroots following. Youthful delegates heard talks from influential conservatives from both sides of the Atlantic. The Young Britons' tenth anniversary conference, at Churchill College, Cambridge, in December 2013, featured appearances from soon-to-be influential Eurosceptic Tory MPs: Douglas Carswell, Steve Baker, Robert Halfon, Conor Burns. Among the speakers was future Trump advisor Steve Bannon. "I knew something big was going to happen in the UK," Bannon told me. "It was the same driving force I could see in the United States."

Bannon began travelling to Britain regularly from the start of 2013, meeting Nigel Farage and others around UKIP such as future *Breitbart* London editor Raheem Kassam, lawyer Matthew Richardson and journalist James Delingpole. "I came over and spoke to the Young Britons," Bannon said. "I started speaking to all those groups." For Bannon, the Tea Party insurrection that propelled Donald Trump into the White House and Brexit were "absolutely aligned".

The source of the very American-inflected Young Britons' funding was unclear. When the organisation opened offices on Regent Street in the centre of London, many Conservatives asked where the cash was coming from.[51] The Young Britons received large donations from an obscure unincorporated association called Healthgear Contracts. Blaney insisted that most of the funds came from him.

There were rumours of American financial involvement, too. The YBF's US sister organisation, the Young America's Foundation, is based at the Ronald Reagan Ranch in California and has received funding from the Koch brothers, the Mercers and Amway billionaires Richard and Helen DeVos, whose daughter-in-law, Betsy, became Donald Trump's education secretary in 2017. The Young Britons' advisory board drew heavily on the same world of US dark money-funded think tanks. The board featured the founder of the Leadership Institute and had representatives from Heritage, the American Conservative Union and the Henry Jackson Society. Vote Leave founder Matthew Elliott was an advisor. The novelist Frederick Forsyth was a patron.

The Cambridge anniversary that Steve Bannon attended was the Young Britons' high-water mark. The organisation was abruptly disbanded in 2015, following a bullying scandal in the wake of the suicide of a 21-year-old activist, Elliott Johnson. His father described the organisation as a "cult". The Conservative Party launched an investigation. Six cabinet ministers who were due to speak at a forthcoming YBF conference pulled out, and it shut down shortly afterwards.[52]

Nevertheless, the ideas – and the transatlantic relationships – that undergirded the Young Britons became even more influential. Many of those involved became key players in British politics, particularly in the European Research Group. Steve Bannon would develop a friendship with Boris Johnson, even claiming that he helped compose the foreign secretary's resignation speech in July 2018.[53] Writing on the Young America's Foundation website in January 2019, Donal Blaney claimed that "treacherous 'Conservatives'" were preventing Brexit and warned of the prospect of violence on the streets.[54]

The demise of the Young Britons did little to temper the growing transatlantic influence on sections of the Conservative Party. In 2012, a quintet of rising Tory stars including future cabinet ministers Dominic Raab, Liz Truss and Priti Patel laid out their neo-imperial vision of a "buccaneering" Britain in a polemical anthology, *Britannia Unchained*. As with their US counterparts, these young libertarians saw government regulations as shackles that had left "the British... among the worst idlers in the world".[55] Once the chains had been slipped, Britain could once again ride the global high seas to prosperity. As historian Robert Saunders noted, "The use of 'trade' as a euphemism for 'empire' became a staple of Brexit ideology."[56]

After the Leave vote, the Anglosphere became an argument for putting clear blue water between Britain and Europe, on both patriotic and practical grounds. Daniel Hannan wrote enthusiastic columns in the *Daily Telegraph* about the coming of a gilded age of the English-speaking nations. A private company was set up to lobby for Canzuk, a union between Canada, Australia, New Zealand and the UK. Conservative historian Andrew Roberts, declared that "of all the many splendid opportunities provided by the British people's heroic Brexit vote, perhaps the greatest is the resuscitation of the idea of a Canzuk Union".[57] Commentator James C. Bennett wrote curious science fiction set in a future Canzuk where carefree office workers shuttle between London and yet-to-be-built cities on the Australian littoral.

In 2017, a cadre of Conservative MPs called the Free Enterprise Group published a paper advocating "reconnecting with the Commonwealth". The group, which included Raab and Patel, was administered by the Institute of Economic Affairs. Tony Abbott wrote the foreword to the Commonwealth paper – the former conservative Australian prime minister had become a frequent pro-Brexit guest on BBC Radio 4's flagship *Today* programme. Abbott's calls for Britain to leave the European Union's customs union and single market and form a new alliance with the

Anglophone world based on mutual recognition of standards were regularly picked up by the European Research Group and its supporters.

Considerable scepticism about the promise of the Anglosphere was expressed by people who actually understood world trade. Economists pointed out the problem of 'trade gravity'. We do a lot more business with our neighbours – like Europe – than with those thousands of miles away. Waggish Whitehall officials dubbed trade secretary Liam Fox's plans "Empire 2.0".[58]

But these were minority voices in government, experts in a political culture that had come to denigrate expertise. Senior ministers continually talked up the prospect of free trade deals around the world, even after India – one of the top targets for a new post-Brexit deal – gave a decidedly lukewarm response to Britain's trade proposals. "I don't think India is in a rush," the country's high commissioner in London said ahead of bilateral talks in April 2018.[59]

Time has borne out the Indian diplomat's words. Liam Fox's promise that Britain would be able to sign 40 trade deals "the second after Brexit" proved misguided.[60] By the end of 2019, Britain had rolled over around twenty trade deals, many with very small territories including the Faroe Islands, the Palestinian Authority and Liechtenstein.[61] Japan, whose extensive free trade deal with the European Union began in early 2019, said that the UK could not expect the same favourable terms as the much larger EU bloc.

Nevertheless, the Anglosphere, and the radical deregulation that would have to go with it, particularly if Trump's US were to be attracted by it, became an accepted part of British political debate. Speaking on a visit to Australia as foreign secretary in 2017, Boris Johnson echoed his idol Winston Churchill's praise for "the special genius of the English-speaking people". Talk of 'Global Britain' increased markedly after Johnson became prime minister. Fox's successor as international trade secretary, Liz Truss, toured the world with a red, white and blue umbrella (and a personal photographer at the taxpayer's expense[62]). John Bew was appointed to the influential Downing Street Policy Unit. Bew, a distinguished historian, had previously led a project called Britain in the World at Policy Exchange, another London think tank funded by anonymous corporate donors.[63]

Even the reality that London would be subservient to Washington in a post-Brexit union was blithely accepted. "Britain will be better off as junior partner of the United States than an EU vassal," historian Andrew Roberts, like Johnson a Churchill biographer, wrote in August 2019.[64] A strange psychology flourished in which equal participation in European affairs was seen as 'vassalage', but further subordination to the US became 'liberation'.

The revival of the idea of the Anglosphere was, says political scientist Nick Pearce, "a product of the extensive links between the UK and the US right" through the early years of the 21st century. As Richard Fink and his acolytes had done so often in the US, a fringe policy nurtured by a small band of corporate-funded Atlanticists had become mainstream.

British politics is starting to look more and more American in other ways, too. A small group of (often very) wealthy individuals have come to dominate the way in which British politics is funded – and to influence what policies make it onto the political agenda.

When it comes to political funding, Britain sits somewhere between the United States and Europe. Unlike in many European states, there is little public funding available for British parties. Parties, and even individual politicians, have to finance themselves through private donations.

Unlike in the US, the amount of money involved in British politics is pretty meagre. The 2018 US midterm elections cost almost $6 billion. In the UK, just about anyone with £50,000 burning a hole in their back pocket can join the Conservative Leader's Group and have an off-the-record dinner with the prime minister and leading cabinet figures.

Britain's largest parties have long relied on funding from sectional interests. Labour, which often raises more money than any other party, is heavily backed by the trade unions. The Conservatives largely rely on private sector funders.

Across the political spectrum, 'cash for access' scandals have been a fixture of British politics. In 2006, Labour peer Lord Levy was arrested but not charged during the 'cash for honours' scandal, in which businessmen who gave loans to the party were subsequently recommended for peerages.[65] Levy denied wrongdoing.

David Cameron agreed to release lists of Leader's Group donors in 2012, after it emerged that the then prime minister was hosting private parties for funders at his Downing Street flat.[66] (The Conservatives have since stopped publishing details of these gatherings.) A fifth of the top Conservative donors have received honours, including knighthoods and seats in the House of Lords.[67] "You have always been able to buy access in British politics," says Alistair Clark, a political scientist at the University of Newcastle. "What has changed is that more people now *realise* that you can buy access."

British political donors have changed as Britain has changed. The early 1970s asset-strippers who championed Ted Heath's Conservative leadership were very different from the privatisation-focused City of London millionaires who bankrolled Margaret Thatcher in the 1980s. Those were the days when the late Lord McAlpine revolutionised Tory fundraising, reputedly turning up in the City with a large sack and asking for bundles of cash to fill it – something that would have been entirely legal at the time. By 2011, with the Conservatives back in power after thirteen years in opposition, fully half of the party's funding came from donors involved in the City of London. Six years previously, it had been a quarter.[68]

Many of the Conservatives' growing ranks of City funders supported David Cameron's Brexit referendum strategy. Big business heavily backed Remain, including Goldman Sachs, Citi Group and The City of London Corporation.[69] Pro-Brexit funding came from the City too, but unlike the stockbrokers and captains of industry that lined up behind Cameron, most of the Leave money came from a small number of individual donors with a background in the high-stakes world of hedge funds.

Veteran fund manager and long-time Conservative funder Jeremy Hosking was a major Vote Leave donor. Numerous other Tory 'hedgies' put money behind a Brexit vote: former Conservative Party treasurer Peter Cruddas, Atlantic Bridge acolyte Michael Hintze, metals fund manager David Lilley. The most infamous hedge fund Brexiter was Crispin Odey, a former UKIP donor and one-time son-in-law to Rupert Murdoch who made £220 million on referendum night betting that sterling would collapse if Leave won – despite donating almost £900,000 to pro-Brexit campaigns. Odey said that the next morning the day broke with "gold in its mouth".[70]

After June 2016, the Conservatives' already narrow funding pool contracted sharply. The pro-European business elite fled the party as factions such as the European Research Group became increasingly powerful. Around two-thirds of existing Tory donors reduced their contributions after the EU referendum, or stopped giving at all. Dislocated from their traditional support, the Conservatives were now largely dependent on funding from a small number of overwhelmingly pro-Leave donors who wanted to cut ties with the EU. These funders' contributions fluctuated in direct correlation with the party's Brexit policy. In the first three months of 2019, as Theresa May tried to force her withdrawal agreement through Westminster, donations to the Conservatives fell by half on the same period the previous year, to £3.7 million. When Boris Johnson took over, promising a hard Brexit, donations increased sharply.

During the subsequent general election, the Tories broke records for the most funds raised in a British campaign.[71] The party raised more than £37 million from large donations for the election. Much of this money came from super-rich donors, many connected to the world of hedge funds and private equity. These speculators often saw themselves as iconoclasts fighting against the establishment. As in the US, Britain's traditional party of government has become increasingly reliant on a handful of very wealthy donors – who only need to spend a fraction of the money the Kochs or the Scaifes spread around in order to wield huge influence.

"The Tory party is now wholly unrepresentative in any way of the UK population. Its source of funds is so restricted," says economist Frances Coppola. "And because they are so dependent on this small group of donors, Tory party policy is going to be skewed."

The Conservatives have close ties to Russian donors who have been given British citizenship. Ahead of the 2019 general election, Johnson was heavily criticised for blocking the release of a report into Russian interference in British politics that reportedly named high-profile Conservative Party donors with links to Russia.[72]

The Conservatives' growing dependence on decentralised private capital, and particularly hedge funds, did not go unnoticed. In September 2019, former chancellor Philip Hammond declared that Boris Johnson was in league with financiers who stood to profit handsomely from a no-deal Brexit. The prime minister's own sister, Rachel, agreed.

But there was a problem with this theory. Hedge funds rely on rapid, largely unforeseen market changes. Johnson's supposed desire to leave the EU on the toughest of terms was widely telegraphed. Instead of a great conspiracy to make a killing on a depreciation of sterling, the most successful party in the history of British politics was being captured by a small group of donors with a professional interest in the buccaneering, free trading Britain envisaged by the cottage industry of libertarian think tanks clustered around Tufton Street. "These are all people who want to see a bonfire of regulation, a Singapore-on-Thames," said Coppola. "They want to dismantle all state regulation, lower taxes to zero."

Their views were not a secret. Months before the referendum, Crispin Odey, Peter Cruddas and over a hundred City executives signed an open letter that called for a slashing of red tape and radical divergence from EU standards after a Brexit vote.

That massive political shocks can be used to push through radical economic change is well documented. Canadian writer Naomi Klein calls it "disaster capitalism".[73] After the Brexit vote, the language of disaster was often used by British politicians and commentators, although often in a positive sense, as an opportunity for collective renewal through suffering. Forgotten in the evocations of Dunkirk and the Blitz were the spivs of the 1940s who made a fortune on the black market. Even at the height of adversity, there is money to be made, especially for speculators. Where factory owners or entrepreneurs generate profits through the productive use of capital – making goods or services – speculators make money from money.

Speculators struggled in the wake of the financial crash. In an era of negative interest rates and low inflation, easy money is much harder to make. A sudden shock to the system, like Brexit, can create volatility, which creates new opportunities for profit. The British sociologist Will Davies describes Boris Johnson and Nigel Farage as "kindred spirits in the project of injecting a bit of chaos into the liberal economic system".[74]

It is striking, too, that many of the most fervent Brexiters in the business world have few or no ties to the British economy. In 2018, an investment fund co-founded by the European Research Group's Jacob Rees-Mogg opened an office in Dublin, to guard against "considerable uncertainty" as Britain left the EU.[75] Vacuum-cleaner tycoon and Leave backer Sir James Dyson no longer produces his machines in the UK. Ineos billionaire Sir James Ratcliffe moved to Monaco despite his vocal support for Brexit. The owners of a number of pro-Brexit newspapers are foreign, like Rupert

Murdoch, or often control their media holdings through offshore companies, like the Barclay brothers.

Meanwhile, in Britain the productive core of the national economy, largely foreign-owned, is no longer tied to British party politics. Where once the Conservatives represented business interests – and were funded by them – now the party is reliant on speculators and hedge funders. David Edgerton, Professor of Modern British History at King's College London, wrote that the Conservatives were taken over by the hard right and its financial backers "because it was no longer stabilised by a powerful organic connection to capital, either nationally or locally".[76]

Business? "Fuck business," Boris Johnson declared.

So, what happens when the party of government is captured by a small group of donors? We can look across the Atlantic to get a rough idea. "A federal election in the US is supposed to be decided by 150 million voters, and yet the policy preferences are being determined by literally 20 people, 20 major donors," says Adav Noti, a US election lawyer with the Campaign Legal Center in Washington DC.

Something similar is happening in the UK. "We should be worried that a major party in Britain is struggling to raise funds," says Frances Coppola. "As that continues they will have to dance ever more to the tune of the cranks who fund it." This will likely mean growing numbers of policies that benefit particular niche interests. Already there are signs of obscure deregulatory projects making their way onto the political agenda.

During the 2019 Conservative leadership contest, Boris Johnson promised to "take back control of our regulatory framework", echoing Vote Leave's referendum slogan. He pledged to review a levy on sugar (designed to curb obesity and other diseases) and backed the quixotic idea of turning almost a dozen UK sites into free ports. The sudden enthusiasm for this fringe proposal was particularly strange. Free ports, which charge no taxes or tariffs, are a money launderer's dream. The EU has been trying to phase them out. So why were they suddenly the future for Britain's post-industrial cities?

Johnson's support followed a well-funded campaign in favour of free ports run by a public affairs consultancy headquartered in Westminster. It is not clear who paid for this lobbying effort, but it had the backing of newspaper commentators and influential, corporate-funded think tanks such as the Institute of Economic Affairs and others.

Two days before Britain left the EU, at the end of January 2020, the Department for International Trade tweeted that it would be "developing ambitious new #Freeports to ensure that towns and cities across the UK can begin to benefit from the trade opportunities that Brexit brings." Free ports were now government policy.

In 2017, Vote Leave founder Matthew Elliott co-authored a report about post-Brexit public opinion for the Legatum think tank. British voters, Elliott found, were far less enamoured with the free market than he might have expected. The report is worth quoting at length:

> On almost every issue, the public tends to favour non-free market ideals rather than those of the free market. Instead of an unregulated economy, the public favours regulation. Instead of companies striving for profit above all else, they want businesses to make less profit and be more socially responsible. Instead of privatised water, electricity, gas and railway sectors, they want public ownership. They favour CEO wage caps, workers at senior executive and board level and for government to rein in big business. They want zero hours contracts to be abolished.[77]

Fewer than one in ten people thought taxes or public spending should be cut.

Yet the very same positions that Elliott identified as publicly unpopular, and which he supports, came to dominate British political debate after June 2016. Free trade and deregulation – issues largely absent during the Brexit referendum – were held up as totemic of the "will of the people". Prominent Leave voices, from Nigel Farage to the ERG, declared that anything less than leaving the European Union's single market and customs union would be Brino: Brexit in Name Only. Donald Trump and senior Republicans in Washington agreed. Britain could simply replace the EU with the Anglosphere, and all would be well.

During the 2019 general election, Boris Johnson pushed a message that was markedly different from his leadership stump speeches. The prime minister-in-waiting promised public investment and state aid for struggling English regions. Voters' concerns would be listened to.

A few weeks after the Conservatives' sweeping victory, I interviewed Steve Bannon. He refused to say whether he was still in contact with Johnson but said that he expected the triumphant prime minister "to adapt his policies to become more populist". Although Johnson was "an elitist" and "a globalist" who had "opportunistically jumped" on Brexit, "he has more economic nationalistic tendencies and he is more populist than he was," Bannon said.

Johnson has shown a populist touch. In his first speech after the general election win, made in Tony Blair's former Sedgefield constituency, the prime minister promised to deliver a "people's government" and thanked former Labour supporters who had "lent" their vote to the Conservatives.

But shortly after his election victory, Johnson reiterated his commitment to ensuring that the UK would be free to deregulate and diverge from EU standards. Global Britain would finally be unchained. Whatever the eventual shape of Britain's new relationship with the European Union, for corporate lobbyists and think tanks, the transatlantic "Brexit influencing game" had already begun.

7

THE BREXIT INFLUENCING GAME

*The IEA... will be like the warm, irresistible tide on that
Brazilian beach – gently, powerfully, sometimes without us
even knowing it, shifting the debate to a whole new place.*

CONSERVATIVE MP DOMINIC RAAB,
IEA's 60th anniversary, 2015

Mark Littlewood leaned back in a chair in his office, just a three-minute walk from the Houses of Parliament.[1] It was a sunny day in early summer 2018. Littlewood, the Institute of Economic Affairs' energetic director-general, had the top button of his white shirt open, his tie pulled slightly down. He was talking business. A keen poker player, Littlewood explained that the IEA, the grandfather of Britain's corporate-funded think tanks, was in "the Brexit influencing game".[2]

The IEA's trade advisor, Shanker Singham, was particularly influential. "Because he is such an expert, he is able to get into ministers and cabinet ministers like that," he said, clicking his fingers.

Sitting opposite Littlewood at the long, dark wood table was a man who said he was an investor in hormone-treated US beef, banned in the EU, who was interested in funding the think tank to write a report about agriculture after Brexit. "I have absolutely no problem with people who have business interests, us facilitating those," said Littlewood, who had previously worked as a press officer for the Liberal Democrats.

The report would cost £42,500. The donation would be kept private. The investor could not change the conclusions of the report, but there would be "substantial content" covering their area of interest and the findings would always support free trade deals.[3] The IEA chief suggested that the report could be written by Matt Ridley, a libertarian commentator and owner of a large estate in the north-east of England who had, he said, already discussed the idea with the environment secretary, Michael Gove. A dinner with the minister was a possibility.[4]

The proposed report was never written. The would-be investor was really an undercover journalist filming the meeting. Greenpeace's investigative unit, *Unearthed*, had been trailing the IEA for months.[5] They had discovered a lot about the institute's activities. At a private club in Manhattan, Littlewood had boasted to potential US funders that Brexit was an opportunity to "shred" EU regulations.[6] He said that Singham had been "writing Gove and Johnson's script" on leaving the customs union.[7] The head of an Oklahoma-based libertarian think tank called the E Foundation said that his organisation was planning to raise money for the IEA's work pushing for a US–UK free trade deal.[8] Singham had also shown an Oklahoma beef and petrochemicals tycoon around Westminster, where he met Brexit Minister Steve Baker, the European Research Group and senior British trade officials.[9] Everyone involved said that no rules had been broken.

The Greenpeace story broke on the last Sunday in July 2018. The next day, Littlewood, Singham and other institute staff gathered to coordinate their response in the Villiers Hotel in Buckingham, near the eponymous private university with which the IEA has long had links. There was a flurry of media interest. Labour called for an investigation, amid accusations that the think tank was offering to broker access to senior politicians for foreign donors seeking to influence the shape of the economy after Brexit.

That evening Singham appeared on BBC *Newsnight* live from the hotel lobby. "We are no different from other think tanks," he said when asked whether anonymous corporate foreign donors were buying access to cabinet ministers. "If ministers want to hear from other people, they are perfectly able to hear from other people." The rest of the IEA contingent watched from an adjacent bar, wondering what tomorrow might bring.

It brought little for them to fear. Greenpeace's story – which just a few years earlier might have sparked a national debate about the role of secretive think tanks in British politics – quickly slipped off the news agenda. Unlike the Atlantic Bridge scandal, where rival journalists vied to outdo one another, the questions about the IEA sank into the morass of the rolling news cycle.

"Three or four years ago, that story would have been a much bigger deal," says writer and transparency campaigner Tamasin Cave. "But Brexit has loomed so large that a lobbying scandal is subservient to the dominant narrative. The obsession with Brexit and a very small number of political actors has meant that the likes of the IEA are easily overlooked."

The brevity of the media's attention span belied the influence that London's think tanks had been exerting on British politics. Staff from the IEA and others frequently supplied supplied sunny analysis about Brexit to the media, and politicians. No-deal was "nothing to fear". A "clean break" with the EU was the road to prosperity. Their research papers were "very important" for maintaining the "fiction" that Britain could easily leave Europe's single market and customs union with little or no economic damage, said a former senior UK trade official. Parliamentary outliers in the European Research Group worked closely with think tanks, frequently citing their work.

From tiny offices dotted around Westminster, a handful of lobbyists backed by anonymous corporate donations were playing a major role in Britain's biggest peacetime policy challenge. How these mavericks managed to exert such influence reveals a lot about how dark money works in British politics. Nowhere is this more apparent than in the story of the Institute of Economic Affairs and a little-known trade lawyer named Shanker Singham.

Singham shifted uncomfortably in his seat as the television cameras rolled. It was September 2014, and he was sitting in a gaudy, white-upholstered armchair in a government office in the unremarkable city of Banja Luka in northern Bosnia. Opposite him was Željka Cvijanović, prime minister of Republika Srpska, an autonomous Serb-run statelet created in the 1990s Balkan wars that has been mired in corruption and political stasis ever since.

Cvijanović was just a little too far away for a comfortable conversation. Singham, diminutive in stature, projected his clipped English accent and gesticulated with his hands. He wanted to "lead this area towards prosperity", he said.[10] Cvijanović pursed her lips and nodded slowly. The prime minister told a handful of local journalists that she hoped to create a low-tax, privatised "enterprise city" in her country, with the help of Singham's firm, a Boston-based university spin-off called Babson Global.[11] Singham smiled politely.

By 2014, Shanker Singham had been in the United States for almost two decades. He was concerned about the direction his adopted nation was going. Two years earlier, Barack Obama had won a second term in the White House. Singham was travelling the world spreading the message of free enterprise but the Beltway was dominated by those who wanted to increase the role of government, not shrink it.[12] His colleagues at Babson complained that the university was working with unsavoury regimes, selling a free market model that would privatise state resources with minimal democratic oversight. Singham disagreed. He lost the argument. The enterprise cities project was quietly wound down.

In many ways, Singham was an unlikely evangelist for free trade. Born in London in 1968 to Sri Lankan immigrants, he went to a leading public school, St Paul's, before studying chemistry at

Balliol College, Oxford. He wrote novels that were never published and left Oxford with a third-class degree. But his real passion was athletics. He ran the 400 metres for the university and had hopes of a career in sport. After rupturing both Achilles tendons ("my body was not designed to run as fast as I was trying to make it run"), he was forced to rethink his future and alighted on the law.

In 1995, Singham moved to Miami to work for a firm called Steel Hector & Davis. The unflinching American legal environment was unsettling at first. But Singham warmed to the more expansive role of a US lawyer, where the ability to lobby and navigate local politics was often just as important as legal advocacy. "Clients liked him," Joseph Klock, the managing partner at Steel Hector at the time, told *Buzzfeed*. "People liked him. The folks at his church liked him."[13]

After a decade in Miami, Singham moved to Washington DC. Most of his legal work in the capital involved helping large companies overcome barriers to international trade. He lobbied for the US cotton industry, a major electrical distributor and a Russian businessman with gold mining operations in Mongolia. He had a relatively junior role representing a group of technology companies on a Washington committee advising the government on trade policy.

In his spare time, Singham began to give speeches and write papers extolling the virtues of free trade. He talked about classical Austrian economics to parents at his son's Opus Dei-run Catholic school in the Maryland suburbs. (Singham and his wife had converted in the US.) In the Florida Keys, he delivered presentations about libertarianism to wealthy conservatives.[14] The Heritage Foundation applauded his ideas.[15] But tangible successes were few and far between.

At the start of 2016, Singham returned to London to head up a small economic policy unit at the Legatum Institute. Although part of the global Atlas Network of privately funded libertarian think tanks, Legatum was widely seen as liberal and pro-European. The US journalist and historian Anne Applebaum and prominent Putin critic Peter Pomerantsev were among the staff at its upmarket Mayfair offices. Singham's role was largely to support Legatum's international philanthropic work. He contributed a chapter to a Heritage Foundation report on economic freedom.

Then came the Brexit referendum.

"When I turned up at Legatum on the morning after the vote, it was like walking into a morgue," says Legatum board member Toby Baxendale. "It was probably only myself and the receptionist who voted for Brexit." But there was one man who had a plan. "Shanker pointed out that he must be the only person in the United Kingdom who knew what to do."

Singham, a reluctant Remainer in the referendum, had thought little about leaving the European Union beforehand. "I just assumed, like everyone else, that they'd vote to remain and that would be the end of it," he told *Buzzfeed*.[16] But when the vote went the other way, the moment Singham must have been waiting for had arrived. A whole array of Brexit-supporting politicians, it was painfully obvious, knew little about trade. Shanker Singham was ready to teach them.

Within weeks of the referendum, Legatum had set up a dedicated "special trade commission" on Brexit. Former officials with experience from around the world were hired. Pro-Brexit staff took senior positions. Vote Leave's Matthew Elliott joined as a research fellow. Singham started writing policy papers and opinion pieces in newspapers. He was called to give evidence to parliamentary committees, where he advised Britain to make a clean break with the EU and seek "deeper agreements" with countries such as Canada, Australia and the United States.[17] He was an enthusiastic supporter of a free trade deal with the US and would later describe a no-deal Brexit as "no worries".

Singham became many Brexiters' go-to trade advisor. Speaking in the House of Commons, Conservative minister Michael Gove said: "I am sanguine about leaving. I take the lead from Shanker Singham." A flattering profile in a Catholic newspaper reported that over coffee Singham's "phone lights up with messages from MPs asking for urgent briefings".[18]

Singham's supporters described him as one of the world's leading trade and competition lawyers.[19] Sympathetic journalists recounted his experience in major economic transactions: US free trade negotiations, China's accession to the World Trade Organisation, Thatcher-era privatisations.

But many experts were less convinced. David Henig, a former UK trade official who worked on the proposed trade deal between the US and EU, told me that during the Transatlantic Trade and Investment Partnership negotiations, "I never came across Singham, even though I had extensive engagement around the EU and with the US administration. Safe to say he wasn't heavily involved."

A biography distributed by a former employer in the US described Singham's work as "assisting governments in the early privatisations during the Thatcher administration". The *Guardian* noted that while Singham had mentioned his work on privatisations in the 1980s in a public speech, his career did not begin until 1992.[20] Singham said that privatisation was an ongoing issue and he had worked on the sales of UK water and gas companies as a young lawyer.

Although Singham claimed to have been a senior trade advisor to Republican presidential hopefuls Mitt Romney and Marco Rubio, key campaign aides of both men had little or no memory of him. "I have no recollection of the name," Kevin Madden, one of Romney's senior staff on both the 2008 and 2012 campaigns, told *Buzzfeed*. "You really aren't a senior advisor unless you were paid, day-to-day staff, and were in regular meetings with the candidate himself." Singham insisted he made an important contribution to the Romney and Rubio campaigns and did talk to both candidates. "I was engaged with them all in putting trade policy proposals on the table for the candidates," he said.[21]

Singham did have one vital quality that many British trade advisors lacked: he took a positive view of Brexit. "There was a role in British politics for someone to make unappealing outcomes seem practical and provide detail that seemed plausible. Shanker filled that need very, very well," says an experienced British trade expert expressing strong opinions who asked to remain anonymous. "Shanker is very polite, very conciliatory. But when you break down what he is saying, it literally doesn't make sense if you understand what the acronyms mean."

In the febrile world of post-referendum Westminster, Singham quickly gained a level of access to cabinet ministers and senior officials that was the envy of London's lobbyists. A crucial moment came in September 2016 when a group of veteran Eurosceptics including John Redwood, Iain Duncan Smith, Peter Lilley and Brexit Minister David Davis met with legal and trade experts at All Soul's College in Oxford to set out a plan for a complete departure from the EU.[22] Singham was a vocal presence at the seminar. Afterwards, Legatum published a report that called for a "great repeal bill" to end EU law in Britain and a timetable for triggering Article 50, which Prime Minister Theresa May subsequently adopted almost in its entirety.

Singham quickly became a fixture in government. He had dozens of face-to-face meetings with senior ministers, far more than any other lobbyist. The IEA's Mark Littlewood would later tell Greenpeace's undercover reporter that Singham spoke with Michael Gove "every three or four days, along with David Davis, Boris Johnson, Liam Fox".[23] In July 2017, Singham was the only think tanker invited to the Brexit department's summit of business leaders at Chevening, the foreign secretary's grace and favour pile in the Kent countryside.[24] A few months later, Singham wrote a letter signed by Boris Johnson and Michael Gove calling for May to adopt a harder Brexit strategy.[25]

Singham was particularly well known in the Brexit departments. Trade Minister Liam Fox appointed him to a committee of experts. (Singham subsequently left the post after it was revealed that he had also taken a job with a lobbying company.[26]) A senior official in Fox's department said he raised concerns about the economic assumptions underlying Legatum's almost uniquely sunny Brexit reports but "it didn't seem to make much difference". The minister liked what he heard too much. A judge later said that the "unstructured nature" of the Brexit policy process enabled Singham "to have a greater degree of access to government than would normally be the case".[27]

Singham was particularly close to Brexit Minister Steve Baker.

Introduced to one another by Legatum's Toby Baxendale, the two men became friends around the time of the referendum. They had plenty in common: both in their mid-40s, they had spent much of their lives as outsiders, believers in a world of apostates. In the months after June 2016, Singham became an influential member of the ERG's central committee with Baker as chair.[28] The group drew heavily on Singham's ideas. In one briefing circulated shortly after the referendum, ERG members were told that whenever World Trade Organisation rules were mentioned they should refer to an answer compiled by Legatum. A 30-page memo sent to Theresa May cited Singham's claim that a new alliance of free trading nations led by the UK would boost the global economy by $2 trillion.[29]

After the disastrous June 2017 snap general election, May appointed Baker as a Brexit minister under David Davis. *Buzzfeed* revealed that as a minister Baker had frequent meetings with Singham that were not disclosed in the official government transparency register.[30] Singham saw Baker and international trade advisor Crawford Falconer out of office hours at the Legatum building in Mayfair. The trio maintained that the meetings were purely social and that they did not discuss government policy. Later, *openDemocracy* found that Singham had been arranging meetings with lobby groups on Baker's behalf.[31]

The press reports about Singham and Baker sparked questions. Could a corporate-funded trade lobbyist advise both ministers and a group of MPs increasingly opposed to their own government? A shadow cabinet minister called for an investigation. Nothing much happened. The government judged that the meetings were not official, as they did not relate to policy, so no rules had been broken. Baker eventually resigned a few months later – because of his strident opposition to May's Chequers proposals.

By then Singham had moved on, too. Life at Legatum had become strained amid a swirl of increasingly fantastical rumours about the think tank's links to Russia. Conservative MP Bob Seely used parliamentary privilege to accuse Legatum's main funder, New Zealand-born, Dubai-based tycoon Christopher Chandler, of having links to Kremlin intelligence agencies.[32] Seely's accusations were lifted from a dossier that had passed around just about every London newsroom without anyone, until that point, seeing fit to print or use it. Chandler, who had made much of his vast fortune in the 1990s privatisation of state-run Soviet businesses, rejected the claims as "complete nonsense".[33] The *Mail on Sunday* subsequently apologised to the businessman.

Nevertheless, the fevered talk of Russia focused unwelcome attention on Legatum, and on Singham's Brexit lobbying. The Charity Commission later found that a paper published by Singham's trade commission, *The Brexit Inflection Point*, breached its rules by being too politically partisan.[34] Legatum removed the report from its website. "We were a charity. Shanker was going off to have these meetings with the ERG. That was difficult for us," said one person close to the think tank.

In March 2018, *City A.M.* reported that Singham and his trade team had been "poached" by the Institute for Economic Affairs.[35] The so-called 'brains of Brexit' was now at the heart of one of the oldest and most influential libertarian think tanks in British politics.

The Institute of Economic Affairs is possibly the most successful British export that most people have never heard of. In 1955, two

eccentric Britons, Old Etonian Antony Fisher and his friend Major
Oliver Smedley, established a new venture from their pokey office
down a nondescript alleyway in the City of London. Its goal was
to promote free market economics. The pair had already set up a
succession of unsuccessful organisations along similar lines: the
Cheap Food League, the Council for the Reduction of Taxation,
the Reliance School of Investment.[36] But the IEA would be different. In the guise of a research institute, it would be a covert weapon
to change political and public opinion. In doing so it would spawn
a multibillion-dollar industry that would change the shape of
politics, particularly in the United States but also in Britain.[37]

The idea for the Institute for Economic Affairs came from
Friedrich Hayek. According to the documentary-maker Adam
Curtis, after the Second World War Fisher paid a visit to Hayek
at the London School of Economics, where the Austrian was an
economics professor.[38] Like Hayek, Fisher feared that communism and socialism would overwhelm the West and believed that
government should have almost no role in people's lives. The
Englishman wanted to know if he should go into politics. Hayek
told him that it was a waste of time. Politicians were led by con-
ventional wisdom.

As Richard Fink would do with the Koch brothers more than
two decades later, Hayek told Fisher that if he wanted to change
politics, he needed to change what politicians thought. He should
establish a "scholarly institute" with a singular aim: to persuade
influencers that the only way to save Britain was to adopt free
market principles. Fisher should set up a think tank.

The IEA's aim was not to generate new ideas, but to change public opinion. Smedley warned Fisher that they needed to be "cagey"
and to appear neutral and dispassionate. They set up as a charity,
which the IEA still is. The major told his colleagues that it was:

imperative that we should give no indication in our literature
that we are working to educate the Public along certain lines

which might be interpreted as having a political bias. In other words, if we said openly that we were teaching the economics of the free-market, it might enable our enemies to question the charitableness of our motives.[39]

The name, the Institute of Economic Affairs, was intentionally bland. This model was later followed almost to the letter by the Heritage Foundation, the Cato Institute and countless other libertarian think tanks that would radically reshape American politics.

Fisher had a flair for picking up economic ideas second-hand and turning them into a marketable commodity.[40] He bankrolled the IEA from the profits of a broiler chicken farming business that he set up after a visit to New York in the early 1950s (ironically paid for by government compensation after all his cattle died of foot and mouth disease[41]). He later sold Buxted Chickens for £20 million.[42]

Fisher eventually moved to North America. Like Richard Fink, he went to Wichita, Kansas, to sell his libertarian think tanks to Charles Koch. George Pearson, Koch's right-hand man, described the meeting as "one of the more memorable dinners of my life": the two business titans compared the merits of cattle ranching and turtle farming (Fisher's new venture) and talked about how to "spread freedom" through think tanks.[43]

Fisher went on to found another 150 or so free market institutes around the world. In 1981, he set up the Atlas Network to act as an umbrella group for libertarian think tanks. Atlas offers coaching in fundraising, messaging and marketing, and connects key figures with potential donors through its regular Liberty Forum gatherings.[44] Current British members of the network include the IEA, the Adam Smith Institute, Legatum and the TaxPayers' Alliance. Atlas does not disclose its funding, but it has previously received money from corporate giants such as ExxonMobil and Mastercard.[45]

Back in late-1950s Britain, Fisher saw the IEA's role as conducting a clandestine political counter-revolution, fighting against Keynesian state control and for open competition. The IEA's books and pamphlets were written by politicians, academics and journalists from both left and right, but the core message, delivered in plain English, was always the same: lower taxes, less government, more freedom for business and consumers.

The problem was that economics was not a very emotive subject. "The free market is a rather cold distillation," said Ralph Harris, the IEA's director from 1957, almost half a century later in an interview with the journalist Andy Beckett.[46] Harris had an idea for how to give capitalism a more human face. He would invite people to the IEA for wine and sandwiches.

Three times a week during the 1960s and 1970s, small groups of opinion-formers came for drinks. The events always started at 12.45 p.m. exactly and ended at half past two, just in time to be back at the office. The refreshments were accompanied by discussions about free market economics. Both Conservative and Labour MPs were invited (though never at the same time).[47]

The IEA's free market ideas began to take root. As industry secretary in 1964, future prime minister Ted Heath was influenced by an IEA pamphlet arguing for an end to the policy of agreements between manufacturers and retailers not to sell a product below a specified price.[48] Tory right-winger Enoch Powell was a particularly passionate advocate, for a time. These minor successes aside, however, the IEA was still a fringe player in British politics. Both Conservatives and their Labour rivals were broadly committed to state management of the economy.

Until, that is, Thatcher came along. "When we set up the Institute, we thought this battle would occupy the rest of our lives," Ralph Harris said. "But twenty years later we had Thatcher. Far quicker than we imagined!"[49]

Thatcher had been a regular at the IEA's drinks parties and lunches. In 1969, Arthur Seldon, a long-serving editorial director at the institute who had been an East End socialist in the 1930s, wrote to express his admiration for the then shadow minister's convictions. "I am particularly glad you did not say that so-and-so policy was eminently desirable but 'politically impossible'."[50] As Thatcher became increasingly influential, so did libertarian think tanks. In 1974, Thatcher set up the Centre for Policy Studies with her close ally Sir Keith Joseph to, in her words, "think the unthinkable". Joseph had also been involved in the IEA.[51]

When Thatcher became Tory leader the following year, she turned to the think tanks to create the policies for her future government.[52] Again, socialising was crucial. Every Saturday, Thatcher's researchers met think tank staff members and columnists and leader writers from *The Times* and the *Telegraph* in a London wine bar, where they "planned strategy for the week ahead".[53] The journalists would then turn the think tanks' ideas into columns while the researchers encouraged shadow ministers to take up their proposals. Like the most effective marketing, the influence was both saturating and almost invisible. "Without the IEA," Chicago University professor Milton Friedman later said, "I doubt very much whether there would have been a Thatcherite revolution."[54] In 1979, the newly elected Conservative prime minister credited the IEA for creating "the climate of opinion which made our victory possible".[55] Thatcher knighted Antony Fisher in 1988, four weeks before his death.

Fisher's quiet revolution had reshaped Britain. Think tanks like the IEA and the Adam Smith Institute facilitated what Stian Westlake, an advisor to the Conservative government under Theresa May, has called "the long march of liberal ideas".[56] State industries were privatised. The City of London boomed. The political landscape was visibly transformed.

Mark Littlewood maintains that the IEA's belief in what he called "bullish libertarianism"[57] has changed little since the days of Fisher and Smedley's tiny office on Austin Friars Passage. But others within the libertarian milieu have been highly critical of what they see as an intellectual decay on the free market right. Where corporate-funded think tanks once provided the ideas for a conservative revolution, now they often appear as one side in an increasingly hyperbolic culture war. Banning smoking in pubs is a full-scale assault on civil liberties; gambling develops numeracy skills; even the overtly economic ideas, such as free ports, feel more like crony capitalism than removing "the dead hand of the state".

Free marketers talk the same language as the deregulators of the 1980s, but their actions are largely "performative", writes Westlake. In his reading, libertarians are "play-acting and position-taking rather than fighting the real battles that would matter to a modern-day market liberal".[58] A former staff member at a prominent British libertarian think tank went even further, telling me: "The IEA used to regularly publish Nobel Prize winners. Now it's driven by money." This veteran of London's corporate-funded think tank world believes that British free marketers tried to take advantage of Brexit to push their agendas, but found themselves ditching their deepest political commitments in the drive to exert influence.

"The think tanks tried to ride the Brexit tiger, and they lost control. They have abandoned a lot of their beliefs. You have [Thatcherite Tory Eurosceptic] John Redwood advocating tariffs," the source said. "The IEA has done for free-market liberals in the UK what Donald Trump has done for the Republican movement in the US. They will condone anything. Brexit encapsulates that."

Most of Tufton Street and its purlieus did not take official stances on Brexit. But their books, pamphlets and conferences often envisaged a Britain freed from European regulations. In the winter of 2013, the IEA offered a €100,000 prize for the best plan for leaving the EU. The six leading entrants all said that the UK could maintain full access to the single market but end freedom of movement.[59] The winner, a civil servant in the British embassy in Manila named

Iain Mansfield, was later briefly appointed as a special advisor in Boris Johnson's pre-election administration.

Once the referendum result was in, think tanks quickly began to frame Brexit as a historic opportunity to radically shrink the state. The morning after the EU referendum, the Centre for Policy Studies said that there was now "a unique political opportunity to drive through a wide-ranging supply-side revolution on a scale similar to that of the 1980s. This must include removing unnecessary regulatory burdens on businesses, such as those related to climate directives and investment fund regulations." In 2017, Mark Littlewood told the Atlas Network's quarterly magazine that the Leave victory had galvanised the libertarian movement: "Brexit provides us with a once-in-a-generation opportunity to radically trim the size of the state and cut the regulatory burden."[60]

The IEA soon emerged as the think tank of choice for Westminster's Brexiters, especially after Singham joined. In late September 2018, the BBC News channel cut live to the launch of an IEA paper entitled *Plan A+: Creating a Prosperous Post-Brexit UK*. In the centre of the shot, David Davis stood behind a rostrum clutching a copy of the report. "It is probably true to say that if this had been the White Paper, I'd still be in government today," said Davis, who had resigned as Brexit secretary earlier in the summer in opposition to Theresa May's Chequers proposals. The IEA's plan, Davis said, offered a chance for Britain "to grasp the Brexit prize".

He raised his voice slightly so it could be heard above the din of photographers furiously snapping. At a long table to his left were a row of familiar faces: Jacob Rees-Mogg, head of the European Research Group; former cabinet minister Theresa Villiers; Vote Leave board member and former Labour MP Gisela Stuart; and Shanker Singham, who had written the report.

Who funded *Plan A+* is unclear, but anonymous corporate donations have long been the biggest source of income for libertarian think tanks. Speaking to Greenpeace's undercover reporter, Littlewood used the example of the drinks industry to explain how the IEA works. "We would go to alcohol companies and say we want to write about the cost of living being too high and actually alcohol consumption is not costing the National Health Service as much money as they often complain," he said.[61]

Given intellectual grifting like this, it is difficult to see the IEA as a neutral research body. Transparency advocate Tamasin Cave says that "the IEA is not an independent think tank. It is a lobby group for private interests". Mark Littlewood has defended the policy of not naming donors, saying it is "perfectly legitimate for people to privately donate to private causes".

Critics of those who ask think tanks "who funds you?" have often pointed out that left-wing and liberal causes have also received private financial support. Defending the IEA's funding model to the *Guardian*, Daniel Hannan noted that Hungarian-American billionaire investor George Soros had funded pro-EU causes. Soros has also supported media outlets around the world, including at times *openDemocracy*, where I work. Unlike the IEA and others, Soros's Open Society Foundations publish extensive details of who they fund. *openDemocracy*'s website lists all of its funders, too. None of this money comes with any editorial control.

Over the years, details of some of the IEA's financial backers have been revealed. Tobacco manufacturers, the gambling and off-shore financial services industries, and Big Oil have all donated.[62] The think tank, which has published numerous books, papers and articles suggesting man-made climate change is disputed or exaggerated, has accepted funding from BP every year since 1967.[63]

Among the businesses that have funded the IEA is Tate & Lyle.[64] The sugar giant is no stranger to lobbying. In 1949, the secretive business lobby group Aims of Industry ran a campaign against sugar nationalisation with the catchy slogans 'Tate not State!' and 'Take the S out of State'.[65] Tate & Lyle were among the most vociferous critics of Britain's EU membership, regularly petitioning government against European duties on sugar cane imports from its vast Belize plantations.[66] Former Brexit secretary David Davis is said to have developed his Euroscepticism during his 17 years working for Tate & Lyle before going into politics.[67]

During the 2016 referendum, the sugar giant was one of the few big firms to support Leave. Tate & Lyle, which has been owned by Cuban sugar magnates the Fanjul Brothers since 2010, wrote to all 800 of its UK staff warning that their jobs could be under threat if Britain voted to remain in the EU. After the Brexit vote, Tate & Lyle pushed for Britain to leave the customs union. As Brexit minister, Steve Baker met the company three times in just a year.

The IEA and the sugar industry remained close, too. At the 2018 Conservative Party conference, the IEA hosted a fringe session about the 'Brexit bonus' from dropping import tariffs. The panel featured Steve Baker, a representative from Tate & Lyle and a *Telegraph* columnist.[68]

The IEA's *Plan A+* arrived at a critical juncture in the fraught Brexit debate. By late September 2018, the clamour to "chuck Chequers" and pivot towards a more hardline vision of Brexit was growing, especially on the Conservative backbenches. The IEA offered an alternative vision to the prime minister's. Rather than shadowing the EU, Britain should dispense with a range of tariffs, quotas and regulations. Environmental protections should be loosened.[69] The National Health Service should be opened up to international competition. It was a none-too-subtle pitch for a free trade deal with the United States.[70]

As we saw previously, Britain's libertarian think tanks often look to America for inspiration – and, it seems, for financial support. In the decade to 2018, the Institute of Economic Affairs raised more than £1.3 million through the American Friends of the IEA.[71] US funders have included the Koch-backed Donors Trust and the conservative Chase Foundation of Virginia. The sums involved are a drop in the ocean of Washington dark money but, as we know, small amounts of money can go a long way in British politics. At the time, the IEA's annual budget was often less than £2 million.

How much of the money raised by the IEA's US wing was passed to the British operation is hard to tell due to the secrecy surrounding the donors, but funds generated in America are often used across the Atlantic. "There are plenty of ways of tapping into Republican funding in the US to bring it over to the UK," says Nick Pearce.

American libertarians have given money to other British causes. From 2016, the Charles Koch Foundation gave \$300,000[72] to the US arm of *Spiked*, a British website that emerged from the ashes of the Revolutionary Communist Party. Once intransigent defenders of the IRA and Bosnian Serb extremists, this tiny Trotskyist sect reinvented itself as a self-styled slayer of liberal holy cows and ardent advocate of anti-environmental and pro-corporate causes. *Spiked*'s cadres regularly feature in the British media, most ubiquitously Claire Fox, who went from BBC Radio's sophistic *Moral Maze* to the European Parliament as a member of Nigel Farage's Brexit Party in May 2019. (When the Koch brothers' funding was revealed by the *Guardian* and *DeSmog*, *Spiked* decried the reporting as spiteful "McCarthyism".)

Elsewhere, the IEA has received funding from the Philadelphia-based John Templeton Foundation for a free market economics magazine that it sends out to thousands of students across the UK. "By influencing today's generation of students, we can create tomorrow's social and economic freedoms," claimed the IEA's successful funding bid. It's a line that Antony Fisher or Major Smedley might have written. Even by US standards, Templeton is a particularly zealous donor. Successful applications have to include a spiritual dimension. "You just talk about the invisible hand of the market," one grantee told me. Edinburgh and St Andrews universities have received money from Templeton in recent years.

A couple of months after the launch of *Plan A+*, Singham, David Davis and former Northern Ireland secretary Owen Paterson travelled to the United States to present their vision of a US free trade deal with post-Brexit Britain. In Oklahoma, the

Three Brexiteers met the state's lieutenant governor. They gave a panel discussion at a centre named after Ronald Reagan in Washington DC. Davis's trip was partly paid for by the IEA and by the Oklahoma-based think tank the E Foundation.[73] Paterson's expenses were covered by a think tank called UK2020, of which he was the sole director. Inevitably based at 55 Tufton Street, the epicentre of the libertarian universe, Paterson's foundation did not have to identify its donors even though it had spent almost £40,000 flying its director around the world over the previous four years.[74]

Plan A+ earned the IEA an official rap over the knuckles. The think tank was temporarily forced to withdraw Singham's paper after the Charity Commission found that it had breached charitable law by advocating for a hard Brexit.[75] But by then it mattered little. The ERG's Jacob Rees-Mogg described it as "the most exciting contribution to this debate in many months". Boris Johnson hailed *Plan A+* as a "fine piece of work". Just as importantly, the report was widely covered in newspapers and on the airwaves. Britain's libertarian think tanks are extremely adept at maximising their media reach in the limited space for public political debate. The IEA alone boasted that while its revenue in 2017 was £2.5 million, it had an advertising value equivalent to £66 million.[76]

Academics who analysed BBC news and current affairs output found that in 2009, when Labour was in power, left- and right-wing think tanks appeared on the national broadcaster in almost equal measure.[77] By 2015, conservative institutes were twice as likely to be called upon. The reasons for this disparity are not inherently party political. Few television producers are supporters of free market pressure groups. But they often solicit voices willing to take up positions that have few obvious advocates, such as opposition to restrictions on smoking. That makes groups like the IEA a valuable commodity for journalists who, sometimes on shaky grounds, feel that they need to editorially balance contributors. "Think tanks tick all the boxes. That's why they are on so much," one BBC producer said. What these putative research institutes actually add to debates often seems a less pressing concern for broadcasters.

Libertarian think tanks fare even better in Britain's traditionally right-wing newspaper market. Comment pages often carry their views, either filtered through regular contributors such as Daniel Hannan or delivered directly in guest editorials. Mark Littlewood frequently writes for *The Times*. Shanker Singham wrote dozens of pro-Brexit opinion pieces for the *Telegraph* alone.

The Barclay brothers' newspaper, which is controlled by an off-shore trust, is particularly enthusiastic about think tanks. In 2015, the *Telegraph* featured Business for Britain's pro-Brexit report 'Change or Go' on its front page four times in a single week. After the EU referendum, the paper hired the political director of the TaxPayers' Alliance as its Brexit editor.

Elsewhere, *City A.M.* editor Christian May sits on the IEA's advisory council. Although the City was at best ambivalent on Brexit, the business freesheet took a very bullish view, regularly publishing columns from IEA staff about the benefits of leaving the EU.

It's not just about personal connections. Think tanks often run slick press operations that are open for business day and night, all year round. "The IEA has more staff dedicated to media and fund-raising than research," complained one source in a rival think tank. "Media is their only metric of success."

Among the strongest selling points of think tanks – of all stripes – is their access to decision-makers. Ministers often need someone outside party politics who can act as an outrider for new ideas. Many of the new generation of Tory MPs elected in 2010 gravitated towards the Thatcherite think tanks. Speaking at the IEA's 60th birthday celebration in 2015, future Brexit minister and foreign secretary Dominic Raab compared his ideological debt to the institute to swimming on a beach in Brazil and emerging from the water only to discover that the current had quietly moved him miles along the shore.[78] A 2019 investigation by the

British Medical Journal found that 32 MPs had financial links, direct and indirect, to the IEA, which had called for the NHS to be privatised.[79] A dozen Tory MPs, including Health Secretary Matt Hancock, had received donations from Neil Record, chair of the IEA's board of trustees.[80] Another IEA trustee, Vote Leave donor and hedge fund boss Michael Hintze, contributed money and gifts to more than a dozen Conservative MPs, including Boris Johnson and Liam Fox.[81]

The IEA also set up an organisation, Freer, to work directly with Conservative MPs to promote "free enterprise and social freedom". Freer has more than a dozen Tory MPs on its roster.[82] Freer is run by the IEA out of the IEA offices, with an IEA phone number and a website registered by the IEA. But technically it is separate from the parent organisation. It is not registered as a charity and so is not subject to the same restrictions on political lobbying and partisanship.

At Freer's launch in the summer of 2018, Liz Truss took inspiration from chart toppers Destiny's Child.[83] "In the merits of capitalism, Beyoncé said it best: 'All the honeys, who making money, throw your hands up at me'," the future international trade secretary declared. Among those looking on were Michael Gove, Dominic Raab and Shanker Singham. The latter would soon have yet another role to play in the "Brexit influencing game" – this time in Northern Ireland.

On 12 June 2019, a flight from London landed in Derry. On board was a former head of the UK Border Force, a senior representative from the Japanese IT giant Fujitsu, Shanker Singham and a British-based American lobbyist named Jennifer Powers, who worked for Singham's private consultancy. The four-person delegation had come to investigate solutions to the thorny issue of how to keep the 310-mile-long Irish border open after Brexit. The Alternative Arrangements Commission had arrived in Northern Ireland.[84]

Stephen Kelly, a local business representative, collected the quartet at City of Derry Airport, from where he brought them over the border to the small Donegal village of Muff. Later he drove the visitors through Derry's Bogside, past Irish Tricolours and murals commemorating Bloody Sunday, before finishing the whistle-stop tour in the Creggan, where dissident Republicans had murdered journalist Lyra McKee three months previously.

"I showed them the reality of life on the border," Kelly told me. "They saw how if a customs official with a clipboard wants to check if the customs duty has been paid on a packet of cigarettes in a corner shop in Creggan they need a battalion of the PSNI [Police Service of Northern Ireland] to support them."

A week after the visit to Derry, the Alternative Arrangements Commission launched its draft report on the Irish border with a day-long conference in the Conrad Hotel in central London. The opening address was delivered by Brexit Secretary Stephen Barclay. Many Eurosceptics attended. The ERG's Suella Braverman and Marcus Fysh spoke, as did the chairman of the AAC's border technical group, the ubiquitous Shanker Singham. Steve Baker and Peter Lilley attended. There were moderate voices, too. Remain-voting Tory MPs Greg Hands and Nicky Morgan headed up the 'commission'. A handful of Labour MPs lent their support.

The Alternative Arrangements Commission looked and sounded like a government propaganda drive. The UK government website described it as a "parliamentary commission", as did some of the AAC's own literature. But it was not an official body. The AAC was a private initiative run by a company called Prosperity UK, which had the catchy tagline 'Coming together to make Brexit a success'. Prosperity UK had been founded by multi-millionaire hedge fund owner and Brexit supporter Paul Marshall. Its board included senior pro-Leave figures, including some, such as Marshall, who had been connected to Singham's former employer Legatum. Vote Leave's outreach director oversaw the self-appointed commission's daily running.

Stephen Kelly was shocked when he read the AAC report. It proposed an unprecedented level of disruption and surveillance along the once deadly border. A 'special economic zone' would be created around Derry and Donegal, effectively turning an invisible border into two customs frontiers. "They completely misrepresented what they saw in Derry," Kelly said. "They deliberately ignored it."

The 'commission' never published the responses to its consultation from Northern Irish groups. I saw more than half a dozen. All raised serious issues with the proposals. The report also seemed geared towards a future UK–US trade deal. There was a lengthy discussion of the 'geographical indications' that appear on products that come from a specific place, like Champagne or feta cheese. Geographical indicators are a major sticking point in American trade talks, but "it doesn't make sense to talk about them" in the context of the Irish border, says trade advisor Sam Lowe. "They're not an issue."

The AAC was hailed as a bipartisan technological solution to the Irish border. At the launch of the Prosperity UK report in London, Hans Maessen, a Dutch customs advisor who had also worked with the European Research Group, said there would be big opportunities from alternative arrangements. "I stood up and said, 'How much are you going to make from this?'" recalled Kelly.

Maessen, who had previously described the Irish border as a "fictitious problem",[85] told me he was never paid for his work with Prosperity UK or the ERG, which he also advised. Others on the AAC technical panel had commercial interests in customs technology. A former senior Swedish custom official, Lars Karlsson, was part of a group given £3 million by the UK Treasury to build an online customs portal for Britain. Fujitsu had met top civil servants in the department for exiting the EU to discuss its proposals for a "drive-through border" in Ireland. The Japanese firm had donated to both the Tories and Labour.

Singham was the animating spirit behind the Alternative Arrangements Commission. He realised early on that the Irish border posed an obstacle to a 'clean break' with Brussels. In 2017, Singham wrote a paper on Ireland for Legatum that suggested a number of possible solutions to the thorny question of how to keep the once militarised border open after Brexit. His proposals included establishing a prize for "innovative solutions" to the border and using airships to police the frontier.[86] (Singham conceded that the unpredictable Irish weather might pose a problem for the dirigible solution.[87])

Other right-wing think tanks were also influential on the Irish border debate. A Policy Exchange paper written by historian Lord Paul Bew and former Northern Ireland first minister David Trimble argued that the backstop itself violated the Good Friday peace agreement, and was frequently adduced by leading pro-Brexit Tories. Again, it is not clear who funded this work; Policy Exchange does not declare its donors.

As Singham moved from Legatum to the IEA, he continued his interest in Ireland. In October 2018, he accompanied Trimble, Iain Duncan Smith and Owen Paterson on a trip to Brussels to present Michel Barnier with the ERG's proposals for the Irish border. They met with the EU chief negotiator's deputy, Sabine Weyand, who said that she could only negotiate with the UK government.[88] Nevertheless, the ERG and Singham kept pushing ahead.

In early 2019, the ERG's Steve Baker and Singham drafted a plan to unite warring factions of the Tory party around a single Brexit strategy. The so-called 'Malthouse compromise' envisioned 'alternative arrangements' on the Irish border to negate the need for a backstop after Brexit. In an attempt to placate her back-benchers, Theresa May allowed the group access to Cabinet Office staff to develop their plans.[89] The prime minister thought she was isolating voluble enemies. Instead, she had given what looked like governmental imprimatur to an ad hoc body run by a private company.

In late April 2019, with May's deal sunk, the Alternative Arrangements Commission formally launched itself. Singham was announced as the head of the group's technical working group. A lobbyist had moved to the fore of the biggest single issue in British and European politics.

The corporate-funded Alternative Arrangements Commission visited Northern Ireland regularly and held press conferences in Brussels and Westminster. It spoke to parliamentarians in Germany and the Netherlands and was frequently cited in the British media. Theresa May seems to have noticed its growing role and looked to counter an initiative that would undermine her withdrawal agreement. One of her last acts as prime minister was to set up a series of official government working groups on the Irish border.

Confusingly, these initiatives also had 'alternative arrangements' in their titles and included a number of key people from the Prosperity UK commission. A suite of Northern Irish trade and customs experts were also invited to join. Many were ambivalent, and wary of being co-opted. "I was worried that we wouldn't be listened to and we would just be a fig leaf," said one member of the government's official technical group. "I was right to be worried."

The UK government knew that technology would not replace the need for physical checks if Northern Ireland and the Irish Republic were in different customs and regulatory orbits, a fact consistently obfuscated by proponents of a hard Brexit. Nevertheless, the government-convened experts were encouraged to consider high-tech proposals for the Irish border, many of which came directly from Prosperity UK. On one occasion Singham was brought in to address the government's technical group.

"Shanker wasn't even on the agenda, but he was there when we arrived for the meeting, saying, 'The Good Friday Agreement is nothing to worry about,'" recalled one expert. (A spokeswoman for Prosperity UK told me that they had been committed to respecting the Good Friday Agreement. The commission's recommendations were "sincerely intentioned, practical, workable and timely", she said.)

The Alternative Arrangements Commission gained influence at the highest levels of the British government. Twice in as many days in late August 2019, newly installed prime minister Boris Johnson publicly endorsed what he called the commission's "excellent paper" on the Irish border. The report was widely cited as offering a compromise between the demands of the European Union for an open border and British concerns about the freedom to sign post-Brexit trade deals.

In early October 2019, Johnson travelled to Brussels to negotiate again with his European counterparts. Writing in the *Telegraph*, Braverman and Hands said that their commission had informed "the British government's thinking and its new offer to the EU".

Instead, Johnson agreed to move the border to the Irish Sea. The market for alternative arrangements had disappeared. The Prosperity UK commission shut up shop, expressing its support for Johnson's withdrawal agreement. Singham and Karlsson were vocal supporters of the prime minister's plan, and both travelled to Belfast to give a presentation to Belfast City Council. Only one DUP councillor turned up. "The DUP invited them, but they spent the whole time trying to convince us," said an Irish nationalist member of the chamber.

Singham also worked with Foyle Port in Derry on a bid to become a free port, an idea close to his earlier 'enterprise cities' initiative. Just days after the Conservative general election victory in December 2019, newspaper reports suggested that Singham was in line for a seat in the House of Lords.

Johnson's volte-face in Brussels removed the need for alternative arrangements on the Irish border, but Prosperity UK's commission showed how much influence a private company could have on a crucial aspect of British government policy. Prominent British politicians and commentators regularly hailed the commission's engagement in Northern Ireland as signalling support for their plans. But many who actually worked in business along the Irish border took a very different view. "They didn't give a toss about Northern Ireland and they didn't care about the border," said one trade representative on the UK government's alternative arrangements group. "They just wanted to push something through so they could get on with a trade deal with the US."

In Derry, Stephen Kelly ruefully remarked that "all the engagement with people with their feet on the ground was completely ignored by the AAC". But, he added, "Some of the people involved seemed to have earned very well out of it."

The word 'lobbyist' dates back to at least the 1800s, when petitioners hung around the rooms outside the chamber where Parliament met, hoping to buttonhole politicians. In some senses, it has not changed much in the intervening centuries. Influence is still the aim. But today, representatives of many vested interests – particularly corporations – are effectively embedded in the political system. As Colin Crouch writes:

> [Lobbyists] are not in the lobby, outside the real decision-making space of government at all. They are right inside the room of political decision-making. They set standards, establish private regulatory systems, act as consultants to government, even have staff seconded to ministers.[90]

Shortly before he became prime minister in 2010, David Cameron called out lobbying as a major scandal waiting to happen. "We all know how it works," the Conservative leader said. "The lunches, the hospitality, the quiet word in your ear, the ex-ministers and ex-advisers for hire, helping big business find the right way to get its way."[91] In government, Cameron introduced measures ostensibly aimed at bringing much-needed sunlight into the dark corners of this shady world. But, if anything, lobbying in British politics is even more opaque now. "In terms of transparency, it's

reverted back to what it was before Cameron made that statement," says Tamasin Cave.

Transparency campaigners such as Cave say that the political
lobbying game grew in size and influence after the EU referendum. Small agencies expanded quickly. Many of Cameron's own
lieutenants got in on the act: former cabinet ministers William
Hague and Francis Maude became consultants, as did Craig
Oliver, who ran the Remain campaign (receiving a knighthood
for his troubles). Former Vote Leave communications chief Paul
Stephenson and ex-Downing Street advisor Ameet Gill set up their
own firm, Hanbury Strategy, which went on to work on the Conservative 2019 general election campaign.[92] The Tories' election-
winning manifesto was written by Rachel Wolf, who co-founded
the lobbying firm Public First with her husband, James Frayne,
formerly of the TaxPayers' Alliance and Dominic Cummings's
path-breaking campaign against a North East Assembly in 2004.

What many of Britain's lobbyists are doing is very hard to
work out. Cameron's reforms bequeathed a confusing mix of
statutory and voluntary registers. Often, those who should sign
up don't. But just as frequently, the rules mean that even lobbyists
with the best access to government are not required to register. In
2019, the Australian spin doctor Sir Lynton Crosby's CTF Partners
masterminded Boris Johnson's successful leadership campaign,
even donating money and personnel to the prime minister's team.
But it did not have to sign up to a lobbying register. Belatedly, the
regulator opened an investigation.[93]

The IEA's Shanker Singham did not have to register, either,
despite owning a personal consultancy and having frequent meetings with many of those sitting around the cabinet table. Britain's
lobbying legislation does not cover in-house lobbying, or require
the disclosure of what is discussed at private meetings, where
policy decisions are often made.

British politics has a revolving door between government and
the lobbying industry. A fifth of new Conservative MPs elected

in 2019 had previously worked as lobbyists. Scores of prominent politicians have gone on to well-paying jobs as lobbyists. In 2018 alone, more than 200 former ministers and senior civil servants took up roles advising and lobbying for different businesses.[94] Within six months of resigning as Brexit secretary, David Davis was earning £3,000 an hour as an "external advisor" to JCB.[95] Prior to the 2019 general election, former environment secretary Owen Paterson lobbied to promote products for two firms that he was paid to advise. He contacted ministers and officials on behalf of companies that he was paid £112,000 to advise, on top of his parliamentary salary of £79,000.[96] (Paterson said his financial interests "have been correctly declared according to the rules of the House of Commons".)

Parliament's anti-corruption watchdog, the Advisory Committee on Business Appointments, is a feeble instrument that seldom, if ever, stands in the way of politicians taking plum jobs outside government. Meanwhile, think tanks operate in a lobbying grey area. They are not counted as lobbyists under the law. Financial transparency is discretionary and decidedly partial.

There is a discernible public good in independent thinkers producing ideas that can feed into policy. But just how autonomous is an organisation that survives on anonymous corporate donations? A 2017 study found that only a third of Britain's think tanks were "highly transparent" about their funding. The same analysis also identified seven influential British think tanks "that take money from hidden hands behind closed doors". Policy Exchange, Civitas, the Adam Smith Institute, the Centre for Policy Studies and the Institute of Economic Affairs were all listed as "highly opaque and deceptive".[97] Most are registered as educational charities, which is a boon for donors looking to bring down their tax bill.

Think tanks with anodyne names have another advantage over commercial lobbyists: they sound like neutral observers. On paper, the Institute for Fiscal Studies – a non-aligned think tank that explains the implications of spending decisions – sounds very similar to the Institute of Economic Affairs. Less than 4 per cent of the British public were able to name a single think tank in a 2019 poll. Just a quarter of one per cent volunteered that they recognised the Institute of Economic Affairs.[98]

Yet these think tanks can exert significant influence on government policy. In February 2016, Matt Hancock announced a ban on recipients of public funds, such as universities and charities, lobbying government. The cabinet office minister cited the IEA's "extensive research" on the issue as a key motivation for the move. The IEA had accepted £15,000 from an unnamed source to develop the proposal.[99] The 'gagging clause' policy was later dropped following extensive criticism.

Regulations do exist to curb the potential for lobbyists to influence ministers. Ministers are supposed to record their meetings in official registers. But ministers often claim meetings are personal rather than political, in which case they do not require disclosure.

There are other ways of circumventing requirements. In footage recorded by Greenpeace, the IEA's Mark Littlewood said he had attended meetings between Shanker Singham and Steve Baker, meaning that the minister could officially record visits as "Mark Littlewood and staff". At none of these meetings were any notes or minutes taken. (A spokeswoman for the IEA said of Littlewood's comments on hiding meetings with Baker: "We do not recognise this version of events."[100])

Think tanks often argue that they advocate certain politics not for the benefit of their funders, but because they are the right thing for the country. But it's impossible to judge that when their lobbying – and their donors – remain cloaked in secrecy. One Tory MP I spoke to gave a blunt assessment of Westminster's libertarian think tanks: "They are corporate lobbyists, nothing more."

*

In early August 2019, a week after Boris Johnson became prime minister, the IEA returned to the Villiers Hotel in Buckingham for the start of a two-day staff retreat. The atmosphere could scarcely have been more different than a year earlier when the Greenpeace video had been aired. Where the mood had been sullen and anxious as Shanker Singham prepared for the *Newsnight* cameras, now the IEA was letting its hair down. Boisterous staff stayed up drinking late into the night.

There was plenty to celebrate. Johnson had just appointed some of the institute's closest political allies to senior roles: Dominic Raab became foreign secretary, Priti Patel took over at the home office, Liz Truss replaced Liam Fox as international trade secretary. In a congratulatory email to its supporters, the IEA declared that 14 of those around the Downing Street table were "alumni" of its initiatives.[101]

During the leadership campaign, Johnson drew on many prominent Tufton Street talking points: a sugar tax was bad; free ports were good; no-deal was nothing to fear. In office, his new administration looked to the libertarian think tank world for key personnel. More than a dozen former staff from the Institute of Economic Affairs, the TaxPayers' Alliance, the Adam Smith Institute and the Centre for Policy Studies were given influential special advisor roles (colloquially known as 'spads').

Right-wing news website *Guido Fawkes* hailed the think tank influx as "good news for free marketeers and lovers of liberty". A few days later a *Guido* reporter, and former Vote Leave staffer, was unveiled as special advisor to the new House of Commons leader, Jacob Rees-Mogg.[102] The revolving door seldom stops spinning.

As the new spads started life in Westminster, more than two dozen IEA staff trooped through the faux-ionic columns of the Vinson Centre at Buckingham University. Buckingham has long been close to the IEA. Its vice-chancellor, biographer Sir Anthony Seldon, is the son of early IEA adopter Arthur. The Vinson Centre is named after its primary funder, entrepreneur and IEA trustee Lord Nigel Vinson, who said it was designed to "cement" the relationship between the think tank and the university.[103]

One of the first speakers at the IEA retreat was Linda Whetstone, daughter of founder Antony Fisher. Whetstone, chairwoman of the Atlas Network and an IEA board member, has been steeped in transatlantic libertarianism for decades. When she addressed the 1978 Tory party conference, Whetstone demanded that the next Conservative government slash regulation. "Don't let's go out of our way to help small businesses, agriculture, the unions, coloured people, women," Whetstone declared before being drowned out by a band playing 'God Save the Queen'.[104]

A libertarian streak runs through the Whetstone family. Linda's daughter, Rachel, worked for Tory central office before becoming a senior executive at some of Silicon Valley's biggest companies. Rachel's husband, Steve Hilton, was director of strategy for David Cameron before joining the think tank Policy Exchange. He later became a vocal Trump supporter, hosting a weekly show on Rupert Murdoch's Fox Network.

In Buckingham, Linda Whetstone delivered a session for IEA staff on "the freedom fighters who put themselves on the line to spread the free market word". Another presentation advised staff how to amplify their research findings. Former Conservative and UKIP MP Douglas Carswell talked about digital disruption. After the referendum, Carswell had opened his own (short-lived) data analytics company with former Vote Leave staffer Thomas Borwick before dedicating himself to his increasingly dyspeptic YouTube channel.

In one of the final talks of the IEA retreat, Mark Littlewood took a look at "life on planet Boris". The director-general noted "the immediate opportunities for the IEA" with Johnson in government. How, Littlewood wondered, might the "IEA exploit the new and potentially fragmented post-Brexit landscape"? The influencing game was very much still on.

*

There are clear parallels between Britain today and the dark money nexus that has underpinned US politics for decades: libertarian think tanks backed by anonymous corporate donations and aided by sympathetic journalists and media outriders; a major party reliant on a handful of wealthy, ideologically motivated donors. Westminster even has its own hardline parliamentary caucus, the European Research Group.

But Britain's dark money problem has its own characteristics. Tufton Street might have ties with America, and look there for inspiration, but it is also a very British phenomenon. The diaphanous rules and regulations that allow clandestine money and influence to flow into UK politics are a product of decisions taken – and not taken – by successive British governments. "Political parties have a vested interest in the status quo," says Labour MP Stephen Kinnock, chair of a parliamentary working group on electoral reform. "They would rather stay with the broken system we have currently, because they know how to maximise their advantage within it."

This is dangerously short-sighted. The US political arms race is already crossing the Atlantic. Kinnock believes that we are in "an Americanised situation whereby dark money and dodgy data are playing an increasing role in our politics. That is a very dangerous place to be. We have been complacent about our democracy. We thought it would just look after itself." These flaws in our democracy are particularly apparent not just in the physical world around us, but in politics' biggest growth market: the online world of digital campaigning.

8

DIGITAL GANGSTERS

*Misinformation affects us all. Our current policies on fact
checking people in political office, or those running for office, are
a threat to what Facebook stands for. We strongly object to this
policy as it stands. It doesn't protect voices, but instead allows
politicians to weaponise our platform by targeting people who
believe that content posted by political figures is trustworthy.*

Open letter from Facebook employees to
CEO Mark Zuckerberg, October 2019

55 New Oxford Street is an unlikely setting for a raid by
a squad of enforcement officials seeking to investigate
election plundering. The office block looks like many in
central London, nine storeys of glass and steel in muted greys
and light blues. When a local estate agent was letting two of the
floors in 2019, it listed the nearby underground stations as one of
the biggest selling points. By then, the name Cambridge Analytica
had been removed from the plaque outside the door. Alexander
Nix had left the building.[1]

At 8 p.m. on 23 March 2018, the British Information Commissioner's Office raided 55 New Oxford Street. I say 'raided' because
that's how it was reported at the time, and because it looked
like a raid. Eighteen people, most in bright blue jackets with

'Enforcement' embossed across the back, filed through the revolving doors and into Cambridge Analytica's offices. The receptionist looked surprised. Behind them television cameras rolled. The cavalry had arrived.

But in one important sense this wasn't a raid: Cambridge Analytica and Nix, its polished chief executive officer, knew the officials were coming. The Information Commissioner had spent much of the preceding week waiting for a judge to grant a warrant to search the building, amid claims that data from tens of millions of illegally acquired Facebook profiles had been used for political campaigns on both sides of the Atlantic.

The commissioner's staff spent seven hours combing through the first and second floors of the office, and at three in the morning a white rental van piled with paperwork and evidence boxes left the building.[2] Within weeks, Cambridge Analytica had filed for insolvency. A company once touted as the future of political campaigning was in ruins. Politicians and parties across the world rushed to play down their links to Nix and the empire he ran from offices in London and New York.

The Cambridge Analytica scandal sparked fevered questions about the unregulated Wild West of digital politics. What exactly are political campaigns doing online? Is technology destroying democracy? Can anything be done to stop what a British parliamentary inquiry called Silicon Valley's "digital gangsters"?

By the time the ICO's enforcement officials walked into 55 New Oxford Street, Cambridge Analytica had already become a byword for political manipulation and malfeasance. Nix, a bespectacled Old Etonian who dresses well but not ostentatiously, had publicly bragged about the power of Cambridge Analytica's sophisticated psychographics and online targeting during the 2016 presidential election. He was even more loose-lipped in private. Speaking with an undercover reporter from *Channel 4 News* posing as a potential client, he boasted that Cambridge Analytica could entrap rival candidates in fake bribery stings. The company, he said, had hired sex workers to seduce opposition politicians and had set up proxy campaigns to feed untraceable political misinformation into social media.[3]

A whistleblower, Cambridge Analytica's pink-haired former research director Chris Wylie, revealed to Carole Cadwalladr that his company had harvested Facebook data from 50 million users and used it for political advertising. (The number of Facebook users potentially compromised was later revised up to 87 million.) The social network lost almost $120 billion in stock value in the wake of the scandal,[4] and it was later fined $5 billion by the US consumer regulator, the Federal Trade Commission, for "deceiving" users about its ability to keep their personal information private.[5]

Cambridge Analytica marketed itself as a "revolutionary" force in political campaigning; counter-revolutionary might be a more accurate description. Cambridge Analytica was a product of the secretive world of the British defence industry where private companies are often closely connected to the state. It was set up in 2013 as an offshoot of a London-based private military contractor called Strategic Communications Laboratories (SCL), which specialised in psychological operations. Cambridge Analytica executives had boasted that it and SCL had worked in more than two hundred elections. Former employee Brittany Kaiser said that the Facebook data scandal was part of a much bigger global influencing operation that worked with governments, intelligence services, commercial companies and political campaigns around the world.[6]

Cambridge Analytica used mass communication 'psy-ops' to disrupt democracy, not enhance it. In Nigeria, the firm created videos that erroneously claimed an opposition Muslim candidate wanted to introduce Sharia law across the country.[7] Its apocalyptic attack ads stoked violence during Kenyan elections.[8] SCL was evidently highly thought of by Whitehall mandarins; the company was awarded contracts by the British government and delivered training to the Ministry of Defence.[9]

Cambridge Analytica took the political techniques developed by SCL and others – including the US government, which has a history of international electoral interference stretching back decades – and applied them to domestic American campaigning. The company had influential financial backers. Robert Mercer, the reclusive billionaire, convinced libertarian and Trump donor, had a major stake in it.

Mercer had a long-standing interest in the marriage of politics and technology. He ran a mammoth New York hedge fund, Renaissance Technologies, which used big data to predict stock market movements.[10] Through Mercer, Cambridge Analytica was plugged deep into Republican politics. It worked for Ted Cruz, then Donald Trump. Steve Bannon sat on Cambridge Analytica's board. Chris Wylie claimed that the alt-right firebrand was personally involved in the company's early stages, shaping its strategy to leverage data-driven technology to push voters towards his populist vision.[11] "Without social media, populist movements wouldn't exist," Bannon told me. "[Matteo] Salvini, [Jair] Bolsonaro, Farage, even Trump would not exist."

For all its revolutionary talk, Cambridge Analytica's core strategy was quite simple, and far from unique: it targeted voters on social media with resonant political messages. More than 300 companies around the world have a similar business model.[12] (Unlike Cambridge Analytica, most don't break the law.)

To target voters online you need data, a lot of data. The first major opportunity Cambridge Analytica had to build profiles of the American electorate came in 2014, when it worked on 44 campaigns across the US.[13] By the time the Trump campaign got rolling, Cambridge Analytica boasted that it had around 5,000 data points on some 230 million Americans. That much data would, Nix said, be enough to profile the entire country.

He claimed that Cambridge Analytica could target voters with political adverts that chimed with their personality type. You're a worn-out working mother worried about the future? Here's a soft focus, pro-Republican video portraying a just-about-managing family. Stressed-out Mom doesn't even see the candidate in the clip on her Facebook feed.

Alexander Nix and his colleagues had more than a whiff of the confidence trickster about them, hamming up their plummy British accents and apparent intellectual self-confidence for marks with deep pockets. The effectiveness of micro-targeting voters on social media is hotly disputed. But whether Cambridge Analytica were a group of hucksters or Machiavellian geniuses matters far less than how they were able to operate without censure for so long and what their story says about how politics operates in the 21st century.

Big data has allowed political parties to know more about their voters than ever before – and to target messages online in ways that are almost impossible to trace. The old rules no longer apply. "Cambridge Analytica is the story of how elections will be run in the future," says journalist Jamie Bartlett, who followed the company closely for his documentary *Secrets of Silicon Valley.* "Cambridge Analytica is not the end of the story, it's the beginning of the story. It will be so much worse in the future. And we haven't been able to do anything about it so far."

In the brave new world of digital politics, truth and falsehood have become malleable concepts. Anything goes. During a TV debate ahead of the 2019 British general election between Boris Johnson and Jeremy Corbyn, the Conservative Party renamed its Twitter account factcheckUK, and then used it to push out partisan messages designed to look like independent verification. When called out, the Conservatives doubled down. Foreign Secretary Dominic Raab said that voters "don't give a toss" about what happens online. His cabinet colleague Michael Gove went even further, refusing to rule out repeating the trick. Twitter publicly upbraided the Conservatives but took no formal action.

This was far from an isolated incident. Barely 24 hours after the televised debate, the Conservatives set up a fake website for those looking for the opposition Labour Party's manifesto. The party paid Google to ensure that its site – which accused Labour of having "no plan for Brexit" – appeared at the top of Internet search results.

The effect of such stunts is less to actively counter opponents' political arguments – how many of the fabled floating voters get their views from largely anonymous websites? – and more to undermine trust in politics itself. Overwhelmed by information, and misinformation, voters are unsure what is real and what is not.

Dirty tactics seem to get results. Donald Trump won a famous victory in 2016. A few weeks after the TV debate, the Conservatives had their best election result in 30 years. The election of 2019 was Britain's "post-truth election", said Katharine Dommett, a political scientist from the University of Sheffield who acted as a special advisor to the House of Lords on electoral reform. "The Conservatives really pushed the boundaries of what is acceptable, and they did it on digital media."

It isn't supposed to be like this. As we have seen, Britain has lots of regulations governing its politics, including restrictive spending limits and campaign finance transparency requirements. But these rules are designed for a pre-Internet age. Campaigns commit vastly increased resources online, but understanding what exactly they are doing has become ever harder.

It's not just adverts on Facebook. There's Instagram and WhatsApp (both owned by Facebook), as well as Google, Snapchat and a growing array of closed messaging platforms. It has never been easier to spread misinformation on an industrial scale, with almost no oversight.

"We don't know what is happening. We can't even describe what is happening. The lack of information is the scariest thing," Dommett told me. "The protections I thought that were in place that meant that the UK system wasn't in danger of being Americanised don't seem to be there anymore."

Of course, misinformation existed long before the Internet. Digital campaigning allows politicians to scale up and refine something they have done for decades – advertise to voters. The modern 'dark arts' of political advertising can be traced back to the work of Edward Bernays in the United States a century ago. A marketing genius, Bernays had previously applied his uncle Sigmund Freud's psychological insights to business.[14] He rebranded cigarettes as "torches of freedom" to promote female smoking, and popularised the morning fry-up, citing a spurious survey of 5,000 doctors that allegedly found bacon and eggs were healthier for breakfast than the traditional tea and toast.

In a 1928 essay, 'Putting Politics on the Market', Bernays encouraged political strategists to imitate the golden rule of business – know your market. "The first thing a sales manager does when he tackles a new sales problem", he wrote, "is to study the public to whom he can sell."

Bernays applied his ideas to practical politics, too. In 1941, William O'Dwyer, the Democratic candidate for mayor of New York, hired Bernays to devise his campaign strategy. Bernays described his plan for O'Dwyer as an "engineering approach"; it relied on the kind of market research and media management that would soon become the norm in American politics.[15] Bernays conducted interviews with voters and collected huge volumes of census data and election results.

He instructed his candidate to use emotional appeals, rather than focusing on dry policy positions, and to tailor his image to appeal to different demographics of his ethnically divided city. When speaking to German Protestants, he should stress his dignity and honesty. In front of Italians, he should play up his commitment to non-discrimination.[16] Bernays recommended that O'Dwyer use photographs and motion pictures to spread the core message. The cost of the campaign was estimated at $100,000, with a tenth going on consulting fees. The equivalent in today's money is roughly $13 million.[17] (Bill de Blasio spent a similar amount in his successful New York mayoral bid in 2013.)

O'Dwyer lost narrowly but won five years later, largely thanks to Jewish voters identified by Bernays as a key constituency.[18] Bernays went on to play a significant role with the United Fruit Company in the CIA-orchestrated overthrow of the democratically elected Guatemalan government in 1954.

Bernays's behavioural manipulation techniques became the mainstay of American political communication. The Mad Men on Madison Avenue marketed politicians the same way they sold mouthwash. First, potential customers were intensely surveyed through polling and what we would now call focus groups.[19] Then they were bombarded with messages that primarily played on fear as a powerful motivation for action. Strong leaders were needed to face down the nation's threats and vanquish its foes, notably Soviet communism and its allies. The vicious television attack ads that have come to characterise US politics have their roots in this world.[20]

American-style political messaging took its time crossing the Atlantic. The first major innovation was in the 1940s, when Gallup began opinion polling. This addition gave parties insights into how voters felt on a range of issues, which could be combined with broad demographic data to create messages that resonated with large population groups. But it was a blunt tool.

Targeted campaigning and direct mail shots only began in the UK in the late 1970s.[21] The real shift came at around the same time, when Margaret Thatcher's Conservatives hired leading advertising agency Saatchi & Saatchi. The two formed an unbeatable team, with style and substance combining in a series of iconic political ads. Saatchi's "Labour isn't Working" poster, showing long lines of miserably unemployed workers, was widely credited with helping Thatcher to victory in the 1979 general election.*

By the 1980s, Labour had followed suit, bringing in expensive political strategists such as Philip Gould, who was very close to the New Labour group around Tony Blair. As the role of consultants grew, the room for expansive political debate shrank. Message discipline – keeping to pithy sound bites – became a key test of any prospective senior politician. At the same time, US-style negative advertising increasingly became the norm. Blair was reimagined with sinister demon eyes. Conservative leader Michael Howard was transformed into a flying pig, sparking accusations of "sly anti-Semitism".[22]

When the digital revolution arrived in politics, US campaigns were the early adopters. The first political video I can remember watching on the Internet was in 2003, for Democratic presidential hopeful Howard Dean. I was a young student living in New York, impressed by the Vermont governor's passionate fury.

It wasn't accidental that I saw the short clip. A bunch of young whizz kids working for Dean were using the Internet to transform the outsider into – for a brief moment – a viable US presidential candidate. Dean soon fizzled out, but his digital team lived on. Many of its former staffers founded Blue State Digital, a multi-million-dollar consultancy that worked on political campaigns on both sides of the Atlantic.

One of the first politicians to recognise the full capabilities of digital social networks was a first-term senator from Illinois. In 2007, Chris Hughes – Mark Zuckerberg's Harvard roommate – left Facebook to join Barack Obama's nascent presidential campaign. The then 24-year-old, who has since become a vocal critic

---

* The slogan was coined by public relations guru Tim Bell, whose company Bell Pottinger collapsed three decades later after it was revealed to be running a secret campaign to stir up racial tension in South Africa on behalf of the billionaire Gupta brothers.

of the tech giant he helped build, set up My.BarackObama.com, or MyBo, which allowed supporters to become active campaign organisers. Around 2 million volunteers organised 200,000 events and raised $30 million in what was dubbed "the Facebook election".[23] Obama won 365 of the 538 Electoral College votes.

Four years later, the incumbent's digital game was even more sophisticated. The second Obama campaign placed voters into 30 'buckets', ranked according to their persuadability. Using a tool called Facebook Connect, the Democrats were able to access information about supporters' friends and build a profile of different voting cohorts. These networks were then used to send tailored messages to millions of people. Obama's digital operation was not confined to Facebook – Google CEO Eric Schmidt was a campaign advisor.[24] Once again, data was widely credited with playing a starring role in Obama's victory.[25]

The 2012 US presidential election also showed that social media could influence people simply to vote. After Facebook added an election button, millions of users told their friends "I voted". Facebook's claim that the widget's nudge effect increased turnout by 340,000 has not been independently verified,[26] but even a slight uptick in turnout can have profound electoral consequences.

Technology allows political parties to do more with less. Instead of copious paper lists of doors to be knocked on, campaigns can create searchable online databases. They can advertise more effectively, and more cheaply, to far more people. Adverts can now be delivered straight to your smartphone, often tailored to what parties think you want to see. Messages can be tweaked and changed based on voters' responses and behaviour, almost in real time.

The effect of this can be slight. Researchers in Berlin found that online adverts increased a party's vote by just 0.7 per cent.[27] But in closely fought elections, even such fine margins can be decisive – especially in non-proportional voting systems like the US or the UK.

In 2016, just 80,000 ballots in the Rust Belt states of Michigan, Wisconsin and Pennsylvania won Donald Trump the White House. In 2019, under first-past-the-post electoral system, Britain's Conservatives won 56.2 per cent of Commons seats with just 43.6 per cent of the vote. A shift of just 51,000 voters across 40 seats would have wiped out Boris Johnson's "stonking" majority entirely. When elections depend on small numbers of swing voters, the influence of a digital campaign only needs to be very, very slight to make a major difference.

The 2016 US presidential election was a watershed for digital politics. Record sums were spent online. Between them, Trump and Hillary Clinton spent more than $80 million on sponsored Facebook ads alone. The tech giants were an integral part of both campaigns. Sympathetic staff from Facebook and Google were seconded to both campaigns, where they worked on the respective digital efforts.

2016 also saw an unprecedented deluge of online political misinformation – and foreign digital interference. Russian operatives spent more than $100,000 on Facebook ads, mostly favouring Trump. Facebook learned about attempts by Russian military intelligence to hack the social network in 2015, but waited two years before coming clean publicly.[28]

American liberals accused Facebook of playing the handmaiden to Trump's victory. But four years earlier, when Obama was inaugurated for a second time, few on the political left had seen any problem with the growing role of big tech and the almost wholly unregulated digital campaigning in politics. "Liberals were apparently extremely comfortable with the idea when their guy was doing it," says tech writer Jamie Bartlett. "That was a mistake."

By then, Britain was already following America down the dark digital path.

*

In the early years of the 21st century, Conservative and Labour staffers looked enviously at the digital revolution flaming across the Atlantic. Britain was having political conversations online – during the televised debates ahead of the 2010 general election, #IAgreewithNick trended on Twitter – but parties kept faith with traditional campaigning techniques: posters, newspaper adverts, direct mailing.

"Britain was a long way behind the US," says Jag Singh, who worked for Democratic presidential candidates, John Kerry in 2004 and prospective nominee Hillary Clinton in 2008, before coming to the UK with Labour's digital team. "Parties didn't see the need to spend money online."

The first time that data and British politics really collided was the referendum on the alternative vote in 2011. The pro-AV camp charged American strategists Blue State Digital with convincing the British electorate to adopt a new voting system. Jag Singh was hired by Matthew Elliott to oversee the 'No' campaign's digital operations.

NotoAV was a training ground for Vote Leave. The campaign pushed dubious statistics about the cost of changing the voting system and photographs of sick babies, as if the choice facing voters was really between "a new cardiac facility" and "an alternative voting system".[29] Elliott used Facebook heavily and built applications to encourage online supporters to turn up at real-world events.

"Some of that stuff had been tried in the US," Singh told me. "By today's standards it was prehistoric." But it was new for British politics.

Smaller parties were often quicker to see the opportunities online. The Liberal Democrats and the Scottish National Party were among the first to take up the new technology. During the early coalition years, the Lib Dems briefly hired a young Chris Wylie as a data specialist. When the SNP won an unexpected majority in the devolved Edinburgh parliament in 2011, the nationalists were using NationBuilder, a tool developed by backroom staff from Obama's second campaign.

As software improved, bigger parties started to invest more in digital campaigning. In 2014, Facebook helpfully layered geographic data provided by the data broker Acxiom onto British Facebook profiles. The result was a finely textured map of the electorate that anyone could advertise to.

"All of a sudden," Martin Moore writes in his book *Democracy Hacked*, "for the first time, a political party could reach every voter in a specific constituency with a specific campaign message. And they did not even have to pay for postage!"[30] (In late March 2018, Acxiom's share price fell by a third in a single day when Facebook announced that it was cutting ties with the company in the wake of the Cambridge Analytica scandal.[31])

As in the US, Facebook fast became the go-to digital platform for British political campaigns. It had the size, the scale and, crucially, the targeting capabilities to allow British campaigners to focus their digital firepower on the marginal constituencies that decide UK elections. During the 2015 general election, the Tories spent £1.2 million on Facebook ads alone, far more than any other UK party.[32] They targeted a blitz of Facebook adverts and direct mailshots at a handful of key swing constituencies, mostly held by their coalition partners, the Liberal Democrats, in the south-west of England. The strategy was called 'black widow', after the venomous spider that kills and consumes its mates.[33] After the Conservatives stole every Lib Dem seat in the south-west, party leader Nick Clegg complained that he hadn't seen any Tory volunteers on the street.[34]

Afterwards, Jim Messina, the US data specialist and Obama 2012 campaign manager hired by the Conservatives, said that he knew three weeks before the election that the party was on course for a majority, even though polls were predicting a hung parliament. "We went in and took very deep dives in the seats and to see what was do-able, what was winnable… who were the voters, and who were potential waverers," Messina said, "and we were able to have very focused messages to all of those people."[35]

Digital campaigning in Britain really came into its own during the 2016 EU referendum. The Brexit vote followed an unprecedented surge in targeted advertising. During the final weeks of the campaign, Vote Leave alone sent more than a billion targeted Facebook ads to some nine million voters identified as persuadable. Arron Banks's truculent Leave.EU pushed out aggressive messages to its massive online following.

Referendum campaigners were under no legal obligation to give any breakdown of their digital spending. Invoices supplied by Canadian data analytics firm AggregateIQ described more than £3 million worth of work for Vote Leave and its affiliates, the Democratic Unionist Party and Veterans for Britain, as simply "digital media spend". Fortunately for posterity and the factual record, Dominic Cummings has been a bit more expansive about what he called "the first campaign in the UK to put almost all our money into digital communication". In one of his lengthy post-referendum jeremiads, the former Vote Leave boss wrote that:

> One of our central ideas was that the campaign had to do things in the field of data that have never been done before. This included a) integrating data from social media, online advertising, websites, apps, canvassing, direct mail, polls, online fundraising, activist feedback, and some new things we tried such as a new way to do polling (about which I will write another time) and b) having experts in physics and machine learning do proper data science in the way only they can – i.e. far beyond the normal skills applied in political campaigns.[36]

Where the Remain campaign was often sluggish and reactive, Vote Leave pushed the digital boundaries. The campaign broke the law, as we've seen, by funnelling funds through the youth group BeLeave to circumvent spending limits. This money was used for AIQ's social media blitz. Cummings pushed ads that peddled shaky narratives, at worst outright falsehoods. Millions of Turks would come flooding into Britain. The NHS would get £350 million a week after Brexit. Early Facebook investor Roger McNamee has said that it seems likely Facebook had a big impact on the Brexit vote "because one side's message was perfect for the algorithms and the other's wasn't".[37]

Vote Leave's adverts were only made public in 2018, two years after the referendum. By then the campaign had long disappeared. Vote Leave and Leave.EU "could be brazen online because they knew that there would be no democratic comeback", said political scientist Katharine Dommett. "There is no accountability mechanism for this kind of campaign." Unsurprisingly, a maximum fine of £20,000 for breaking the existing law is little deterrent to a campaign that can dispense many millions of pounds.

Where traditional campaign tactics changed slowly – the importation of US-style consultants into British politics took years – digital strategies often change radically from one election to the next. By the time Theresa May called a snap general election in the middle of 2017, targeted digital advertising had become a major weapon in almost every party's arsenal. During the campaign, the Tories splurged an estimated £2.1 million on Facebook.[38] Labour spent just over half a million pounds on the platform, but successfully used targeted adverts to spread highly emotive content to the most fervent supporters – particularly in the tech-savvy left-wing Momentum campaign – who in turn shared it among their friends. Partisan Labour news sites like the *Canary* amplified the message.

On polling day, the Conservatives – who had the same digital wizards that had supposedly won the 2015 election – lost their majority and only clung on to power after fashioning a deal with the Democratic Unionist Party.

For the 2019 general election, the Conservatives changed tack completely. Out went Jim Messina and his fine-grained data targeting of swing voters on Facebook. In came Vote Leave's online operation and Dominic Cummings's ruthless will to win. Former senior Vote Leave staff played key roles. Lee Cain, who had worked with Boris Johnson since the referendum, moved across to Downing Street to run the media operation with another Brexit veteran, Paul Stephenson.

The campaign itself was run by a hirsute Australian political strategist named Isaac Levido who had helped secure a surprise general election triumph for Scott Morrison's Liberal Party in his native land a few months earlier. Levido – a protégé of another Conservative Australian spin doctor, Sir Lynton Crosby – had been approached by Cummings on the day Johnson entered Downing Street in July 2019.[39] Levido brought with him a pair of hard-nosed 20-something Antipodean digital consultants called Sean Topham and Ben Guerin, who had won Australia's online election battle by pushing large volumes of very basic social media messages that played on voters' emotions.[40]

"You have got to shock people," Guerin told a conference shortly after Morrison's unexpected win. "The particular emotions that we need to unlock are arousal emotions. We are talking anger, excitement, pride, fear. Your content should be relating to one of these emotions for anyone to give a damn about it."

In Britain, Levido and his young team crafted Johnson's election slogan: "Get Brexit Done". The mantra was endlessly repeated by just about every Conservative politician who came within spitting distance of a microphone.

Online, Boris Johnson's party ripped up the British political rule book. There were combative digital messages, dubious claims delivered in comic sans across numerous tech platforms, and an unprecedented level of media manipulation. Tory social media channels shared a doctored video of Labour's Keir Starmer on a morning television show, edited to look as if the shadow Brexit secretary had been unable to answer a question about his party's position on the EU, when he had in fact spoken at length. Host Piers Morgan – hardly a paragon of journalistic virtue – called the ploy "misleading and unfair".[41] It was viewed three million times.[42]

Like their leader, the Conservatives lied with an abandon that would have been reckless if it had come at any discernible electoral cost. The party took advantage of Facebook's refusal to fact-check paid-for political adverts; a study by First Draft News found that 88 per cent of Tory online ads posted over four days in the run-up to the election featured misleading claims.[43] "I don't think a mainstream party in Britain has ever done this kind of thing before," Katharine Dommett told me.

The Conservatives were not the only party pulling digital stunts. Pro-Labour 'ginger' groups bought anonymous 'dark ads' on Facebook. An analysis for *Tortoise Media* found that Labour had told the most untruths about poverty during the campaign.[44] Anti-Brexit tactical voting sites encouraged a Liberal Democrat vote even in seats where the party had no chance. But these were tame by comparison. The Conservatives were the only party to rebrand their Twitter account as a fact-checking site during a TV debate and then pretended it was a perfectly normal thing to do.

The effect of a party's social media strategy on its election performance is often difficult to judge, much as the impact of traditional campaigning on results is an exercise in educated guesswork. In 2019, the Liberal Democrats poured resources into targeted Facebook adverts in key constituencies and ended the general election with twice as many votes and one fewer seats. Labour was widely seen as running a strong social media campaign – often topping metrics of online engagement – and lost 60 seats in a heavy defeat.

The winning Tories focused less on Facebook than in previous years, instead investing in display ads on YouTube, Google and other platforms. Where the Conservatives had significant success was in generating huge amounts of low-cost online publicity. They trolled opponents on Twitter and 'shit-posted', circulating intentionally poor-quality memes that were often shared as much in mockery as in earnest – but the message still got out. Surreally, the Tories posted a 71-minute YouTube video of Boris Johnson sitting on a train.

In a post-election blog post, Dominic Cummings noted how "the world of digital advertising has changed very fast since I was last involved in 2016." While "so many journalists wrongly looked at things like Corbyn's Facebook stats and thought Labour was doing better than us" the online ecosystem had shifted radically, away from paid-for Facebook ads and towards more effective, almost ironic messaging across a range of platforms. "The digital people involved in the last campaign really knew what they are doing, which is incredibly rare in this world of charlatans and clients who don't know what they should be buying," Cummings wrote.[45]

There was a sinister edge to some of the online campaigning, too. Anonymous WhatsApp messages warned British Hindus to vote against Labour;[46] extreme political content spread on closed Facebook groups. One Labour MP who nearly lost their Brexit-supporting seat told the *Guardian* that on the doorstep voters continually brought up Corbyn's connections with the IRA, after seeing memes and images on Facebook. "It was never used by the Tories in the campaign, but there was a separate election going on, which was a Facebook-orientated campaign."[47]

Ordinary voters were often the most prolific producers of fake content. When, a few days before polls opened, the Tory campaign was briefly derailed by a photograph of a young child on a hospital floor, a viral message spread among Conservative outriders that the image was a hoax created by Labour supporters. The falsehood spread rapidly across the Internet, boosted by prominent journalists and influencers.

A few hours earlier, senior Conservative Party advisors had briefed that an aide to Health Secretary Matt Hancock had been punched. The incident never happened, but it was tweeted out by senior broadcast journalists, seemingly too eager to be first to the story to take the time to stand it up.

Such digital malfeasance was often picked up quickly. For the first time, almost every major British news outlet had a dedicated team of journalists focused on social media. Endless fact-checks corrected the record. But they were a finger in the dyke against a flood of disinformation. Conspiracy theories swirled, in some cases actively encouraged by political parties.

In Britain, as in many other countries, digital politics has become a chaotic void where almost anything goes. Politicians have allowed electoral law to be outpaced by technological change and have ignored calls for change from regulators.

Election candidates, for instance, are legally required to ensure that all their printed election material is clearly labelled: a leaflet pushed through a voter's door has to say who paid for it. But online political ads do not even have to carry an identifying imprint, and political parties have to provide no more than the most cursory accounting of how money is spent.

Former Labour MP Ian Lucas told me that "social media is by far the biggest change" he had seen in more than three decades as a political campaigner. "Online is essentially a completely unregulated environment where you can do whatever you want," said the former member of the Department of Culture, Media and Sport select committee's fake news inquiry. "We have never had the political debate about whether we want to have targeted advertising in the UK. At some stage in the past, we made the decision not to have political adverts like in the US. But online is a free-for-all."

The UK ban on paid-for broadcast adverts – long the bane of sections of the Conservative right – has been rendered rather meaningless in the digital age. Even if they could, who would want to spend a fortune on a television commercial when social media allows anyone to circulate political videos to a mass audience at minimal cost with (so far) no restrictions. "Effectively, you are free to do what you want," says Sam Jeffers, who founded Who Targets Me, a project that monitors political adverts on social media. "The cost of delivery is so low. The barrier for entry is almost non-existent."

Online campaigning is also barely constrained by Britain's tight election finance laws. Each candidate for Parliament has a spending ceiling of around £15,000 (the exact limit varies by constituency size). The impetus behind these strict limits is to provide a level playing field and prevent the kind of spending wars that can characterise even minor contests in the US.

Digital campaigning, however, can easily be kept off constituency expenses. So while an election candidate has to keep carefully within unrealistically low spending limits, a party can spend six figures targeting voters in the same constituency without breaking any rules.

With ever fewer activists on the ground, the online platforms give parties the opportunity to vastly extend their reach. Data has become political hard currency. Before the Brexit referendum, the Liberal Democrats sold personal information about their members to the Remain campaign for £100,000.[48] Political parties now employ in-house staff dedicated to processing and analysing personal data. Campaigns can work out voters' employment and marital status. Even ethnicity can be estimated.

During the 2016 London mayoral election, losing candidate Conservative Zac Goldsmith sent leaflets to British Indians accusing his Labour opponent Sadiq Khan, who is of Pakistani Muslim origin, of being hostile to the Hindu Indian prime minister Narendra Modi.[49] (In December 2019, Goldsmith was given a life peerage after losing his seat in the Commons for the second time in three years.[50] Goldsmith's views had clearly changed a lot since 2012, when he tweeted that the "seedy" House of Lords rewarded "party apparatchiks" who faced "no democratic pressure".[51])

What can be done about the digital Wild West? New legislation would be a start. Election lawyer Gavin Millar believes that one solution is to treat highly targeted political messaging as a form of 'undue influence', which is prohibited under electoral law. "We are back in the 19th century because we have no measure of undue influence in the digital age," he said.

But even if the way politicians spend money online was circumscribed, would it stem the rising tide of lies and disinformation?

Voters themselves are already conduits for mistruths and false-hoods. Tighter constraints on parties would also do little to stop another growing source of online interference: the rise of a British version of America's dark money vehicle of choice, the super Pac.

As politicians have increasingly come to believe that elections are won and lost online, a sprawling influence industry has developed on both sides of the Atlantic. Behind shiny brass plaques, teams of political consultants and strategists promise parties that they can sway voters' behaviour. One such outfit is the College Green Group.

From the usual well-preserved Georgian townhouse (so many of these companies inhabit buildings from the glory days of rotten boroughs and political oligarchy) a stone's throw from West-minster in central London, College Green promises clients that "change is our mission, digital is our means". Plenty of campaigns have taken up the offer: the firm, previously known as Kanto, was hired by anti-abortion activists in Ireland,[52] has run elections for a pharmaceutical trade body and even worked with trade unions. Cambridge Analytica's parent company, SCL, bought its mobile canvassing app.* College Green's offices have also hosted events with visiting Republican Party activists.[53]

The moving spirit behind College Green – though there was no mention of his name on the company website when I last checked – is Thomas Borwick, a tall, thin, serious young man with a clipped Home Counties accent. The son of former Con-servative MP Victoria Borwick and Tory Lord James Borwick, Thomas started in the political data business around 2012, shortly after graduating from university. In Isaiah Berlin's schema, he is

---

* After Cambridge Analytica's overnight collapse, two of its most senior data scientists, Tadas Jucikas and the aptly named Brent Clickard, came to work at College Green's 15 Great George Street headquarters.

less the fox, who knows many things, and more the hedgehog, who knows one big thing.

Thomas Borwick's key insight is that elections in the digital age are won by splitting the electorate into fragments that can be bombarded with targeted messages. As chief technology officer at Vote Leave, Borwick divided the UK into 72 groups of voters who were sent different Facebook ads. The advertising did, however, have one common theme: the European Union was always clearly defined as the over-reaching behemoth from which Britain needed to "take back control". "I believe that a well-identified enemy is probably a 20 per cent kicker to your vote," Borwick told the writer Peter Pomerantsev.[54]

In late 2017, one of Borwick's numerous companies, Voter Consultancy, began buying ads targeting the constituencies of Conservative MPs opposed to Brexit. These ads accused the MPs of "sabotage". Tory MP Anna Soubry said Borwick was "stoking and fuelling the fire" of online hate. Borwick declined to say where the funding for the ads came from. He didn't have to.*

In the run-up to the 2019 British general election, Green Party activists in a number of swing constituencies in England noticed something unusual on Facebook. Paid-for adverts had started appearing, calling on voters to "support your local Green candidate". The ads, illustrated with a photograph of fresh-faced climate activist Greta Thunberg, were not posted by the Greens. They had been bought by Thomas Borwick in the name of a company he owned called 3rd Party Ltd.[55] (One Twitter user

---

* Many seasoned political operatives have moved into digital campaigning. After the Brexit vote, Borwick's boss at Vote Leave, Matthew Elliott, became a partner in a technology firm called Awareness Analytics Partners which boasted of having a database of 115 million social media profiles and the ability to "micro-target your ads to the people most likely to take your desired action". The company's founding partner, Sean Noble, was a consultant for the Koch brothers, distributing political donations to conservative causes during the 2010 and 2012 US election cycles.

joked that the name Plausible Deniability must have already been taken.)

Why was the deputy chairman of a local Conservative association buying ads in support of the Greens? To split the left-wing vote? To muddy the waters? Borwick told me over email that "green causes are very important to some of our patrons" so he wanted to send "a message to politicians about the strength of feeling on this issue".[56]

Borwick sent messages about lots of other election causes, too. During the campaign, 3rd Party bought thousands of pounds worth of ads on a dizzying range of subjects. Facebook users in Belfast who liked the military saw adverts extolling them to "save Brexit"; voters in East Dunbartonshire were told to back the Scottish National Party in order to defeat Liberal Democrat leader Jo Swinson (she lost by fewer than 150 votes); Borwick ran ads supporting Conservative Iain Duncan Smith's re-election bid and macabre messages asking if Labour was "really on the side" of residents in Grenfell Tower, where 72 people died in a 2017 fire. When I emailed Borwick again to ask who paid for all these ads, he did not respond.

Third-party consultancies – like Borwick's – can obscure how money is spent to influence politics. In a period of a few weeks before the 2019 general election, so-called 'non-party campaigns' bought more than half a million pounds worth of adverts on Facebook and its subsidiary Instagram, as well as on Google and Snapchat.[57] The sums involved were significant by British standards and are almost certainly a major underestimate, given the weakness of digital campaign spending oversight. A handful of sites advertised Labour, others recommended tactical voting around Brexit, but most pushed Conservative talking points – often to the extreme.

One group, the incongruously named Capitalist Worker, campaigned specifically against the Labour Party's sweeping nationalisation plans. Created just five weeks before the vote and closely linked to Brexit Party MEP Brian Monteith, Capitalist Worker spent almost £40,000 on Facebook ads that predominantly targeted men aged between 18 and 34. The adverts were most frequently viewed in a number of working-class Labour 'red wall' seats that were key to the Conservatives' election strategy.[58] Another new Facebook page spent more than £55,000 on adverts attacking Jeremy Corbyn's housing policy, warning that "landlords will lose their livelihood overnight".[59]

The ads were bought in the name of Jennifer Powers, the lobbyist who worked for Shanker Singham's private consultancy and had been a member of the Alternative Arrangements Commission alongside the Institute of Economic Affairs' trade advisor. Powers, who was criticised for incorrectly attributing anti-Corbyn quotes to estate agents on her campaign's website, said that she funded the ads herself and raised money through crowdfunding.[60]

Individually, many of these groups flew under the regulatory radar. If you spend less than £20,000 on electioneering in England (or £10,000 in Scotland, Wales or Northern Ireland), you don't need to register with the Electoral Commission or declare who's funding you. But collectively, they're ferocious. Together, these groups reached tens of millions of voters, often multiple times.

The parallels with the super Pacs that can spend limitless amounts of dark money in American elections are not hard to spot. "It feels like what happens in the US," said Katharine Dommett. "These external actors go in and set the tone of the debate without parties having to take responsibility for what they say. The unanswered question is whether there is any coordination" with political parties.

Secretive, super Pac-style digital campaigning had already emerged in Britain in the years after the EU referendum. In a few months around the turn of 2019, a website called Britain's Future spent more than £400,000 on targeted Facebook adverts encouraging millions of voters to tell their local MP to push for a no-deal Brexit.[61]

Once again, the source of the money behind this advertising

barrage was a mystery. The only name associated with Britain's Future was Tim Dawson, a 30-year-old freelance writer who had run unsuccessfully as a Conservative council candidate for Manchester City Council and was part of a network of Tory activists aligned to the European Research Group.[62] Dawson declined to say who was bankrolling his campaign.

The reasonable suspicion was that rich Brexit supporters were using so-called 'dark ads' booked by groups like Britain's Future to anonymously influence public debate. Damian Collins told me that these ads showed how easy it is to "bypass all these rules we have created to try to make elections transparent and honest". Campaigns "can easily just put up a front person without disclosing who is really behind it and why", the Conservative MP said.

Britain's Future had done just that. The apparently grassroots campaign was actually what experts in these dark arts call 'astroturf' – the masking of tendentious messages as if they emerged spontaneously from individual citizens. Fake grass and fake roots. This particular artificial surface was laid by staff at the Mayfair offices of CTF Partners, the blue-chip lobbying firm run by the Australian spin doctor and Conservative election strategist Sir Lynton Crosby.

In all, CTF Partners administered a range of pro-Brexit pages that spent upwards of £1 million on Facebook adverts at a crucial juncture in British politics.[63] Some had been running since late 2017, suggesting that the influencing campaign to push voters towards a harder Brexit had been operating online long before it was picked up by the press. Around the same time as these ads were flooding British social media, it was reported that Crosby's firm was also running dozens of unbranded Facebook pages on behalf of the autocratic Saudi government and in support of coal and tobacco interests. The main trade body for British lobbyists said the company's behaviour was "entirely unethical".[64] (CTF Partners has said that it "carries out its work in strict adherence to all relevant laws and regulations".[65])

Once reports about Britain's Future started to surface, the ads abruptly vanished. As happened in the EU referendum, key information about the digital campaigns was deleted before it could be analysed.

None of this was supposed to be happening. On a wet morning in late November 2018, I made my way to the committee room in Portcullis House, overlooking the River Thames in Westminster, for an evidence session of Parliament's fake news inquiry. Facebook's then European director of policy – and former Liberal Democrat MP – Richard Allan was explaining that his company was committed to supporting democracy. Having been cited as a factor in the genocide against the Rohingya in Myanmar, Facebook had hired more Burmese speakers to stem the flow of inflammatory content. It had suspended political advertisements ahead of a referendum on abortion in Ireland in 2018 after evidence emerged of foreign, mainly American, 'pro-life' donors buying adverts targeted at Irish voters.* Facebook was, he said, introducing a comprehensive library of all paid-for political advertising.

Richard Allan was a flinty witness. I could only see the back of his white-haired head and his gesticulating hands. His answers were often short and testy. He said that Mark Zuckerberg – who had been invited – would like to have attended but couldn't find the time.

The politicians were not impressed. A green seat was left vacant with the Facebook founder's name on it. One lawmaker complained that democracy had "been upended by frat boy billionaires from California". A month earlier, the British Information Commissioner had issued Facebook with its maximum fine – half a million pounds – for failing to protect user data.[66]

---

* The ban on foreign political adverts during the Irish referendum could be circumvented without much difficulty. My colleagues and I were able to post ads from abroad about abortion targeted at Facebook users in Ireland hours after the policy came into force.

Allan looked most uncomfortable when he was asked about his second job, as a life peer in the House of Lords. Was there not a conflict of interest between being a senior Facebook executive and being Baron Allan of Hallam, with a free pass to wander through Westminster? He admitted it didn't look "great". But there are no rules against members of Parliament working as consultants. A few weeks earlier, Facebook had announced that former deputy prime minister Nick Clegg was moving to California to become the company's head of global affairs. Clegg had succeeded Richard Allan as Lib Dem MP for Sheffield Hallam in 2005. (British politics is a vanishingly small world.)

Facebook's ad library did bring some transparency to digital campaigning. For the first time, anyone could see who was posting adverts, how much they were spending, and even ballpark figures for how many eyeballs saw each message. But there was no requirement to provide any information about who is actually paying for these messages. Groups such as Britain's Future and the anti-Brexit campaigners Best for Britain and People's Vote bought millions of dark ads without having to say who was really footing the bill.

In 2019, Internet not-for-profit Mozilla complained that Facebook's political ad library was "failing" and "doesn't provide necessary data".[67] Facebook pledged to expand the ad library. But Mark Zuckerberg has so far refused calls for his platform to moderate paid-for political adverts that spread lies.

The pressure on Facebook to tackle misinformation more aggressively has been increasing. In October 2019, Twitter announced that it was banning paid political ads outright.* That same month, around 250 Facebook employees signed an open letter warning

* At the time of writing, it was still relatively easy to pay for political messaging on Twitter, too. In January 2020, the microblogging site apologised after a BBC investigation was able to buy adverts micro-targeted at neo-Nazis, homophobes and other hate groups.

that the platform was damaging democracy.[68] The company's senior management present the issue rather differently. Nick Clegg compared the platform to the organiser of a tennis tournament.

"Our job", he said in a public statement a few weeks before Twitter's announcement, "is to make sure the court is ready – the surface is flat, the lines painted, the net at the correct height. But we don't pick up a racket and start playing. How the players play the game is up to them, not us."[69]

Damian Collins told me that "Facebook actively seeks to get away with disclosing as little as possible. They try to keep real decision-makers in the company, people who really know what's going on, away from scrutiny." The former Saatchi advertising executive was particularly riled by Zuckerberg's refusal to come to London and face his committee. The social media behemoth had been "deliberately evasive". There were, he said, still so many unanswered questions.

The fake news inquiry's final report denounced Facebook for breaking privacy and competition law and accused Zuckerberg of treating Parliament with contempt. The committee called for the "digital gangsters" to be subject to urgent statutory regulation in order to protect British democracy.[70] Nothing happened.

So, if the rules of political engagement are being set by recalcitrant tech multinationals, is a fair fight even possible? To find out, I went to meet Louise Edwards, director of regulation at the Electoral Commission.

It was a Friday afternoon in late summer as I took the elevator to the ninth floor of a glass-fronted office block in central London. I had expected a cagey half-hour with a tight-lipped bureaucrat. Instead, we had a lively, wide-ranging chat that went on until the end of the working day. Our conversation often circled back to two issues: the weakness of British election laws and the role of big tech in our politics.

The Electoral Commission has asked for more powers to trace digital campaigning. So far, little has been done. Whether the regulator could handle more power is debatable. Its budget was cut significantly during the long years of austerity. A former employee told me that during the 2017 general election, the electoral watch-dog's online monitoring team consisted of two young interns looking at social media, supplemented by a cardboard box for staff to deposit any suspicious-looking printed material. "We got a whole bunch of leaflets from north London and that was pretty much it," one of them said.

Louise Edwards said the Electoral Commission wanted to work with tech companies. "Facebook are really keen to help," she said, with what sounded like forced optimism in her voice. The reality is more like European colonisers overrunning native tribes centuries ago. The election regulator has around 140 staff. Facebook employs roughly 3,000 in London alone.

The commission is only able to obtain a limited amount of information from social media companies. Even if Facebook did a complete policy reversal, digital campaigning is already migrat-ing to other platforms, mostly also owned by Mark Zuckerberg's company. While journalists tend to focus on Facebook – the ad library was a constant source of stories during Britain's 2019 general election – there is little or no transparency on other platforms.

Private messaging channels are fast becoming the new frontier in digital campaigning. Here, almost untraceable misinformation spreads like digital wildfire. Ahead of the Brazilian general election in 2018, four out of every ten viral political messages on WhatsApp contained verified falsehoods. (Only 3 per cent had factual infor-mation.[71]) Organic false content, shared by peers not faceless cam-paigns, can be even more effective than paid-for political advertising. The digital genie is already out of the bottle.

"There is a danger", Edwards said, with masterly understate-ment, "that Britain runs the real risk of coming out of an election soon that isn't well run."

*

It is not easy to be optimistic about democracy in the digital age. Anonymous, dark money-funded influence campaigns offer a dystopian vision of where we could be headed. Digital campaigns with anodyne names like Britain's Future are cheap to run, easy to dispose of, leave few tracks that investigators can follow, and can be extremely effective.

Humans are far more receptive to messages that we think come from an independent source. In one study, British political scientists showed participants three identical political ads. One ad was branded as Labour, the other as Conservative, the third as an ambiguous new campaign. The responses were predictably partisan. Labour voters were more likely to click on the ad if it had a red rosette. Conservatives engaged more when it was in bright Tory blue. But supporters of both parties showed interest in the putatively non-aligned campaign, even if its message chimed with the policies of a particular party.

"We risk losing our political compass and our ability to navigate political messaging because of the rise of third-party groups, and there is absolutely no transparency about who these organisations are and where their money has come from," says Katharine Dommett.

Political strategists can use sophisticated 'shadow campaigns' to undermine trust in democracy itself and actually dissuade political participation. This is what happened in Trinidad and Tobago in 2010. Politics on these tiny islands has long been divided along ethnic lines, between Indo- and Afro-Caribbeans. Ahead of a general election, a spontaneous youth revolt sprung up against the whole system. It was called 'Do So' – Don't vote. Don't get involved in politics. On the country's walls, bright yellow posters appeared, with a pair of arms, wrists crossed. Stand up against corruption. Boycott the election. Videos appeared on YouTube.

It looked like the epitome of grassroots politics, just as the Arab Spring was about to awaken on the other side of the world. It was in fact a covert strategy to suppress turnout among Afro-Caribbean voters, devised and coordinated by Cambridge Analytica's parent company, SCL. It worked. The Indo-Caribbean party won, on a reduced turnout.

As Alexander Nix explained to Brittany Kaiser half a dozen years later,[72] "when it came to voting, all the Afro-Caribbean kids wouldn't vote, because they 'Do So'. But all the Indian kids would do what their parents told them to do, which is go out and vote. And so all the Indians went out and voted, and the difference on the 18–35-year-old turnout is like 40 per cent, and that swung the election by about 6 per cent – which is all we needed!"

The lessons learned in Trinidad and Tobago were applied around the world. SCL worked with AggregateIQ to "create a political customer relationship management software tool" for the islands' elections. This was later used by Cambridge Analytica during US elections.[73]

Nix denied that Cambridge Analytica had engaged in voter suppression, but research suggests that this kind of negative campaigning does dissuade people from voting. The same study in Berlin that found a small positive boost for a party from running online advertising found a much bigger *negative* impact on the party's main competitors. Instead of persuading voters to switch parties, targeted adverts were far more effective at "demobilising opponents" and making them less likely to vote, the research found.[74]

Russia has been accused of running interference operations to suppress turnout in foreign elections. The Kremlin operation during the 2016 US presidential election often seemed geared less towards changing how people voted and more at influencing who voted – and who didn't. Russia spent only a fraction of the amount that the official campaigns did on paid-for advertising on Facebook and Google, but its organic content, amplified by bots, often spread quickly.

The Kremlin passed emails about Hillary Clinton to Wikileaks, allegedly hacked from her campaign chairman John Podesta's account. These emails were used to powerful effect, feeding into established narratives about Clinton as untrustworthy and duplicitous. Trolls pushed out an almost endless stream of pro-Trump and anti-Clinton messages, flooding social media with what looked like grassroots support for the Republican candidate. That this content did not *look* as if it was aligned with a party increased its take-up. Propaganda generated by Russian operatives on Facebook reached an estimated 126 million US voters.[75]

The impact of this social media onslaught could be felt on the ground. In the weeks leading up to the American presidential election, I drove across the Midwest meeting voters. I spoke to dozens who said that they normally voted Democrat but were uncertain about Clinton. When I asked why, almost all listed the same concern: "Emails." Few offered more detail than that.

The 2016 US presidential election also showed how online disinformation can be used not just to support a particular candidate, but also to sow discord and chaos. While the Kremlin weighed in on Trump's side, Russian-backed fake social media accounts often seemed primarily concerned with stoking division. One example occurred in Minneapolis in July 2016 after a young African American named Philando Castile was shot dead by traffic police.[76] On Facebook, a militant black activist page called 'Don't Shoot' started running paid-for ads promoting a protest in Castile's name. Thousands signed up for a demonstration outside the local police department. Racial tensions were high after a slew of similar shootings.

But when local activists in Minnesota started asking questions about 'Don't Shoot', they received some strange and cryptic answers from the administrators of the group's Facebook page. "They were completely making up everything that they had been saying," one Black Lives Matter activist later said. 'Don't Shoot' faded from memory until, almost a year and a half later, long after the presidential election, CNN revealed that the page had actually been set up and run by trolls at the Internet Research Agency, 4,000 miles away in St Petersburg.

Russian social media accounts had even organised rival pro-Trump and anti-Trump demonstrations, including one in Florida in which someone was paid to portray Hillary Clinton in a prison uniform while standing in a cage built on a flatbed truck. At another demonstration, in July 2016 in Washington, a Facebook group allegedly created by the Russians held a rally called 'Support Hillary. Save American Muslims' at which an American held a sign depicting Clinton and a fake quote attributed to her: "I think Sharia Law will be a powerful new direction of freedom."[77]

This kind of behaviour might not swing elections, but it does something even more serious. It corrodes public confidence and trust in democracy itself.

Have similar techniques been used in the UK? On the day Britain voted to leave the EU, a network of Twitter accounts linked to the Internet Research Agency pushed pro-Brexit messages.[78] That's hardly surprising. Western intelligence agencies knew back in 2014 that Putin had launched a major campaign of political destabilisation intended, among other things, to target and weaken the European Union.

But it is difficult to tell exactly what Russian interference occurred in the 2016 Brexit vote. Facebook declined to give Parliament's fake news inquiry information about pro-Brexit Russian propaganda that circulated on influential closed groups ahead of the referendum. British political leaders have been equally hesitant.

In 2017, Theresa May accused Russia of trying to "undermine free societies" by "planting fake stories" to sow disharmony and distort elections. Conspicuously, the then prime minister didn't mention the Brexit vote. Shortly before she left office, May did introduce ambitious proposals to bring about online transparency, but the measures were not implemented – apparently because of fears that any revamp of electoral law would raise awkward questions about the legality of the Brexit referendum, according to a November 2019 report in *Politico*.[79]

Around the same time, May's successor Boris Johnson took the highly unusual step of refusing to publish a report by Parliament's Intelligence and Security Committee into Russian meddling in British politics, citing the impending general election. The committee's chair, former Tory MP and Attorney General Dominic Grieve, called the decision "jaw dropping". Hillary Clinton described it as "inexplicable and shameful". The Electoral Commission warned that until rules were changed, British elections would remain vulnerable to foreign interference.

Some commentators think the evidence that digital electoral interference really works is patchy, at best. Suspected Russian meddling failed to change the outcome in a number of European elections. Cambridge Analytica's candidates often lost. Are we overestimating the size of the threat to democracy? Do a few dodgy ads and untruths on social media really make a difference on polling day?

These are the wrong questions to ask, according to transparency campaigner Gavin Sheridan.

"The issue isn't what did Cambridge Analytica do and did it work. It isn't even what did Russia do and did it work," he says. "It's the entire ecosystem within which these campaigns take place. Facebook ads, social media memes, bots and all the other tactics create a worldview in which it becomes increasingly difficult for voters to know what is believable and what isn't. And politicians don't want to seriously ask what's going on, because they don't think it's in their interests to know – or worse, they want to use those techniques themselves."

In April 2018, Facebook announced that it would be working with academics to research the effect of social media on elections. Scholars from around the world would be able to examine the sharing patterns of fake and polarised news, among other topics. Facebook's huge data stockpile would provide an invaluable academic resource.

This rosy prospect was tarnished when the tech giant prevaricated over giving the promised access. By August 2019, almost eighteen months later, the researchers were so fed up that the Social Science Research Council took the unusual step of publicly telling Facebook that they would pull their support for the project if the data was not made available by the end of the following month. David Lazer, a professor of political science at Northeastern University, told *Buzzfeed* that Facebook had "thrown major talent at the issue; but ultimately, the proof is in whether we ever get to eat the pudding".[80] (The academics were eventually given access to some of the Facebook data in early 2020.)

So far, few sovereign governments have shown as much resolve as the Social Science Research Council in the face of the social media giant. Britain's attempts to rein in Facebook were largely confined to Westminster's inquiry into fake news. Its chair Damian Collins told me that he regarded online political advertising and messaging "as a threat to our democracy".

Yet there is little sign of politicians mobilising to act. What changes have been introduced – like Facebook's ad library – have come from big tech companies themselves, not government. Many politicians seem content to outsource the regulation of democracy to Silicon Valley companies that have a financial interest in maintaining the status quo.

Even if Facebook has a change of heart about paid-for political adverts spreading misinformation ahead of the 2020 US presidential election, it will almost certainly be too little, too late. Digital campaigning has already migrated to other, even more opaque platforms.

"The stuff that is happening that everyone should be worried about is peer-to-peer, Facebook groups, Discord, 4chan, Reddit," says Claire Wardle, co-founder of First Draft News, a non-profit dedicated to tackling misinformation. It is hard to see how any amount of regulation can dampen this raging digital wildfire.

The online influence campaigns facilitated by Facebook and

other tech giants have fundamentally altered the nature of politics itself. Where political parties once had to craft messages that would appeal across the country, now an influence industry can micro-target specific key groups, or intentionally spread misinformation to divide communities or dissuade voters from engaging with politics at all. "Because different voters can be communicated with, using different messages, in inconsistent ways without them realising it, the very concept of *the commons* is being challenged," says political commentator Paul Evans.[81]

There is a grim irony in the way consultants like Thomas Borwick carve up the electorate in order to target messages in the name of supposedly grand unifying campaigns like Brexit. As Peter Pomerantsev notes, "In an age in which all the old ideologies have vanished and there is no competition over coherent political ideas, the aim becomes to lasso together disparate groups around a new notion of the people, an amorphous but powerful emotion that each can interpret in their own way, and then seal it by conjuring up phantom enemies who threaten to undermine it."[82]

The technological revolution in politics is more likely to speed up than slow down. A few weeks before the 2019 British general election, a video showing Boris Johnson and Jeremy Corbyn endorsing each other for prime minister spread online. It was obviously a fake – created in an attempt to demonstrate the potential for 'deepfake' videos to undermine democracy – but it was real enough to show what could soon be available to unscrupulous and well-funded operators.

Britain faces "a perfect storm" of digital disruption and weak rules, Louise Edwards told me as we sat in a nondescript meeting room in the Electoral Commission's offices. "There should be a real urgency to sort this out," said Edwards. "This is our democracy, there should be an impetus to do it right."

9

THE DEAD CAT

The politician who wants to target the swing voter via television tries to seem as normal as possible. The politician who seeks to mobilise support online will do precisely the opposite.

WILL DAVIES, *London Review of Books,*
June 2019[1]

Life was going well for Nigel Farage in January 2015. Or at least it looked that way. The party he led, UKIP, was riding high in the polls. Prominent Conservative defectors had crossed the floor to join him. A referendum on Britain's membership of the European Union was now a formal commitment of David Cameron's Conservatives. But behind the scenes, Farage had problems. Internally UKIP was a mess, riven by in-fighting and disorganisation.[2]

Farage decided that he needed to build a new political vehicle, one that he could truly control. So he travelled with his advisors Raheem Kassam and Liz Bilney, who worked for Arron Banks, to a quiet residential street in an upmarket neighbourhood of Milan. The trio stopped at a set of heavy wooden doors. On the other side were the offices of Casaleggio Associates, the private company behind the anti-establishment Five Star Movement.[3]

In Milan, Farage and his entourage met Gianroberto Casaleggio. A 60-year-old tech utopian with a mane of shaggy hair,

Casaleggio was the digital wizard who had orchestrated Five Star's remarkable ascent from political start-up to Italy's largest party. Casaleggio had devised and orchestrated the web platform where Five Star's legions of supporters log on to vote for policy, stand for election and donate to the self-styled "movement".

Although it all looks like a grassroots movement, the reality is very different: Five Star is actually micro-managed from the top. Five Star's Rousseau web platform is run by Casaleggio Associates. Legally Casaleggio's son Davide has control over the party's data.[4] It is almost impossible to say where Five Star the party begins, and the private company ends. This is not a spontaneous democratic movement welling up from the streets, like the anti-war movements of the 1960s or the Solidarity movement that transformed Poland. It is a carefully managed form of protest.

Farage liked what he saw in Milan. The UKIP leader returned to Britain with the zeal of the convert. He began to talk about digital democracy, about building a new party online. "I learned a lot from Five Star," he later said. "They used the Internet to build up a grassroots movement. I was impressed by their energy and the commitment of their supporters, who were willing to pay €25–30 a year to participate in the movement."[5]

But Farage bided his time. In early 2019, more than four years after his trip to Milan and a year after Five Star had become the largest party in Italy at a general election and entered government for the first time, the by now ex-UKIP leader re-emerged into electoral politics. As Theresa May's EU withdrawal agreement turned to ash in the House of Commons, Farage presented himself as the reluctant saviour of the British public from the nefarious elite in Westminster. Out went the herring-bone suits, the blokey bonhomie and his old party's tarnished, fascist-leaning brand; in came headsets, sharp suits and the shiny new Brexit Party. Farage had reinvented himself as a televangelist, preaching politics for the digital age.

The Brexit Party was officially launched in April 2019, in a crowded warehouse belonging to an industrial cleaning company in Coventry. One reporter noted that the atmosphere was "like a pop concert for the Leave-voting pensioners of Middle England". There were Brexit Party t-shirts and posters and official lanyards.[6] Farage confidently told journalists that he would "change politics for good".[7]

New parties often make bold statements only to later flounder. A few weeks before the Brexit Party's launch, a cadre of rebel centrist Tory and Labour MPs formed by the Blairite era left their parties to form a new 'independent group'. What became the optimistically named Change UK soon sank without trace. Farage was far more buoyant. His new party's belligerent press conferences and media briefings set the news agenda.

Support surged. Farage claimed that in the Brexit Party's first ten days it raised a record £750,000 in anonymous online donations.[8] Less than two months after its launch, Farage rode a wave of popular anger to top the polls in elections to the European Parliament that Britain was never supposed to contest, winning 30 per cent of the vote. Even when the Brexit Party failed to win a seat in Westminster in the general election a few months later, Farage's party played a significant role in framing the contest that led to Boris Johnson's sweeping victory.

In many ways, the Brexit Party is nothing new. A political chameleon with a populist touch spots an opening and seizes it. Opportunists and grifters have long abounded in politics. But there is something different about this tale, too. The Brexit Party encapsulates how the Internet has radically reshaped politics, from the rise of untraceable online fundraising to the splintering of a relatively homogenous media landscape into myriad shards, all competing for attention.

The declining power of traditional media is arguably the most profound political change in living memory, opening up new possibilities for political influence. Loosely connected networks spread misinformation into the digital ether. From bedrooms and pokey offices across Britain, hyper-partisan websites increasingly deliver highly partial news and views to millions of voters. Political half-truths and rumours travel at warp speed online, from old media to new and vice versa, propelled by anonymous digital armies.

Where the last generation of politicians needed to appear plausible in front of the television cameras, the leaders who thrive now are those who can best control a fragmented and disoriented media, harnessing the power of social networks as they push us towards extremes. In the long run, it is this misinformation revolution that could have the biggest impact of all on the future of democracy. Or on whether we have a democracy at all.

In early 2019, Steve Bannon organised a dinner for Nigel Farage ahead of the annual Conservative Political Action Conference in Oxon Hill, Maryland. Afterwards, the two men talked privately. As they talked, Farage outlined his plans for the as-yet-unannounced Brexit Party. Bannon was sceptical, at first. "I strongly recommended to Nigel that he stick with UKIP," he recalled. "I thought it would be too big a risk. If they didn't have a great showing in the European elections, I'm not that sure that the momentum would have been there to drive (Brexit) home." But Farage won Bannon over.

"He had a very detailed plan," Bannon told me. Farage wanted to be "just like Five Star. Make it an online party. He had this thing thought through and he pulled it off."

Among the lessons that Farage gleaned from Five Star was the electoral benefit of being seen as coming from outside traditional politics altogether. Beppe Grillo, the pugnacious former comedian who fronted Five Star's rise, often said that his movement was neither left nor right. It was, he said, direct democracy in action.

Farage did the same. The Brexit Party's only substantive policy was its name. Its European election slate spanned the spectrum of

British politics. The former Tory minister, ardent Roman Catholic and death penalty and gay conversion therapy evangelist Ann Widdecombe took a seat. So did Claire Fox, one-time Revolutionary Communist Party cadre and full-time controversialist, whose positions on many matters are often difficult to distinguish from those of the furthest extremes of the libertarian right.

A few months after her election, I went to meet Fox. She had just returned from Strasbourg. "I'm knackered," she said with a gravelly laugh shortly before lighting the first of numerous cigarettes (she is an opponent of bans on smoking indoors) as we sat in the sun outside a bare brick south London café. On the table in front of us were two dictaphones, one for me and one for her. Hers was bigger.

Fox talked me through her rapid journey from being a regular on the BBC to the corridors of the European Parliament. In mid-March 2019, as it became apparent that the UK would not be leaving the EU at the end of the month as originally scheduled, Fox started attending more pro-Brexit meetings. She was invited to speak at a large rally in London. In early April, she met Farage and Leave.EU co-founder Richard Tice, the Brexit Party's chairman.

Why, I asked, had someone who still describes themselves as a Marxist joined a pop-up party created by a former commodities trader and a rich businessman? "I felt it was important that there was a left-leaning Leave voice among the MEPs," Fox said. A few minutes later, she compared the battle for Brexit to the suffragettes winning the vote for women. "Progressive change is disruptive."

Fox certainly knows about political change. Over three decades, like her former Trotskyite colleagues such as Brendan O'Neill and Mick Hume, she has surfed the tides of British politics in remarkable ways. From supporting the IRA and accusing other far-left groups of being insufficiently rigorous in their support for the 'armed struggle', and defending Saddam Hussein and Slobodan Milošević in the 1980s and 1990s, the ranks of the Revolutionary Communist Party have provided some of the loudest – and most ubiquitous – media voices arguing against environmentalism, liberalism and the European Union.

Although the Revolutionary Communist Party formally disbanded in 1997, it has not exactly disappeared. I collected Fox from her office at the Academy of Ideas, a think tank that grew out of the RCP. Another RCP spin-off, the online magazine *Spiked*, is a fixture on the frontlines of Britain's nascent culture war. *Spiked*'s stock in trade is a contrarianism so predictable you could set your watch by it. According to *Spiked*'s small stable of writers, vegetarians are bad. Climate change is overhyped. Corporations are good.

There's money to be made in such intellectual promiscuity. In the years after the Brexit vote, *Spiked*'s US funding arm received $300,000 from the Koch brothers.[9] Its writers regularly appear on British television, willing to defend almost any position. Meanwhile, former RCP comrades have gained influence in the heart of British politics; the drafting of the Conservatives' winning 2019 election manifesto was overseen by Munira Mirza, a one-time RCP member who later worked for Boris Johnson as London mayor and prime minister.[10]

For Fox, there is no contradiction between taking money from American oil billionaires and claiming to represent ordinary voters against a corrupt establishment. She says: "What the Brexit Party did was to give voice to millions of frustrated people who were asking, 'What happened to my vote?' If you come along and say, 'We are the Brexit Party,' they say, 'Yes, what a relief,' because they had been left shouting at the television."

When I posed a question about what the Brexit Party's policies were beyond the self-explanatory, Fox chuckled. "Don't ask me, I don't know. You can quote me on that."

Five Star and the Brexit Party are textbook examples of what sociologist Paolo Gerbaudo calls "digital parties".[11] They take a populist message, fronted by a strong leader, and mix it with the organisational techniques of the Internet age. Supporters register online. They watch party videos on their smartphones and share party messages across social media. As with the Internet itself, the digital party is disaggregated and fluid. There are few structures or hierarchies. Everyone can participate.

Or at least it *looks* as if they can. The Silicon Valley rhetoric of engagement and empowerment often masks the concentration of power at the top of the digital party. Much like Five Star, the Brexit Party is, as Farage put it, "a company, not a political party".[12] The former UKIP leader owns 60 per cent of the party,[13] and the constitution effectively gives him total control. In late 2019, the Brexit Party had just three officers: a secretary, who was a little-known European election candidate, and two directors, Farage and Tice, who founded Leave Means Leave after the Brexit vote. Farage is the only person who can appoint and remove directors.

Traditional political parties spend time and money trying to build their membership, but the Brexit Party is a closed shop. Fewer than half a dozen senior officials are actual members. (The Brexit Party's very corporate structure is highly unusual in British politics – but not completely unique. Change UK also registered as a non-trading company, headed by a former Labour MP. Britain could be set for an era where private enterprise and political parties become structurally inseparable.)

The promise of digital democracy often rings hollow. In May 2019, less than two weeks before the European elections, Farage told listeners to his regular LBC radio show that he was building an app that would allow supporters to "shape policy and shape our future direction".[14] When the app launched, it featured only lists of party candidates and videos of Farage and his colleagues speaking. There was no way for supporters to interact with the party, much less vote on policies.

One early reviewer on Google's app store complained that it looked like it had been "created by a first-year computer science student and not a very talented one". Another wrote: "I support Brexit, but this has to be said: For a party which is supposedly slick and media-savvy, this app is so awful it can hardly be classed as such. I can only hope the party's MEPs perform far better." This was a take-it-or-leave-it form of politics, not even a simulacrum of democratic decision-making.

The 100,000 or so people who each donated £25 to become "supporters" during the Brexit Party's first couple of months were given no power over its policies. When, in November 2019, Nigel Farage unilaterally announced that his new party was standing down from 317 Conservative-held seats in the general election, candidates complained that they had not been consulted. Like more than 3,000 others, they had each paid £100 to apply to run under the Brexit Party's colours. Farage – who refused to say whether any of these luckless candidates would be reimbursed – broke the news of his election climbdown at a rally in Hartlepool filled with supporters who had paid £2.50 to hear him speak for less than ten minutes.

Spiked declared that "the Brexit Party has betrayed us".[15] But there was nothing they could do about it. There was only one voice that mattered: Farage's.

The importance of controlling a digital party's internal machinery was not the only lesson Farage and his colleagues learned in Milan. The Brexiters were particularly struck by how Five Star was amassing data from the party's Rousseau voting platform to hone its political strategy.[16]

Five Star's digital approach to politics was the life's work of Gianroberto Casaleggio. In the 1990s, Casaleggio ran a web consulting business and waxed lyrical about the "radical social and revolutionary" force of the Internet.[17] He initially grew Five Star on the networking website Meetup, which had been popularised by Howard Dean's 2004 presidential campaign. Through Meetup, Beppe Grillo communicated with supporters and encouraged them to coordinate local meetings. Often the topics discussed were not directly political. 'No incinerators'. 'Ethical consumerism'. 'Currency'. In June 2007, Grillo launched Vaffanculo Day in Bologna. 'Fuck Off Day' quickly spread across Italy, a ribald two fingers to a corrupt political elite. Casaleggio had set up and ghost-written Grillo's blog, from which Five Star emerged.

As Meetup's popularity faded and Five Star became an electoral force, many of the groups moved onto Facebook, again orchestrated by Casaleggio. Through closed Facebook forums, Five Star supporters often pushed misinformation and attacked their political opponents, just as Casaleggio had expected they would.

Casaleggio said he wanted to fight the corruption of the Italian political system and to provide an alternative to the "fake news" of traditional media, but Five Star ran a clandestine network of websites that actively spread, among other things, anti-vaccination conspiracy theories and Kremlin propaganda.[18] One blog with more than a million followers posted articles that claimed that the United States – backed by George Soros – was smuggling migrants from Libya to Italy, and that Obama wanted to topple the Syrian regime to prevent China accessing Middle Eastern oil. A Five Star member of parliament was criticised for tweeting a link to an anti-Semitic website claiming that Jews controlled the world's banking system.[19]

Even though he had no official position with the Five Star Movement, Casaleggio had an iron grip on the organisation. He owned the web platform and the data that it gathered. "Casaleggio was far cleverer than Cambridge Analytica," says Jacopo Iacoboni, an Italian journalist who has written two books on Five Star. "He never needed to steal data. With Five Star, the web company created a party, with the owner directly possessing all the data."

The Rousseau online platform was formally launched on 13 April 2016. The previous day, Gianroberto Casaleggio had died following a long illness with a brain tumour.[20] In what Iacoboni called a "dynastic succession", Casaleggio's son, Davide, 40 at the time, took control of the family business. Since then, Davide has held an annual convention on the anniversary of his father's death. Each year some of the biggest names in Italian tech and business, including Google's CEO in Italy, travel to the city of Ivrea, where Casaleggio began his career.[21]

Such is Davide's control of the party that the *New York Times* described him as the "mystery man who runs Italy's Five Star from the shadows".[22] Questions have been raised about the digital party's online operation. Italy's privacy regulator has said that it is impossible to guarantee that votes on Five Star's web platform are not being manipulated from within by party staff.[23]

Five Star's sophisticated set-up appealed to Farage, Kassam and, particularly, Arron Banks. After Liz Bilney came back from Milan, she wrote a report for Banks about the possibilities of digital campaigning. Bilney told Banks that he could, if he wished, build a new party on the Internet. "There is not currently any party in the UK with any true Internet presence," her report said.[24] Like Five Star, Banks's new digital party should engage followers in a conversation. Bilney compared the approach to running his business empire.

"If you look at insurance, you want people to renew their policies," Bilney wrote.[25] Just like selling insurance policies, a political campaign should aim to "upgrade" a follower to a paying "supporter" through frequent contact and engagement. Leave.EU – the pro-Brexit movement Banks founded and Bilney ran – was fashioned in Five Star's image. The political 'movement' was in fact a company, controlled by Banks. Everything was done online.

Even before Brexit had been won, Banks was thinking about building a post-UKIP political vehicle in Five Star's image. He spoke to sympathetic Tory MPs about his admiration for Grillo's anti-establishment movement. When the Brexit Party finally emerged, Arron Banks saw the Italian parallels clearly. "What the Five Star did, and what the Brexit Party is doing, is having a tightly controlled central structure, almost a dictatorship at the centre," he told journalist Darren Loucaides, with remarkable frankness.[26]

There was one major difference between Five Star and the Brexit Party. Where Five Star had largely grown organically under Casaleggio's tutelage, the Brexit Party was bootstrapped by paid-for Facebook ads combined with the huge social media reach of Farage and his allies. As soon as it launched, Arron Banks's Leave.EU sent out a constant stream of supportive posts to its almost one million followers. Many suspected that Banks was also funding this slick new party, but Farage was at pains to stress that the Brexit high roller was not involved. The authorities were soon asking, however, where exactly Britain's first digital party was raising its cash.

A few days before the European Parliament elections in May 2019, Gordon Brown gave a speech in Glasgow. The former prime minister covered familiar themes: the threat of Scottish independence; the Tories "banging on" about Europe; the need for investment in health and education. Brown also zeroed in on a new target: the millions of pounds that the Brexit Party was raising online.

"Democracy is fatally undermined if unexplained, unreported and thus undeclared and perhaps under the counter and under-hand campaign finance – from whom and from where we do not know – is being used to influence the very elections that are at the heart of our democratic system," Brown said.[27]

Farage responded angrily, accusing the one-time Labour leader of an "absolutely disgusting smear" against his party.[28] Brown's former party had, Farage correctly noted, installed several of its biggest donors in the House of Lords. Brexit Party co-founder Richard Tice dismissed the complaints as "jealous Westminster people who are just aghast at how we can capture the mood of the country".[29]

Certainly, the Brexit Party had found that there was money to be made in Britain's feverish political atmosphere. Within a month of launching, the party raised £2 million in online donations.[30] Farage himself encouraged supporters to give money via PayPal.

Yet questions about the party's record digital donations still swirled. When the BBC's Nick Robinson asked Tice about the possibility that foreign donors could be giving money to the party online, the Brexit Party chairman said that he didn't "sit in front of the PayPal account all day, so I don't know what currencies people are paying in".[31] This was hardly a ringing denial of the possibility of foreign interference in British politics.

The Brexit Party had a £500 limit on PayPal contributions – the point at which British political donations must be declared – but there was nothing to stop individuals breaking those limits by donating multiple times. Eyebrows were raised when *The Times* reported that the Brexit Party's fundraising team included George Cottrell, a former Farage aide who had spent time in jail in the United States for wire fraud, after offering to launder drug pushers' money.[32] A fresh-faced aristocrat who went by the nickname 'Posh George', Cottrell had served as UKIP's head of fundraising until he was arrested on his return from the 2016 Republican National Convention.[33]

Shortly after Gordon Brown's intervention, the Electoral Commission decided to take a closer look at the Brexit Party's finances. After a visit to the party's London headquarters, the regulator reported that it was concerned about "the potential for individuals or organisations to evade the permissibility rules, which primarily seek to prevent significant sums entering UK politics from overseas".[34] In June, the watchdog said that the Brexit Party's online funding left it open to "a high and on-going risk" of impermissible donations, and ordered the party to tighten its reporting procedures.[35]

By then, of course, the European elections were already over. Once again the stable door was being closed after the horse had been given ample time to bolt. "What people have been very good at is spotting loopholes in the law and exploiting them," says electoral law expert Gavin Millar. "It is so easy to mask where money is coming from."

The Brexit Party's online funding model, borrowed directly from Five Star, could easily be replicated by others. It is the quintessence of murky digital politics: dispersed, loosely connected yet centrally controlled, and almost impossible to scrutinise. The old analogue system of political donations – of cheques posted off to fusty central party offices – is being replaced by contributions made with the click of a mouse. Tracing donations will likely become even more difficult in the coming years.

"In the future, people will use online payment systems to give, say, £1 million in multiple micro-donations that won't be picked up," says Conservative MP Damian Collins. "Facebook is launching its own platform currency – Libra – which could be a mechanism to launder money into campaigns with no transparency at all."

One possible solution is to make political parties responsible for ensuring that the money they receive is untainted. The Electoral Commission's head of regulation Louise Edwards suggested adopting the same anti-money laundering checks used by banks, art dealers and others for political donations. In the summer of 2019, the Electoral Commission had private meetings with the anti-money laundering team at the Treasury to discuss how the proposal might work.

But as so often in British politics, the talk of change did not develop into action. There were "a lot of chats but there didn't seem to be any clear political will to do anything", said someone close to the Treasury's discussions with the elections watchdog. "It seemed there had already been nudges from Number 10 – 'Don't make life too difficult for our donors.'"

Donors are the lifeblood of British politics. As well as PayPal donations, the Brexit Party received more than £8 million from named donors between its launch in April 2019 and December's general election. (By comparison, Change UK raised less than £275,000 in the same period.) Some of the Brexit Party's biggest contributors had previously given money to the Conservatives and worked in finance.

Many of the names and the networks were very familiar. Brexit donor Jeremy Hosking, who donated heavily to Tory candidates in the 2017 general election, announced that he was backing the Brexit Party. Jon Wood, who donated to Boris Johnson's Tory leadership campaign, gave money; Christopher Harborne, a Thailand-based businessman and one-time member of the 'leader's group' of senior Conservative donors, was dubbed "the new Arron Banks" by an online news site after donating an eye-watering £6.7 million to the Brexit Party.[36]

Other donors had links to the opaque world of libertarian think tanks. Richard Smith, who owns the building at 55 Tufton Street, contributed, as did George Farmer, the 20-something former chairman of the alt-right group Turning Point UK.

In September 2019, as a potential general election loomed, Banks's right-hand man Andy Wigmore tweeted that Conservative and Brexit Party donors had been "having secret meetings on how to cooperate",[37] warning that if Boris Johnson did not do a deal with Farage "then Tories may be in for a financial surprise". Newspapers reported that the Conservatives were offering honours to senior Brexit Party figures in return for standing aside.[38] In the end, Johnson eschewed a formal pact with Farage, but the Brexit Party's European elections success had already paved the way for Johnson to become Conservative leader and had galvanised his party around the pledge to "Get Brexit Done".

Questions about the Brexit Party's funding did little to blunt its appeal ahead of the European elections in May 2019. Criticism by the likes of Gordon Brown was dismissed as yet another manifestation of a compromised pro-EU establishment trying to protect itself. Negative newspaper stories gained little traction either. Voters seemed uninterested in Claire Fox's past defence of an Irish Republican bomb that killed two and injured 56 in Warrington,[39] or whether a Brexit Party candidate John Kennedy had shared a platform with Radovan Karadžić[40] or secretly worked for Cambridge Analytica in Kenya.[41] Meanwhile, Farage's party adeptly harnessed new online tools to grab the attention of voters and spread its no-deal Brexit message. (The party's only other substantive policy was a pledge to get rid of inheritance tax.)

A digital party can appear chaotic, but it is often carefully micromanaged. Like a multinational launching a new product line, the digital party carefully tests its offer with consumers. Voters are bombarded with targeted online messages to see what sticks, and what doesn't.

Before the European elections, the Brexit Party appointed Steven Edginton, a 19-year-old former digital strategist at the TaxPayers' Alliance, to head its online campaign. Just as Leave.EU did before the Brexit referendum, the Brexit Party specifically targeted Labour voters on Facebook. It spent hundreds of thousands of pounds on slick ads. Attacks on the British political establishment for failing to take the country out of the EU at the end of March 2019 were mixed with a more hopeful message: change politics for good.

"We knew that there was basically a ceiling with fucked-off people," a party insider told *Wired*.[42] "In order to open our horizons and reach out to more voters, we wanted a much more optimistic message."

Like Farage's clipped, emotive prose, the Brexit Party's social media was succinct and powerful: its average Facebook post was 19 words long, compared with 71 for the doomed centrist party Change UK.[43] It was wildly successful. By the end of the European elections campaign the Brexit Party had more than 120,000 Facebook likes, five times more than Change UK.[44] Its content was shared more than all the other parties' combined.[45]

Social networks and smartphones have not just changed how parties market themselves to voters. The digital age has ushered in a new type of politician. The Internet, as Will Davies writes, calls for "a very different set of political and personal talents: confrontation, wit, defiance, spontaneity and rule-breaking".[46] Where Bill Clinton or Tony Blair tried desperately to appear normal for the TV camera, digital politicians intentionally court the *lulz*. In his first speech in the European Parliament, the Brexit Party's Martin Daubney called the EU's key negotiator, Guy Verhofstadt, the "Darth Vader of Europe". The clip was widely shared on social media.

Unlike the overproduced television politicians of the 1980s and 1990s, who needed to appeal to the news editors and producers that guarded access to the media, digital politicians can build their own media and their own following. The Brexit Party set up highly professional social media channels. Viewers on YouTube could watch a dedicated news-panel-style show called *Brexbox*. The party's ersatz newspaper, the *Brexiteer*, was distributed in town centres and pubs by a small army of volunteers.[47]

"We are completely circumnavigating the traditional media stream who, let's face it, are often hostile to us and don't like us. And more to the point, our voters don't watch them," said Martin Daubney, himself a former editor of lads' magazine *Loaded*. Rather than relying on journalists who, Daubney complained, tell "different versions of truth", the Brexit Party decided to "be the news source", the MEP told *Wired*.[48]

In becoming its own media, the Brexit Party was helped by another digital innovation: the rise of an almost invisible network of do-it-yourself, hyper-partisan websites that push political messages deep into the digital echo chambers where many voters increasingly get their views of the world.

When Jordan James was growing up, he dreamed of being a journalist. At school, James, who describes himself as "a mixed race lad from a broken family" on "the rough side of Bolton" in north-west England, walked around with a copy of the *Sun* folded under his arm. He studied media at a regional university and applied for jobs in journalism, but the closest he got to Fleet Street was the final round of the *Sun*'s apprenticeship scheme. So he decided to set up his own tabloid online.

James launched *Politicalite.com* in spring 2017. The site's style was bombastic. Sensationalist headlines. Showbiz gossip side-by-side with hard-right talking points.[49] On a good day, he was getting 50,000 visitors. His most-read stories covered three closely related subjects: the far-right activist Stephen Yaxley-Lennon (better known as Tommy Robinson); Islam; and Brexit.

"That's what people wanted. That's what people wanted to share, the things that aren't usually said in the 'PC media bubble'. We fed the monster," James told me during one of our many long text message conversations in the second half of 2019.

Politicalite is one node in a loosely connected network of avowedly partisan, hard-right British political websites that have sprung up in recent years. Their names are little-known beyond the depths of the Internet. Their stories are not read out on the morning media round-up on BBC Radio 4's *Today* programme, which has traditionally set the Westminster agenda. But these highly partial, anything-but-neutral outlets increasingly supply opinions to a vast swathe of the British public.

"People don't trust the mainstream media anymore," says David Clews, who set up the right-wing website *Unity News Network* in Glasgow with a couple of young UKIP activists in early 2018. "People don't have an issue with partisan reporting. What they have an issue with is the mainstream media who dress up partisan reporting as news."

These wildly opinionated websites can exert political influence far beyond their relatively meagre resources. The 2016 US presidential election was often framed as a victory for fake news. False stories proliferated. The Pope had endorsed Donald Trump. Hillary Clinton was involved in an apocryphal child abuse ring operating out of a suburban Washington pizza parlour.

Reports blamed the tsunami of misinformation on youths working for online 'troll farms' in Macedonia – which were subsequently found to have involved highly coordinated international efforts[50] – but the most enduring pro-Trump messaging was crafted by hyper-partisan media much closer to home.

Breitbart, the site funded by Robert Mercer and overseen by Steve Bannon, was the most popular conservative news outlet in the 2016 campaign.[51] Fringe right-wing outfits such as *Gateway Pundit*, *Conservative Tribune* and *Truthfeed* supplied jaundiced reporting to millions of readers.[52] Fox News broadcast almost hourly attacks on the Democrats. This insular ecosystem played up conspiratorial thinking and minimised negative stories about Trump.

Ahead of the 2020 US presidential election, the Columbia Journalism School documented the sudden appearance of at least 450 websites that looked like local news portals, but which were actually pushing right-wing propaganda, mostly written by algorithms rather than human reporters.[53] Most misinformation is not outright falsehood – which can be disproved – but "genuine content taken out of context", says Claire Wardle of First Draft News. "You take things that work in the mainstream media, whether on the left or the right, and you just twist it further."

The 2016 EU referendum had a similar effect on British political media as the Trump campaign in the US. New political websites opened up in its aftermath. Vote Leave's Matthew Elliott established *Brexit Central* and hired former staff such as Darren Grimes to pump out pro-Brexit content. *Brexit Central* was even granted a journalistic pass to Parliament.[54] Arron Banks bankrolled *Westmonster*, which was as belligerent as it sounds before going into abeyance in the middle of 2019. On the left of politics, the *Canary*, *Skwawkbox* and other sites became lightning rods for supporters of Jeremy Corbyn, often spreading partisan stories targeting political opponents and established media outlets, particularly the BBC.

You don't necessarily need a financial backer or deep ties to a political party to run a successful news site. The barrier for entry to the media has fallen almost to zero. Registering a domain and setting up a basic WordPress site costs less than a family ticket to the cinema. At the same time, entrepreneurial young journalists have little chance of a job in an established newspaper or broadcaster. There are few opportunities in Bolton to intern at a Tufton Street think tank or write for a Fleet Street title. "I just thought, 'Well I may as well do something myself,'" said Jordan James.

How does a website with no staff and no money mushroom into a platform with millions of page views? There is a long answer and a short answer. The long answer is about human psychology, the Internet and our attraction to highly emotive stories. The short answer is one word: Facebook.

When *Politicalite* first started, James mainly published stories praising Trump, but he quickly realised that readers were far more likely to click on radical home-grown content. But he needed an audience to know his stories existed. So James started to pay Facebook to promote his site in specific areas. He targeted working-class towns in England ("not the cities or Scotland"). A Facebook user living in Blackpool would see a story about a Traveller ploughing his car into a crowd outside a nightclub. If they lived in the next town, they got a similarly themed story from their own locality. James told me that he focused on "immigration, religion and talking about the things people say you aren't allowed to say in the politically correct world".

James did not just buy ads on Facebook, he seeded his pro-Brexit, anti-immigration stories into closed Facebook groups. This allowed him to push stories to an audience of hundreds of thousands, if not millions, almost completely below the radar. Facebook groups offer a positive experience to many users – mothers can talk about child-rearing, sports fans can chat about their beloved games and teams – but they are also a honey pot for fake news, conspiracies and misinformation. Through these private groups, stories can spread rapidly across a massive organic online network.

Once he had built an audience through Facebook, "Big hitters in the right-wing media world started working with us," said James. The most significant was Stephen Yaxley-Lennon, better known as Tommy Robinson. James, of mixed heritage, had once viewed the anti-Muslim activist as a racist. James said he had even fallen out with his stepfather when his mother's partner had joined an early incarnation of Yaxley-Lennon's far-right English Defence League in Bolton.

But after the terrorist attack on an Ariana Grande concert in Manchester that killed 22 people in May 2017, he started following Yaxley-Lennon's videos on an extremist YouTube channel.* When Yaxley-Lennon appeared on breakfast television show *Good Morning Britain* with Piers Morgan, James wrote a positive report on his website. "I thought Tommy was standing up, saying what needed to be said," he told me.

James met Yaxley-Lennon and was invited to meet Republican congressman Paul Gosar at a pro-Robinson rally in London in July 2018. James could not make the event, at which Gosar described Muslim men as a "scourge"[55] on society, but by then Yaxley-Lennon was frequently sharing *Politicalite* stories. As UKIP shifted hard to the right – then party leader Gerard Batten hired Yaxley-Lennon as a political advisor in November 2018 – *Politicalite* became an important part of its digital support base. Farage's former assistant Raheem Kassam wrote for the site. When the Brexit Party appeared, *Politicalite* ran positive stories about the new party, too.

James had graduated from a WordPress blog to the centre of the nascent alt-right British world. He was making enough money, mainly from Facebook ads, that he was able to quit his job to concentrate on *Politicalite*. "It was like winning the lottery," he said.

That rise was brought to a juddering halt when Facebook banned *Politicalite* in 2019 for breaching its hate-speech policies. James said he was taking legal advice to overturn the decision, but he wore the ban as a badge of honour. The site carried the

---

* The YouTube channel was run by a British nationalist based in the north of England who listed Nigel Farage and Enoch Powell as his political heroes.

strapline "Britain's most CENSORED news outlet". (Caps are very popular in the partisan online world.) Without Facebook, however, *Politicalite*'s donations slowed markedly. Page views declined. James had to go back to work as a labourer.

Facebook had targeted others, too. A couple of months earlier, Yaxley-Lennon's Facebook page, with about a million followers, was closed. (Moderators at the social media giant had previously been wary of taking action against prominent far-right pages because of their huge following, a *Channel 4* investigation found.[56]) Yaxley-Lennon was later given a nine-month prison sentence for contempt of court after his Facebook Live videos almost caused the collapse of the trial of a gang in northern England that had groomed young women for sex.[57] The *Guardian* also revealed that Yaxley-Lennon was heavily funded by US libertarian think tanks linked to Robert Mercer, among others.[58]

Over months of messaging, James told me that he wanted to move away from the alt-right and become a mainstream journalist. He said that he had been "groomed" and that, after briefly working for Yaxley-Lennon, he had seen a different side to his former hero. "Tommy isn't working class like he says he is," he told me. "I just thought, 'Wow, I've been slogging away, blogging, supporting you, struggling to make ends meet, thinking you were this man of the people and you're not.'"

In late December 2019, a week after Boris Johnson's election victory, James published *Politicalite*'s final story. He gave it the headline "Populism won… we're done". The valedictory post included a photograph of him shaking hands with Yaxley-Lennon more than a year earlier. James was smiling.

Politicalite is unlikely to have been mourned for long. There are dozens of news sites like it. Often the most basic are among the most popular. *PoliticalUK* is run by just one person, a former UKIP member from Essex who declined to give his name when I contacted him. It launched in early 2018, and within eight months the site's populist stories about immigration and Brexit had accumulated more than three million interactions on social media.[59]

On average, these articles are far more popular than stories on their left-wing equivalents. "There is a reason that the right does so well online," says Claire Wardle. "The right is generally better at generating fear, which is the driving motivation for engagement."

Once again, Facebook is crucial. Almost every *PoliticalUK* story is also posted to a Facebook group called 'EU – I Voted Leave', which has more than a quarter of a million members. The algorithms used by tech platforms often drive users to more extreme content. A 2019 study of 360 alt-right channels on YouTube found that users were often recommended increasingly hardcore, racist videos.[60]

When I looked at the 'EU – I Voted Leave' Facebook page, Facebook itself suggested I might like "related" pages including the alt-right Turning Point UK and the Football Lads Alliance, a radical anti-Muslim group which the English Premier League has warned clubs to avoid. *PoliticalUK*'s proprietor stressed that his site had been given a positive rating by Newsguard, an online tool that rates the trustworthiness of news sites.

The popularity of proudly partisan news sites is partly a product of a very human response to sensory overload. We all employ cognitive biases to navigate the unending sea of information we face every day. We seek out information that confirms our beliefs. Conflicting opinions are often rejected. These feverishly biased websites go even further, providing an almost hermetically sealed worldview of good and evil, delivered with flashing arrays and screaming all-caps headlines.

"It's all about making us angry," tech writer Jamie Bartlett told me. "How the message is being delivered really matters. The way you consume it. How your faculties are being used. The medium is driving you to hyper-partisanship."

These 'news' sites also have a social function. Their audiences are older, predominantly men with time on their hands. In an increasingly atomised world, the online rabbit hole is a place to make friends, and to win status. "So much misinformation is people sharing content because they want to be the performative person at the centre of things," says Wardle. "There is a dopamine hit from online engagement."

These websites are businesses too, often run by canny entrepreneurs with a sophisticated understanding of the changed economics of news media. The key challenge is to gain a big enough audience to make money from clicks, while also delivering something that readers will consider paying for.

Unity News's David Clews told me that he knows "what buttons to push". He talked about the Overton window, the notion that the range of ideas that are acceptable to the public can be shifted. "We cater our content to suit our audience, which is what any business would do," he said.

As well as subscribers, *Unity News* runs an online shop selling pro-Brexit gimcrack. One of the more popular items is a badge with Winston Churchill flashing the V-sign, embossed with the legends "We want our country back" and "We will never surrender". When I saw it, I was surprised that the *Mail* or the *Express* had not thought of it already.

It is very tempting to divide the media into 'good' established outlets in large offices holding power to account, and 'bad' insurgents spreading 'fake news' from their bedrooms. (As a journalist, I am particularly keen to cleave to this professional distinction. We've all got bills to pay.) But, really, how different are old and new media?

Let's take a look at the front page of *Unity News* on a random day in September 2019. There was a story about Boris Johnson, another on the Brexit Party. A dispatch from Germany about the far-right Alternative for Germany, and an attack on London mayor Sadiq Khan.

The most outlandish piece claimed that Britain had actually already left the European Union due to a legal technicality. It was straight misinformation, or what would once have been called a glaring lie.

It also seemed strangely familiar. I did some more digging around. The online story was lifted almost entirely from a blog on the *Spectator* website that had appeared a few months earlier, tantalisingly titled "Does this EU small print mean Brexit has already happened?"[61] It did, the writer concluded. A very similar story ran in the *Express* around the same time. The new fake news is not always that different from the old.

The young men who run partisan websites – they are almost all young men – often speak about themselves as inheritors of Fleet Street's mantle. "Once upon a time the red tops were dominant for the more populist message, the *Sun*, the *Express*," said *Unity News*'s David Clews. "Now their influence is waning." Jordan James told me he was inspired by Rupert Murdoch. "He fucking owns what he does like a boss," James said of the man who owns Fox News, the *Sun* and a vast empire of other media outlets.

The distance between a cottage industry run out of a bedroom in Bolton and the offices of a national newspaper should be measured more in degrees than absolutes. I have lost count of the number of times 'established' media have spun stories I have written elsewhere to suit their own narratives. A few years ago, one repeat offender produced an entire web story based on a handful of cherry-picked quotes from a long piece about Brexit I had written for a major European outlet. I called to complain. A tired-sounding sub-editor picked up the phone. He apologised profusely but assured me there was nothing he could do. "This is just how it is now," he said.

Newspaper sales in Britain have declined markedly, as has trust in the press. A 2019 study by the Reuters Institute for the Study of Journalism at Oxford University found that just two-fifths of the British public felt they could "trust most news most of the time".[62] The figure had dropped by ten points in just four years. Reflecting on possible reasons for the decline in trust, the authors noted the growth of political polarisation, the rise of 'clickbait' news in an age of declining revenues and the proliferation of misinformation.

Another source of mistrust, of course, is the culture of the British press itself, which is often tolerant of mistruths, especially when the solecisms are committed by members of the elite that dominate its upper echelons. Boris Johnson's career is a case in point.

As a cub reporter, Johnson was sacked by *The Times* for fabricating a quote about the 14th-century King Edward II's catamite lover and attributing it to his godfather, the historian Colin Lucas. In many walks of life, that would be a career-ending deceit. Instead, the *Daily Telegraph* hired Johnson to run the paper's Brussels bureau. (He was 24, the same age as Jordan James when he bought an off-the-shelf website and a domain name for £9.99.)

At the *Telegraph*, Johnson excelled in an emerging newspaper genre: the confected European Union story. Eurocrats, he told his readers, wanted to ban prawn cocktail crisps and limit the size of condoms, to the dismay of Italian men. Editors on other papers ordered their often staid Brussels correspondents to follow suit. When Johnson left the European beat to become the *Telegraph*'s chief political correspondent in 1994, James Landale, then a reporter at *The Times*, marked his departure by penning a satirical poem based on Hilaire Belloc's 'Matilda'. "Boris", Landale wrote, "told such dreadful lies/It made one gasp and stretch one's eyes."[63]

Johnson was far from a lone voice punting stories about the EU that strained credibility. Rupert Murdoch was stridently Eurosceptic long before most of the British public felt so strongly about the issue. An infamous 1990 *Sun* front page declared "Up Yours Delors". Just in case the headline was too subtle, it was accompanied by a picture of two V-shaped fingers protruding from a Union Jack shirt cuff and aimed at the European Commission's then president.

Britain's predominantly right-wing tabloid culture has exerted an almost uniquely strong pull on the nation's politics. At times, the red tops have rushed to follow political changes – the *Sun* endorsed Tony Blair's New Labour – but more often it has been a jingoistic press that has succeeded in pushing fringe positions into the centre of political debate. The Conservative right's obsession with Europe went mainstream on the pages of its newspapers. Through the 1990s and into the early years of the new millennium, there were almost endless stories about how Brussels bureaucrats were meddling with the venerable traditions of British life.

In a 1999 "exclusive", the *Sun* told its readers that a new EU labour law meant the Queen would suddenly have to make her own tea, as her servants would be forced to clock off. (The working time directive had actually been agreed by the British government, six years earlier.) The *Daily Star* once declared that the EU was going to limit the speed of children's playground roundabouts. (It wasn't.)

There were so many mistruths about the EU that the European Commission set up a rebuttal website ahead of the EU referendum. Around a thousand people read each meticulous fact check; by contrast, the *Mail*'s website, which frequently featured dubious stories about the European institutions, had an average monthly audience of around 225 million at the time.[64] Intriguingly, a study has even suggested that a long-running boycott of the *Sun* on Merseyside following the Hillsborough Stadium disaster in 1989 – which the paper blamed on Liverpool fans – contributed to the largely working-class city voting Remain in 2016.[65]

The power of the British press is concentrated in a handful of owners. In 2019, just three companies – the Daily Mail and General Trust, Reach and Murdoch's News UK – controlled 83 per cent of the British newspaper market (up from 71 per cent in 2015).[66] The agendas of these newspapers, and their owners, matter. Successive prime ministers have been said to have made decisions based on the front page of the mid-market *Daily Mail*.

The press has fed Britain's growing polarisation. In November 2016, less than six months after Jo Cox MP was murdered by a neo-Nazi sympathiser, the *Mail* declared High Court judges "enemies of the people" after a ruling that Parliament would have to vote to give notice on leaving the EU. A year later, the *Daily Telegraph* published on its front page mugshots of 15 Tory MPs who had indicated that they would vote against a government proposal to enshrine the putative Brexit date in law. The paper, owned by the billionaire Barclay brothers via an offshore trust, labelled the parliamentarians "mutineers".

The barrier between Fleet Street and Westminster has long been porous.* Winston Churchill, Michael Foot and Nigel Lawson all worked as journalists before going into politics. After being elected to the Commons in 2001, Boris Johnson spent his first four years in the House combining his job as an MP with editing the *Spectator*. When the *Spectator*'s new chief executive Andrew Neil replaced him in 2005, Johnson continued to write for the *Daily Telegraph*, renegotiating the fee for his weekly columns up to a quarter of a million pounds a year.

During the 2019 Tory leadership contest, while he was still a columnist, Johnson appeared on the *Telegraph*'s front page 22 times in a single month. As is often the case, these stories were regularly picked up by broadcasters. The sound of BBC morning bulletins

---

* There is often a revolving door between journalism and political communication, too. Party press offices tend to be heavily populated by former hacks. There is also movement in the other direction. In the middle of 2019, Steven Edginton made a dramatic move from the Brexit Party comms team into journalism when he published, with Isabel Oakeshott, leaked British diplomatic cables about Donald Trump that led to the resignation of the UK ambassador to Washington, Kim Darroch. Edginton soon joined *Guido Fawkes*. After just two weeks, he was hired by the *Sun*.

being led by reports of Johnson's latest op-eds was so frequent that the former Conservative minister Chris Patten rhetorically asked, "What did our poor country do to deserve government by the editorial columns of the *Daily Telegraph*?"[67]

When Johnson became prime minister a few weeks later, a message congratulating the paper's star columnist ran on a big screen in the lobby of the *Telegraph*'s offices in central London. "The *Telegraph* has become like Fox News in the US, a for-profit commercial press outfit for a single political figure," says media scholar Martin Moore. On 31 January 2020, the day Britain officially left the European Union, red, white and blue Union Jack bunting was hung up in the *Telegraph*'s newsroom.

As in the US, British political reporting has become increasingly histrionic. There are flashing lights and countdown clocks. Celebrity reporters narrate politics as a theatre played out by sniping, bickering personalities. The public are tacitly encouraged to root for one side or another – Boris or Jeremy? – and to treat them all with equal disdain and disbelief. "They're all liars anyway," was a frequent refrain among British voters in 2019.

Instead of debates about policy, the couches of late-night political discussion shows are filled by cadres of ever more partisan commentators from the left and the right who often have little, if any, discernible expertise beyond the ability to parrot party political talking points. No wonder so many are switching off the news completely.

An alienated, disengaged electorate and a media that, in the name of balance, often creates a false equivalence between facts and lies is as much a boon for populists and political snake oil sellers as dark money and disinformation. The shift to high-octane, 24/7 reporting has made it easier for those in power to manipulate journalistic conventions.

Almost as soon as Boris Johnson became prime minister – bringing with him Vote Leave's press operation – on-the-record interviews almost completely ceased. In their place, a rash of stories appeared citing only anonymous government sources, widely assumed to be senior advisor Dominic Cummings: Downing Street was investigating pro-Remain MPs for "collusion" with foreign governments; on a private phone call, German chancellor Angela Merkel had accused the prime minister of trying to play "a stupid blame game" over Brexit; Johnson's Irish counterpart Leo Varadkar had "reneged on a secret deal" with the prime minister ahead of a crunch Brussels summit.

Many of these stories were subsequently proven to be false or vastly exaggerated, but they frequently led the news agenda while giving the government plausible deniability. British journalists were being "played like an instrument", warned Rasmus Nielsen, director of the Reuters Institute for the Study of Journalism.

Politicians spinning stories is not new. Margaret Thatcher's press secretary, Bernard Ingham, frequently briefed the media to settle internal party scores. Alastair Campbell was so successful at controlling the press that he became immortalised as the sweary spin doctor in Armando Iannucci's satirical sitcom *The Thick of It*. But, as with so much else, the Internet has changed the rules of the game. Where once the news day started with a set piece interview on the BBC, it now increasingly kicks off with a tweet thread from a prominent journalist setting out the government's key talking points for the day. There is no space for rebuttal. By the time scrutiny arrives, hours or even days later, the message is already out.

Linguist George Lakoff calls this "framing the narrative" – what is being talked about matters far more than whether it is true or false. Boris Johnson and Australian spin doctor Sir Lynton Crosby have another name for the same strategy: the dead cat. Chuck a lifeless feline on the table, and it will immediately dominate the conversation.

Johnson has been a master of the dead cat. The only time he looked under severe pressure in the 2019 general election was when a television journalist, during a live interview, showed the

Conservative leader a photograph on his phone of a sick child forced to sleep on the floor of a full hospital in Leeds. Johnson refused to look at the image, and instead snatched the reporter's phone and put it in his pocket. The clip quickly went viral on social media. For almost the first time in the campaign, a Labour message – that the NHS was in crisis – was cutting through.

What happened next was classic dead cat. Conservative advisors briefed senior political journalists that an aide to Health Secretary Matt Hancock – who had been dispatched to the Leeds hospital – had been punched during a mass protest by Labour supporters. The reporters tweeted out the news, and it spread like digital wildfire.

But it wasn't true. Footage soon emerged showing that rather than a melee of Labour protesters, there were only half a dozen people and no punches had been thrown. The journalists who had amplified this disinformation apologised for their mistake, but it was too late. The dead cat had become the story.

Journalists have struggled to react to this rising tide of distraction and dissembling. "We are just reporting what politicians say," is a common defence, rooted very reasonably in the commitment to fair and balanced reporting. But as politics has become another form of entertainment, it is very easy for journalists to be manipulated by skilful, self-serving political disruptors. Boris Johnson, Nigel Farage, Donald Trump – all know how to frame narratives that will spread quickly through established media and onto partisan news sites.

A good example of this is an interview that Farage gave to Talkradio in September 2019. The Brexit Party leader said that the BBC had treated him "like a war criminal" at Nuremberg during the European elections. His comments were quickly picked up by the *Sun*, a Murdoch stablemate of Talkradio. The pro-Brexit *Daily Express* carried the story on its website. *PoliticalUK* followed suit, reporting that "VOTERS SAY 'NIGEL IS RIGHT' AS FARAGE LOSES TEMPER WITH REMARKS AGAINST THE BBC". In less than 24 hours, the *PoliticalUK* story was liked more than 1,500 times on the 'EU – I Voted Leave' Facebook page. Hundreds of commenters agreed with Farage.*

It is a grim irony that the more journalists are successfully manipulated by populist-minded politicians, the easier it is for the very same leaders to delegitimise and undermine one of the few potential sources that could scrutinise and hold them to account. The BBC has been assailed from the left and the right. After an error-prone general election, trust in the corporation declined markedly, according to a post-election opinion poll.[68]

Perfect timing, then, for a politician to attack the public sector broadcaster. Having unexpectedly announced on the campaign trail that he was "looking at" the licence fee that pays for the BBC – another dead cat that was dutifully pored over – Boris Johnson issued a diktat banning his ministers from appearing on Radio 4's *Today* in the immediate aftermath of his election victory.[69] Other than the show's editor complaining that the move was "Trumpian",[70] the reaction was muted.

Similarly, when Nigel Farage compares his experience on the BBC to a Nazi on trial in Nuremberg, he can be sure that heads will nod in agreement, from the news desks of red tops to the febrile audiences in Facebook groups and message forums. It also makes it even more likely that he will be invited back onto the BBC. Farage, who has stood seven times for election to Parliament and never won, has appeared more than thirty times on its main political debate show *Question Time*. Few politicians have appeared so regularly.

Farage "learned from Five Star in Italy how to bludgeon the

---

* Steve Bannon used very similar tactics ahead of the 2016 US presidential election. The then *Breitbart* boss fed stories about Hillary Clinton's finances to the *New York Times* that were subsequently reported by his own site with links to respected mainstream titles adding credibility. From *Breitbart*, the stories soon spread across the hyper-partisan right-wing media world and into the news feeds of tens of millions of American voters.

media", a public relations expert told trade magazine *Campaign* shortly after the Brexit Party's launch. "He gets so much airtime on *Question Time* because he has, with the help of the tabloid press, cowed the BBC. The focus on the media as biased servants of the liberal elite is relentless."[71] And it's relentless because it works.

There has seldom been a better time to be a prevaricating politician. Where once a run of negative headlines could end a career, now it can all be dismissed as "fake news". Established arbiters of truth have been decentred. The nightly news bulletin and the front page of a broadsheet paper still exist, but they carry much less weight. Fewer and fewer families crowd around their television set each evening to receive a shared view of the world.

The decline of once almost monolithic media has had many positive effects. Fresh voices have emerged. The 'official' version is far more open to contestation. But the 'post-truth' epoch has also been a boon for misinformation and political disruption.

Already, digital parties are pointing the way to a new version of politics, supercharged by almost invisible networks of aggressively partisan websites. The digital democracy promised by Five Star and the Brexit Party has, according to sociologist Paolo Gerbaudo, "mostly proven a sham".[72] Behind the digital party's glittering egalitarian promise sits a tiny leadership cabal. Decisions taken on high are rubber-stamped by a pliant movement that does not have the same rights and powers as traditional party members. Crepuscular hyper-partisan news sites flood social media, often aided by a disoriented established media that has played up the very same narratives of fear and betrayal.

Rather than demonstrating utopian transparency, digital parties are often extremely opaque. Money flows in from anonymous sources. The elision of the political party and the private business hints at a dystopian digital future, in which democracy becomes even less participative and pluralist. (This is a particularly worrying vista in Britain, where the first-past-the-post electoral system and the consequent marginalisation of smaller parties has already reduced much of the country to political irrelevance.)

Digital parties have, of course, struggled in the face of real-world politics. In Italy, Five Star's support has plummeted since 2018, when Beppe Grillo went into government with the far-right League led by Matteo Salvini, who is a far more ruthless political operator. The two parties had plenty in common: Eurosceptic, anti-immigrant and pro-Russian. But after less than eighteen months, the coalition collapsed when Salvini walked out, with his League party far ahead in opinion polls.[73]

In Britain, the Brexit Party did not win a single seat in the general election in December 2019. Despite President Trump calling in to Nigel Farage's radio show to tell Boris Johnson that he should form a pact with the Brexit Party – foreign political interference is often far less subtle than Russian bots on social media – the Conservatives refused to countenance a 'Leave Alliance'. Under pressure from his former patron Arron Banks and his Leave.EU digital juggernaut, Farage stood down in all Conservative-held seats. But the Brexit Party still took over half a million votes, mostly in working-class constituencies. On election night, Farage claimed, with some justification, that the Brexit Party had allowed the Conservatives to come through the middle to take a swathe of once solidly Labour seats in northern England and the Midlands. Farage "accomplished everything that he said," Steve Bannon told me. "Nigel eventually got the Brexit he had always fought for."

The Brexit Party is unlikely to be a lasting force in British politics. After the general election, Farage sacked the party's staff, despite having raised at least £11.5 million in less than a year.[74] Farage told journalists that he intended to campaign for Trump in the 2020 US presidential election.

His digital party, however, is less the final word in how the Internet has changed politics, and more a taste of things to come.

What does democracy look like in a world of political grifters, echo chambers and orchestrated misinformation? Will any safeguards really be able to stop the flow of anonymous online funding? Can the digital-era politician ever be held to account?

The UK is far from the only state facing such existential questions. It is time to take a deeper look at how dark money and hidden influence are feeding a global populist surge.

10

MAKING EUROPE GREAT AGAIN

*The EU is managed by lobbies and is ever more distant from
the people, but things are changing... I want to be part of an
international front that includes Donald Trump, who will
be re-elected, Boris Johnson, [Brazil's] Jair Bolsonaro and
[Israel's] Benjamin Netanyahu.*

MATTEO SALVINI, December 2019[1]

In April 2016, Matteo Salvini, leader of Italy's secessionist
Northern League, attended a Donald Trump campaign rally in
Wilkes-Barre, Pennsylvania. At the time, Salvini, a charismatic
43-year-old with the physique of a rugby player, was already one
of the leading figures on the Italian far right. In the Mohegan
Sun Arena in Wilkes-Barre, he sat among a group of supporters
holding a banner that read 'Make America Great Again'.[2]

Afterwards Trump and Salvini chatted and posed for a photograph beside an American flag. Trump was in trademark campaign
mode – broad smile, thumb up, blond thatch reflecting the harsh
overhead light. Salvini had the air of an expectant schoolboy. The
top button of his shirt was undone, tie askew. He grinned widely.
Salvini told Italian reporters that Trump had confided, "Matteo, I
hope you become prime minister of Italy soon."[3]

Trump later denied meeting Salvini at all.[4] But the digital-savvy

Italian, making the most of his brief moment, had already tweeted the picture out to his army of followers. Steve Bannon noticed it. Within 48 hours, Salvini was in Washington with the man who would become Donald Trump's chief strategist.[5] Bannon would later talk of Salvini as a brother-in-arms at the vanguard of a global right-wing populist resurgence.

Before the 2018 Italian election, Salvini rebranded his party as the League. The party's xenophobic, anti-EU message was now pitched at all of Italy, not just the prosperous north. Voters responded positively. The League took almost a fifth of the vote and ended up in an anti-establishment coalition government with the Five Star Movement.

Afterwards, Bannon provided a pen portrait of Salvini for *Time*'s list of 2019's most influential people. "He came, he saw, he Facebooked – live," Bannon wrote of Italy's then deputy prime minister and interior minister. "The most unconventional of politicians ran the most unconventional of campaigns, a whirlwind of rallies, speeches, energy, all captured live in the moment on social media, financed on a shoestring, with grit and determination and a message."[6]

The depiction of Salvini – and fellow travellers across Europe such as France's Marine Le Pen, Hungary's Viktor Orbán and, of course, Nigel Farage – as grassroots insurgents storming the citadel with little more than an Internet connection and a nativist dream is compelling. Certainly, this new generation of nationalists have tapped into a deep well of popular anger and frustration with the status quo. Their advance, however, is also undergirded by networks of dark money and hidden influence, much as we have seen in Britain. Armies of digital supporters spread disinformation across the borderless Internet. Electoral rules, where they exist, are there to be broken.

Europe's populists often share similar campaigning styles and talking points, too. While pro-Brexit campaigns conjured up images of hordes of Turks arriving on British shores ahead of the

2016 referendum, Europe's far-right insurgents have been even more explicit in playing on fears around immigration and identity. Matteo Salvini has claimed that Jewish financier George Soros "wants to fill Italy and Europe with migrants". For Viktor Orbán Muslim immigration threatens the future of a "Christian Hungary in a Christian Europe".

Increasingly, across the continent, nationalist leaders such as Salvini and Orbán are using the language of religion and identity to pursue culture wars characterised not only by racism, but by sexism, homophobia and aggressive anti-environmentalism. At the same time, many of these populists benefit from networks of funding and support that cross national frontiers, through pressure groups and opaque campaign finance vehicles.

A revealing example of this is the way in which an obscure religious movement set up by American and Russian ultra-conservatives in the late 1990s became a hugely influential network supporting organisations on Europe's radical right. Meet the World Congress of Families.

In late March 2019, almost three years to the day since meeting Donald Trump in the green room in that Pennsylvania ice hockey stadium, Matteo Salvini strode onto the stage to a hero's welcome at the 13th meeting of the now-annual World Congress of Families at Gran Guardia Palace in Verona. In front of him sat the elite of the global conservative right: American anti-abortionists, Australian supporters of gay conversion therapy, Russian Orthodox priests, delegates from Brazilian prime minister Jair Bolsonaro's misnamed Social Liberal Party, and the various factions of Europe's far right.[7]

Salvini did not disappoint. With the sleeves of his white shirt rolled up, the League's leader railed against Islamic extremism, population decline and Europe's crisis of "empty cribs". The crowd applauded wildly when Salvini pulled on a dark blue and white t-shirt with silhouettes of a man, a woman and two small children. "You are the vanguard... that keeps the flame alive for what 99.9 per cent of people want," he declared.[8]

In front of Salvini sat a few hundred ultra-conservative activists (as well as a couple of undercover reporters from *openDemocracy*'s 'Tracking the Backlash' project). Outside the conference centre thousands of protesters against the Congress swarmed Verona's cobblestone streets, carrying colourful banners and chanting slogans against racism and fascism. Italian riot police and paramilitary *carabinieri* formed a human wall around the beautiful 17th-century Gran Guardia Palace.[9]

After Salvini, other speakers claimed that the "natural family" was under such systematic assault that the West was on the precipice of a "demographic winter" because not enough babies will be born.[10] At an informal press conference on the venue's steps, an Italian neo-fascist party announced the launch of a campaign for a referendum to overturn the country's abortion law.[11] (In the US, the Southern Poverty Law Center, which monitors extremist movements, has described the World Congress of Families as an "anti-LGBT hate group".)

Salvini is an unlikely figure to be proclaiming the virtues of family life. He is not known as a particularly god-fearing man. He is divorced, with two children by different women, and has a girlfriend 20 years his junior. He once posed half-naked for a series of "sexy" photos that were auctioned on eBay for charities including an anti-abortion group.[12]

But, like many of Europe's (and America's) far-right politicians, Salvini has used the language of religion for political expediency, even setting himself up in opposition to the relatively liberal Pope Francis. In Verona, the city of Romeo and Juliet, Salvini played the penitent sinner. Before an applauding audience, he talked up his personal failings while also presenting himself as the strongman who could save Italy from homosexuals, feminists, immigrants and Muslims. The pitch was crude, xenophobic and very successful.

By the time the World Congress of Families arrived in Verona, the League was ahead in the polls.

Salvini's best-known policy was a punitive ban on migrant rescue boats entering Italy's waters. Refugees were left to fend for themselves in overcrowded small boats on the open sea. Countless numbers perished. In one night in July 2019 alone, almost 150 died when their dilapidated boat sank off the north African coast.[13] Those that survived were returned to Libya, where migrants have been held in brutal detention centres. Salvini even criminalised Italians who helped migrants with food and shelter. A Catholic priest who had been nominated for the Nobel Peace Prize for his work supporting refugees was placed under police investigation.[14]

This might not sound very Christian, yet it chimes with the World Congress of Families' philosophical outlook. Founded in 1997 after meetings between ultra-conservative religious figures in the US and Russia, the Congress is the closest Europe's radical right has to Davos. Dozens of far-right politicians have attended over the last decade, as have cardinals, bishops and a ragtag crew of minor continental royalty.[15]

Princess Gloria of Thurn und Taxis was once famous for her wild parties and even wilder punk mohawk hair; latterly, she is better known as a WCF regular and a friend of Steve Bannon.[16] Bannon had hoped Princess Gloria would offer the use of her family castle in Regensburg, Germany, for a summer school to educate and train right-wing Catholics, but the aristocrat demurred.*

The Congress's brand of social conservatism has also become part of the new political discourse that is fast becoming normal in many countries. In Hungary, Viktor Orbán has vowed to defend "Christian Europe" from Muslim migration. Poland's Law and Justice party have put in place restrictive limits on women's access to contraception and demonised LGBT people. This has

---

* The princess is also close to Hillary Clinton and was one of about a dozen women to attend her birthday party in 2016.

enthusiastic support from Poland's Catholic establishment, which warns of a "rainbow plague" that has replaced the "red plague" which blighted the country in the communist era.[17] Matteo Salvini – who was upbraided by Pope Francis, who urged Italy to reopen its ports to boats carrying migrants – has claimed that he is "the last of the good Christians".[18] Support for the League among practising Catholics is high. In America, more than 80 per cent of evangelical Christians voted for the thrice-married Donald Trump in 2016.

Many explanations have been offered to account for this rising tide of reaction: economic uncertainty; cultural anxiety; a backlash against liberal attitudes to religion and sexuality. The failures of market capitalism, especially in Eastern Europe. Austerity measures introduced after the financial crisis. The migration crisis on Europe's borders. What is often missed, however, is the role that global flows of political money and influence have played in bringing once diffuse nativist movements together for set-piece occasions such as the gathering in Verona.

The WCF network's support has come primarily from two supposed mortal enemies: the US and Russia. One of the key figures is Konstantin Malofeev, a Kremlin-linked oligarch who made a fortune in private equity then set up his own right-wing think tank.[19] Malofeev, who was placed on international sanctions lists for his support of Russia's annexation of Crimea, is closely aligned with Vladimir Putin. The billionaire businessman's television station spreads a conservative message laced with disinformation. Frequent guests on his programmes include influential Putin acolyte Aleksandr Dugin, a neo-fascist thinker and proponent of 'Eurasianism' – a dream of a revived Russian empire radically opposed to liberal values – and the rabble-rousing fantasist Alex Jones of *Infowars*.

The World Congress of Families has also attracted influential figures from America's powerful religious conservative movements. The WCF's head, Brian Brown, is a father of nine who was raised a Quaker but converted to Catholicism as an adult and made his name fighting against marriage equality in his native California.

(Brown once declared that gay marriage could lead to "a serious push to normalise paedophilia", the kind of statement considered normal in this alternative world.)[20] Brown chose Verona to host the 2019 Congress after the League-led local government defied Italy's abortion laws to declare itself a "pro-life city" and gave public funding to anti-abortion groups.[21]

From the stage in Verona, Brown told delegates that the Congress theme was "the Winds of Change" because "we're seeing a lot of good indications" from countries like Hungary "standing up for the family". Another American, a Missouri lawyer and Republican activist named Ed Marton, arrived at the podium in a red MAGA hat and declared that "Brexit, the Bible and borders" would "make Europe great again".[22]

American ultra-conservatives have a long history of trying to influence international politics.* They have backed homophobic campaigns in Africa and supported draconian anti-abortion laws across Latin America. In Europe, conservative evangelists and libertarians have sent teams of lobbyists to Brussels to petition EU officials and challenge laws against discrimination and hate speech in European courts.[23] They have supported campaigns against LGBT rights in the Czech Republic and Romania, and funded a network of 'grassroots' anti-abortion campaigns in Italy and Spain.

Some of the richest organisations on the US Christian right have spent tens of millions of dollars in Europe: the Billy Graham

---

* The influence of American religious conservatives on European politics extends far beyond the confines of obscure conferences and seminars. In early 2019, another *openDemocracy* investigation found that a dozen groups on the US religious right had spent at least $50 million in Europe, on various causes, over the previous decade. The pattern is similar to the dark money that has long flowed through Washington's sprawling libertarian think tanks. Funds are often raised from anonymous sources. Official filings give very limited insight into how much is really being spent, or where the money is coming from. The true figures are likely to be much higher, but the payments offer a glimpse into how these funds have contributed to the nativist political shift across the Atlantic.

Evangelistic Association; the Alliance Defending Freedom; the American Center for Law and Justice. The latter group, which praised Vladimir Putin's laws banning "gay propaganda", is particularly well connected to the Trump White House – its chief counsel Jay Sekulow was on Trump's legal team during the high-profile Mueller inquiry into Russian interference in the 2016 presidential election.

As in the US, much of the funding for the Christian right's outreach comes from plutocrats and corporations. The Alliance Defending Freedom has received money from the billionaire Prince family of Betsy DeVos, appointed as Trump's education secretary, and her brother Erik Prince, founder of the huge Blackwater security firm.[24] Prince is yet another convert to a defiantly traditionalist version of Catholicism, which he combines with a notably uncharitable vision of the state's social obligations.

US conservative money has had a very tangible impact on Europe's streets. If you are a woman in Italy who unexpectedly becomes pregnant, you might find yourself in one of numerous free counselling services that have popped up across the country run by an Italian charity called Movimento Per la Vita (Movement for Life), modelled on the 'crisis pregnancy centers' in the US. In the clinics, Italian women are told that having an abortion causes cancer and promised financial help if they do not have a termination.[25] These Italian clinics are supported and partly funded from thousands of miles away in Columbus, Ohio, by an organisation called Heartbeat International.

Another high-spending US Christian funder in Europe, the Acton Institute for the Study of Religion and Liberty, was involved through its Italian branch in Steve Bannon's ill-fated plans to turn an ancient abbey into what he called a "gladiator school" for the "next generation of nationalist and populist leaders". From an 800-year-old hilltop monastery in Trisulti, nearly two hours outside Rome, Bannon hoped to propagate populism across Europe. He had already encouraged Salvini to undermine Pope Francis.[26]

(These movements are full of ardent Catholics who hate their own Pope.)

Day-to-day operations at Bannon's "Academy for the Judeo-Christian West" were handled by the Dignitatis Humanae Institute, an anti-abortion group set up by Bannon's friend Benjamin Harnwell while he worked for former British Conservative MEP Nirj Deva in the European Parliament.[27] The academy never got off the ground. Acton's founder publicly distanced himself from Bannon, saying that the Rome office had acted without his knowledge in supporting the project.[28]

But much of the coverage of the controversy surrounding Bannon's scheme missed a significant point about Acton's work. The think tank has an explicit mission to fuse support for free market capitalism with social conservatism. Its funders have included a foundation belonging to the Kochs, the oil magnates who have spent billions pushing libertarian causes and climate change denial in the US. The unholy alliance of fundamentalist Christianity and pro-corporate lobbying has been part of American political life for decades.[29]

Steve Bannon wanted to set himself up as the key broker in the transatlantic conservative network. After his meeting with Matteo Salvini in Washington in April 2016, Bannon and his acolytes stayed in contact with the rising star of the Italian far right. Ted Malloch, an American professor and friend of Nigel Farage based in England, met Salvini on a number of occasions. Ahead of the Brexit referendum, Salvini met Farage and promised to celebrate the demise of the European Union if the UK voted to leave.[30]

In America, intermediaries between the League and Donald Trump's entourage attempted to engineer a second, more substantial encounter between the pair. It never came to pass, but Bannon and Salvini did meet again, in Milan in March 2018. The timing was significant. Just five days earlier, the League had recorded its best performance in an Italian general election. Bannon actively encouraged Salvini to go into the coalition with the Five

Star Movement. "I had gone over [to Italy] and pitched quite hard to Salvini to put the Five Star and the League together, to form a coalition government, because I thought they were both populists," Bannon told me.

Ultimately, Bannon's direct influence on European electoral politics was muted, despite his typically overblown claims. When Bannon announced that he had set up "the Movement" to unite the far right ahead of the 2019 European elections, there was fevered press speculation that Trumpism was coming to Europe. But Salvini and other right-wingers snubbed Bannon's advances. "We don't need him," said Jörg Meuthen, a leader of the far-right Alternative for Germany.[31] Europe's populists had already learned what they needed from Bannon: how to create political momentum by combining fears about immigration with conservative rhetoric about 'family values', and were canny enough to know that an explicit association with Trump and his fixers could be electoral poison in Europe.

Populists were widely expected to make historic gains in the European elections in May 2019. They did win a record number of seats in the European Parliament; however, as a bloc they fell short of their most optimistic predictions, not least because many traditional right and centrist parties adopted similarly hardline stances on immigration in order to draw the sting of their proto-fascist rivals. But in Italy, the openly racist League topped the poll for the first time in its history. Salvini celebrated by holding up a rosary and kissing a small crucifix.

Brian Brown claimed partial credit for what he called the League's "huge victory".[32] The World Congress of Families was on the rise.

Among the most effective speakers in Verona was a telegenic Spaniard with salt-and-pepper stubble named Ignacio Arsuaga. A World Congress of Families veteran, Arsuaga knew how to work the ultra-conservative room for applause. In slow, deliberate tones he told delegates that they were fighting a global "culture war" against "cultural Marxists", "radical feminists" and "LGBT totalitarians".[33] The only way to win was by taking power directly through "parties and elected officials" – and, indirectly, by shifting public opinion. Just as Richard Fink had advised the Kochs four decades earlier, Arsuaga told his audience that they must change the subjects discussed by politicians and voters, making ultra-conservative ideas the new common sense of the 21st century.

Europe's ultra-conservatives had long been planning their rise. In January 2013, around twenty pro-life leaders from Europe and the US met for a retreat in London. There were two issues up for discussion: establishing a Christian-inspired European think tank, and developing ways of advancing conservative policies across the continent. The network – which christened itself Agenda Europe – proposed that lobbyists petition governments to repeal all legislation allowing for divorce, civil partnerships or same-sex adoption, according to a private document called *Restoring the Natural Order*.[34] "Anti-sodomy" laws should be introduced, and all LGBT organisations defunded. By 2018, Agenda Europe had grown to over 100 organisations in more than 30 countries,[35] meeting in secret to implement "a detailed strategy to roll back human rights".[36]

As in the US, Agenda Europe's professional advocacy has had successes. Prohibitions on marriage equality were passed in several Central European countries; the EU created a special envoy on religious discrimination and intolerance (the post was filled by an Agenda Europe member); the Polish government introduced a bill to ban abortion in all cases (which ultimately failed amid mass women's protests).

Ignacio Arsuaga founded one of the most influential groups in these networks: CitizenGo. Launched after the 2013 Congress in Madrid, CitizenGo is the European religious right's answer to online campaign platforms like Avaaz and Change.org that have been popular on the progressive left. CitizenGo has often promoted online petitions around conservative causes. One petition called for a boycott of Netflix after the streaming service announced that it was supporting opponents of a draconian anti-abortion bill in the US state of Georgia. Another asked Disneyland Paris to cancel a gay pride parade.[37] (The Walt Disney Company refused.)

CitizenGo has a presence in a number of European states and is close to conservative American think tanks such as the Leadership Institute. But it is most active in Arsuaga's homeland, where it is known as HazteOir ('Make yourself heard'). When Spain's parliament proposed a law banning discrimination based on sexual orientation, the group hired a plane to carry a banner warning: "They are coming for your children."[38]

HazteOir helped popularise the phrase 'gender ideology', a faux academic catch-all term that depicts feminists and supporters of gay and transgender rights as ideological extremists out to subvert traditional family values. Buses with the word "feminazis" emblazoned across the side, next to an image of Adolf Hitler wearing lipstick, have been driven across Spanish cities. In 2019, HazteOir lost its charitable status after the Spanish government ruled that it "denigrated and devalued" gay people.[39]

Although nominally non-party political, CitizenGo is particularly close to Spain's far-right party, Vox. Since the fall of the dictatorship in the mid-1970s, Spain had been one of the few European states without a serious ultra-conservative political force. That changed in 2014 when a small group of radicals broke away from the conservative Popular Party – which had long contained people nostalgic for the Franco regime – to form Vox.[40]

The new party rose quickly. It captured headlines, promising to deport extremist imams and crush the "criminal" separatist government in Catalonia that was pushing for independence. Vox would take back Gibraltar and reassert Spain's Catholic identity. *Hacer España grande otra vez*: Make Spain great again.

Vox quickly built international alliances. Steve Bannon was, unsurprisingly, a fan. And in an indication of the rightward drift of Britain's historic party of government, Vox was given an audience by British Conservatives. In early 2019, Vox's international spokesperson Ivan Espinosa de los Monteros met with a trio of Tory MPs, including Brexit Minister Chris Heaton-Harris. Afterwards, Espinosa de los Montero told me that he wanted to "establish relationships with parties such as the Conservatives, which I think is our natural ally in the UK".[41]

But while Vox was making friends and influencing people abroad, domestic matters were pressing. By the time the WCF arrived in Verona in late March 2019, Spain was facing a snap general election. Vox needed to raise money, fast.

Spain, like most European countries, has strict political finance laws that cap spending and usually require donor transparency. One way to circumvent funding limits is through third-party campaign groups that can lobby for a party's policies without being formally aligned to them.

In Verona, a senior Vox official told an undercover journalist from *openDemocracy* – posing as an upper-class Scot with a recently acquired inheritance – that he could support the party by giving money "indirectly" to CitizenGo.[42] The Vox staff member compared CitizenGo to a super Pac, the election vehicles that can spend limitless amounts of dark money in American elections without having to reveal their donors.

There have been other signs of super Pac-style dark money on Europe's far right. The Alternative for Germany has been embroiled in a number of funding scandals, including receiving anonymous donations routed through Swiss companies and €150,000 from an obscure Dutch political organisation called the European Identity Foundation.[43] In Germany, donations from non-EU states are prohibited and there are tight controls on anonymous political contributions. AfD was issued with a hefty fine. (The party appealed.)[44]

Third-party campaigns can help political parties in other ways. In Verona, CitizenGo's president Ignacio Arsuaga told the undercover reporter that his funders included Patrick Slim, son of Mexican telecoms magnate Carlos, Mexico's richest man, and that the group was planning a pre-election advertising blitz that would attack negative comments other leaders had made about Vox and support the party's policies on abortion and same-sex marriage.[45] "We're never going to ask people to vote for Vox," Arsuaga said, "but the campaign is going to help Vox indirectly."

CitizenGo's ad campaign was launched a few weeks later. On polling day in April 2019, Vox won 10 per cent of the vote and its first ever seats in parliament. (Arsuaga told *openDemocracy* that "the destination of our funds has always been legal and public".)

CitizenGo exemplifies the ultra-conservative movement's transnationalism. Its board includes the World Congress of Families' Brian Brown and Alexey Komov, a close business associate of the so-called 'Orthodox Oligarch' Konstantin Malofeev. The American political consultant Darian Rafie gave CitizenGo advice on digital campaigning. In Verona, Rafie, a specialist in running clandestine political influence campaigns, boasted to *openDemocracy*'s undercover reporter about his connections with Trump's campaign and far-right parties across Europe.[46]

American political consultants have often brought the most hard-nosed techniques to European politics. During Ireland's abortion referendum in 2018, US conservatives targeted Irish voters on social media, though their efforts seem to have had little impact on the outcome. In Verona, Rafie bragged about the ways in which voters' mobile phone data could be extracted for targeted advertising in the 2020 elections in the US. "There is a lot of stuff to be done with mobile phones and geo-fencing areas,' he told the reporter, adding:

Say there's a rally somewhere, like one of these big Trump campaign rallies, what we'll do is we'll draw a polygon around that

event and then we'll register all the phones that were there…
Then we follow those phones home, and then we know who
they are, and what they do, and now I know what your Netflix
unique ID is, and I've got your Facebook unique ID, so then I
can communicate with you through a whole variety of ways.

Rafie said of this technology: "We can do it in Europe, too." In a
later email, he said that his company's approach was the same as
"many political campaigns and businesses in the United States",
adding that "we should all be frightened by the amount of data
routinely collected, collated and sold by ad networks".[47]

Rafie is right. Google, Facebook and a host of other big tech
giants *are* constantly surveilling us. Our phones track us wherever
we go. Political campaigns are already trying to use this surveillance to their advantage. The Trump 2020 campaign was reported
to be working with a firm that specialises in the mass collection
of smartphone location data for targeted political advertising.[48]
(A Democratic campaign had previously hired the same company.)
The scope for invisible influence campaigns like the ones Rafie
outlined is terrifyingly vast.

Shortly after the World Congress of Families, I called up a
man who knows a lot about the corrosive effect of dark money
in politics. Former US Democratic senator Russ Feingold spent
years trying to clean up American finance laws with his Republican counterpart John McCain. Their bipartisan legislation, which
severely curtailed the scope for dark money in American politics,
was hailed as a major advance in the early years of this century.

What became known as the McCain–Feingold Act did not last
long, however. Citizens United – a 'political action committee' that
funded conservative causes – challenged the law. In 2010, the US
Supreme Court decided that corporations and rich foundations
should be treated as individuals whose free speech needed
protection, paving the way for unlimited anonymous political
spending and ushering in the super Pac revolution in American

politics. In 2016, super Pacs in the US spent more than $1.4 billion on political campaigns.

Feingold, who has a friendly demeanour and a thick Midwestern drawl, highlighted the contradiction between the nativist appeals of Europe's insurgent far right and their reliance on international networks of finance and patronage.

> They are trying to appeal to ultra-nationalist sentiments, but they are using tactics that are completely contrary to the sovereignty of those countries. These are international actors, oligarchs and others who are trying to control the political processes of these countries. Even if you are a nationalist, one would think you would be a little bit concerned about that.

Feingold told me that Europe needed to be wary of making "the same mistakes that were made here in the United States".

It might be too late for that. Already the use of supposedly independent pressure groups to push party political messages and act as super Pacs is making it harder to trace where political funding is coming from. Europe's nativist surge has not just benefited from international money and expertise. It is also aided by a sprawling, global network of far-right activists online who have sought to manipulate and distort elections at home and abroad.

In early February 2018, Luca Traini drove his black Alfa Romeo into the centre of Macerata, a small city in central Italy. Over the course of two mid-morning hours, he shot six African migrants. A Ghanaian man on his way to get a haircut was hit in the chest. People fled for their lives through busy shopping streets. Remarkably, nobody was killed.[49]

Police quickly apprehended Traini, parked in front of a monumental archway built during the Mussolini era. He was wrapped in an Italian flag and had a neo-Nazi tattoo on his forehead. When police searched his home, they found a copy of *Mein Kampf*.[50]

Three days earlier, the body of an Italian teenage girl had been found mutilated, hidden in two suitcases, allegedly murdered by a Nigerian drug dealer. Traini, a 28-year-old former local election candidate for the League, had vowed to take revenge.

The reaction to Traini's shooting spree was deeply partisan. Many blamed the victims for the racist attack that had targeted them. On the general election campaign trail, Matteo Salvini said that Traini had been provoked by an influx of "hundreds of thousands of illegal migrants".[51] Traini was hailed as a hero on the websites and forums where far-right supporters from around the world increasingly congregate. The spike in traffic on neo-Nazi message boards in the immediate aftermath of the attack was so pronounced that far-right activists dubbed it the 'Traini effect'. This was the new reactionary internationalism in action. The gunman who killed 51 at a mosque in Christchurch, New Zealand, in March 2019 had scrawled Traini's name on a rifle cartridge used in the massacre.[52]

The Traini effect was not confined to the darkest reaches of white nationalism. In the aftermath of the shooting, memes quickly spread across mainstream social media lionising Traini as the "god" of a coming race war. Far-right activists from across Europe and the US pushed depictions of Traini as Neo, the protagonist of *The Matrix*.[53] Italian fascists even copied the format of an American far-right campus campaign – "It's OK to be white" – and encouraged supporters to circulate fliers with Traini's image in universities, in an attempt to spark confrontations with left-wing students. In the US, the neo-Nazi *Daily Stormer* ran articles in praise of Traini. (The American alt-right has often used the prospect of racially motivated violence in Europe, and exaggerated its extent, to build support at home.)

Traini fed into an unprecedented surge in online far-right activity ahead of Italy's general election. The same Italian extremist groups who had vaunted Traini as a "god of war" pushed out fascist comments and slogans on the messaging app Telegram. Far-right articles, memes and hashtags fanned out across Facebook, Instagram and Twitter.[54] The aim was, in a US alt-right phrase lifted from *The Matrix*, to 'red pill the normies' – radicalise the mainstream.

Online activity fed offline influence operations, too. Far-right supporters organised street stalls, especially on campuses, to support both the League and the Brothers of Italy, a party that emerged from Italy's post-fascist right and was a member of the same European Parliament group as the British Conservatives before Brexit.

The Italian far right also had international assistance. Message boards on 4chan and 8chan served as multilingual global hubs. An analysis by the London-based Institute for Strategic Dialogue concluded that the 2018 Italian election campaign showed "the maturation of an international consciousness around tactics which have previously worked well for extreme-right activists".[55]

The League were the main beneficiaries. Memes superimposed Matteo Salvini onto Pepe the Frog. (In alt-right circles, being depicted as this green, anthropomorphic cartoon character is a high honour.) One Italian far-right activist told his colleagues: "I have redpilled my friends, so we have six more votes for Matteo."[56]

Salvini himself has long been a master social media manipulator. As he demonstrated with Donald Trump, his campaign trick is the smiling selfie. "Salvini is a chameleon who learned how to control consensus through social media," says Italian investigative journalist Jacopo Iacoboni. Steve Bannon told me that Salvini is a "real master" of online organisation "like Bolsonaro and Farage".

The League spent heavily on targeted Facebook ads playing on Salvini's personal brand. This mix of mainstream coverage for the League's anti-system, anti-immigrant, anti-EU message and its more shadowy far-right online support helped the party more than triple its share of the vote to over 17 per cent in the 2018 Italian general election. Afterwards, Salvini declared, "Thank God for the

Internet, thank God for social media, thank God for Facebook."[57]

He was not the only xenophobic politician to be grateful to the god of Facebook. In Spain, Vox consciously bypassed traditional media outlets to appeal directly to voters with emotive images. Ultra-nationalist videos told frightening stories about immigration.[58] Others provided a hopeful vision of the future; Vox's leader Santiago Abascal on horseback or standing in the rain looking out over fields and vineyards.[59]

This dual digital strategy has been very successful, especially with young people, who are often thought less likely to be attracted to conservative politics. Vox has more followers on Instagram than the Socialists and the left-wing Podemos combined.[60]

In a second Spanish general election in November 2019, Vox put the "menace" of migrant children at the centre of an aggressively racist campaign.[61] Amid widespread disillusionment at the country's gridlocked politics, the far-right party's support surged. Vox finished third, more than doubling its seats in parliament.

Xavier Arbos, a professor of constitutional law at the University of Barcelona, said that Vox had tapped a growing wave of reaction. "Just as happened with Trump in the US and with Brexit in Britain, there are obviously Spaniards who feel isolated by the political system in an era of globalisation," he told the *Independent*.[62]

Vox also benefited from a huge social media reach that exhibited some suspicious characteristics. Many of the most prolific pro-Vox accounts displayed behaviour that digital researchers would call unusual, according to research published in early 2019. Over the course of a year, some 3,000 Twitter accounts sent four and a half million pro-Vox and anti-Islamic tweets.[63] They often published identical posts that were designed to look spontaneous but were in fact coordinated disinformation. In one instance, a raft of pro-Vox accounts tweeted images of a riot said to be happening in a Muslim district in France. The photographs were actually of anti-government protests in Algeria.

Vox supporters were particularly likely to share conspiracy

theories. There were stories about "white genocide" and myriad mentions of Jewish billionaire George Soros, who had barely featured in Spanish politics until Vox started talking about him. Similar hyper-partisan political news sites had also proliferated in Italy and Brazil ahead of their elections in 2018. In both countries, these far-right portals amplified narratives – about immigration in Italy, corruption in Brazil – before they had become part of the mainstream discourse.

"Americans will recognise these types of sites," *Washington Post* columnist Anne Applebaum wrote of Vox's anonymous digital boosters. "They function not unlike *Infowars*, *Breitbart*, the infamous partisan sites that operated from Macedonia during the U.S. presidential campaign or, indeed, the Facebook pages created by Russian military intelligence, all of which produced hypercharged, conspiratorial, partisan news and outraged headlines that could then be pumped into hypercharged, conspiratorial echo chambers."[64]

Many of Vox's digital echo chambers pushed religiously tinged disinformation. Muslims wanted to take Spain back to the time of the Moors. Leftists were encouraging children to have abortions. Highly emotive messages about moral issues – especially those that spark feelings of fear – are a particularly effective way to spread disinformation. Similar tactics were used during the 2016 presidential election, when pro-Kremlin accounts appealed directly to Christian fundamentalists by sharing images that showed Hillary Clinton, devil horns protruding, arm-wrestling with Jesus.[65] Religion, as digital expert Claire Wardle explained to me, "is one of the best ways to spread disinformation online."

Digital disinformation and wealthy foreign donors are not the only sources of electoral interference. States often meddle in each other's politics. Between 1946 and 1989, the US intervened in more than 60 international elections, mostly in secret without announcing their covert operations to the world.[66] Britain and

France routinely interfered in their former colonies. The Soviet Union funded communist parties around the world. Eastern bloc intelligence services even bought up pliant British Labour MPs. More recently, of course, Russia has been implicated in a spate of high-profile foreign electoral influence campaigns.

Aside from the 2016 US presidential election, Moscow's best-documented external electoral interest is in Europe's populist right. French National Rally leader Marine Le Pen took €11 million in loans from Russian banks, including one close to the Kremlin. (She insisted that the deal was commercial, not political.) Ahead of the 2016 EU referendum, Brexit's most generous backer, Arron Banks, discussed lucrative gold and diamond investment deals offered through the Russian embassy in London. Banks has said that he declined the offers. The leader of Austria's far-right FPÖ party, Heinz-Christian Strache, was forced to resign in 2019 after being filmed in an elaborate sting operation discussing the exchange of public contracts for Russian campaign support.[67]

The Kremlin is particularly well connected to Matteo Salvini and the League. The party has long courted Russian influence. The openly fascist Russian philosopher Aleksandr Dugin has often been invited to League events in Italy. After Salvini took over the leadership in late 2013, the party became more overtly pro-Kremlin.[68]

In February 2014, Salvini established a cultural association to build links with Moscow. Its honorary chair was Aleksey Komov, Russia's representative at the World Congress of Families. The association's president, Gianluca Savoini, a journalist and advisor on Russia for the League, said the goal was to make the Italian public aware that "it is absurd and counterproductive for the EU to view Russia as an enemy and not as a fundamental geopolitical, military, as well as economic ally".[69]

The League's affinities with Vladimir Putin's authoritarian state were hardly a secret. In 2014, Salvini led a party delegation on a visit to Crimea, by then annexed by Russia. He travelled to Moscow numerous times and met Putin to discuss the "absurd sanctions against Russia" imposed by the EU. In early 2017, Salvini returned to Russia to sign a cooperation agreement between the League and the United Russia party.[70] Putin's party had signed similar pacts with the Austrian Freedom Party.*

The relationship between the League and the Kremlin seems to have extended beyond fraternal visits. In October 2018, three Russian officials and three Italians, including Gianluca Savoini from the League's Russian cultural association, convened in Moscow's Metropol Hotel to discuss plans for a "great alliance". In an espresso-fuelled conversation in the hotel lobby, the men negotiated the terms of a deal to covertly channel tens of millions of dollars of Russian money to the League. At least three million metric tonnes of diesel fuel would be sold at a discount to an Italian oil company by a group close to Putin's government. The profits – estimated at $65 million – would be secretly funnelled to the League, via intermediaries, to fund its political campaign ahead of the European elections.[71]

It is not clear if the oil deal was ever done. Salvini – who did not attend the meeting himself but was in Moscow at the time – dismissed the story as "fake news" when reports originally surfaced in the Italian media in early 2019. But *Buzzfeed* later released a tape of a detailed conversation between the Russians and Italians that discussed clandestine political funding. Savoini can be heard saying that the Italian party wanted "a new Europe" that is "close to Russia".[72]

That private chat in the Metropol Hotel was politically explosive. Italian electoral law bans political parties from accepting foreign donations. Amid questions about Russian influence, Salvini walked out of government in August 2019, in an attempt to force a general

---

* The Freedom Party and the League are sister parties, but fell out in 2018 when the Austrians proposed allowing German speakers in the Italian province of South Tyrol to apply for Austrian passports. Despite all the talk of international populist alliances, Europe's nationalists are still, well, nationalists.

election. He failed. The Five Star Movement formed a new coalition partnership with the centre-left, leaving the League in the cold.

Salvini, it seemed, had over-reached. He had shown himself to be callow and prone to political misjudgements. "I don't think he played it right," Steve Bannon said of his one-time mentee. "He made a couple of tactical mistakes."

But there is little sign that the allegations about Kremlin interference have cost the League very much in electoral terms. "Even though he's out of government he is more popular than ever," Bannon said of Salvini. In October 2019, a League-led coalition swept into power in Umbria, ending half a century of left-wing rule in that region.

Yet Salvini's grip on power in Italy has been shaky. At the end of 2019, he was in opposition, still competing with other parties for control of Italy's democratic institutions. We don't have to look far, however, to find a European state where disinformation and targeted influence campaigns have already created a much more solidly grounded 'illiberal democracy'.

In late 2017, I arrived in an icy Budapest to give a journalism workshop at the Central European University. One of the first things I noticed when I disembarked from the airport bus in the centre of the Hungarian capital was the posters. They seemed to be everywhere. From billboards and bus shelters a craggy, ageing face framed by a thin smile and an aquiline nose looked down. I recognised it instantly as the CEU's Hungarian-born founder George Soros. Next to the image was a line of text: "Don't let Soros have the last laugh."[73]

This propaganda drive cost the Hungarian government almost €20 million. For Viktor Orbán, it was small change in his almost decade-long campaign to portray Soros as the number one enemy of the Hungarian people. Its success inspired far-right leaders and activists around the world.

Orbán, a well-built man with the broad shoulders of a weight-lifter, has revelled in his status as Europe's most successful national-ist demagogue. As Brussels looks askance, Orbán has built barbed wire fences to repel immigrants. Laws have been introduced to protect 'family values': marriage is defined as solely between a man and a woman; human life begins at the moment of conception; large families get mortgage breaks; there are tax incentives for stay-at-home mums. Hungary's media and civil society are tightly controlled, too. Many of the institutions that Soros funded – including the Central European University – have effectively been forced out of the country.

A few months after I gave my talk at the CEU in Budapest, Orbán made a pre-election address in front of the Hungarian parliament. Even by Orbán's standards it was more foghorn than dog whistle. The prime minister told his compatriots that they were "fighting an enemy that is different from us. Not open but hid-ing. Not straightforward but crafty. Not honest but unprincipled. Not national but international. Does not believe in working but speculates with money. Does not have its own homeland but feels it owns the whole world."[74]

Orbán's words could have been lifted from *The Protocols of the Elders of Zion*. When Jewish leaders accused him of anti-Semitism, Orbán decried them as enemies of free speech.[75] In April 2018, his Fidesz party won a third consecutive term in office.

It is easy to forget that in the late 1980s, Viktor Orbán was one of the most articulate voices of a new liberal generation railing against the moribund communist system. He began working at the Central European Research Group, which was funded by the Soros Foundation. Orbán soon received a Soros-funded scholar-ship to study at Oxford, but only stayed in England for three months before returning to Hungary to run in the first free elec-tions in 1990,[76] winning a seat for the recently created Fidesz. He was just 26. Within eight years, he was prime minister and widely seen as one of the most trenchant anti-authoritarian voices in

Eastern European politics. But after a single term, he lost power in 2002.

Defeat hit Orbán hard. Out of office and languishing in opposition, he vowed to regain power. The one-time Hayekian libertarian reinvented himself as the nationalist protector of Hungarian minorities in neighbouring states. He made stirring speeches defending the Catholic Church. "Personally, Orbán has never been very religious," says Kim Lane Scheppele, a legal scholar at Princeton who studies Hungary and first met Orbán in the 1990s. "He used this new uniform as a route to power. That's all that matters to him. Power."

Orbán's ultra-conservative reinvention was not an overnight success. In 2006, Fidesz unexpectedly lost a second successive election. Now, Orbán looked abroad for strategic advice, to the world of highly paid political consultants. Israeli president Benjamin Netanyahu introduced his Hungarian friend to the legendary US pollster Arthur J. Finkelstein.[77]

Few lobbyists were as well connected in Republican politics as Finkelstein. Having worked for Barry Goldwater, Richard Nixon and Ronald Reagan, and once shared a college radio show with the radical libertarian Ayn Rand, Finkelstein had begun running a consultancy that specialised in working in post-communist states in Eastern Europe. In Ukraine, Finkelstein introduced another veteran Republican lobbyist, Paul Manafort, to pro-Russian Ukrainian oligarchs.*

A long-time New York associate of Donald Trump, Finkelstein

---

* Manafort went on to advise Ukraine's then president Viktor Yanukovych. The American political consultant told Yanukovych, an old-school autocrat from the Russian-speaking east, to play on the country's geographic and linguistic divisions to foster grievances. In 2014, Yanukovych was overthrown in a revolution that continues to divide Ukraine. As chair of the Trump campaign in 2016, Manafort encouraged the Republican presidential nominee to adopt similarly divisive tactics, playing on America's ethnic and racial tensions.

also had a hand in Manafort becoming the Republican candidate's campaign chair for five months in 2016. (Manafort was later given a seven-and-a-half-year prison sentence after pleading guilty to fraud and conspiracy in his lobbying for pro-Kremlin politicians in Ukraine. A federal judge in Washington denounced him as a man who "spent a significant portion of his career gaming the system".[78])

Finkelstein made Hungary the centre of his political consulting empire. He relocated to Budapest and began working for Viktor Orbán. Just like Vote Leave's Thomas Borwick, 'Finkie', as Orbán liked to call him, believed that the most successful political campaigns united voters against a clearly defined enemy.

It wasn't hard to find a villain in crisis-stricken Hungary. The country was a financial mess. In 2008, Hungary was bailed out by the 'Troika' – the World Bank, the EU and the International Monetary Fund – who demanded harsh austerity measures. Finkelstein and his protégé and business partner George Birnbaum told Orbán to target "the bureaucrats" and "foreign capital".[79]

The strategy was a huge success. In 2010, Orbán won two-thirds of the vote. Safely returned as prime minister, he now sought to consolidate his rule. "We had an incumbent with a historic majority, something that had never happened in Hungary before," George Birnbaum later told Swiss journalist Hannes Grassegger.[80] "You need to keep the base energised, make sure that on Election Day they have a reason to go out and vote."

Finkelstein set about finding a new foe for Orbán. This time, however, the adversary would have a face. "Arthur always said that you did not fight against the Nazis but against Adolf Hitler. Not against al-Qaeda, but against Osama bin Laden," Birnbaum said.[81] Finkelstein had an idea for the perfect guy in the black hat. Someone who was hated by the right as a Jewish funder of progressive causes, and despised by the left as the embodiment of big capital: George Soros. Orbán's friendship with Netanyahu and vocal support for Israel gave political cover against accusations of anti-Semitism.

With uncanny prescience, Finkelstein had come up with a "campaign idea, so big and so Mephistophelian, that it will outlive itself". It was a grim irony that the Soros bogeyman was created by two Jews whose families had fled Europe. Birnbaum's father was an Auschwitz survivor.

Soros was already a hate figure on the American right by the time Finkelstein pitched up in Budapest. He had spent huge sums funding political movements around the world, including in the US. Soros first attracted the attention of the Republican right after speaking out against the Iraq War and donating money to the Democrats against George W. Bush in 2004. On Fox News, Bill O'Reilly described Soros as "an extremist who wants open borders, a one-world foreign policy, legalised drugs, euthanasia, and on and on".[82]

Orbán went further. With Finkelstein's guidance, he constructed Soros as an existential threat to Hungary's very way of life. Soros's support for democracy and open societies was really a stalking horse for a globalist plot to destroy the nation state itself. This was a new model for attack politics in an era of global division, one that the far right would exploit to devastating effect.[83]

During the 2016 US presidential campaign, Soros went from obscure Fox News talking point to moral panic. As I drove across the United States in the months before the election, I was bewildered by the number of voters who mentioned Soros. His name came up in blue-collar bars in Bethlehem, Pennsylvania, and outside upmarket shopping malls in Cleveland, Ohio.

At the time, I was barely aware of Soros. I knew he had 'broken the Bank of England', making $1 billion on Black Wednesday in 1992 as Britain was forced to withdraw from the European Exchange Rate Mechanism. I knew he was a major philanthropist. But that was about it. By the end of my reporting trip through America, I was a Soros aficionado. I had seen his face surrounded by flames in a poster in the window of a suburban house and been told that he was masterminding a communist takeover of America. Trump's final TV ad featured Soros as a visual representative of "global special interests".

It subsequently emerged that accounts connected to the GRU, the Kremlin's military-intelligence agency, were pushing Soros conspiracy theories on Facebook ahead of the presidential election.[84] Russia had long criticised Soros, wary of the democratic revolutions in Ukraine, Georgia and other post-communist states on its borders that it believed Soros had supported.[85] In office, Trump would often spread anti-Soros propaganda, mendaciously accusing him of funding a caravan of migrants on America's southern border.

Soros has also emerged as a cipher in British political debate. He openly spent millions funding anti-Brexit campaigns after the EU referendum, much to the chagrin of right-wing newspapers. During the 2019 British general election, Conservative candidates were accused of having shared Soros conspiracy theories on social media.[86] Labour was also embroiled in a long-running controversy over anti-Semitism in the party.

All of this would be familiar to watchers of Hungarian politics. Orbán, as his confidant Steve Bannon pointed out, was "Trump before Trump". He was the only EU leader to endorse Trump in 2016, and he had taken the anti-Soros mythology and run with it. After Orbán's re-election in 2018, the crackdown on Soros-funded organisations intensified. An Act of Parliament was passed to change the licensing of foreign universities and limit international-funded non-governmental organisations. Vladimir Putin had done the very same. Orbán's move was directed very precisely at Soros-funded institutions.

The Central European University, which had promoted independent academic research in the region since 1991, eventually announced that it was moving much of its operations to Vienna, though the Budapest campus remains open. "In Hungary, the law is a tool of power," Michael Ignatieff, the university's rector, said at the time.[87] The Hungarian office of Open Society Foundations, the main vehicle for Soros's philanthropy, closed.

The relentless focus on Soros gave Orbán the cover to dismantle the pillars of Hungarian democracy. In 2011, a year after re-election, he introduced an entirely new constitution in just nine days.[88] Veteran judges on the constitutional court were forced to retire so that their seats could be filled with more Fidesz-friendly jurists.[89] Most of the media was taken over by the party's oligarch supporters.

Laws were introduced that distorted the popular ballot. Orbán gerrymandered electoral districts to ensure his dominance. Liberal strongholds, predominantly in cities, were divided so that large numbers of voters were packed into a handful of parliamentary seats, while districts in Hungary's conservative countryside have far fewer people. Fake parties were created to split the anti-Fidesz vote.[90]

In 2014, Fidesz received fewer votes than it had in 2002 and 2006, when it lost elections, but it ended up with the parliamentary supermajority that it needed to push through radical constitutional changes.[91] In 2018, Fidesz won more than two-thirds of the seats in the Hungarian parliament despite taking less than half of the vote. "Orbán combined American-style gerrymandering with the British first-past-the-post system," legal scholar Kim Lane Scheppele told me. "He has turned Hungary into a dictatorship in plain sight."

Orbán is a master of distraction and political sleight of hand. Often when he introduces a legislative change that cements his power, it has been accompanied by a contentious symbolic gesture that flames Hungary's culture wars and grabs the attention of the opposition and international media. "When Orbán wants to do something in Parliament, he will announce that he is building a statue to a wartime anti-Semite or something equally appalling, and everyone runs off to cover that," said Lane Scheppele. "It's the same tactics that Boris Johnson and Dominic Cummings use in Britain."

Ahead of the 2018 general election, Israeli private intelligence firm Black Cube was reportedly involved in a campaign to discredit Hungarian NGOs, especially those linked to Soros. Black Cube agents using false identities secretly recorded prominent civil society activists.[92] The tapes were released to a Hungarian government-controlled daily newspaper three weeks before the vote. Orbán used the revelations to attack civil society organisations.

Black Cube had previously been hired by disgraced Hollywood mogul Harvey Weinstein to collect information on actresses and journalists investigating his sexual predations, but this was the first time that the firm, created by former Israeli intelligence officers, had been cited in an election campaign. Black Cube refused to confirm or deny whether it had worked in Hungary but said it fully complied with the law and took "legal advice from the world's leading law firms".

Orbán's political takeover – buttressed by a German industrial lobby that relies on cheap labour in Hungarian plants – has largely been bankrolled by cash plundered from the European Union that he rails so fervently against. A 2019 *New York Times* investigation found that Orbán uses billions of euros in EU subsidies as a patronage fund that enriches his allies, protects his political interests and punishes his rivals.[93] "The ideology is a ruse. The money is where the action is," said Lane Scheppele.

Brussels has done little to stem the tide of Hungary's rampant corruption. Instead, Orbán has treated his frequent public dressing-downs in the European Parliament as a PR opportunity. He smiles for the cameras as Western politicians berate him. His florid responses – anti-liberal, anti-globalist, anti-EU – are clipped and circulated across social media.

It is a message that chimed with voters across post-communist Europe, frustrated after decades of being told that there was no alternative to a market-led liberal democracy that often enriched the elite and left the majority disenfranchised and alienated. As Bulgarian political scientist Ivan Krastev and US law professor

Stephen Holmes wrote: "The very conceit that 'there is no other way' provided an independent motive for the wave of populist xenophobia and reactionary nativism that began in central and eastern Europe, and is now washing across much of the world."[94]

Europe's migration crisis gave Orbán the chance to take his message of 'illiberal democracy' to an international stage. In July 2015, as the number of Syrians coming through Turkey and Greece increased, Orbán adopted a very aggressive stance against accepting refugees. As the Hungarian government hastily erected holding centres along its border with Serbia, he warned of invading Muslim hordes. When Angela Merkel announced that Germany would admit hundreds of thousands of refugees, Orbán and other leaders of the so-called Visegrád group – the Czech Republic, Hungary, Poland and Slovakia – publicly rejected the German prime minister's humanitarian appeal. "I think it is just bullshit," said Mária Schmidt, one of Orbán's closest political advisors.[95]

For most refugees, Hungary was only a staging point on the way to Western Europe. The numbers settling in Central and Eastern Europe have been relatively small. But immigration plays into wider demographic concerns in many post-socialist states. More citizens have left the EU's eastern states in the wake of the 2009 financial crisis than have arrived as migrants.[96] Images of crowds of migrants outside Budapest's Keleti train station fed a perception that Hungary was being overrun.

Orbán declared that the gravest threat to the survival of the white Christian majority in Europe was the incapacity of Western societies to defend themselves. Hungary's government passed a series of anti-immigration measures, including a 'Stop Soros' bill in 2018, which makes it a criminal offence to provide assistance to undocumented migrants applying for asylum or residency permits.

The Hungarian Helsinki Committee, a human rights organisation, has accused Orbán of systematically denying food to failed asylum seekers held in detention camps on Hungary's border – an action it described as "an unprecedented human rights violation in 21st-century Europe". He has also made homelessness a criminal offence.[97]

The migration crisis elevated Orbán's status among global ultra-conservatives. When the World Congress of Families met in Budapest in 2017, Orbán was met with rapt applause. Playing to both his domestic audience and the Christian gallery, Orbán announced that he was setting up a think tank to address the biggest issue facing Europe – white people not having enough children. Afterwards, he posed for photographs with WCF chief Brian Brown.

Orbán's appeals to 'Christian liberty' may be just rhetoric, but he has actively sought to turn Budapest into a capital of conservative thought. American white nationalist Richard Spencer has been a frequent guest, as have numerous leading Russian conservatives and former Australian prime minister Tony Abbott. Steve Bannon told me that he was "very close" to Orbán and had to cancel a scheduled visit to Budapest in late 2019 to assist President Trump's battle against impeachment.

British Tories looked eastwards, too. Conservative MPs such as Daniel Kawczynski expressed their admiration for Orbán's regime. A group of pro-Brexit libertarians, including leading figures from the TaxPayers' Alliance and the Adam Smith Institute, lobbied for the establishment of a Museum of Communist Terror in London inspired by the similarly titled Budapest attraction.* Elsewhere, former Thatcher speech writer John O'Sullivan – a prominent advocate of the Anglosphere at the turn of the millennium – has run the Orbán-friendly Danube Institute think tank in Budapest.

In December 2019, shortly after the British general election,

---

* The House of Terror in Budapest has been criticised for largely blaming Communist crimes on foreigners, principally Russians, and for failing to accurately portray the fate of hundreds of thousands of Hungarian Jews who perished during the Holocaust.

Tim Montgomerie, an advisor on social justice to Boris Johnson, addressed a Danube Institute meeting in Budapest. Montgomerie praised Hungary's "interesting early thinking" on "the limits of liberalism". "I think we are seeing that in the UK as well," he said, adding that Britain should forge a "special relationship" with Hungary after Brexit.[98] It's hard not to see traces of Orbán's ostentatious populism in Prime Minister Boris Johnson.

Orbán, however, demurred when Brexiters called on him to come to their aid. Despite pleas from his long-time ally Nigel Farage, Orbán refused to block the European Union's extension to Brexit in September 2019.

That same month, at an international demography conference in Budapest, Orbán returned to his favourite themes: immigration and George Soros. "Political forces", he said, wanted to replace the white European population with "others". What more openly fascist thinkers call 'the great replacement' is promoted by the Hungarian head of state.

"The political vision nurtured by the World Congress of Families has become frighteningly mainstream," says my *openDemocracy* colleague Claire Provost, an investigative journalist who has spent years tracking the backlash against rights for women, LGBTQI people and minorities. "The longer I spend with these groups, the less I think they're actually fixated on specific issues like abortion. While they talk a lot about women's wombs, theirs is a much wider political project, to support authoritarian societies led by 'strongmen'."

As this book has looked primarily at the effect of dark money and disinformation on Britain, this chapter has focused on examples of the nativist surge in some of the UK's European neighbours: Italy, Spain and Hungary. In all three, nationalist appeals to religion and identity have been underpinned by international networks of political influence and digital disinformation. The effects of this can be seen most dramatically in Hungary, where Viktor Orbán has shown how quickly supposedly liberal democratic norms and conventions can be defanged and dismantled.

Of course, autocrats are also on the rise in many other parts of the world, bolstered by many of the same American and Russian networks and socio-political dynamics that are helping to upend politics in Europe. From the Philippines and Brazil to Turkey and India, a new generation of strongmen has emerged. They often use similar tactics – weaponising religion and mobilising fear of the 'other' – but have adapted these strategies to local circumstances.

The authoritarian model "moves around not as a caravan but as spare parts", says Princeton legal scholar Kim Lane Scheppele. Populists take inspiration from one another but also buy advice from "political consultants that go from place to place and help the new autocrats set up shop". Steve Bannon boasted to me in early 2020 that he talked to Europe's populist leaders "on a fairly regular basis" and was "still working behind the scenes driving stuff".

Dark money and demagogic online campaigns have been particularly effective in societies where democracy is comparatively young (although, as this book has explored, this offers no grounds for complacency in so-called 'established' democracies like the UK and the US). We often assume that, in Europe, 1945 was a kind of year zero in which fascist, anti-Semitic and other political traditions of the pre-war right were eradicated, but that was far from the case. In painting George Soros as a mortal enemy of the Hungarian people, Orbán draws on local fears of the Jewish 'other' that are centuries old.

Like the Law and Justice Party in Poland, Fidesz has tapped into traditions of anti-Semitism that are deeply rooted in these staunchly Catholic, largely rural societies. Orbán often celebrates Hungary's inter-war dictatorship, in which anti-Semitism was rampant. The post-war seizure of power by a Stalinist clique backed by the Red Army did little more than drive those attitudes underground, out of sight but not out of mind. In the Soviet Union and across the Eastern Bloc, 'cosmopolitanism' was often a synonym for Jews. Orbán's rhetoric is less *sui generis* and more a product of deep, divisive histories.

Similarly, in Italy and Spain the fascist past has in many important respects never been fully faced. After the war, Italy eschewed any serious process of restitution. Bureaucrats and lawyers loyal to the regime continued in post. Neo-fascist parties were allowed to operate openly. Shrines to Mussolini can still be found all over the country. All the while, there was a single party in power with enormous scope for patronage and corruption. Italy was a very qualified democracy in which the main opposition party could never attain power.

Since the 1990s, there has been a determined effort to push back Italy's post-war anti-fascist consensus, which permeated literature and culture more generally but was never really shared by the dominant Christian Democratic Party. Matteo Salvini draws on this history and is supported by a flourishing subculture of identitarian grouplets and magazines and football fan clubs. (Silvio Berlusconi pioneered much of this strategy in the early 1990s, whipping up rage against a corrupt and incompetent political elite just as Trump did two decades later.)

In Spain, Vox draws from a barely repressed legacy of Franco, which remains politically incendiary. In October 2019, protests broke out when *El Caudillo*'s body was exhumed from a monumental state-built mausoleum and reburied in a low-key municipal cemetery;[99] two weeks later, Vox won 15 per cent of the vote in the general election.

There is often a temptation to believe that your country is immune, or at least inoculated, from the worst authoritarian excesses. I watched the early hours of Donald Trump's election victory in 2016 in a bar in New York's East Village, surrounded by young liberals. As Republican victories mounted up and Clinton's path to the White House became ever more vertiginous, one turned to me and said, "Even if Trump wins, it doesn't matter that much. The constitution will protect us."

I heard a similar sentiment dozens of times in the hours and days that followed. But in truth, the American system of checks and balances had already been eroded long before Trump arrived on Pennsylvania Avenue. Previous presidents routinely used executive orders to bypass Congress, especially after the end of the Cold War.

In the UK, the limits of an uncodified constitution have become increasingly apparent. Brexit has seen executive power increase markedly. In the name of popular sovereignty, long-held conventions of British parliamentary politics have been abrogated. The Supreme Court may have ruled it unlawful, but many voters seem to have little problem with a prime minister misleading the Queen, as Boris Johnson did when proroguing Parliament in late 2019. The end, it seems, justifies the means.

As the rise of nativist movements in Europe graphically shows, hard-won political battles can quickly be reversed. Change does not always mean progress: it can bring fewer rights, freedoms and opportunities. Dark money and shadowy, unaccountable networks of political influence and persuasion, empowered and amplified by powerful and largely unregulated technology, are swiftly bending democracy out of shape. Worse still, they are destroying faith in the idea that politics can and should be transparent, and accountable to citizens.

What, if anything, can be done to reverse the crisis in democracy? Can we halt the seemingly unstoppable rise of disinformation and dirty politics? Or has democracy already gone dark?

11

DEMOCRACY GOING DARK

On a wet morning in late November 2019, two weeks before Boris Johnson won his "stonking" majority in the British general election, I filed into an overcrowded room on the first floor of a cream-coloured 19th-century mansion in the wealthiest corner of London's West End. The Institute for Government, one of Britain's most respected independent think tanks, was hosting a lunchtime panel discussion on the subject: 'Can we trust our electoral system?'

The lugubrious title was apt. The election campaign had already witnessed an unprecedented surge in dirty tricks, with social media the key staging ground. The Conservatives were promoting a website pretending to be the Labour manifesto. Partisans had bought up countless 'dark ads' on Facebook. A few days earlier, the Tories had shamelessly rebranded their Twitter account as a fact-checking site during a debate between Boris Johnson and Jeremy Corbyn. Ten days later, senior party advisors would spread the rumour that an aide had been punched by a Labour supporter outside a hospital in Leeds where a sick child had been photographed on the floor. The falsehood would blaze across the Internet long after it was debunked.

Roughly four dozen people had given up their lunch hour that damp day in London to hear about the state of British democracy. It wasn't pretty. Every one of the five panellists on stage at the

Institute for Government, ranging from academics and policy wonks to the chair of the Electoral Commission, warned that the country's democratic process was failing.

The biggest source of disinformation "is the governing party, and they are the ones charged with changing the law", said Will Moy, chief executive of Full Fact, an independent fact-checking website that vainly tried to hold politicians to account during the election campaign. Irish transparency campaigner Liz Carolan – whom I had first met while writing about online misinformation during Ireland's 2018 abortion referendum – warned that Britain's hidebound electoral system was ripe for foreign interference. She singled out a potential post-Brexit border poll on Irish unity as a particular concern.

The Electoral Commission's Sir John Holmes, a former career diplomat, was the most circumspect speaker. But even he noted that Britain's "electoral laws are fundamentally unfit for purpose". Shell companies, he said, could donate to British political parties; a maximum fine of £20,000 was insufficient deterrent for bad behaviour; campaign spending needed to be disclosed in real time, not after the fact.

As we have seen throughout this book, the rules of the democratic game are not fit for purpose. It is increasingly difficult for voters to evaluate the accuracy of the information they receive. In Britain, laws designed to prevent elections being bought have been rendered obsolete when huge sums can be spent outside regulated periods, or by super Pac-style campaign surrogates. Politicians wilfully spread disinformation. We are being targeted online in ways that we cannot fully understand, partly because campaigns and tech platforms have to disclose so little about how money is spent. Far from taking back control, law-makers have largely outsourced decisions about the integrity of democracy to the CEOs of large American technology companies.

All this has happened with minimal public protest, or even acknowledgement. The dire warnings from the Institute for

Government were barely covered in the press, lost in the pre-election scrum of rolling news. Few in power seem particularly concerned that the electoral system can't be trusted. But they should be. As political theorist Martin Moore told the lunchtime audience in west London: "Our entire democratic system needs to be rewritten for the digital age."

A few months earlier, I had interviewed Moore for this book. One of Britain's sharpest writers on how tech is changing democracy, he has documented how unaccountable corporate monopolies have taken over key functions of government. The Chinese state has developed a social credit system that aims to monitor and evaluate citizens' behaviour in real time. In America, most schoolchildren use Google's education apps, which can track everything from how many times they go to the bathroom to how long they spend on specific exercises.[1] (And, of course, Google collects all the data.)

Moore told me that if democracy is to survive in an age of surveillance capitalism, two very different things need to change: the laws that govern politics, and how we conceive of democracy itself.

"Our regulations need to be updated for the digital age," he said. "But electoral laws are not the only thing. We need to re-think how we do liberal democracy. We need to ask what kind of democracy we want to live in. Do we want six massive US platforms dominating the public sphere? How do we want people to engage in politics? We need to think about all that. But we're not."

As I write this, at the start of January 2020, it is difficult to be upbeat about the prospect that Britain's electoral system will be reformed – much less that democracy itself can be imagined anew. In his first Queen's Speech, delivered a week after his general election victory, Boris Johnson promised to tackle social media abuse and to set up a commission on restoring trust in democracy. One of the prime minister's few concrete proposals for electoral reform was the introduction of mandatory photographic identification for all British voters.

If Johnson genuinely wanted to strengthen British democracy, he was picking a strange issue to start with. Of the 44.4 million ballots cast in 2017, there were just 28 allegations of voter impersonation, of which only one resulted in a conviction. Forcing American voters to carry photographic ID has been found to lower turnout among minorities, to the benefit of the Republican Party.[2] The Electoral Reform Society said it was "dismayed" by Prime Minister Johnson's proposals which "would make it harder for millions of citizens to exercise their democratic rights."

The voter ID announcement chimed with a cynical, populist general election campaign. The policy was trumpeted by outriders on the right and earned a few quick headlines. But already Britain's political conversation had moved on. There were few post-mortems about the dismal campaign, little talk of how electoral laws had failed and how misinformation had run wild. It was almost as if the dirtiest British election in living memory had never happened.

What the Conservatives did better than anyone else in 2019 was to actively stoke the growing frustration with politics and politicians among many British voters. Unlike the Brexit referendum's promise to "take back control", Johnson's winning campaign promised to make politics go away. Get Brexit Done. No more politicians squabbling on voters' television screens. As Adam Ramsay pointed out, Johnson profited from a culture of mistrust in politics that his party had itself helped cultivate.[3] One analysis found that almost 90 per cent of a sample of Conservative Facebook adverts posted before the general election contained misleading information.[4] The Tories were not alone. Hundreds of targeted Liberal Democrat adverts featured dubious graphics that wildly overstated their chances of "winning here". Fact-checkers also found a number of Labour ads misleading.

No wonder many voters don't trust politicians when so few lawmakers seem to care about protecting democracy. Only a handful of British parliamentarians spoke up when it turned out that the most important political campaign in living memory, Vote Leave, broke the law. Imagine the response if something similar happened in, say, a European neighbour. Would the British political class shrug their shoulders then too, or would they ask why a Western democracy was allowing its electoral system to be undermined and debased? Surely the *Telegraph* would at least run a couple of editorials bemoaning Europe's venal elites.

As this book has documented, it is extraordinarily easy to funnel dark money into British politics. You and I can do it, right now. First, we declare ourselves an unincorporated association, just like Richard Cook's Constitutional Research Council or the pro-Brexit European Research Group. (Don't worry, we don't actually have to register anywhere or say where our money comes from.)

Then we can start giving money to British politicians. What if our funders are offshore? That's no problem, either. As long as our backers can vote in the UK, they can route money through the opaque financial world that orbits the City of London.

Maybe there is a specific issue we are particularly interested in, say an obscure business regulation that we would like to see changed after Brexit. We could lobby politicians. But why stop there? We could also fund a think tank that doesn't declare its donors to produce a report on our specialist subject. Friendly journalists and grifters would talk up our interest in newspaper columns and on broadcast shows. A junior government minister might even take an interest. We could buy adverts on Facebook to support politicians and parties sympathetic to our concerns.

All of this is perfectly legal. And, if we do inadvertently break any rules, the fines are so low that we can write them off as the cost of doing business.

*

British politics, of course, is not alone in becoming increasingly Americanised. The global nexus of dark money and political disinformation that we have seen is part of an escalating war against the basic tenets of democracy. Nationalists and xenophobes from Italy to Hungary have tapped into international circuits of influence and money. Such electoral manipulation has become transnational, and global.

In early 2020, new documents reportedly revealed that the scale of the Cambridge Analytica operation was far greater than previously estimated, stretching to 68 countries around the world.[5] Former Cambridge Analytica employee Brittany Kaiser claimed that emails showed major Trump donors discussing ways to obscure the source of their donations through different financial vehicles. The same dark money machinery had, she said, been deployed in other countries that Cambridge Analytica worked in, including the UK. Electoral interference is likely to get worse, not better.

So how will we respond to the growing crisis of dark money and disinformation? Will we all sit back and mutely watch it unfold, complaining bitterly on social media but struggling, atomised, to find avenues to channel our anger productively?

There are plenty of reasons to be gloomy. Donald Trump, Boris Johnson and many others have learned that waging war on truth pays political dividends. Established media outlets are easily manipulated. Falsehoods spread rapidly across hyper-partisan websites. Targeted advertising and social platform algorithms aimed at maximising 'likes' and engagement have split the electorate into myriad fragments, undermining the very idea of a national political conversation.

Vastly richer, and more powerful, than many nation states, big tech platforms have little motivation to change their behaviour. Debates around the role of tech in democracy are often dominated by lobbyists and professional contrarians who sophistically decry almost every proposed reform as an attack on free speech.

But there are also reasons to be, if not quite cheerful, then at least hopeful.

Anger at the intrusive role of tech companies in our everyday lives is growing. In September 2019, activists with loudhailers and hi-vis jackets targeted Palantir, a data-mining defence contractor co-founded by a controversial Trump-supporting tech billionaire.[6] Two months later, roughly 200 Google employees and their supporters demonstrated outside of their own company's San Francisco offices after the tech giant dismissed two employees – ironically, for organising protests against the tech giant's own behaviour including its work on a project to build a censored search engine for China and cloud services for the fossil fuel industry.[7] And after the Cambridge Analytica scandal broke in 2018, a group of 'Raging Grannies' demonstrated outside Facebook's sprawling, Frank Gehry-designed head office in Silicon Valley, declaring that "privacy should be the default setting". Whereas once the primary focus of privacy campaigners was on state surveillance, the role of private tech companies in our lives has become a political issue in ways that would have been unimaginable a decade ago.

But it's not enough. Almost every one of us willingly carries a device that allows us to be tracked, traced and, quite easily, identified: a smartphone. The companies that gather all this data say that people give consent and that their information is secure and anonymous. This is patently untrue. In late 2019, the *New York Times* showed how a single file of smartphone location data could be used to trace more than 12 million Americans as they moved through major US cities. Smartphone data is routinely paired with other sources of information, such as mobile advertising IDs, to create the detailed profiles needed to target adverts. "The data can change hands in almost real time, so fast that your location could be transferred from your smartphone to the app's servers and exported to third parties in milliseconds," the *New York Times* journalists wrote. "This is how, for example, you might see an ad for a new car some time after walking through a dealership."

This byzantine system – all perfectly legal, of course – was built for a single purpose: to sell advertising.[8] But the possibilities of using such data for targeted political messaging are already being realised. (Some states have gone much further. Chinese authorities use smartphone tech to track down and target dissidents.)

The impact of technology and dark money on democracy is belatedly edging up the political agenda. Elizabeth Warren made taking money out of American politics a central plank of her bid for the 2020 Democratic nomination.[9] Warren vowed to ban lobbyists from donating to, or fundraising for, candidates, and to end the bipartisan practice of giving plum ambassadorial posts around the world to big donors.*

Warren also proposed banning donations from foreign businesses and making it illegal for corporate political action committees (Pacs) to donate to federal election candidates. Super Pacs would be forced to declare their donors in full, and individual contribution limits would be reduced.†

Many of Warren's measures could be easily adapted and introduced in the UK. Others are needed, too. The most obvious is dramatically increasing the maximum fines for breaking political finance rules. The false distinction in electoral law between online and offline political advertising – which allows campaigns to send

* In 2018, Donald Trump appointed Gordon Sondland as America's man in Brussels. A self-made hotel magnate, Sondland was a diplomatic neophyte with little experience of the European Union, but he was a major Republican donor who gave $1 million to the president's inaugural committee. Sondland was later at the centre of the Trump impeachment inquiry after the ambassador said that he was following the president's orders when he pressured Ukraine to conduct investigations into Trump's political rivals.

† Embarrassingly for Warren, in November 2019 a dark money group bought an advert in support of her candidacy in the influential Des Moines Register ahead of the crucial Iowa Caucus. The funders of the ad, which boasted that "Warren doesn't take corporate or super Pac money", were not disclosed. The Warren campaign asked the people behind it to stop.

digital adverts without even an imprint – must end. Digital spending should be accounted for transparently, and voters should be
able to see how they are being targeted by political campaigns.

The role of money in British politics also has to change. A ban
on donations from individuals who are not domiciled in the UK
and who are non-resident for tax purposes would go some way to
stemming the flow of dark money, as would preventing the use
of shell companies to hide the true source of donations. Offshore
firms – such as that used by Arron Banks to bankroll his Brexit
campaigns – should be barred from making political contributions.

Political parties could be forced to publish the names of significant donors that also attend private party events. This would
end the secrecy of elite donation clubs like the Conservatives'
Leader's Group and give us better information about which donors
have access to the highest levels of British government.

The surest way to reduce the power of money in politics is
to replace a handful of super-rich donors with large numbers of
smaller contributions. If the maximum donation was, say, £10,000
a year, political parties would be forced to rely on a far wider, and
more inclusive, donor base. That, of course, would leave many
parties with an income shortfall. One way around that could be
for the state to step in and match-fund small donations, say below
£250. The scheme could even be paid for by a much-needed tax
on the tech giants. Another option to encourage political participation is to make the cost of party membership tax deductible.

The stick needs to be used as well as the carrot. Think tanks
such as the Institute of Economic Affairs should be forced to
declare their donors, and Britain's ineffective, diaphanous lobbying
register completely overhauled. Any system where corporates can
plough anonymous money into putative research institutes that
influence public debate, and a consultant such as Shanker Singham
can meet government ministers multiple times without having to
register as a lobbyist, is hardly fit for purpose.

Even finding out how registered lobbyists operate is almost

impossible, given the poverty of much of the transparency data that comes out of the British government. We had to go all the way to the courts just to get hold of the European Research Group's taxpayer-funded briefings. Lobbyists should have to declare far more about what conversations they are having, and with whom. Proper sanctions need to be introduced for breaking the rules or not complying, including bans on future meetings with public officials as well as monetary fines.

A dramatic alternative to the dysfunctional status quo is suggested by the title of political commentator Paul Evans's Swiftian provocation *Save Democracy – Abolish Voting*. Instead of trudging to polling stations every few years, Evans proposes putting the whole world of MPs, lobbyists, think tanks, even the civil service, under public ownership. Every voter would be given a "universal basic income for democracy" – Evans envisages £20 a month – that they can spend only on supporting different aspects of the political process. A fan of the IEA? Well, give them a tenner. Want to see reform of housing legislation? Put your money into a white paper on affordable rents. Politics would become a constant marketplace of ideas.

Rather than trying to ban dark money and clandestine influence, Evans suggest that it can be side-stepped altogether. "Our elected representatives would be a lot more transparent in their dealings. They'd do their job properly, and not be spoon-fed by lobbyists and opaquely funded political think-tanks. They'd probably be more interested in what voters' concerns are and less worried about what newspaper editors and the peer group that haunts the political village thinks."

It's a radical proposal – and for that reason alone, there is little chance of a basic income for democracy any time soon. But even if lawmakers did actually heed calls for some measure of electoral reform – say, by introducing new regulations on political funding and lobbying – it is unlikely to be sufficient to rebuild trust in British democracy. There are a number of reasons for this. Firstly, as we have seen time and again, the watchdogs charged with overseeing democracy are often easily outmanoeuvred by both wealthy corporations and small-time players willing to bend the rules until they break, safe in the knowledge that they are about as likely to face prosecution as win the lottery. Under-resourced and institutionally risk-adverse, these regulators are more like paper tigers than attack dogs.

And they could become even less effective in years to come; many on the right of British politics have long been calling for a "bonfire of the regulators". Twice in as many weeks in the wake of the Conservatives' general election win in December 2019, Theresa May's former special advisor Nick Timothy wrote in his weekly *Telegraph* column that the Electoral Commission should be disbanded. And what would replace it? Nothing, apparently.

A second, and related, issue is that even if politicians do introduce new electoral legislation overseen by robust regulators, it is practically impossible for even the most cutting-edge law-making to keep pace with technology and the global networks out to exploit it. Legislation is slow-moving, considered and deliberative. Meanwhile, outside of Parliament, tech companies and lobbyists move swiftly and with little care for the putative rules of engagement. Like a game of whack-a-mole, whenever one loophole is closed, another quickly opens up.

The third, and biggest, obstacle to meaningful democratic reform is the political class itself. As long as politicians think that disinformation wins elections, dirty habits are unlikely to change. Not only are the fines for breaking the rules of our democracy meagre; funding politics through anonymous donations and spreading disinformation seems to come at little political or reputational cost. In 2019, the Conservatives faced no electoral comeback for 'shitposting' on social media, lying with impunity and banning ministers from appearing on some public broadcasters. Until politicians are incentivised – by much stronger public demands – to overhaul the system, they won't.

Occasional protests outside the headquarters of tech giants hint at growing frustrations, but where are the mass movements needed to push dark money and disinformation from a niche concern to the top of the political agenda? If proven law-breaking – as in the Brexit referendum – and obvious electoral manipulation is not enough to make us all stand up and take notice, what would be? And even if public anger at the crisis in democracy did catch fire, could a different system be built that is genuinely free, open and transparent? Or are we already too late?

After the Second World War, a widely shared consensus pervaded across most Western liberal democracies. Mindful of the communist enemy that needed to be kept at bay, both left and right broadly agreed on high taxes, heavy regulation and a generous welfare state that, on some level, demonstrated its respect for social cohesion and solidarity.

The breakdown of this post-war consensus began in the mid-1970s, and was exacerbated by the end of the Cold War. Since the fall of the Eastern Bloc, the drive to revert to a more ruthless market fundamentalism and a minimal state has been increasingly strong, promoted, of course, by the numerous libertarian think tanks documented in this book. Taxes should be lowered. State assets should be privatised. In the process, the assumptions about democracy, ethics and human rights absorbed by the West's educated middle class can much more easily be undermined, and the institutions that underpin those attitudes weakened.

The effective destruction of trade unions, and the decline of the industries that made them possible, has also hugely frayed the bonds tying workers to historic labour parties and led to the well-documented crisis of social democracy. In Britain, Labour's 'red wall' was crumbling long before Isaac Levido instructed Tory MPs to repeat "get Brexit done" as if it was a Buddhist mantra. While the established Western political consensus slowly crumbled, huge spaces opened up through which the old right-wing press and the new social media attack vehicles were able to advance.

These huge political shifts have coincided with a revolution in digital communication. A handful of corporations, most of which did not even exist when the Berlin Wall fell, have amassed unparalleled influence over politicians and the economy. Almost 90 per cent of all Internet searches go through Google.[10] Between them, Facebook, Google and Amazon account for nearly 70 per cent of all digital ad spending.[11] The scions of Big Tech are plugged into the highest levels of power. Ahead of the 2020 presidential election, Mark Zuckerberg met privately with Donald Trump. No details of their discussion were released.

Silicon Valley titans are the modern-day equivalent of the Gilded Age's steel magnates, railroad tycoons and oil monopolists. Back then, the power of a tiny number of super-rich men such as John D. Rockefeller, J.P. Morgan and William H. "the public be damned" Vanderbilt[12] was eventually checked only by growing public agitation for regulation to curb their excesses.* Out of the backlash came the Federal Trade Commission which broke up coercive monopolies and introduced laws against reducing competition. The question now is whether the unbridled power of today's digital 'robber barons' can be similarly tamed.

Facebook and others, unsurprisingly, have insisted that concerns about the effect of tech monopolies on democracy are overstated. Zuckerberg's platform has introduced changes aimed at limiting the spread of disinformation. Doubtless Facebook will launch more initiatives. But promises have been made before and have failed to deliver.

Meanwhile, digital influence campaigns are already migrating to other platforms. During the 2018 Brazilian general election,

---

* In 1912, three-quarters of Americans voted for presidential candidates who pledged to limit corporate power. The establishment Republican candidate, William Taft, finished a distant third.

companies supporting far-right candidate Jair Bolsonaro spent millions of dollars on WhatsApp messages.[13] Widely circulated false reports accused Bolsonaro's left-wing rival of, among other things, handing out baby bottles with penis-shaped tops at schools to combat homophobia. The following year, in India, legions of online trolls spread fake WhatsApp stories in support of Narendra Modi to hundreds of millions of voters.

The misuse of technology poses an existential threat to democracy. So what can be done to curb these digital excesses? For a start, companies who deal in information and personal data could be seriously policed and penalised for cybersecurity or data protection failures – to the same extent that financial institutions in most Western states are for money laundering, for example.

Legislation already exists in many countries. The European Union's General Data Protection Regulation (GDPR) includes substantial safeguards against data misuse, including fines of up to 4 per cent of a company's turnover (for tech platforms with multi-billion-dollar revenues that's a lot of money). But in its first year in operation, European regulators only issued around £100 million in fines. Hardly a stinging deterrent for companies with market caps measured in the hundreds of billions.

Some have proposed breaking up Facebook, Google and other tech behemoths. Yet while dismantling the modern-day equivalent of the railroad monopolies might help, it's not clear how such a move would stem the flow of disinformation, especially on the closed groups and anonymous forums from which armies of online trolls are feeding a populist surge across the world.

There have been other proposals. GDPR laws could be used to check the worst abuses of a sprawling online advertising technology industry that shares huge amounts of personal data with companies across the Internet. Tim Berners-Lee, the founder of the World Wide Web, has warned of a "digital dystopia" if disinformation and invasion of privacy are not stopped. In 2019, dozens of tech companies including Facebook and Google signed

Berners-Lee's 'Contract for the Web' calling for a safe, free and open Internet.

But self-regulation will only ever go so far. When Facebook ignored Berners-Lee's request to cease running targeted political adverts in the 2019 UK general election, one British columnist understandably dismissed the contract as a PR opportunity "for the megalomaniacs who will carry on doing their worst".[14]

Others are attempting to bypass the tech monopolies by building an open, decentralised cloud to host the next generation of software and services. Whether or not any of these ideas come to fruition, their emergence attests to the depth of concerns about the overweening influence of a handful of tech conglomerates – and speaks to the scale of the ambition needed to tackle them.

The power of Big Tech is not the only pressing concern. Liberal democracy cannot function without trust, and people across the Western world are increasingly disenchanted with democracy. Over two-thirds of older Americans believe it is essential to live in a democracy; among millennials, less than one-third do.[15] In Britain, support for democracy has fallen sharply over the last decade. More than half of the respondents to a 2019 study agreed that "Britain needs a strong ruler willing to break the rules".[16]

The crisis in British democracy has been accompanied by a crisis in the British state itself. The UK is an increasingly disunited kingdom. Scottish independence and even Irish unification are distinct possibilities in the coming years. The ongoing inability of Westminster's political system to even understand these nationalist movements – the union barely featured during the 2019 general election campaign, beyond bromides – attests to deeper structural failings.

All the while, the institutions and interests which shape the British state remain fundamentally unreformed. The City of London is the epicentre of a global network of financial secrecy – and reputation laundering – that no prime minister has ever seriously tried to rein in. Foreign magnates and British elites can funnel their money offshore with ease. Despite his 'one nation' rhetoric, Boris Johnson is particularly close to the oligarch set. The day after his landslide election win in December 2019, Johnson attended a champagne-and-caviar Christmas party in London hosted by Alexander Lebedev and his son Evgeny. The former was once a senior KGB officer; the latter owns the *Independent*, the *Evening Standard* and a little-watched London TV channel. Not exactly 'Workington man'.

There seems little prospect, either, of reorienting Britain's lop-sided first-past-the-post electoral system. It is hardly a coincidence that political polarisation has been so acute in the UK and America, two countries united by a voting system that punishes consensus-building and vastly over-rewards winners. No wonder Viktor Orbán looked to the 'Westminster model' when he decided to gerry-mander Hungary's electoral system to his advantage.

Ironically, the communications revolution that has so im-perilled the very idea of democracy could provide the means to transform how democracy is done. The constraints on how we participate in public life are fast disappearing. The challenge is to create a more responsive version of the public sphere for the digital age, one which is not controlled by giant tech companies and which, unlike the sham 'digital democracy' preached by Five Star and the Brexit Party, is genuinely participative.

Like the climate, democracy is fast reaching a tipping point. If the opportunity for change is not seized, the worst aspects of the present malaise – disinformation, dark money and spiralling polarisation – could well push us beyond a point of no return.

It is not too late. I am still an optimist, just as I was as a teenager growing up in rural Ireland two decades ago. Democracy faces many perils, but there is still time to act. We can build better systems, we can imagine more democratic forms of politics, and conversation. But we should be in no doubt about the urgency and scale of the challenge.

ACKNOWLEDGEMENTS

Few books are written in a vacuum, but more than most this book was the product of the diligence and hard work of many other people. First, this book would never have been possible without the tireless team at *openDemocracy* and, in particular, Mary Fitzgerald, who realised early on the importance of dark money and disinformation in British politics and has been prepared to fight tooth-and-nail to tell many of the stories in this book. She has been my ideal reader, reviewer and editor.

This book has drawn heavily on excellent reporting and research produced by a host of colleagues on both sides of the Atlantic. I have been fortunate to count many of these great journalists and researchers as friends and to rely on their counsel in writing this book. I would particularly like to thank Carole Cadwalladr, Cynthia O'Murchu, Leigh Baldwin, Marcus Leroux, Jim Fitzpatrick, Guy Grandjean, Manveen Rana, Jacopo Iacoboni, Peter Jukes, Mat Hope and Iain Campbell. Your generosity and comradery during the long months of writing this book was invaluable.

Thanks to those who had the patience to wade through early drafts of chapters: Gavin Sheridan, Jess Black, Zach Boren, Michael John McCarthy, Maxim Edwards, Liz Carolan, Oliver Bullough. Thanks also to colleagues and friends who provided invaluable advice at crucial moments: Seth Thévoz, Tom McTague, Martin Moore, Tamasin Cave, Sam Jeffers, Gavin Millar, Katharine Dommett, Alistair Clark, Kim Lane Scheppele, Daniel Trilling, Andrew Dolan, Oliver Norgrove, Shaunagh Connaire, Tom Brookes and others who would rather their names were kept out of the public domain. A very special thanks to my old college roommate, Nicholas Hamilton, who very kindly put me up at his family's beautiful home at Belle Isle, Co. Fermanagh, in the summer of 2019 while I was writing this book.

This book was based on dozens of interviews often done on very tight deadlines. I would like to thank everyone who generously gave me their time, and their insights. Many of these interviews were conducted 'on the record' and are referred to in the book directly, but many others spoke on condition of anonymity. Thanks, one and all.

This book would never have happened without the great faith that Róisín Davis showed in me. When Róisín first suggested I write a book proposal, in March 2019, I spent half an hour trying to convince her that it was a terrible idea. I'm glad that I failed. My agent, David Grossman, has been a source of calm and expert advice. At Head of Zeus, Neil Belton has been a guiding presence. Clare Gordon helped enormously to turn a scattered manuscript into this book, as did Martin Soames.

I would also like to thank all my wonderful colleagues. When Adam Ramsay phoned, back in early 2017, to talk about the DUP's Brexit funding, little did either of us realise how far down the dark money rabbit hole we would end up. Jim Cusick, Claire Provost, Nandini Archer, Emily Falconer, Julian Richards, Adam Bychawski, Ally Tibbitt, Caroline Molloy, Matt Linares, Tom Rowley and everyone else at *openDemocracy* have been constant sources of guidance, advice and good cheer. Thanks also to our funders at Luminate and to the thousands of readers who support *openDemocracy*'s work. Without them this book would never have happened.

I am indebted, too, to everyone at the *Ferret* and to Paul Evans and his family for providing me with a home away from home in London. Thanks to Ben McMahon for being there to distract me with beer and good food when I needed it most. A very special thanks goes to Jenna Corderoy, who worked so closely with me on this book, to Nick Holdstock, for his sound guidance throughout, and to my family and particularly my mother, Mary Melvin Geoghegan. Thanks for always being there for me.

Notes

Chapter 1: Introduction

1 Anne Applebaum, 'The more we learn about Brexit, the more crooked it looks', *Washington Post*, March 2019.
2 Sean Coughlan, 'Dissatisfaction with democracy "at record high"', *BBC*, January 2020.

Chapter 2: Democracy on Leave?

1 'Investigation: Vote Leave Ltd, Mr Darren Grimes, BeLeave and Veterans for Britain', *The Electoral Commission*, July 2018.
2 Alex Spence, 'Boris Johnson Secretly Asked For A Massive Amount Of User Data To Be Tracked. Dominic Cummings Said It's "TOP PRIORITY"', *Buzzfeed*, September 2019.
3 William Norton, *White Elephant: How the North East Said No* (London, 2008), p. 200.
4 Dominic Cummings, 'On the referendum #20: the campaign, physics and data science – Vote Leave's 'Voter Intention Collection System' (VICS) now available for all', *Dominic Cummings's Blog*, October 2016. See also https://dominiccummings.com/2016/10/29/on-the-referendum-20-the-campaign-physics-and-data-science-vote-leaves-voter-intention-collection-system-vics-now-available-for-all/; accessed 19 Jan. 2020.
5 Alice Thomson and Rachel Sylvester, 'Sir Nicholas Soames interview: "Johnson is nothing like Churchill and Jacob Rees-Mogg is an absolute fraud"', *The Times*, September 2019.
6 Sam Knight, 'The man who brought you Brexit', *Guardian*, September 2016.
7 Tim Shipman, *All Out War: The Full Story of Brexit* (London, 2017), p. 27.

8 George Eaton, 'Vote Leave head Matthew Elliott: "The Brexiteers won the battle but we could lose the war"', *New Statesman*, September 2018.

9 Chloe Farand and Mat Hope, 'Matthew and Sarah Elliott: How a UK Power Couple Links US Libertarians and Fossil Fuel Lobbyists to Brexit', *DeSmog UK*, November 2018.

10 Robert Booth, 'Who is behind the Taxpayers' Alliance?', *Guardian*, October 2009.

11 '08/09 Review', *TaxPayers' Alliance*. See also http://d3n8a8pro7vhmx. cloudfront.net/themes/534b9dfd01925b57ba000001/attachments/original/1402669714/TPA_Review_08_09.pdf? 1402669714

12 Robert Booth, 'Taxpayers' Alliance admits director doesn't pay British tax', *Guardian*, October 2009.

13 George Eaton, 'Vote Leave head Matthew Elliott: "The Brexiteers won the battle but we could lose the war"', *New Statesman*, September 2018.

14 Tom Bawden, 'The address where Eurosceptics and climate change sceptics rub shoulders', *Independent*, February 2016.

15 Phillip Inman, 'US Tea Party in London to spread low tax message', *Guardian*, September 2010.

16 Andrew Hough, 'TaxPayers' Alliance seeks advice from Tea Party movement leaders', *Telegraph*, September 2010.

17 Robert Booth, 'A very British Tea Party: US anti-tax activists advise UK counterparts', *Guardian*, September 2010.

18 Tamasin Cave and Andy Rowell, *A Quiet Word: Lobbying, Crony Capitalism and Broken Politics in Britain* (London, 2015), pp. 39–40.

19 Tim Shipman, *All Out War: The Full Story of Brexit* (London, 2017), p. 28.

20 Ibid., p. 37.

21 Oliver Wright, 'Dominic Cummings aims a wrecking ball at Whitehall', *The Times*, August 2019.

22 Jonny Ball, 'John Prescott: the Northern Powerhouse is "not devolution, really"', *New Statesman*, February 2019.

23 Johnny McDevitt, 'Dominic Cummings honed strategy in 2004 vote, video reveals', *Guardian*, November 2019.

24 William Norton, *White Elephant: How the North East Said No*, (London, 2008), p. 70.

25 Frederick Studemann, 'US conservatives cast wary eye at EU treaty', *Financial Times*, November 2004.

26 Tim Shipman, *All Out War: The Full Story of Brexit* (London, 2017), p. 622.

27 Christopher Hope, 'Conservative donors prepare to sink £5million into Brexit campaign amid anger about pro-EU leaflet', *Telegraph*, April 2016.

28 Jim Waterson, 'Darren Grimes: the pro-Brexit student activist fined £20k', *Guardian*, July 2018.

29 Darren Grimes, 'Darren Grimes: Why I am a Conservative', *Conservatives for Liberty*, December 2015.

30 Public Administration and Constitutional Affairs, 'Lessons Learned from the EU Referendum', *House of Commons*, November 2016. See also http://data.parliament.uk/writtenevidence/committeeevidence.svc/evidencedocument/public-administration-and-constitutional-affairs-committee/lessons-learned-from-the-eu-referendum/oral/42639.html; accessed 19 Jan. 2020.

31 Tim Shipman, *All Out War: The Full Story of Brexit* (London, 2017), p. 28.

32 Sam Coates, 'Brexit group's plot to break campaign spending limit', *The Times*, February 2016.

33 Carole Cadwalladr, 'The Brexit whistleblower: "Did Vote Leave use me? Was I naive?"', *Guardian*, March 2018.

34 'Report of an investigation in respect of Vote Leave Limited, Mr Darren Grimes, BeLeave and Veterans for Britain concerning campaign funding and spending for the 2016 referendum on the UK's membership of the EU', *The Electoral Commission*, July 2018.

35 Ibid.

36 Pamela Duncan and David Pegg, 'City millionaire says Vote Leave directed his donation decision', *Guardian*, December 2017.

37 Adam Ramsay and Peter Geoghegan, 'Revealed: how loopholes allowed pro-Brexit campaign to spend "as much as necessary to win"', *openDemocracy*, September 2017.

38 Sean Morrison, 'Electoral Commission under fire from Remainers for launching probe into Leave campaign's spending 18 months after Brexit', *Evening Standard*, November 2017.

39 Carole Cadwalladr, Emma Graham-Harrison and Mark Townsend, 'Revealed: Brexit insider claims Vote Leave team may have breached spending limits', *Guardian*, March 2018.

40 Dominic Casciani, 'Lobby group admits unlawful whistleblower dismissal', *BBC*, November 2018.

41 'Darren Grimes: Brexit campaigner wins appeal against £20,000 fine', *BBC*, July 2019.

42 David Pegg, 'Vote Leave drops appeal against fine for electoral offences', *Guardian*, March 2019.

43 'Brexit: Police hand Vote Leave file to Crown Prosecution Service', *BBC*, November 2019.

44 James Cusick and Adam Ramsay, 'Police still not investigating Leave campaigns, citing "political sensitivities"', *openDemocracy*, October 2018.

45 Dominic Cummings, 'Dominic Cummings: how the Brexit referendum was won', *Spectator*, January 2017.

46 Tim Shipman, *All Out War: The Full Story of Brexit* (London, 2017), pp. 415–416.

47 Carole Cadwalladr, 'Vote Leave donations: the dark ads, the mystery "letter" – and Brexit's online guru', *Guardian*, November 2017.

48 'Vote Leave launches £50m Euro 2016 football contest', *BBC*, May 2016.

49 Dominic Cummings, 'On the referendum #20: the campaign, physics and data science – Vote Leave's 'Voter Intention Collection System' (VICS) now available for all', *Dominic Cummings's Blog*, October 2016. See also https://dominiccummings.com/2016/10/29/on-the-referendum-20-the-campaign-physics-and-data-science-vote-leaves-voter-intention-collection-system-vics-now-available-for-all/; accessed 19 Jan. 2020.

50 Monetary penalty notice to Vote Leave Limited, *Information Commissioner's Office*, March 2019. See also https://ico.org.uk/media/action-weve-taken/mpns/2614565/vote-leave-limited-monetary-penalty-notice.pdf; accessed 19 Jan. 2020.

51 'Vote Leave's targeted Brexit ads released by Facebook', *BBC*, July 2018.

52 Anoosh Chakelian, 'Facebook releases Brexit campaign ads for the fake news inquiry – but what's wrong with them?', *New Statesman*, July 2018.

53 Dominic Cummings, 'Dominic Cummings: how the Brexit referendum was won', *Spectator*, January 2017.

54 Carole Cadwalladr and Mark Townsend, 'Revealed: the ties that bound Vote Leave's data firm to controversial Cambridge Analytica', *Guardian*, March 2018.

55 Carole Cadwalladr, '"I made Steve Bannon's psychological warfare tool": meet the data war whistleblower', *Guardian*, March 2018.

56 Sam Coates, 'Vote Leave dodged limits on spending, says insider', *The Times*, April 2018.

57 Thomas Claburn, 'Political ad campaign biz AggregateIQ exposes tools, DB logins online', *The Register*, March 2018.

58 Natasha Lomas, 'Brexit ad blitz data firm paid by Vote Leave broke privacy laws, watchdogs find', *TechCrunch*, November 2019.

Chapter 3: The Bad Boys of Brexit

1 Arron Banks, *The Bad Boys of Brexit: Tales of Mischief, Mayhem & Guerrilla Warfare in the EU Referendum Campaign* (London, 2017), p. 306.

2 Digital, Culture, Media and Sport Committee, 'Fake News', *House of Commons*, June 2018. See also http://data.parliament.uk/writtenevidence/committeeevidence.svc/evidencedocument/digital-culture-media-and-sport-committee/disinformation-and-fake-news/oral/85344.html; accessed 19 Jan. 2020.

3 Ed Caesar, 'The Chaotic Triumph of Arron Banks, the "Bad Boy of Brexit"', *New Yorker*, March 2019.

4 Danny Dorling and Sally Tomlinson, *Rule Britannia: Brexit and the End of Empire* (London, 2019), p. 37.

5 Ed Caesar, 'The Chaotic Triumph of Arron Banks, the "Bad Boy of Brexit"', *New Yorker*, March 2019.

6 Robert Wright, 'Arron Banks and the mystery Brexit campaign funds', *Financial Times*, November 2018.

7   Ed Caesar, 'The Chaotic Triumph of Arron Banks, the "Bad Boy of Brexit"', *New Yorker*, March 2019.

8   Ibid.

9   Martin Fletcher, 'Arron Banks: the man who bought Brexit', *New Statesman*, October 2016.

10   Ed Caesar, 'The Chaotic Triumph of Arron Banks, the "Bad Boy of Brexit"', *New Yorker*, March 2019.

11   Tim Shipman, *All Out War: The Full Story of Brexit* (London, 2017), p. 43.

12   Alastair Sloan and Iain Campbell, 'How did Arron Banks afford Brexit?', *openDemocracy*, October 2017; accessed 19 Jan. 2020.

13   Ibid.

14   Martin Fletcher, 'Arron Banks: the man who bought Brexit', *New Statesman*, October 2016.

15   Tim Shipman, *All Out War: The Full Story of Brexit* (London, 2017), p. 42.

16   Alastair McCall and Robert Watts, 'Five of UK's richest men bankrolled Brexit', *Sunday Times*, April 2017.

17   Tom Metcalf and Stephanie Baker, 'The Mysterious Finances of the Brexit Campaign's Biggest Backer', *Bloomberg*, February 2019.

18   Alastair Sloan and Iain Campbell, 'How did Arron Banks afford Brexit?', *openDemocracy*, October 2017.

19   Lionel Barber, *Twitter*, June 2017. See also https://twitter.com/lionelbarber/status/880682552809443331; accessed 19 Jan. 2020.

20   Arron Banks, *Twitter*, June 2017. See also https://twitter.com/arron_banks/status/880839135828860931?lang=en-gb; accessed 19 Jan. 2020.

21   Ed Caesar, 'The Chaotic Triumph of Arron Banks, the "Bad Boy of Brexit"', *New Yorker*, March 2019.

22   Cynthia O'Murchu and Henry Mance, 'How the businesses of Brexit campaigner "King" Arron Banks overlap', *Financial Times*, June 2017.

23   Alex Hawkes, 'Brexit "bad boy"' Arron Banks widens the net as he prepares to pump more cash into his Isle of Man bank', *thisismoney.co.uk*, September 2017.

24   Cynthia O'Murchu and Henry Mance, 'How the businesses of

Brexit campaigner "King" Arron Banks overlap', *Financial Times*, June 2017.

25 Martin Fletcher, 'Arron Banks: the man who bought Brexit', *New Statesman*, October 2016.

26 Alastair Sloan and Iain Campbell, 'How did Arron Banks afford Brexit?', *openDemocracy*, October 2017.

27 Ibid.

28 Cynthia O'Murchu and Henry Mance, 'How the businesses of Brexit campaigner "King" Arron Banks overlap', *Financial Times*, June 2017.

29 Leigh Baldwin and Marcus Leroux, 'Arron Banks and Brexit's offshore secrets', *openDemocracy*, April 2018.

30 Ed Caesar, 'The Chaotic Triumph of Arron Banks, the "Bad Boy of Brexit"', *New Yorker*, March 2019.

31 'Taking Stock: No humble pie after anti-PwC newspaper ad', *AccountancyAge*, September 2014.

32 Arron Banks, *The Bad Boys of Brexit: Tales of Mischief, Mayhem & Guerrilla Warfare in the EU Referendum Campaign* (London, 2017), p. xxii.

33 Richard Kay, 'Portillo is up for sale', *MailOnline*, October 2003.

34 Rajeev Syal and Rebecca Davis, 'Ukip donor has links to Belize and mining in southern Africa', *Guardian*, October 2014.

35 Digital, Culture, Media and Sport Committee, 'Chair comments on the decision to refer Arron Banks to the National Crime Agency', *House of Commons*, November 2018. See also www.parliament.uk/business/committees/committees-a-z/commons-select/digital-culture-media-and-sport-committee/news/arron-banks-nca-quote-17-19/; accessed 19 Jan. 2020.

36 Alastair McCall and Robert Watts, 'Five of UK's richest men bankrolled Brexit', *Sunday Times*, April 2017.

37 Ed Caesar, 'The Chaotic Triumph of Arron Banks, the "Bad Boy of Brexit"', *New Yorker*, March 2019.

38 'Arron Banks, Better for the Country and others referred to the National Crime Agency for multiple suspected offences', *The Electoral Commission*, November 2018.

39 'Arron Banks faces Brexit referendum spending probe', *BBC*, November 2018.

40   Arron Banks, *The Bad Boys of Brexit: Tales of Mischief, Mayhem &*
     Guerrilla Warfare in the EU Referendum Campaign (London, 2017), p. 84.

41   Harry Davies, 'Ted Cruz using firm that harvested data on millions
     of unwitting Facebook users', *Guardian*, December 2015.

42   Peter Geoghegan, 'Brexit bankroller Arron Banks, Cambridge
     Analytica and Steve Bannon – explosive emails reveal fresh links',
     openDemocracy, November 2018.

43   Arron Banks, *The Bad Boys of Brexit: Tales of Mischief, Mayhem &*
     Guerrilla Warfare in the EU Referendum Campaign (London, 2016), p. 84.

44   Martin Shipton, 'Controversial Ukip funder and Brexit supporter
     Arron Banks was Cardiff's Honorary Consul from Belize',
     WalesOnline, July 2018.

45   Arron Banks, *The Bad Boys of Brexit: Tales of Mischief, Mayhem &*
     Guerrilla Warfare in the EU Referendum Campaign (London, 2016),
     p. 9.

46   Peter Geoghegan, 'Brexit bankroller Arron Banks, Cambridge
     Analytica and Steve Bannon – explosive emails reveal fresh links',
     openDemocracy, November 2018.

47   Peter Geoghegan and Jenna Corderoy, 'Revealed: Arron Banks
     Brexit campaign's "secret" meetings with Cambridge Analytica',
     openDemocracy, December 2018.

48   Carole Cadwalladr, 'Revealed: how US billionaire helped to back
     Brexit', *Guardian*, February 2017.

49   Elaina Plott, 'Five Questions for Gerry Gunster, the DC Strategist
     Who Ran the "Leave" Campaign', *Washingtonian*, June 2016.

50   Peter Geoghegan, 'Brexit bankroller Arron Banks, Cambridge
     Analytica and Steve Bannon – explosive emails reveal fresh links',
     openDemocracy, November 2018.

51   Peter Geoghegan and Jenna Corderoy, 'Revealed: Arron Banks
     Brexit campaign's "secret" meetings with Cambridge Analytica',
     openDemocracy, December 2018.

52   Ed Caesar, 'The Chaotic Triumph of Arron Banks, the "Bad Boy
     of Brexit"', *New Yorker*, March 2019.

53   Digital, Culture, Media and Sport Committee, 'Written testimony
     to the Fake News Inquiry', *House of Commons*. See also https://
     www.parliament.uk/documents/commons-committees/culture-

media-and-sport/Brittany%20Kaiser%20Parliamentary%20
testimony%20FINAL.pdf; accessed 19 Jan. 2020.

54 Digital, Culture, Media and Sport Committee, 'Additional
Submissions to Parliament in Support of Inquiries Regarding
Brexit', *House of Commons*, July 2019. See also https://www.
parliament.uk/documents/commons-committees/culture-media-
and-sport/Britanny-Kaiser-July-2019-submission.pdf; accessed 19
Jan. 2020.

55 Digital, Culture, Media and Sport Committee, 'Written testimony
to the Fake News Inquiry', *House of Commons*. See also https://
www.parliament.uk/documents/commons-committees/culture-
media-and-sport/Brittany%20Kaiser%20Parliamentary%20
testimony%20FINAL.pdf; accessed 19 Jan. 2020.

56 Carole Cadwalladr, 'Leave.EU, Arron Banks and new questions
about referendum funding', *Guardian*, April 2018.

57 Arron Banks, *The Bad Boys of Brexit: Tales of Mischief, Mayhem &
Guerrilla Warfare in the EU Referendum Campaign* (London, 2016), p. 96.

58 David Gilbert, 'Everything you need to know about the bombshell
report linking Russia to Brexit', *Vice News*, June 2018.

59 Carole Cadwalladr and Peter Jukes, 'Arron Banks "met Russian
officials multiple times before Brexit vote"', *Guardian*, June 2018.

60 David D. Kirkpatrick and Matthew Rosenberg, 'Russians Offered
Business Deals to Brexit's Biggest Backer', *New York Times*, June 2018.

61 Luke Harding, 'Revealed: details of exclusive Russian deal offered
to Arron Banks in Brexit run-up', *Guardian*, August 2018.

62 David D. Kirkpatrick and Matthew Rosenberg, 'Russians Offered
Business Deals to Brexit's Biggest Backer', *New York Times*, June 2018.

63 'The Banks Files: How Brexit "bad boy" Arron Banks was eyeing a
massive Russian gold deal', *Channel 4*, March 2019.

64 Ibid.

65 Ed Caesar, 'The Chaotic Triumph of Arron Banks, the "Bad Boy
of Brexit"', *New Yorker*, March 2019.

66 Manuel Roig-Franzia, Rosalind S. Helderman, William Booth and
Tom Hamburger, 'How the "Bad Boys of Brexit" forged ties with
Russia and the Trump campaign – and came under investigators'
scrutiny', *Washington Post*, June 2018.

67   Carole Cadwalladr and Peter Jukes, 'Arron Banks "met Russian officials multiple times before Brexit vote"', *Guardian*, June 2018.

68   Tom Harper, Caroline Wheeler and Shingi Mararike, 'More meetings, more offers: truth emerges of Arron Banks's Russia links', *Sunday Times*, July 2018.

69   David Gilbert, 'Everything you need to know about the bombshell report linking Russia to Brexit', *Vice News*, June 2018.

70   Jim Waterson, 'Five things we learned from Arron Banks' questioning by MPs', *Guardian*, June 2018.

71   Martin Fletcher, 'Arron Banks: the man who bought Brexit', *New Statesman*, October 2016.

72   Dominic Kennedy, '007 blonde and the Russian connection', *The Times*, April 2016. Tom Harper, 'From Urals to Ukip: racy tale of Arron Banks's Russian wife', *Sunday Times*, September 2017.

73   James Murray, 'The story of Mrs Arron Banks' extraordinary first marriage', *Daily Express*, November 2018.

74   Ed Caesar, 'The Chaotic Triumph of Arron Banks, the "Bad Boy of Brexit"', *New Yorker*, March 2019.

75   Steven Swinford and Gordon Rayner, 'Russian "spy" case: Liberal Democrat MP "helped second Russian girl"', *Telegraph*, December 2010.

76   Caroline Wheeler and Tom Harper, 'The name's Banks, Katya Banks: Russia's belle at Trump ball', *Sunday Times*, June 2018.

77   Arron Banks, *The Bad Boys of Brexit: Tales of Mischief, Mayhem & Guerrilla Warfare in the EU Referendum Campaign* (London, 2016), pp. 24–25.

78   Ed Howker, 'Revealed: Arron Banks puts controversial diamond mine up for sale', *Channel 4*, September 2019.

79   Tom Harper, Caroline Wheeler and Iggy Ostanin, 'Smuggling claims cast shadow over Brexit's £8m diamond geezer Arron Banks', *Sunday Times*, August 2019.

80   'Long Read: The Arron Banks allegations', *Channel 4*, July 2018.

81   Tom Harper, Caroline Wheeler and Iggy Ostanin, 'Smuggling claims cast shadow over Brexit's £8m diamond geezer Arron Banks', *Sunday Times*, August 2019.

82   'Public statement on NCA investigation into suspected EU referendum offences', *National Crime Agency*, September 2019. See

also https://nationalcrimeagency.gov.uk/news/public-statement-on-nca-investigation-into-suspected-eu-referendum-offences; accessed 19 Jan. 2020.

83 Charles Hymas, 'Arron Banks threatens to sue Electoral Commission after being cleared by National Crime Agency over loans in Brexit referendum campaign', *Telegraph*, September 2019.

84 Andrew Marr Show, *BBC*, November 2018.

85 Ian Cobain, 'Ashcroft's millions: from Belize tax haven to Tories via Southampton', *Guardian*, March 2010.

86 Joe Lo, 'Revealed: How Britain First Disguised the Source of a £200,000 Donation', *Vice*, July 2019.

87 Billy Kenber, Paul Morgan-Bentley and Louis Goddard, 'Tories under attack after tax haven donations', *The Times*, March 2019.

88 Ian Cobain and Matthew Taylor, 'Far-right terrorist Thomas Mair jailed for life for Jo Cox murder', *Guardian*, November 2016.

89 'The Banks Files: Brexit funder urged campaign to "press it harder" after Jo Cox murder', *Channel 4*, March 2019.

90 Rowena Mason, 'Leave.EU condemned for linking Orlando attack to referendum vote', *Guardian*, June 2016.

91 Ibid.

92 'Revealed: How Leave.EU faked migrant footage', *Channel 4*, April 2019.

93 Digital, Culture, Media and Sport Committee, 'Fake News', *House of Commons*, June 2018. See also http://data.parliament.uk/writtenevidence/committeeevidence.svc/evidencedocument/digital-culture-media-and-sport-committee/disinformation-and-fake-news/oral/85344.html; accessed 19 Jan. 2020.

94 Peter Geoghegan and Jenna Corderoy, 'Arron Banks lied to Parliament about his Brexit campaign, say whistleblowers', *openDemocracy*, November 2018.

95 Arron Banks, *The Bad Boys of Brexit: Tales of Mischief, Mayhem & Guerrilla Warfare in the EU Referendum Campaign* (London, 2016), pp. 308–309.

96 Ed Howker, 'Arron Banks and the UKIP data hijack', *Channel 4*, December 2019.

97 Peter Geoghegan and Jenna Corderoy, 'Revealed: Arron Banks's

staff crunched millions of voters' data after Brexit vote',
openDemocracy, November 2019.

98 Ibid.

99 Alex Hern, 'Leave.EU and Arron Banks insurance firm fined
£120,000 for data breaches', *Guardian*, February 2019.

100 Jen Frost, 'Tribunal throws out Eldon and Leave EU appeals
against ICO', *InsurancePost*, February 2020.

101 David Pegg, 'Met to take no further action over Leave.EU
spending breaches', *Guardian*, September 2019.

102 Andrew Pierce and James Tapsfield, 'Your gold door's worth more
than my house! The riotous inside story of Farage and his Ukip
posse's astonishing coup as he became the first foreign politician
to meet President-elect Trump', *MailOnline*, November 2016.

103 Ed Howker, 'Arron Banks and the UKIP data hijack', *Channel 4*,
December 2019.

104 Jen Mills, 'Man jailed for sending Anna Soubry MP letter saying
"Cox was first you are next"', *Metro*, November 2019.

105 Carole Cadwalladr, 'Threats, bullying, vindictiveness: how Arron
Banks repels charges against him', *Guardian*, November 2018.

106 Peter Walker, 'Arron Banks gave "£450,000 funding to Nigel
Farage after Brexit vote"', *Guardian*, May 2019.

107 Jim Pickard and Gillian Tett, 'Nigel Farage teams up with Trump
supporters to raise Brexit funds', *Financial Times*, July 2019.

Chapter 4: The DUP's Dark Money

1 Richard Cook, 'Political credibility relies on displaying good
judgement', November 2009. See also http://voterichardcook.
blogspot.com/; accessed 20 Jan. 2020.

2 'Sir Teddy Taylor, Eurosceptic Scottish Tory MP – obituary',
Telegraph, September 2017.

3 Adam Ramsay and Peter Geoghegan, 'Meet the Scottish Tory
behind the £435,000 DUP Brexit donation', *openDemocracy*, May 2017.

4 'Better off out campaign', *The Freedom Association*. See also
https://www.tfa.net/better_off_out; accessed 20 Jan. 2020.

5   Adam Ramsay and Peter Geoghegan, 'Meet the Scottish Tory behind the £435,000 DUP Brexit donation', *openDemocracy*, May 2017.

6   Adam Ramsay and Peter Geoghegan, 'The "dark money" that paid for Brexit', *openDemocracy*, February 2017.

7   Ibid.

8   Amanda Ferguson, 'Pro-unionist group gave DUP £425,622 for Brexit campaign', *Irish Times*, February 2017.

9   Peter Geoghegan, 'Revealed: the dirty secrets of the DUP's "dark money" Brexit donor', *openDemocracy*, January 2019.

10   Ibid.

11   Ibid.

12   Jim Fitzpatrick, 'BBC Spotlight: Brexit, Dark Money and the DUP', *BBC*, June 2018.

13   Ibid.

14   Peter Geoghegan, 'Revealed: the dirty secrets of the DUP's "dark money" Brexit donor', *openDemocracy*, January 2019.

15   Adam Ramsay and Peter Geoghegan, 'The strange link between the DUP Brexit donation and a notorious Indian gun running trial', *openDemocracy*, February 2017.

16   Peter Popham, 'Up in arms: The bizarre case of the British gun-runner, the Indian rebels and the missing Dane', *Independent*, March 2011.

17   Adam Ramsay and Peter Geoghegan, 'Secretive DUP Brexit donor links to the Saudi intelligence service', *openDemocracy*, February 2017.

18   Paul Hutcheon, 'Richard Cook: Chair of the shadowy Constitutional Research Council talks to the Sunday Herald', *The Herald*, May 2017.

19   Adam Ramsay and Peter Geoghegan, 'The DUP's Facebook ads for Brexit targeted voters outside Northern Ireland', *openDemocracy*, July 2018.

20   Adam Ramsay and Peter Geoghegan, 'Meet the Soopa Doopa branding agency that delivered Brexit', *openDemocracy*, June 2017.

21   Previously unpublished email, sent 1 May 2016.

22   Jim Fitzpatrick, 'BBC Spotlight: Brexit, Dark Money and the DUP', *BBC*, June 2018.

23 Digital, Culture, Media and Sport Committee, 'Fake News', *House of Commons*, May 2018. See also http://data.parliament.uk/writtenevidence/committeeevidence.svc/evidencedocument/digital-culture-media-and-sport-committee/disinformation-and-fake-news/oral/82471.html; accessed 20 Jan. 2020.

24 Peter Geoghegan and Jenna Corderoy, 'How the Electoral Commission turned blind eye to DUP's shady Brexit cash', *openDemocracy*, October 2018.

25 Peter Geoghegan and Jenna Corderoy, '"Not in the public interest": why the Electoral Commission didn't investigate Vote Leave and DUP donation', *openDemocracy*, April 2019.

26 Peter Geoghegan and Jenna Corderoy, 'How the Electoral Commission turned blind eye to DUP's shady Brexit cash', *openDemocracy*, October 2018.

27 'DUP confirms £435,000 Brexit donation', *BBC*, February 2017.

28 Delegated Legislation Committee, 'Draft Transparency of Donations and Loans etc. (Northern Ireland political parties) order 2018', *House of Commons*, December 2017. See also https://hansard.parliament.uk/Commons/2017-12-19/debates/718e887a-4f01-44f6-a250-a56449cd1bbf/DraftTransparencyOf DonationsAndLoansEtc (NorthernIrelandPoliticalParties) Order2018; accessed 20 Jan. 2020.

29 Jessica Elgot, 'Labour criticises move to let past donations to DUP stay hidden', *Guardian*, December 2017.

30 Niall McCracken, 'Brexit donation: DUP received further £13,000 from CRC', *BBC*, April 2019.

31 Niall McCracken, 'Brexit technology firm used by DUP in Northern Ireland elections', *thedetail*, June 2017.

32 Laura Hughes and Jim Pickard, 'Curious tale of Boris Johnson's Irish flight with party backer', *Financial Times*, January 2019.

33 'Ian Paisley: DUP MP "stunned" and "humbled" at keeping seat', *BBC*, September 2018.

34 Sammy Wilson MP, *Twitter*, November 2018. See also https://twitter.com/eastantrimmp/status/1066330424585187337; accessed 20 Jan. 2020.

35 Peter Geoghegan, Seth Thévoz and Jenna Corderoy, 'Revealed:

The elite dining club behind £130m+ donations to the Tories', *openDemocracy*, November 2019.

36   Seth Thévoz, 'Inside the elite Tory fundraising machine', *openDemocracy*, December 2019.

37   Nicholas Watt, '"Secretive" Tory dining clubs bankrolling election campaign in key seats', *Guardian*, November 2014.

38   Jamie Mann and Ally Tibbitt, 'Electoral Commission probes £319,000 Tory "dark money" trust', *The Ferret*, June 2018.

39   'Fifth of Tory election donations from "dark money" trust', *STV News*, July 2018.

40   Niall McCracken, 'CRC Brexit donation to DUP not reported to watchdog', *BBC*, December 2018.

41   Paul Hutcheon, 'Scots Tory in £435,000 Brexit "dark money" row facing questions by MPs', *The Herald*, November 2018.

42   Letters to and from Digital, Culture, Media and Sport Committee, *House of Commons*. See also www.parliament.uk/documents/commons-committees/culture-media-and-sport/181126-Correspondence-between-Richard-Cook-CRC-and-the-Chair.pdf; accessed 20 Jan. 2020.

43   Digital, Culture, Media and Sport Committee, 'Disinformation and "fake news": Final Report', *House of Commons*, February 2019. See also https://publications.parliament.uk/pa/cm201719/cmselect/cmcumeds/1791/179112.htm; accessed 20 Jan. 2020.

44   'Electoral Funding: Unincorporated Associations', *House of Commons*, February 2019. See also https://hansard.parliament.uk/Commons/2019-02-27/debates/1016EB2E-9610-406B-913B-E20A2D5D9281/ElectoralFundingUnincorporatedAssociations; accessed 20 Jan. 2020.

Chapter 5: The Party Within a Party

1   Christopher Hope, 'Trump aide asked Brexiteers how President can help secure a clean Brexit before intervention', *Telegraph*, July 2018.

2   Tom Newton Dunn, 'TRUMP'S BREXIT BLAST Donald Trump told Theresa May how to do Brexit "but she wrecked it" – and says the US trade deal is off', *Sun*, July 2018.

3   Mattha Busby, 'UK-US trade deal discussed in secret meeting between Brexiteers and top Trump advisor', *Independent*, July 2018.

4   Adam Ramsay, 'MPs demand "urgent investigation" into Cabinet ministers' support for hard-Brexit lobby group', *openDemocracy*, January 2018.

5   Sam Knight, 'The man who brought you Brexit', *Guardian*, September 2016.

6   David Willetts and Anthony Teasdale, 'How the seed of Brexit was planted 30 years ago', *Prospect*, September 2018.

7   Paul Vallely, 'A big Little Englander', *Independent*, April 1996.

8   Martin Bright, 'Desperate Lucan dreamt of fascist coup', *Guardian*, January 2005.

9   Zac Goldsmith, 'Zac Goldsmith: How my dad saved Britain', *Spectator*, February 2015.

10   Tim Shipman, *All Out War: The Full Story of Brexit* (London, 2017), p. 25.

11   Michael Spicer, 'Move over Ukip, Jacob Rees-Mogg and the ERG are now the real Brexit watchdogs', *Telegraph*, January 2018.

12   Sam Knight, 'The man who brought you Brexit', *Guardian*, September 2016.

13   Roger Boyes, 'Austrian far Right plans euro ambush', *The Times*, November 1996.

14   Adam Ramsay, 'MPs demand "urgent investigation" into Cabinet ministers' support for hard-Brexit lobby group', *openDemocracy*, January 2018.

15   Jennifer Rankin, 'Daniel Hannan's MEP group told to repay €535,000 in EU funds', *Guardian*, December 2018.

16   Sam Knight, 'The man who brought you Brexit', *Guardian*, September 2016.

17   Daniel Hannan, 'I helped found the ERG – accusations of extremism are ridiculous', *Telegraph*, February 2019. Denis Doherty, 'Brexit: The history of the Tories' influential European Research Group', *BBC*, January 2018.

18 'The group that broke British politics', *The Economist*, February 2019.

19 Tom Embury-Dennis and Joe Watts, 'Brexit: Minister appointed to negotiate Britain's withdrawal wants European Union "wholly torn down"', *Independent*, July 2017.

20 Rowena Mason, 'EU referendum: David Cameron suffers defeat in parliament over "purdah" rules', *Guardian*, September 2015.

21 Adam Ramsay, 'MPs demand "urgent investigation" into Cabinet ministers' support for hard-Brexit lobby group', *openDemocracy*, January 2018.

22 Peter Geoghegan and Jenna Corderoy, 'Key members of Jacob-Rees Mogg's pro-Brexit MP lobby group finally revealed', *openDemocracy*, May 2019.

23 Sam Coates, 'Brexit-backing MPs plot their attacks on WhatsApp', *The Times*, February 2017.

24 Patrick Maguire, 'Meet Steve Baker, the Brexiteers' shop steward', *New Statesman*, July 2018.

25 Adam Ramsay and Peter Geoghegan, 'The new Brexit minister, the arms industry, the American hard right… and Equatorial Guinea', *openDemocracy*, July 2017.

26 Ian Birrell, 'I met Brexiter Steve Baker in Equatorial Guinea. His plan there was just as daft', *Guardian*, September 2018.

27 Mikey Smith, 'Ex-Brexit minister invested £70,000 in firm urging people to buy gold as "insurance" against no-deal', *Mirror*, August 2018.

28 Adam Ramsay and Peter Geoghegan, 'The new Brexit minister, the arms industry, the American hard right… and Equatorial Guinea', *openDemocracy*, July 2017.

29 Steve Baker, 'On complaining to the BBC', *stevebaker.info*, January 2011. See also www.stevebaker.info/2011/01/on-complaining-to-the-bbc/; accessed 21 Jan. 2020.

30 Tim Walker, 'BBC apology over suggestion that Norris McWhirter was a fascist', *Telegraph*, June 2011.

31 Alex Spence, 'The Definitive Story Of How A Former Washington Lobbyist Became "The Brexiteers' Brain"', *Buzzfeed*, May 2018. James Cusick, Peter Geoghegan and Jenna Corderoy, 'Ex-Brexit

minister Steve Baker remained in charge of secretive Tory ultra faction', *openDemocracy*, August 2018.

32 Anna Fazackerley, 'Universities deplore "McCarthyism" as MP demands list of tutors lecturing on Brexit', *Guardian*, October 2017.

33 Krishnan Guru-Murthy, 'Conservative MP Suella Fernandes warns Theresa May not to keep Britain in Single Market', *Channel 4*, September 2017.

34 James Cusick, 'MPs demand full investigation of hard-Brexit backing Tory "party within a party"', *openDemocracy*, September 2017.

35 David Pegg, Felicity Lawrence and Rob Evans, 'Tory Brexit faction censured for using public funds for campaigning', *Guardian*, September 2018.

36 James Cusick, Peter Geoghegan and Jenna Corderoy, 'Parliament watchdog probes Rees-Mogg's hard Brexit lobby group over "other sources of funding"', *openDemocracy*, September 2018.

37 Alex Spence, 'These Leaked WhatsApp Chats Reveal Just How Brexiteer Tories Fight The "Smeary" BBC', *Buzzfeed*, March 2018.

38 David Pegg, Felicity Lawrence and Rob Evans, 'Tory Brexit faction censured for using public funds for campaigning', *Guardian*, September 2018.

39 Ibid.

40 Ibid.

41 Peter Geoghegan, 'Revealed: the dirty secrets of the DUP's "dark money" Brexit donor', *openDemocracy*, January 2019.

42 James Cusick, Peter Geoghegan and Jenna Corderoy, 'Parliament watchdog probes Rees-Mogg's hard Brexit lobby group over "other sources of funding"', *openDemocracy*, September 2018.

43 James Cusick, Jenna Corderoy and Peter Geoghegan, 'Revealed: the files that expose ERG as a militant "party within a party"', *openDemocracy*, July 2019.

44 'Freedom of Information', *Institute for Government*. See also www.instituteforgovernment.org.uk/explainers/freedom-of-information; accessed 21 Jan. 2020.

Chapter 6: The Atlantic Bridge to Global Britain

1 Daniel Schulman, 'Charles Koch's Brain', *Politico*, September 2014.
2 Jane Mayer, *Dark Money: The Hidden History of the Billionaires Behind the Rise of the Radical Right* (London, 2018), pp. 141–142.
3 Ibid.
4 Daniel Schulman, 'Charles Koch's Brain', *Politico*, September 2014.
5 Jane Mayer, *Dark Money: The Hidden History of the Billionaires Behind the Rise of the Radical Right* (London, 2018), pp. 141–142.
6 Ibid.
7 Ibid., p. 79.
8 Ibid., p. 89.
9 Nadja Popovich, Livia Albeck-Ripka and Kendra Pierre-Louis, '95 Environmental Rules Being Rolled Back Under Trump', *New York Times*, December 2019.
10 George Monbiot, 'A rightwing insurrection is usurping our democracy', *Guardian*, October 2012.
11 Ibid.
12 Tamasin Cave and Andy Rowell, *A Quiet Word: Lobbying, Crony Capitalism and Broken Politics in Britain* (London, 2015), p. 130.
13 David Frum, 'When Did the GOP Lose Touch With Reality?', *New York Magazine*, November 2011.
14 Doug Palmer, 'UK hopes for trade Christmas gift from Trump', *Politico*, July 2018.
15 Jeremy W. Peters, 'Heritage Foundation Says Trump Has Embraced Two-Thirds of Its Agenda', *New York Times*, January 2018.
16 Dominic Kennedy, 'Cash raised for Margaret Thatcher centre spent on rightwing events', *The Times*, February 2019.
17 Peter Walker and Anushka Asthana, 'Brexit thinktank scrambles to remove institute from its name', *Guardian*, December 2017.
18 Felicity Lawrence, David Pegg and Rob Evans, 'Rightwing thinktanks unveil radical plan for US-UK Brexit trade deal', *Guardian*, September 2018.
19 George Monbiot, 'How corporate dark money is taking power on both sides of the Atlantic', *Guardian*, February 2017.

20   Jamie Doward, 'Liam Fox's Atlantic Bridge linked top Tories and Tea Party activists', *Guardian*, October 2011.

21   'Conservative Liam Fox is Britain's "Almost" Donald Rumsfeld', *Human Events*, October 2006.

22   Molly Jackman, 'ALEC's Influence over Lawmaking in State Legislatures', *Brookings*, December 2013. See also www.brookings. edu/articles/alecs-influence-over-lawmaking-in-state-legislatures/; accessed 23 Jan. 2020.

23   Ed Pilkington, 'How a powerful rightwing lobby is plotting to stop minimum wage hikes', *Guardian*, February 2015.

24   'Atlantic Bridge and the climate skeptic connection', *Carbon Brief*, October 2011.

25   Jamie Doward, 'Liam Fox's Atlantic Bridge linked top Tories and Tea Party activists', *Guardian*, October 2011.

26   Ibid.

27   Jane Mayer, *Dark Money: The Hidden History of the Billionaires Behind the Rise of the Radical Right* (London, 2018), p. 19.

28   Simon Bowers, 'Climate-sceptic US senator given funds by BP political action committee', *Guardian*, March 2015.

29   Toby Harnden and Rosa Prince, 'Senior Tories' links with Republican NHS-bashers revealed', *Telegraph*, August 2009.

30   Deborah Summers and Lee Glendinning, 'Cameron rebukes Tory MEP who rubbished NHS in America', *Guardian*, August 2009.

31   Jamie Doward, 'Liam Fox's Atlantic Bridge linked top Tories and Tea Party activists', *Guardian*, October 2011.

32   Rupert Neate, Robert Booth, Rajeev Syal, '"Adviser" Adam Werritty ran charity from Liam Fox's office', *Guardian*, October 2011.

33   Rupert Neate, 'Charity created by Liam Fox axed after watchdog issues criticism', *Guardian*, October 2011.

34   'Adam Werritty: Fox's friend, flatmate and business partner', *BBC*, October 2011.

35   Tamasin Cave and Andy Rowell, *A Quiet Word: Lobbying, Crony Capitalism and Broken Politics in Britain* (London, 2015), p. 46.

36   Rupert Neate, 'Adam Werritty paid £70,000 by Tory donor-funded Pargav Limited', *Guardian*, March 2012. 'Liam Fox donor Jon Moulton felt "mugged"', *BBC*, November 2011.

37 Rupert Neate, 'Defence minister Gerald Howarth met firm funding Werritty trips', *Guardian*, October 2011.

38 Sir Gus O'Donnell, 'Allegations against Rt Hon Dr Liam Fox MP'. See also https://assets.publishing.service.gov.uk/government/uploads/system/uploads/attachment_data/file/60517/allegations-fox.pdf; accessed 23 Jan. 2020.

39 'Cotton, Colleagues Pen Letter Pledging to Back Britain After Brexit', August 2019. See also www.cotton.senate.gov/?p=press_release&id=1191; accessed 23 Jan. 2020.

40 Ewen MacAskill, 'Thatcher returns to fight old battles', *Guardian*, October 1999.

41 Duncan Bell, 'The Anglosphere: new enthusiasm for an old dream', *Prospect*, January 2017.

42 Michael Kenny and Nick Pearce, *Shadows of Empire: The Anglosphere in British Politics* (Cambridge, 2018), pp. 122–123.

43 Ibid.

44 John Lloyd, 'The Anglosphere Project', *New Statesman*, March 2000.

45 Felicity Lawrence, Rob Evans, David Pegg, Caelainn Barr and Pamela Duncan, 'How the right's radical thinktanks reshaped the Conservative party', *Guardian*, November 2019.

46 'How to use Brexit as an example for future policy changes', *Atlas Network*, September 2017.

47 Tom Happold, 'Tory youth group accused of take-over plot', *Guardian*, October 2003.

48 Hannah Barnes, 'What is the Young Britons' Foundation?', *BBC*, December 2015.

49 Robert Booth, 'Radicalised Tories ready to take on Labour's big guns', *Guardian*, March 2010.

50 Robert Booth, 'David Cameron accused of being dishonest over links with "Conservative madrasa"', *Guardian*, May 2010.

51 Tom Happold, 'Tory youth group accused of take-over plot', *Guardian*, October 2003.

52 Josh Boswell, 'Strippers, booze and Tatler Tories', *The Times*, December 2015.

53 Carole Cadwalladr, 'Steve Bannon: "We went back and forth" on the themes of Johnson's big speech', *Guardian*, June 2019.

54 'Blaney on Brexit: What The Hell Has Happened?!', *Young America's Foundation*, January 2019. See also www.yaf.org/news/blaney-on-brexit-what-the-hell-has-happened/; accessed 23 Jan. 2020.

55 Fintan O'Toole, *Heroic Failure: Brexit and the Politics of Pain* (London, 2018), p. 83.

56 Robert Saunders, 'Myths from a small island: the dangers of a buccaneering view of British history', *New Statesman*, October 2019.

57 Andrew Roberts, 'CANZUK: after Brexit, Canada, Australia, New Zealand and Britain can unite as a pillar of Western civilisation', *Telegraph*, September 2016.

58 Sam Coates and Marcus Leroux, 'Ministers aim to build "empire 2.0" with African Commonwealth', *The Times*, March 2017.

59 Annabelle Dickson, 'India in no rush to do a trade deal with post-Brexit Britain', *Politico*, April 2018.

60 Adam Bienkov, 'Liam Fox will break his promise to sign 40 free trade deals the "second after" Brexit', *Business Insider*, January 2019.

61 Tom Edgington, 'Brexit: What trade deals has the UK done so far?', *BBC*, January 2020.

62 Alex Wickham, 'Liz Truss Charged The Taxpayer To Hire A Photographer For Her World Trade Tour', *Buzzfeed*, October 2019.

63 'The Downing Street Policy Unit, Boris Johnson's brain', *The Economist*, August 2019.

64 Andrew Roberts, 'Britain will be better off as a junior partner of the United States than an EU vassal', *Telegraph*, August 2019.

65 'Q&A: Cash-for-honours', *BBC*, July 2007.

66 Nicholas Watt, 'David Cameron publishes details of donor dinners in cash-for-access row', *Guardian*, March 2012.

67 Peter Geoghegan, Seth Thévoz and Jenna Corderoy, 'Cabinet Office urged to investigate fresh Tory "cash for honours" scandal', *openDemocracy*, December 2019.

68 Nick Mathiason and Yuba Bessaoud, 'Tory Party funding from City doubles under Cameron', *The Bureau of Investigative Journalism*, February 2011. See also www.thebureauinvestigates.com/stories/2011-02-08/tory-party-funding-from-city-doubles-under-cameron; accessed 23 Jan. 2020.

69   David Hellier, 'Why are hedge funds supporting Brexit?', *Guardian*, November 2015.

70   Caroline Wheeler and Rosamund Urwin, 'Boris Johnson's donor Crispin Odey eyes Brexit jackpot with £300m bet against British firms', *The Times*, August 2019.

71   Stefan Boscia, 'Conservatives break election donations record while unions turn on the taps for Labour', *City A.M.*, November 2019.

72   Seth Thévoz and Peter Geoghegan, 'Revealed: Russian donors have stepped up Tory funding', *openDemocracy*, November 2019.

73   Naomi Klein, *The Shock Doctrine: The Rise of Disaster Capitalism* (London, 2008).

74   William Davies, 'England's rentier alliance is driving support for a no-deal Brexit', *New Statesman*, August 2019.

75   Ashley Cowburn, 'Jacob Rees-Mogg's investment firm opens second Ireland fund but insists it "has nothing to do with Brexit"', *Independent*, July 2018.

76   David Edgerton, 'Brexit is a necessary crisis – it reveals Britain's true place in the world', *Guardian*, October 2019.

77   Matthew Elliott and James Kanagasooriam, 'Public opinion in the post-Brexit era: Economic attitudes in modern Britain', *Legatum Institute*, October 2017. See also https://lif.blob.core.windows.net/lif/docs/default-source/default-library/1710-public-opinion-in-the-post-brexit-era-final.pdf?sfvrsn=0; accessed 23 Jan. 2020.

Chapter 7: The Brexit Influencing Game

1   'Undercover: How the IEA lets donors influence Brexit', *Unearthed*, July 2018. See also www.youtube.com/watch?v=OXyaLhkBaJ4; accessed 23 Jan. 2020.

2   Robert Booth, 'Rightwing UK thinktank "offered ministerial access" to potential US donors', *Guardian*, July 2018.

3   Ibid.

4   Alice Ross and Lawrence Carter, 'A hard Brexit think tank told a potential donor it could influence its research reports in exchange

for funding', *Unearthed*, July 2018. See also https://unearthed.
greenpeace.org/2018/07/29/a-hard-brexit-think-tank-offered-a-
prospective-us-agribusiness-donor-the-chance-to-influence-its-
report-on-green-brexit/; accessed 23 Jan. 2020.

5   Lawrence Carter and Alice Ross, 'A leading think tank brokered
access to ministers for US donors looking to influence Brexit',
Unearthed, July 2018. See also https://unearthed.greenpeace.
org/2018/07/29/iea-hard-brexit-think-tank-access-ministers/;
accessed 23 Jan. 2020.

6   Alice Ross and Lawrence Carter, 'How the IEA teamed up with
US donors to push for environmental deregulation post-Brexit',
Unearthed, July 2018. See also https://energydesk.greenpeace.
org/2018/07/30/iea-brexit-shanker-singham-mark-littlewood-us-
donors/; accessed 23 Jan. 2020.

7   Lawrence Carter and Alice Ross, 'A leading think tank brokered
access to ministers for US donors looking to influence Brexit',
Unearthed, July 2018. See also https://unearthed.greenpeace.
org/2018/07/29/iea-hard-brexit-think-tank-access-ministers/;
accessed 23 Jan. 2020.

8   Robert Booth and Damian Carrington, 'The Brexit-influencing
game: how IEA got involved with a US rancher', *Guardian*,
July 2018.

9   Ibid.

10 'RTRS Shanker Singham / Danielle Sremac Interview Enterprise
City RS', SerbianInstituteTV, October 2014. See also www.youtube.
com/watch?v=koGzYswoUqI; accessed 23 Jan. 2020.

11 'Prime Minister Cvijanovic signs a Letter of Intent with Babson
Global from Boston', *Republic of Srpska Government*, September
2014. See also http://www.vladars.net/eng/vlada/prime_
minister/media/news/Pages/Prime_Minister_Cvijanovic_
signs_a_Letter_of_Intent_with_Babson_Global_from_Boston.
aspx; accessed 23 Jan. 2020.

12 Alex Spence, 'The Definitive Story Of How A Former Washington
Lobbyist Became "The Brexiteers' Brain"', *Buzzfeed*, May 2018.

13 Ibid.

14 Ibid.

15 Alden Abbott, 'Enterprise Cities, Competition, and Economic Growth', *The Heritage Foundation*, September 2014. See also www.heritage.org/budget-and-spending/commentary/enterprise-cities-competition-and-economic-growth; accessed 23 Jan. 2020.

16 Alex Spence, 'The Definitive Story Of How A Former Washington Lobbyist Became "The Brexiteers' Brain"', *Buzzfeed*, May 2018.

17 Treasury Committee, 'Committee questions economic experts on Brexit', *House of Commons*, July 2016. See also www.parliament.uk/business/committees/committees-a-z/commons-select/treasury-committee/news-parliament-2015/future-economic-relationship-with-eu-evidence-16-17/; accessed 23 Jan. 2020.

18 Luke Coppen, 'Brexit's Catholic Mr Fixit', *Catholic Herald*, July 2017.

19 'About Shanker Singham', *IEA*. See also https://iea.org.uk/wp-content/uploads/2018/05/Shanker-Singham-about.pdf; accessed 23 Jan. 2020.

20 David Pegg, Felicity Lawrence and Rob Evans, 'Pro-Brexit adviser admits UK would be better off staying in EU', *Guardian*, November 2018.

21 Alex Spence, 'The Definitive Story Of How A Former Washington Lobbyist Became "The Brexiteers' Brain"', *Buzzfeed*, May 2018.

22 Patrick Wintour, 'David Davis went to seminar that drew up hard Brexit blueprint', *Guardian*, October 2016.

23 Lawrence Carter and Alice Ross, 'A leading think tank brokered access to ministers for US donors looking to influence Brexit', *Unearthed*, July 2018. See also https://unearthed.greenpeace.org/2018/07/29/iea-hard-brexit-think-tank-access-ministers/; accessed 23 Jan. 2020.

24 Cynthia O'Murchu and Henry Mance, 'Legatum: the think-tank at intellectual heart of "hard" Brexit', *Financial Times*, December 2017.

25 Simon Walters and Glen Owen, 'Putin's link to Boris and Gove's Brexit "coup" revealed: Tycoon who netted millions from Russian gas deal funds think tank that helped write the ministers letter demanding May take a tougher stance on leaving the EU', *Daily Mail*, November 2017.

26 Adam Ramsay and Peter Geoghegan, 'Liam Fox caught in fresh "lobbyists as advisers" scandal', *openDemocracy*, June 2018. Henry Zeffman, 'Trade guru Shanker Singham quits over role at lobbying firm', *The Times*, June 2018.

27 Peter Geoghegan and Jenna Corderoy, 'Freedom of Information is broken – help us fix it', *openDemocracy*, January 2020.

28 James Cusick, Jenna Corderoy and Peter Geoghegan, 'Revealed: the files that expose ERG as a militant "party within a party"', *openDemocracy*, July 2019.

29 Alex Spence, 'The Definitive Story Of How A Former Washington Lobbyist Became "The Brexiteers' Brain"', *Buzzfeed*, May 2018.

30 Ibid.

31 Peter Geoghegan and Jenna Corderoy, 'Revealed: How dark money is winning "the Brexit influencing game"', *openDemocracy*, February 2019.

32 Alex Spence, 'This Billionaire Was Accused Of Being A Russian Spy. Now He's Suing The Man He Says Is To Blame', *Buzzfeed*, October 2018.

33 Dan Bloom, 'Founder of Brexiteer Legatum Institute think tank "was suspected of working for Russian intelligence"', *Mirror*, May 2018.

34 Peter Geoghegan, 'Legatum breached charity regulations with Brexit work, Charity Commission finds', *openDemocracy*, May 2018.

35 Catherine Neilan, 'IEA poaches Legatum's top Brexit adviser Shanker Singham and team', *City A.M.*, March 2018.

36 Adam Curtis, 'The Curse of Tina', *BBC*, September 2011.

37 Jane Mayer, *Dark Money: The Hidden History of the Billionaires Behind the Rise of the Radical Right* (London, 2018), p. 80.

38 Adam Curtis, 'The Curse of Tina', *BBC*, September 2011.

39 Ibid.

40 Richard Cockett, *Thinking the Unthinkable: Think-Tanks and the Economic Counter-Revolution, 1931–83* (London, 1995), p. 166.

41 Adam Curtis, 'The Curse of Tina', *BBC*, September 2011.

42 Peter Clarke, 'Serial Evangelists', *London Review of Books*, June 1994.

43 Felicity Lawrence, Rob Evans, David Pegg, Caelainn Barr and Pamela Duncan, 'How the right's radical thinktanks reshaped the Conservative party', *Guardian*, November 2019.

44 Ibid.

45 Lee Fang, 'Sphere of Influence: How American Libertarians Are Remaking Latin American Politics', *The Intercept*, August 2017.

46 Andy Beckett, *When the Lights Went Out: Britain in the Seventies* (London, 2010), p. 274.

47 Ibid., p. 276.

48 Ibid., p. 48.

49 Ibid., p. 276.

50 Peter Clarke, 'Serial Evangelists', *London Review of Books*, June 1994.

51 'Commanding Heights', *PBS*. See also www.pbs.org/wgbh/ commandingheights/shared/minitext/prof_keithjoseph.html; accessed 23 Jan. 2020.

52 Adam Curtis, 'The Curse of Tina', *BBC*, September 2011.

53 George Monbiot, 'A rightwing insurrection is usurping our democracy', *Guardian*, October 2012.

54 David Parker, *The Official History of Privatisation Volume 1: The Formative Years 1970–1987* (London, 2009), p. 42.

55 Jonathan Gornall, 'Big tobacco, the new politics, and the threat to public health', *The BMJ*, May 2019.

56 Stian Westlake, 'The strange death of Tory economic thinking', *Capx*, April 2019.

57 Mark Littlewood, 'The next Tory leader must be a bullish libertarian, not a bland managerialist', *Telegraph*, March 2019.

58 Stian Westlake, 'The strange death of Tory economic thinking', *Capx*, April 2019.

59 Nick Cohen, 'Brexiters never had a real exit plan. No wonder they avoided the issue', *Guardian*, January 2019.

60 Felicity Lawrence, Rob Evans, David Pegg, Caelainn Barr and Pamela Duncan, 'How the right's radical thinktanks reshaped the Conservative party', *Guardian*, November 2019.

61 Lawrence Carter and Alice Ross, 'Revealed: BP and gambling interests fund secretive free market think tank', *Unearthed*, July 2018. See also https://energydesk.greenpeace.org/2018/07/30/bp-funding-institute-of-economic-affairs-gambling/; accessed 23 Jan. 2020.

62 Ibid.

63   David Pegg and Rob Evans, 'Revealed: Top UK thinktank spent decades undermining climate science', *Guardian*, October 2019.

64   Jonathan Gornall, 'Big tobacco, the new politics, and the threat to public health', *The BMJ*, May 2019.

65   Tamasin Cave and Andy Rowell, *A Quiet Word: Lobbying, Crony Capitalism and Broken Politics in Britain* (London, 2014), p. 28.

66   Dan Roberts, 'Sweet Brexit: what sugar tells us about Britain's future outside the EU', *Guardian*, March 2017.

67   Tom McTague, 'The Brawler', *Politico*, December 2017.

68   'Think Tent 2018 | Global Trade: Producers versus Consumers. Where does the balance lie?', *IEA*, October 2018. See also https://iea.org.uk/events/think-tent-2018-global-trade-producers-versus-consumers-where-does-the-balance-lie/; accessed 23 Jan. 2020.

69   Chloe Farand, 'Hard-Brexit Lobbyists Demand UK Roll-Back Environmental Standards to Strike Free Trade Deals with India, China and US', *DeSmog*, September 2018.

70   Felicity Lawrence, 'Who is behind the push for a post-Brexit free trade deal with the US?', *Guardian*, December 2018.

71   Rob Evans, Felicity Lawrence and David Pegg, 'US groups raise millions to support rightwing UK thinktanks', *Guardian*, September 2018.

72   George Monbiot, 'How US billionaires are fuelling the hard-right cause in Britain', *Guardian*, December 2018.

73   Rob Evans, Felicity Lawrence and David Pegg, 'US agribusiness lobbyists paid for trip by David Davis', *Guardian*, December 2018.

74   David Pegg, Rob Evans and Felicity Lawrence, 'Owen Paterson trips worth £39,000 funded by unknown donors', *Guardian*, January 2019.

75   Lawrence Carter and Alice Ross, 'Leading Brexiteers' trip to meet Trump trade officials funded by US business interests', *Unearthed*, December 2018. See also https://unearthed.greenpeace.org/2018/12/21/brexit-oklahoma-david-davis-owen-paterson/; accessed 23 Jan. 2020.

76   Lawrence Carter and Alice Ross, 'A leading think tank brokered access to ministers for US donors looking to influence Brexit', *Unearthed*, July 2018. See also https://unearthed.greenpeace.

org/2018/07/29/iea-hard-brexit-think-tank-access-ministers/; accessed 23 Jan. 2020.

77 Justin Lewis and Stephen Cushion, 'Think Tanks, Television News and Impartiality', *Journalism Studies*, October 2017. See also www. tandfonline.com/doi/pdf/10.1080/1461670X.2017.1389295; accessed 23 Jan. 2020.

78 Adam Ramsay and Peter Geoghegan, 'Dominic Raab: is he the IEA's man in government?', *openDemocracy*, July 2018.

79 Jonathan Gornall, 'Big tobacco, the new politics, and the threat to public health', *The BMJ*, May 2019.

80 Ibid.

81 Ibid.

82 Solomon Hughes, 'Making the IEA "Freer" to espouse Tory ideology', *Morning Star*, April 2018.

83 Taylor Heyman, 'An MP quoted Destiny's Child in a speech and Twitter doesn't know what to think', *Independent.ie*, July 2018.

84 Tony Connelly, 'Alternative arrangements: Holy grail or fig leaf?', *RTÉ*, June 2019.

85 John Campbell, 'Brexit: Irish border a "fictitious problem"', *BBC*, November 2018.

86 Peter Geoghegan, 'Legatum: the Brexiteers' favourite think tank. Who is behind them?', *openDemocracy*, November 2017.

87 Shanker Singham, Austen Morgan, Victoria Hewson and Alice Brooks, 'Mutual Interest: How the UK and EU can resolve the Irish border issue after Brexit', *Legatum Institute*, September 2017. See also https://img1.wsimg.com/blobby/go/bf4d316c-4c0b-4e87-8edb-350f819ee031/downloads/1cstfufh8_214588. pdf?ver=1566163477846; accessed 23 Jan. 2020.

88 Peter Geoghegan and Jenna Corderoy, 'Revealed: How dark money is winning "the Brexit influencing game"', *openDemocracy*, February 2019.

89 'The Malthouse Compromise explained as May appoints Working Group to take the proposals forward', *BrexitCentral*, February 2019.

90 Colin Crouch, *The Strange Death of Neo-liberalism* (Cambridge, 2011), p. 131.

91   Andrew Sparrow, 'David Cameron vows to tackle "secret corporate lobbying"', *Guardian*, February 2010.

92   Steven Swinford, 'Election 2019: Isaac Levido secured Tory triumph with skill and sharp slogan', *The Times*, December 2019.

93   Jim Waterson, 'Lynton Crosby's firm in illegal lobbying inquiry over Boris Johnson link', *Guardian*, October 2019.

94   Advisory Committee on Business Appointments (ACOBA) Annual Report 2017–2018. See also www.gov.uk/government/publications/advisory-committee-on-business-appointments-acoba-annual-report-2017-2018; accessed 23 Jan. 2020.

95   Peter Walker, 'David Davis trousering £96,000 for part-time roles since cabinet exit', *Guardian*, January 2019.

96   Rob Evans, Felicity Lawrence and David Pegg, 'Revealed: Owen Paterson lobbied for firms he was paid to advise', *Guardian*, September 2019.

97   'Think Tanks in the UK 2017: Transparency, Lobbying and Fake News in Brexit Britain', *Transparify*, February 2017.

98   'New think tank ranking: less than 4% of the UK public can name a think tank', *Cast From Clay*, June 2019. See also https://weareflint.co.uk/blog/2019/6/25/new-research-less-than-4-of-the-uk-public-can-name-a-think-tank; accessed 23 Jan. 2020.

99   Cahal Milmo, 'Right-wing think-tank secured change in Government policy after £15,000 gift from mystery donor', *Independent*, February 2016.

100 Lawrence Carter and Alice Ross, 'A leading think tank brokered access to ministers for US donors looking to influence Brexit', *Unearthed*, July 2018. See also https://unearthed.greenpeace.org/2018/07/29/iea-hard-brexit-think-tank-access-ministers/; accessed 23 Jan. 2020.

101 Felicity Lawrence, Rob Evans, David Pegg, Caelainn Barr and Pamela Duncan, 'How the right's radical thinktanks reshaped the Conservative party', *Guardian*, November 2019.

102 Charlotte Tobitt, 'Guido Fawkes news editor made special adviser to Jacob Rees-Mogg', *Press Gazette*, August 2019.

103 'Buckingham launches new centre for economics and entrepreneurship', *University of Buckingham*, November 2018. See

also www.buckingham.ac.uk/news/buckingham-launches-new-centre-for-entrepreneurship/; accessed 23 Jan. 2020.

104 Adam Curtis, 'The Curse of Tina', *BBC*, September 2011.

Chapter 8: Digital Gangsters

1 Stephanie Baker, 'Cambridge Analytica Won't Be Revived Under New Company Name', *Bloomberg*, May 2018.

2 Katie French and Martin Robinson, 'Information commissioners leave Cambridge Analytica with a van full of evidence after searching data firm's London offices for seven hours amid Facebook privacy scandal', *Daily Mail*, March 2018.

3 'Revealed: Trump's election consultants filmed saying they use bribes and sex workers to entrap politicians', *Channel 4*, March 2018.

4 'Facebook: Explaining the company's massive share slump', *BBC*, July 2018.

5 Rob Davies and Dominic Rushe, 'Facebook to pay $5bn fine as regulator settles Cambridge Analytica complaint', *Guardian*, July 2019.

6 Carole Cadwalladr, 'Fresh Cambridge Analytica leak "shows global manipulation is out of control"', *Guardian*, January 2020.

7 Carole Cadwalladr, 'Cambridge Analytica's ruthless bid to sway the vote in Nigeria', *Guardian*, March 2018.

8 Larry Madowo, 'How Cambridge Analytica poisoned Kenya's democracy', *Washington Post*, March 2018.

9 Holly Watt, 'MoD granted "List X" status to Cambridge Analytica parent company', *Guardian*, March 2018.

10 Jane Mayer, 'The Reclusive Hedge-Fund Tycoon Behind the Trump Presidency', *New Yorker*, March 2017.

11 Curt Devine, Donie O'Sullivan and Drew Griffin, 'How Steve Bannon used Cambridge Analytica to further his alt-right vision for America', *CNN*, May 2018.

12 Amber Macintyre, 'Who's Working for Your Vote', *Tactical Tech*, November 2018. See also https://ourdataourselves.tacticaltech.org/posts/whos-working-for-vote/; accessed 26 Jan. 2020.

13   Martin Moore, *Democracy Hacked: Political Turmoil and Information Warfare in the Digital Age* (London, 2018), p. 66.

14   Alix Spiegel, 'Freud's Nephew and the Origins of Public Relations', *npr*, April 2005.

15   Adam Sheingate, *Building a Business of Politics: The Rise of Political Consulting and the Transformation of American Democracy* (2016), pp. 59–64.

16   Ibid.

17   Ibid.

18   Ibid.

19   Liza Featherstone, 'Talk is cheap: the myth of the focus group', *Guardian*, February 2018.

20   Adam Sheingate, *Building a Business of Politics: The Rise of Political Consulting and the Transformation of American Democracy* (2016), pp. 59–64.

21   Amber Macintyre, Gary Wright and Stephanie Hankey, 'Data and Democracy in the UK: A report by Tactical Tech's Data and Politics Team', *Tactical Tech*. See also https://cdn.ttc.io/s/ourdataourselves.tacticaltech.org/ttc-influence-industry-uk.pdf; accessed 26 Jan. 2020.

22   Matt Tempest and Julia Day, 'Labour chief defends "flying pigs" ad', *Guardian*, February 2005.

23   Martin Moore, *Democracy Hacked: Political Turmoil and Information Warfare in the Digital Age* (London, 2018), p. 113.

24   Monica Langley and Jessica E. Vascellaro, 'Google CEO Backs Obama', *Wall Street Journal*, October 2008.

25   Maggie Dalton-Hoffman, 'The Effect of Social Media in the 2012 Presidential Election', *Trinity College Digital Repository*, summer 2012. See also https://digitalrepository.trincoll.edu/cgi/viewcontent.cgi?article=1035&context=fypapers; accessed 26 Jan. 2020.

26   Jamie Bartlett, *The People Vs Tech: How the Internet is Killing Democracy (and How We Save It)* (London, 2018), p. 81.

27   Anselm Hager, 'Do Online Ads Influence Vote Choice?', *Political Communication*, January 2019. See also www.tandfonline.com/doi/abs/10.1080/10584609.2018.1548529?journalCode=upcp20; accessed 26 Jan. 2020.

28 Leighton Andrews, *Facebook, the Media and Democracy: Big Tech, Small State?* (Abingdon, 2019), p. 248.

29 Tamasin Cave and Andy Rowell, *A Quiet Word: Lobbying, Crony Capitalism and Broken Politics in Britain* (London, 2015), pp. 39–40.

30 Martin Moore, *Democracy Hacked: Political Turmoil and Information Warfare in the Digital Age* (London, 2018), p. 126.

31 Sonam Rai, 'Acxiom shares tank after Facebook cuts ties with data brokers', *Reuters*, March 2018.

32 Jim Waterson, 'How The Tories Spent £1.2 Million On Facebook Adverts In Run-Up To Election', *Buzzfeed*, January 2016.

33 Amber Macintyre, Gary Wright and Stephanie Hankey, 'Data and Democracy in the UK: A report by Tactical Tech's Data and Politics Team', *Tactical Tech*. See also https://cdn.ttc.io/s/ourdataourselves.tacticaltech.org/ttc-influence-industry-uk.pdf; accessed 26 Jan. 2020.

34 Martin Moore, *Democracy Hacked: Political Turmoil and Information Warfare in the Digital Age* (London, 2018), p. 127.

35 David Taylor, 'Tories knew they would win election three weeks before vote', *The Times*, May 2015.

36 Dominic Cummings, 'On the referendum #20: the campaign, physics and data science – Vote Leave's "Voter Intention Collection System" (VICS) now available for all', *Dominic Cummings's Blog*, October 2016. See also https://dominiccummings.com/2016/10/29/on-the-referendum-20-the-campaign-physics-and-data-science-vote-leaves-voter-intention-collection-system-vics-now-available-for-all/; accessed 26 Jan. 2020.

37 Leighton Andrews, *Facebook, the Media and Democracy: Big Tech, Small State?* (Abingdon, 2019), p. 243.

38 Dan Sabbagh, 'Rise of digital politics: why UK parties spend big on Facebook', *Guardian*, March 2018.

39 Sebastian Payne, 'UK election: how the Tories "got it done"', *Financial Times*, December 2019.

40 Steven Swinford, 'Election 2019: meet the whizzkids fighting the social media war', *The Times*, November 2019.

41 Jim Waterson and Rajeev Syal, 'Keir Starmer: Tories' doctored TV footage is "act of desperation"', *Guardian*, November 2019.

42   Sebastian Payne, 'UK election: how the Tories "got it done"',
     Financial Times, December 2019.

43   Alastair Reid and Carlotta Dotto, 'Thousands of misleading
     Conservative ads side-step scrutiny thanks to Facebook policy',
     First Draft, December 2019. See also https://firstdraftnews.org/
     latest/thousands-of-misleading-conservative-ads-side-step-scrutiny-
     thanks-to-facebook-policy/; accessed 26 Jan. 2020.

44   Ella Hollowood and Matthew D'Ancona, 'Big little lies', *Tortoise*,
     December 2019. See also https://members.tortoisemedia.
     com/2019/12/11/lies-191211/content.html; accessed 26 Jan. 2020.

45   Dominic Cummings, '"Two hands are a lot" – we're hiring data
     scientists, project managers, policy experts, assorted weirdos...',
     Dominic Cummings's Blog, January 2020. See also https://
     dominiccummings.com/2020/01/02/two-hands-are-a-lot-were-
     hiring-data-scientists-project-managers-policy-experts-assorted-
     weirdos/; accessed 26 Jan. 2020.

46   Rowland Manthorpe, 'General election: WhatsApp messages urge
     British Hindus to vote against Labour', *Sky News*, November 2019.

47   Jim Waterson, 'What we learned about the media this election',
     Guardian, December 2019.

48   James Cusick, 'New evidence that LibDems sold voter data for
     £100,000 held back till after election', *openDemocracy*, November 2019.

49   Rowland Manthorpe, 'Data protection experts want watchdog to
     investigate Conservative and Labour parties', *Sky News*, October
     2019.

50   'General election 2019: Zac Goldsmith loses seat to Lib Dems
     again', *BBC*, December 2019.

51   Kate Proctor, 'Johnson accused of "rewarding racism" after Zac
     Goldsmith peerage', *Guardian*, December 2019.

52   Isobel Thompson, 'How Irish anti-abortion activists are drawing
     on Brexit and Trump campaigns to influence referendum',
     openDemocracy, May 2018.

53   'Republicans Overseas UK: An Evening with GOP Strategist Matt
     Mackowiak', *Republicans Overseas UK*. See also www.eventbrite.
     co.uk/e/republicans-overseas-uk-an-evening-with-gop-strategist-
     matt-mackowiak-tickets-56806612106#; accessed 26 Jan. 2020.

54 Peter Pomerantsev, *This is Not Propaganda: Adventures in the War Against Reality Paperback* (London, 2019), p. 365.

55 Gian Volpicelli, 'An ex-Vote Leave staffer is running Facebook ads pushing the Greens', *Wired*, November 2019.

56 Peter Geoghegan, 'Revealed: Former Vote Leave data chief accused of pro-Tory "disinformation"', *openDemocracy*, November 2019.

57 Jemima Kelly, Cynthia O'Murchu and David Blood, 'Voters left in the dark over money behind online election ads', *Financial Times*, December 2019.

58 Ibid.

59 Rowland Manthorpe, 'General election: Woman accused after posting ads costing £17,000 on Facebook attacking Labour', *Sky News*, December 2019.

60 Ibid.

61 Peter Geoghegan, 'Revealed: The dark-money Brexit ads flooding social media', *openDemocracy*, February 2019.

62 Alex Spence, 'A Mysterious Hard Brexit Group Run By A Young Tory Writer Is Now Britain's Biggest Spending Political Campaign On Facebook', *Buzzfeed*, March 2019.

63 Jim Waterson, 'Facebook Brexit ads secretly run by staff of Lynton Crosby firm', *Guardian*, April 2019.

64 Jim Waterson, 'Johnson ally Lynton Crosby could be called to give evidence to MPs', *Guardian*, August 2019.

65 Jim Waterson, 'Lynton Crosby's firm in illegal lobbying inquiry over Boris Johnson link', *Guardian*, October 2019.

66 Hadas Gold, 'Facebook agrees to pay fine over Cambridge Analytica', *CNN*, October 2019.

67 Patrick Howell O'Neill, 'Mozilla Calls Out Facebook for "Failing" on Ad Transparency', *Gizmodo*, April 2019.

68 Kari Paul, 'Facebook employees "strongly object" to policy allowing false claims in political ads', *Guardian*, October 2019.

69 'Facebook, Elections and Political Speech', *Facebook*, September 2019. See also https://about.fb.com/news/2019/09/elections-and-political-speech/; accessed 26 Jan. 2020.

70 Digital, Culture, Media and Sport Committee, 'Disinformation and "fake news": Final Report published', *House of Commons*,

February 2019. See also www.parliament.uk/business/
committees/committees-a-z/commons-select/digital-
culture-media-and-sport-committee/news/fake-news-report-
published-17-19/; accessed 26 Jan. 2020.

71 Cristina Tardáguila, 'Falsehoods outperform facts in Brazilian
WhatsApp groups, study shows', *Poynter*, October 2019.

72 Paul Hilder, '"They were planning on stealing the election":
Explosive new tapes reveal Cambridge Analytica CEO's boasts
of voter suppression, manipulation and bribery', *openDemocracy*,
January 2019.

73 Digital, Culture, Media and Sport Committee, 'Disinformation
and "fake news": Final Report published', *House of Commons*,
February 2019. See also https://publications.parliament.uk/pa/
cm201719/cmselect/cmcumeds/1791/179107.htm; accessed 26 Jan.
2020.

74 Anselm Hager, 'Do Online Ads Influence Vote Choice?', *Political
Communication*, January 2019. See also www.tandfonline.com/doi/
abs/10.1080/10584609.2018.1548529?journalCode=upcp20; accessed
26 Jan. 2020.

75 Jane Mayer, 'How Russia Helped Swing the Election for Trump',
New Yorker, September 2018.

76 Donie O'Sullivan, 'Her son was killed — then came the Russian
trolls', *CNN*, June 2018.

77 'Russians Staged Rallies For and Against Trump to Promote
Discord, Indictment Says', *Fortune*, February 2018.

78 Donie O'Sullivan, 'Russian trolls pushed pro-Brexit spin on day of
referendum', *CNN*, November 2017.

79 Mark Scott, 'UK ignores warnings of digital election interference',
Politico, November 2019.

80 Craig Silverman, 'Facebook Said It Would Give Detailed Data To
Academics. They're Still Waiting', *Buzzfeed*, August 2019.

81 Paul Evans, *Save Democracy – Abolish Voting* (Brussels, 2017), p. 27.

82 Peter Pomerantsev, *This is Not Propaganda: Adventures in the War
Against Reality Paperback* (London, 2019), p. 381.

Chapter 9: The Dead Cat

1 William Davies, 'They don't even need ideas', *London Review of Books*, June 2019.

2 Rowena Mason and Frances Perraudin, 'Ukip infighting just party "blowing off steam", says Nigel Farage', *Guardian*, May 2015.

3 Darren Loucaides, 'Building the Brexit party: how Nigel Farage copied Italy's digital populists', *Guardian*, May 2019.

4 Jason Horowitz, 'The Mystery Man Who Runs Italy's "Five Star" From the Shadows', *New York Times*, February 2018.

5 Paul Simpson, 'Nigel Farage exclusive: "Advertising? I might fancy it myself one day"', *Campaign*, July 2019.

6 Jennifer O'Connell, '"No more Mr Nice Guy" – Farage is back with his Brexit Party and this time he's Mr Angry', *Irish Times*, April 2019.

7 'Nigel Farage launches Brexit Party ahead of European elections', *BBC*, April 2019.

8 Turlough Conway, 'Brexit Party Donations – "It Couldn't Be Less Secure"', *Byline Times*, May 2019.

9 George Monbiot, 'How US billionaires are fuelling the hard-right cause in Britain', *Guardian*, December 2018.

10 Caroline Wheeler, 'Women behind Boris Johnson's blueprint', *The Times*, November 2019.

11 Paolo Gerbaudo, 'Are digital parties more democratic than traditional parties? Evaluating Podemos and Movimento 5 Stelle's online decision-making platforms', *Sage Journals*, November 2019.

12 Edward Malnick, 'Nigel Farage interview: "At the end of this campaign the Brexit Party will be a lot bigger than the Conservatives"', *Telegraph*, May 2019.

13 Darren Loucaides, 'Inside the Brexit Party's general election war machine', *Wired*, October 2019.

14 Darren Loucaides, 'Building the Brexit party: how Nigel Farage copied Italy's digital populists', *Guardian*, May 2019.

15 Steve Roberts, 'The Brexit Party has betrayed us', *Spiked*, December 2019.

16   Darren Loucaides, 'Building the Brexit party: how Nigel Farage copied Italy's digital populists', *Guardian*, May 2019.

17   Darren Loucaides, 'What Happens When Techno-Utopians Actually Run a Country', *Wired*, February 2019.

18   Alberto Nardelli and Craig Silverman, 'Italy's Most Popular Political Party Is Leading Europe In Fake News And Kremlin Propaganda', *Buzzfeed*, November 2016.

19   'Italian lawmaker lambasted for anti-Semitic tweet', *The Times of Israel*, January 2019.

20   Darren Loucaides, 'What Happens When Techno-Utopians Actually Run a Country', *Wired*, February 2019.

21   Darren Loucaides, 'In Italy, Five Star Movement's war on journalism is picking up pace', *Columbia Journalism Review*, June 2019.

22   Jason Horowitz, 'The Mystery Man Who Runs Italy's "Five Star" From the Shadows', *New York Times*, February 2018.

23   'The failures of the Five Star Movement's Rousseau', *Privacy International*, April 2019.

24   Darren Loucaides, 'Building the Brexit party: how Nigel Farage copied Italy's digital populists', *Guardian*, May 2019.

25   Ibid.

26   Ibid.

27   Matt Honeycombe-Foster, 'Gordon Brown demands probe into funding of Nigel Farage's Brexit Party', *PoliticsHome*, May 2019.

28   'Electoral watchdog to review Brexit Party finances after Gordon Brown raises concerns over PayPal payments from abroad', *ITV*, May 2019.

29   James Randerson, '"Dirty money" claims "ridiculous," says Brexit Party chair', *Politico*, May 2019.

30   Tom Payne, 'Top Tory donor gives £200,000 to Nigel Farage's surging Brexit Party and defiantly blasts "the stormtroopers of the politically correct Brexit reversal conspiracy"', *Daily Mail*, May 2019.

31   Dan Bloom, 'Squirming Brexit Party chief repeatedly fails to say if party takes foreign cash', *Mirror*, May 2019.

32   Gabriel Pogrund, Tom Harper and Caroline Wheeler, 'Brexit Party fundraiser is "Posh George", once jailed in US after money-laundering sting', *The Times*, May 2019.

33 Ibid.

34 Rob Merrick, 'Farage's fundraising for Brexit Party allows foreign donors to "break rules", warns elections watchdog', *Independent*, May 2019.

35 'Brexit Party "at high risk" of accepting illegal donations', *BBC*, June 2019.

36 Sam Bright, 'The new Arron Banks? Meet the man bankrolling Nigel Farage's Brexit Party', *Scram News*, November 2019.

37 Andy Wigmore, *Twitter*, September 2019. See also https://twitter.com/andywigmore/status/1168632307902820354; accessed 26 Jan. 2020.

38 Mattha Busby, 'Police assessing claims that Tories offered peerages to Brexit party', *Guardian*, November 2019.

39 Adam Forrest, 'Brexit Party candidate denies being "insensitive" following condemnation for her past defence of IRA bombing', *Independent*, April 2019.

40 Leigh Baldwin, Peter Geoghegan and Marcus Leroux, 'Revealed: Nigel Farage's Brexit Party candidate spread "propaganda" for Balkan warlord, was "bugged" by MI6', *openDemocracy*, May 2019.

41 Narjas Zatat, 'Brexit Party MEP admits secretly working for Cambridge Analytica, Channel 4 investigation shows', *Independent*, July 2019.

42 Darren Loucaides, 'Inside the Brexit Party's general election war machine', *Wired*, October 2019.

43 Michael Savage, 'How Brexit party won Euro elections on social media – simple, negative messages to older voters', *Guardian*, June 2019.

44 Darren Loucaides, 'Inside the Brexit Party's general election war machine', *Wired*, October 2019.

45 Will Bedingfield, 'The Brexit Party is winning social media. These numbers prove it', *Wired*, May 2019.

46 William Davies, 'They don't even need ideas', *London Review of Books*, June 2019.

47 Darren Loucaides, 'Inside the Brexit Party's general election war machine', *Wired*, October 2019.

48 Ibid.

49 Mark Di Stefano, 'A Hyperpartisan Pro-Tommy Robinson News

Website Has Been Permanently Banned From Facebook', *Buzzfeed*, May 2019.

50 Saska Cvetkovska, Aubrey Belford, Craig Silverman and J. Lester Feder, 'The Secret Players Behind Macedonia's Fake News Sites', *OCCRP*, July 2018. See also www.occrp.org/en/spooksandspin/ the-secret-players-behind-macedonias-fake-news-sites; accessed 26 Jan. 2020.

51 Rob Faris, Hal Roberts, Bruce Etling, Nikki Bourassa, Ethan Zuckerman and Yochai Benkler, 'Partisanship, Propaganda, & Disinformation: Online Media & the 2016 U.S. Presidential Election', *Berkman Klein Center for Internet & Society at Harvard University*, August 2017. See also https://cyber.harvard.edu/sites/ cyber.harvard.edu/files/2017-08_electionReport.pdf; accessed 26 Jan. 2020.

52 Ibid.

53 Priyanjana Bengani, 'Hundreds of "pink slime" local news outlets are distributing algorithmic stories and conservative talking points', *Tow Center for Digital Journalism*, December 2019. See also www.cjr.org/tow_center_reports/hundreds-of-pink-slime-local- news-outlets-are-distributing-algorithmic-stories-conservative- talking-points.php; accessed 26 Jan. 2020.

54 Jim Waterson, 'This Pro-Brexit News Website Is Actually Run By Former Vote Leave Campaigners', *Buzzfeed*, August 2017.

55 Lucy Pasha-Robinson, 'Tommy Robinson march: Arizona congressman labelled a "disgrace" after calling Muslim men "scourge" in speech', *Independent*, July 2018.

56 'Dispatches investigation reveals how Facebook moderates content', *Channel 4*, July 2018.

57 Lizzie Dearden, 'Tommy Robinson caused Huddersfield grooming gang member to appeal conviction, court ruling reveals', *Independent*, July 2019.

58 Josh Halliday, Lois Beckett and Caelainn Barr, 'Revealed: the hidden global network behind Tommy Robinson', *Guardian*, December 2018.

59 Tom McTague, 'How Britain grapples with nationalist dark web', *Politico*, December 2018.

60 Agha Ali, 'Research on YouTube's recommendation algorithm reveals extremist content', *Digital Information World*, September 2019.

61 Charles Day, 'Does this EU small print mean Brexit has already happened?', *Spectator*, July 2019.

62 Jacob Granger, '2019 Reuters Digital News Report finds that trust in the media continues to fall', *journalism.co.uk*, June 2019.

63 Sam Knight, 'The Empty Promise of Boris Johnson', *New Yorker*, June 2019.

64 'Debunking years of tabloid claims about Europe', *The Economist*, June 2016.

65 Andy Bounds, 'Sun boycott reduced Euroscepticism on Merseyside, study shows', *Financial Times*, August 2019.

66 'New Report: Who Owns the UK Media?', *Media Reform Coalition*, March 2019.

67 Chris Cook, *Defeated by Brexit* (London, 2019), p. 9.

68 Sarah Provan, Adam Samson, Charlotte Middlehurst, Philip Georgiadis and Myles McCormick, 'General election 2019: Boris Johnson declares "powerful mandate to get Brexit done" – as it happened', *Financial Times*, December 2019.

69 Ibid.

70 Patrick Grafton-Green, 'Boris Johnson "orders review of BBC licence fee" amid "boycott" of flagship Radio 4 Today programme over "pro-Remain bias"', *Evening Standard*, December 2019.

71 Paul Simpson, 'Nigel Farage exclusive: "Advertising? I might fancy it myself one day"', *Campaign*, July 2019.

72 Paolo Gerbaudo, 'Digital parties on the rise: a mass politics for the era of platforms', *openDemocracy*, December 2018.

73 Angela Guiffrida, 'Italy's Matteo Salvini calls for fresh elections as coalition fractures', *Guardian*, August 2019.

74 Hugo Gye, 'Nigel Farage sacks Brexit Party staff after general election disaster', *The i*, December 2019.

Chapter 10: Making Europe Great Again

1 Silvia Sciorilli Borrelli, 'Matteo Salvini plans return as PM, wants alliance with Trump', *Politico*, December 2019.

2   Jacob Bojesson, 'Trump Does Meet And Greet With Italian National-ist Party Leader, Mussolini Defender', *Daily Caller*, April 2016.

3   Corinna Harrison, 'Salvini meets Trump in Philadelphia', the *Italian Insider*, April 2016.

4   Dan Mangan, 'Former Trump advisor Steve Bannon hits Rome as far-right candidate runs for prime minister of Italy', *CNBC*, March 2018.

5   SourceMaterial, Stefano Vergine and Claudia Torrisi, 'The heretic in the Vatican: How Pope Francis became a hate figure for the far right', *Source Material*, April 2019.

6   Steve Bannon, 'Matteo Salvini', *Time*, 2019.

7   Nandini Archer and Claire Provost, 'Revealed: dozens of European politicians linked to US "incubator for extremism"', *openDemocracy*, March 2019.

8   Claire Provost, 'How the far right is weaponising "the family"', *The Face*, April 2019.

9   Ibid.

10   Ibid.

11   Maya Oppenheim, 'Verona protests: Tens of thousands of cam-paigners march against "medieval" anti-LGBT+ and anti-abortion conference', *Independent*, April 2019.

12   Claudia Torrisi, Claire Provost and Mary Fitzgerald, 'A deep dive into "dark money"', *The Face*, August 2019.

13   'Up to 150 feared dead in "year's worst Mediterranean tragedy"', *Al Jazeera*, July 2019.

14   Nandini Archer, Claudia Torrisi, Claire Provost, Alexander Nabert and Belen Lobos, 'Hundreds of Europeans "criminalised" for helping migrants – as far right aims to win big in European elections', *openDemocracy*, May 2019.

15   Isobel Thompson, 'Europe's aristocratic elite in the fight against women's and LGBT rights', *openDemocracy*, March 2019.

16   Jason Horowitz, 'The "It" '80s Party Girl Is Now a Defender of the Catholic Faith', *New York Times*, December 2018.

17   'The *Guardian* view on the rise of Christian-nativist populists: a troubling sign of things to come', *Guardian*, December 2019.

18   Mattia Ferraresi, 'How the Catholic Church Lost Italy to the Far Right', *New York Times*, July 2019.

19 Tom Kington, 'World Congress of Families: Russia plays happy Christian families with Europe's populists', *The Times*, March 2019.

20 Sheryl Gay Stolberg, 'Ready to Fight Gay Marriage at Court Door', *New York Times*, March 2013.

21 J. Lester Feder and Giulia Alagna, 'Italy Is Ground Zero For The War On Women – Which Is Why These Far-Right Groups Are Meeting There', *Buzzfeed*, March 2019.

22 Claire Provost, 'How the far right is weaponising "the family"', *The Face*, April 2019.

23 Claire Provost and Adam Ramsay, 'Revealed: Trump-linked US Christian "fundamentalists" pour millions of "dark money" into Europe, boosting the far right', *openDemocracy*, March 2019. .

24 Anya Kamenetz, 'DeVos Family Money Is All Over The News Right Now', *npr*, August 2018.

25 Claudia Torrisi, Claire Provost and Mary Fitzgerald, 'A deep dive into "dark money"', *The Face*, August 2019.

26 Leigh Baldwin, Marcus Leroux, Claudia Torrisi and Stefano Vergine, 'How Pope Francis became a hate figure for the far right', *openDemocracy*, April 2019.

27 Jon Stone, 'Revealed: Tory links to Steve Bannon's far-right training school', *Independent*, May 2019.

28 Leigh Baldwin, Marcus Leroux, Claudia Torrisi and Stefano Vergine, 'How Pope Francis became a hate figure for the far right', *openDemocracy*, April 2019.

29 Mary Fitzgerald and Claire Provost, 'The American Dark Money Behind Europe's Far Right', *The New York Review of Books*.

30 'EU referendum: Key quotes from European figures', *BBC*, March 2016.

31 Adam Nossiter and Jason Horowitz, 'Bannon's Populists, Once a "Movement," Keep Him at Arm's Length', *New York Times*, May 2019.

32 'American-led "pro-family" summit in Ghana condemned for "shocking" white supremacist, Islamophobic links', *openDemocracy*, October 2019.

33 Mary Fitzgerald and Claire Provost, 'The American dark money behind Europe's far right', *openDemocracy*, July 2019.

34 '"Restoring the Natural Order": The religious extremists' vision

to mobilize European societies against human rights on sexuality and reproduction', *European Parliamentary Forum for Sexual & Reproductive Rights*, April 2018. See also https://www.epfweb.org/node/690; accessed 26 Jan. 2020.

35   Ibid.

36   According to Neil Datta, secretary of the European Parliamentary Forum for Sexual and Reproductive Rights.

37   'STOP LGBT indoctrination at Disneyland', *CitizenGo*, May 2019.

38   Lara Whyte, '"They are coming for your children" – the rise of CitizenGo', *openDemocracy*, August 2017.

39   Adam Ramsay and Claire Provost, 'Revealed: the Trump-linked "Super PAC" working behind the scenes to drive Europe's voters to the far right', *openDemocracy*, April 2019.

40   Guy Hedgecoe, 'Spanish elections: How the far-right Vox party found its footing', *BBC*, November 2019.

41   Peter Geoghegan and Jenna Corderoy, 'Revealed: Former Brexit minister accused of breaching ministerial code in meeting with Spanish far right', *openDemocracy*, May 2019.

42   Adam Ramsay and Claire Provost, 'Revealed: the Trump-linked "Super PAC" working behind the scenes to drive Europe's voters to the far right', *openDemocracy*, April 2019.

43   'AfD donation scandal deepens as party conference kicks off', *DW*, November 2018.

44   Galaxy Henry, 'Germany's AfD hit with hefty fine in donations scandal', *Politico*, April 2019.

45   Adam Ramsay and Claire Provost, 'Revealed: the Trump-linked "Super PAC" working behind the scenes to drive Europe's voters to the far right', *openDemocracy*, April 2019.

46   Ibid.

47   Ibid.

48   Lee Fang, 'The Trump Campaign Is Deploying Phone Location-Tracking Technology', *The Intercept*, December 2019.

49   Jason Horowitz, 'This Italian Town Once Welcomed Migrants. Now, It's a Symbol for Right-Wing Politics', *New York Times*, July 2018.

50   'Italy shooting: Mein Kampf found in home of suspect', *Guardian*, February 2018.

51 'Italy's League party under pressure over racist shootings', *Irish Times*, February 2018.

52 Charles Miranda and Cindy Wockner, 'Christchurch mosque shootings: "Smug" Tarrant faces court as New Zealand Prime Minister Jacinda Ardern pledges action', *The West Australian*, March 2019.

53 Julia Ebner and Jacob Davey, 'Mainstreaming Mussolini: How the Extreme Right Attempted to "Make Italy Great Again" in the 2018 Italian Election', *Institute for Strategic Dialogue*, March 2018. See also www.isdglobal.org/wp-content/uploads/2018/03/Mainstreaming-Mussolini-Report-28.03.18.pdf; accessed 26 Jan. 2020.

54 Ibid.

55 Ibid.

56 Ibid.

57 Mark Di Stefano, 'Italy's New Far-Right Star Specifically Thanked Facebook For The Election Result Because Of Course He Did', *Buzzfeed*, March 2018.

58 Emma Graham-Harrison and Sam Jones, 'Facebook takes down far-right groups days before Spanish election', *Guardian*, April 2019.

59 Carmen Aguilera-Carnerero, 'Beers for Spain and Instagram: VOX and the youth vote', *openDemocracy*, August 2019.

60 Ibid.

61 Sam Jones, 'Vox party puts "menace" of migrant children at centre of election drive', *Guardian*, November 2019.

62 Graham Keeley, 'Wristbands and a sense of belonging: How Spain's far-right Vox party has entered the mainstream', *Independent*, November 2019.

63 Anne Applebaum, 'Want to build a far-right movement? Spain's Vox party shows how', *Washington Post*, May 2019.

64 Ibid.

65 Jane Mayer, 'How Russia Helped Swing the Election For Trump', *New Yorker*, September 2018.

66 Peter Beinart, 'The U.S. Needs to Face Up to Its Long History of Election Meddling', *The Atlantic*, July 2018.

67 Alberto Nardelli, 'Revealed: The Explosive Secret Recording That Shows How Russia Tried To Funnel Millions To The "European Trump"', *Buzzfeed*, July 2019.

68   Alina Polyakova, Markos Kounalakis et al., 'The Kremlin's Trojan Horses', *Atlantic Council*, November 2017.

69   Ibid.

70   Ibid.

71   Alberto Nardelli, 'Revealed: The Explosive Secret Recording That Shows How Russia Tried To Funnel Millions To The "European Trump"', *Buzzfeed*, July 2019.

72   Ibid.

73   Nick Thorpe, 'Hungary vilifies financier Soros with crude poster campaign', *BBC*, July 2017.

74   'In speech, Hungary's Orbán attacks "enemy" who "speculates with money"', *The Times of Israel*, March 2018.

75   Bernard-Henri Lévy, 'How an Anti-totalitarian Militant Discovered Ultranationalism', *The Atlantic*, May 2019.

76   Elisabeth Zerofsky, 'Viktor Orbán's Far-Right Vision for Europe', *New Yorker*, January 2019.

77   Hannes Grassegger, 'The Unbelievable Story Of The Plot Against George Soros', *Buzzfeed*, January 2019.

78   Sharon LaFraniere, 'Paul Manafort's Prison Sentence Is Nearly Doubled to 7½ Years', *New York Times*, March 2019.

79   Hannes Grassegger, 'The Unbelievable Story Of The Plot Against George Soros', *Buzzfeed*, January 2019.

80   Ibid.

81   Ibid.

82   Elisabeth Zerofsky, 'Viktor Orbán's Far-Right Vision for Europe', *New Yorker*, January 2019.

83   Hannes Grassegger, 'The Unbelievable Story Of The Plot Against George Soros', *Buzzfeed*, January 2019.

84   Jane Mayer, 'How Russia Helped Swing the Election For Trump', *New Yorker*, September 2018.

85   Oleg Boldyrev and Erika Benke, 'Is Hungary copying Russia by targeting Soros-backed university?', *BBC*, April 2017.

86   Kate Proctor, 'Tories investigate three candidates over alleged antisemitism', *Guardian*, December 2019.

87   Elisabeth Zerofsky, 'Viktor Orbán's Far-Right Vision for Europe', *New Yorker*, January 2019.

88   Ibid.

89   Zack Beauchamp, 'It happened there: how democracy died in Hungary', *Vox*, September 2018.

90   Ibid.

91   Elisabeth Zerofsky, 'Viktor Orbán's Far-Right Vision for Europe', *New Yorker*, January 2019.

92   Lili Bayer, 'Israeli intelligence firm targeted NGOs during Hungary's election campaign', *Politico*, June 2018.

93   Selam Gebrekidan, Matt Apuzzo and Benjamin Novak, 'The Money Farmers: How Oligarchs and Populists Milk the E.U. for Millions', *New York Times*, November 2019.

94   Ivan Krastev and Stephen Holmes, 'How liberalism became "the god that failed" in eastern Europe', *Guardian*, October 2019.

95   Anne Applebaum, 'A Warning From Europe: The Worst Is Yet to Come', *The Atlantic*, October 2018.

96   Ivan Krastev and Stephen Holmes, 'How liberalism became 'the god that failed' in eastern Europe', *Guardian*, October 2019.

97   'The *Guardian* view on the rise of Christian-nativist populists: a troubling sign of things to come', *Guardian*, December 2019.

98   Alex Wickham, 'A Top Boris Johnson Aide Says The UK Will Have A "Special Relationship" With Viktor Orbán's Hungary After Brexit', *Buzzfeed*, January 2020.

99   Raphael Minder, 'Franco's Remains Are Exhumed and Reburied After Bitter Battle', *New York Times*, October 2019.

Chapter 11: Democracy Going Dark

1   Heather Kelly, 'School apps track students from classroom to bathroom, and parents are struggling to keep up', *Washington Post*, October 2019.

2   Zoltan L. Hajnal, Nazita Lajevardi and Linday Nielson, 'Do voter identification laws suppress minority voting? Yes. We did the research', *Washington Post*, February 2017.

3   Adam Ramsay, 'Boris Johnson made politics awful, then asked people to vote it away', *openDemocracy*, December 2019.

4   Alastair Reid and Carlotta Dotto, 'Thousands of misleading
    Conservative ads side-step scrutiny thanks to Facebook policy',
    First Draft, December 2019.

5   Carole Cadwalladr, 'Fresh Cambridge Analytica leak "shows global
    manipulation is out of control"', *Guardian*, January 2020.

6   Rick Paulas and Jana Ašenbrennerová, 'How Workers Are Fighting
    Back Against Big Tech', *Vice*, November 2019.

7   Mark Bergen, 'Google Workers Protest Company's "Brute Force
    Intimidation"', *Bloomberg*, November 2019.

8   Stuart A. Thompson and Charlie Warzel, 'Twelve Million Phones,
    One Dataset, Zero Privacy', *New York Times*, December 2019.

9   'Getting Big Money Out of Politics', *elizabethwarren.com*. See also
    https://elizabethwarren.com/plans/campaign-finance-reform;
    accessed 30 Jan. 2020.

10 Robert Reich, 'Elizabeth Warren is right – we must break up
    Facebook, Google and Amazon', *Guardian*, March 2019.

11 Greg Sterling, 'Almost 70% of digital ad spending going to Google,
    Facebook, Amazon, says analyst firm', *Marketing Land*, June
    2019. See also https://marketingland.com/almost-70-of-digital-
    ad-spending-going-to-google-facebook-amazon-says-analyst-
    firm-262565; accessed 30 Jan. 2020.

12 Robert Reich, 'Elizabeth Warren is right – we must break up
    Facebook, Google and Amazon', *Guardian*, March 2019.

13 Tai Nalon, 'Did WhatsApp help Bolsonaro win the Brazilian
    presidency?', *Washington Post*, November 2018.

14 Yasmin Alibhai-Brown, 'The new "contract for the web" is just
    good PR for the tech megalomaniacs who will carry on doing their
    worst', *The i*, November 2019.

15 David Frum, 'If America's Democracy Fails, Can Other Ones
    Survive?', *The Atlantic*, March 2018.

16 '2019 Audit of Political Engagement', *Hansard Society*, 2019. See
    also www.hansardsociety.org.uk/publications/reports/audit-of-
    political-engagement-16; accessed 30 Jan. 2020.

Index

Liverpool 246
Lloyd George, David 4
Lloyd's of London 47
lobbyists 178–81, 299–300
London mayoral election (2016) 204
London School of Economics 17, 161
Long, Naomi 93
Loucaides, Darren 230
Lowe, Sam 174
Lucas, Colin 245
Lucas, Ian 30–1, 32, 203

Maastricht Treaty (1992) 74–5, 103
McAlpine, Lord 144
McCain, John 269
McCain-Feingold Act 269
McCorquodale, Donald 84, 85
Maciver, Andy 74
MacKinlay, Andrew 106
McMillan-Scott, Edward 107
McNamee, Roger 199
Madden, Kevin 157
Maessen, Hans 174
Magee, Seamus 93
Mair, Thomas 63–4
Major, John 74–5, 78–9
Malloch, Ted 263
Malofeev, Konstantin 260, 268
'Malthouse compromise' 175
Manafort, Paul 279–80 and n.
Mandela, Nelson 75
Mansfield, Iain 166
Margaret Thatcher Center for
   Freedom 129
marketing, political 191–3
Marr, Andrew 61
Marshall, Paul 173
Marton, Ed 261
Massingham, Zack 34, 39
Maude, Francis 179
Maugham, Jolyon 28
May, Christian 171

May, Theresa 29, 158
   2017 general election 91, 112, 199
   Chequers plan 101, 102–3, 113, 117,
      160, 166, 168
   and the ERG 114
   and the Irish border 175, 176
   Lancaster House speech 112
   resignation 108, 114
   on Russian interference 217
   and Singham 159
   visits Trump 134
   vote of no confidence 113, 121
   withdrawal deal 40, 70, 94, 95, 113,
      114, 117, 121, 122, 145, 222
Mayer, Jane 4, 132
Meetup 228–9
Mellon Scaife family 136, 137
Mellor, David 105
Mercer, Rebekah 53, 55, 126, 129, 140
Mercer, Robert 4, 53, 55, 111, 126, 129,
      140, 188, 238, 241
Merkel, Angela 249, 285
Messina, Jim 197, 199
Metro 2, 80, 88, 90
Metropolitan Police 30, 32, 69
Meuthen, Jörg 264
Midlands Industrial Council 18, 24
Militant Tendency 112
Millar, Gavin 24, 30, 31, 32, 89, 204, 232
Mills, John 21, 31
Ministry of Defence 188
Minneapolis 216
Mirza, Munira 226
Mises, Ludwig von 124
Modi, Narendra 8, 204, 304
Momentum 199
Monday Club 112
money laundering 148–9, 233, 304
Monteith, Brian 207–8
Montgomerie, Tim 287
Montgomery, Christopher 78, 117
Moore, Martin 8, 67, 197, 248, 293